JOHN·FORD·MADE·WESTERNS

☎ 01603 773114
email: tis@ccn.ac.uk ▼ @CCN_Library Ⓦ ccnlibraryblog.wordpress.com
f /ccninformationstore

21 DAY LOAN ITEM

JOHN·FORD
MADE·WESTERNS

FILMING THE LEGEND IN THE SOUND ERA

EDITED BY GAYLYN STUDLAR AND MATTHEW BERNSTEIN

INDIANA UNIVERSITY PRESS
Bloomington and Indianapolis

This book is a publication of

Indiana University Press
601 North Morton Street
Bloomington, IN 47404-3797 USA

http://www.indiana.edu/~iupress
Telephone orders   800-842-6796
Fax orders   812-855-7931
Orders by e-mail   iuporder@indiana.edu

© 2001 by Indiana University Press

All rights reserved

The paper used in this publication meets the minimum requirements of American National Standard for Information Sciences—Permanence of Paper for Printed Library Materials, ANSI Z39.48-1984.

Manufactured in the United States of America

Library of Congress Cataloging-in-Publication Data

John Ford made westerns : filming the legend in the sound era / edited by
Gaylyn Studlar and Matthew Bernstein.
p.   cm.
Includes bibliographical references and index.
ISBN 0-253-33798-4 (alk. paper) — ISBN 0-253-21414-9 (pbk. : alk. paper)
1. Ford, John, 1894–1973.   I. Studlar, Gaylyn.   II. Bernstein, Matthew.

PN1998.F65 J65 2001
791.43′0233′092—dc21

00-040971

1   2   3   4   5   06   05   04   03   02   01

For
CHARLES MUSSER,
an extraordinary historian,
a valued colleague,
and a superb editor

CONTENTS

Part II · Dossier

ACKNOWLEDGMENTS

We are indebted to many individuals and organizations for their help in preparing this volume. First, we thank our contributors for their intellectual efforts and for their remarkable patience in staying the course with us for a much longer period than any of us had anticipated.

We would also like to thank the many individuals and institutions who granted, supplied, or facilitated permission to use photographs: Dan Ford; Tag Gallagher (himself a major Ford film scholar); Barry Grant; Kay Kalinak; Charles Maland; *Esquire* magazine and the Hearst Corporation; Paramount Pictures; the University of California at Los Angeles Special Collections Music Library; the Margaret Herrick Library at the Academy of Motion Picture Arts and Sciences; the Buffalo Bill Historical Museum, Cody, Wyoming (Elizabeth Holmes); the Frederic Remington Art Museum, Ogdensburg, New York (Laura Shea); the Woolaroc Museum, Bartlesville, Oklahoma (Linda Stone); and the Gerald Peters Gallery, Santa Fe, New Mexico (Ashley Waechter and Amy Scott). Special thanks to Ben Brewster and Maxine Fleckner Ducey at the Wisconsin Center for Film and Theater Research, Terry Geesken and Mary Corliss at the Museum of Modern Art Film Stills Archive, and Saundra Taylor and her staff at the Lilly Library at Indiana University. Thanks also to Jamie Martin of Emory University's Woodruff Library Media Center. Most of all, we thank the University of Michigan, College of Literature, Science, and the Arts, for a generous subvention that helped defray the costs of using the many photographs that this book—or any book on Ford's films—deserves by virtue of its subject matter. We here acknowledge that most of the illustrations are production stills that approximate the actual look of shots in the films.

We owe special thanks to the following for their help and permission in reprinting articles: Dan Ford for "John Wayne—My Pal" (and Piera Petat for tracking it down); Richard Jameson of *Film Comment* and Robin Wood for permission to reprint "'*Shall* We Gather at the River?': The Late Films of John Ford"; the *Saturday Evening Post* and the Curtis Publishing Company (Steve C. Pettinger) for permission to reprint "Hollywood's Favorite Rebel"; David Shepard for "Fighting Irish"; *Cinema Journal*, the University of Texas Press (Julie Martin), and Ed Buscombe for "Painting the Legend: Frederic Remington and the Western"; the Directors Guild of America (Charles Warn) for permission to reprint "About John Ford" from *Action* magazine; and *Cosmopolitan* for

"The Old Wrangler Rides Again." For other assistance, we thank Annie Hall, Sue Kirby, Carl Derrick, Connie Ejarque, and David Pratt.

Thanks also go to Joan Catapano and Michael Lundell for cheerfully and capably ushering us through the publication process at Indiana University Press. John Belton, a leading Ford scholar, provided an incredibly astute and helpful reader's report.

The very idea of an anthology of new work on John Ford came from Charles Musser, a leading light in the fields of film history and criticism. Having suggested the topic, Charles encouraged and gently prodded us to make this the best volume it could possibly be. For his marvelous ideas, sage scholarly advice, and unfaltering support of this project, we are greatly indebted. That is why we dedicate *John Ford Made Westerns* to him.

JOHN·FORD·MADE·WESTERNS

INTRODUCTION
GAYLYN STUDLAR AND MATTHEW BERNSTEIN

John Ford Made Westerns is a title that shamelessly plays with the most famous understatement in Hollywood history: "My name's John Ford. I make Westerns."[1] This remark is cited by many of the contributors to this volume—and with good reason. The utterance and the circumstances that originally provoked it combine to reveal something of the abiding appeal of a legendary filmmaker whose name is now attached to the Western genre more than that of any other single director.

At a Directors Guild meeting in October 1950, director Cecil B. DeMille led a right-wing faction in accusing guild president Joseph L. Mankiewicz of being a Communist. At one point during the meeting, a guild member rose from his seat to comment. Since the proceedings were being recorded by a court stenographer, the man, in rumpled clothes and dark glasses, identified himself for

John Ford about the time of his "I make Westerns" declaration.
With Maureen O'Hara and John Wayne on location for *Rio Grande* (1950).
Courtesy of the Museum of Modern Art Film Stills Archive.

the record: "My name's John Ford. I make Westerns." Ford called for a motion demanding that DeMille and the board of directors resign. He then asked the membership to endorse Mankiewicz's presidency so they could "all go home and get some sleep. We've got some pictures to make tomorrow."[2]

Anyone familiar with American film history knows that in 1950, John Ford (1894–1973) needed no introduction to his filmmaking peers, just as he needed no introduction to critics and audiences around the world.[3] He was nothing less than Hollywood's preeminent director, and the American film industry's most honored one. Some two years after the Directors Guild meeting he would win the last of his six Academy Awards (including two for documentaries), and he held almost as many New York Film Critics awards. In 1973, he became the first recipient of the Lifetime Achievement Award of the American Film Institute in a ceremony in which the then president of the United States, Richard M. Nixon, also awarded him the Presidential Medal of Freedom.[4]

The Directors Guild statement "for the record" is always read as "classic" Ford. Here was a director who garnered as many awards and as much praise as his profession had to offer, yet he was not ashamed to publicly proclaim his association with Westerns, a perennially popular genre but one often disdained as children's Saturday-afternoon fare. His call to endorse Mankiewicz is couched not in political terms, but in hard-nosed practicality. He's a yeoman (not an artist or an ideologue) who needs his sleep to get his job done the next day. Over twenty years later, a scant two years before his death, Ford reiterated both the plain-spoken tenor and the anti-elitist message of his self-introduction when he remarked, "When I pass on, I want to be remembered as 'John Ford—a guy that made Westerns.'"[5]

Ford's attachment to the Western became an important part of his image as a rebel, a rule-breaker who sneered at all pretensions of artistry. Director-critic Peter Bogdanovich's interview-based monograph, which was perhaps the most widely read book on Ford in the 1970s, praised the director for "the singular poetic vision with which he sees all life."[6] Nor was Bogdanovich the first to praise the "poetry" of Ford's films. Ford himself was quoted as saying, "I am not a poet, and I don't know what a Western saga is. I would say that is horseshit."[7] In 1980, Robin Wood targeted one of the central dilemmas of talking about Ford: "Few would now wish to question that Ford is among the greatest artists the cinema has so far produced, yet the nature of his greatness has proved difficult to define."[8] The director's gift for visual composition, his ability to use film as an eloquent, often wordless means of expression, his insight into human psychology, and the vigor of his storytelling have all been cited as reasons for his greatness as a director. Yet Ford's importance in the history of the Western remains the easiest thing to tangibly identify among his artistic achievements.

As Charles Maland suggests in his essay in this volume, John Ford's association with the Western may now seem inevitable or natural, but it is the result of an evolution in the director's public reputation that began with his entry into the film business in 1914 and still continues over a quarter of a century after his death. Ford's first directorial assignment, in 1917, was a Western, *The Tornado,* for his brother Francis's production unit at 101 Bison-Universal. Also written by Ford, it tells the story of an Irish immigrant in the American West who thwarts a bank robbery by the colorfully named "Coyote Gang" and rescues the mayor's daughter.[9] Ford continued with Westerns, and they formed the bulk of his prodigious output in the 1910s. Ford's many Western films of this period in his career, now almost all lost to us, established him as a successful and notable director in the genre. Certainly, the sheer number of films he shot (over sixty before 1930) offer some indication of his work's positive reception with audiences. However, his Westerns' success was no doubt also related to the popularity of the genre itself.

If the Western is now one of the most instantly recognizable genres in the history of cinema (in no small part due to the iconography of Ford's Westerns), its even greater importance to early film history must also be acknowledged. Western films have been an important part of commercial U.S. filmmaking at

Director Ford—closely associated with the Western from the very beginning. Ford and unidentified man on the set of *3 Bad Men* (1926).

Courtesy of the Margaret Herrick Library, Academy of Motion Picture Arts and Sciences.

least since the appearance of Edwin S. Porter's watershed example of cinematic storytelling, *The Great Train Robbery* (1903). As Edward Buscombe's essay in this volume demonstrates, when movies appeared as a mass medium, Western conventions of character and narrative formula were already well established in photography and painting, popular literature, and stage plays, as well as other entertainments such as the Wild West show. But it was film, with its ability to show movement and record "authentic" landscapes, that seemed ideally suited to recording and restaging a historical West that was fast passing away even as it was embraced in myriad popular-culture entertainments for its spectacle, its action, its romance, and its nostalgia.

Through the influence of both popular culture and eminent social commentators (such as Theodore Roosevelt and historian Frederick Jackson Turner), the history of U.S. westward expansion was incorporated into the fictional Western and became an important site for explaining the values of a people and a nation perceived to be in danger from the increasing encroachment of a softening civilization centered on urbanity, consumerism, and technological "progress." Ford's own interest in Westerns reflects something of these same cultural fascinations and anxieties, ideals and disappointments in a changing society. Like D. W. Griffith, Ford was a pioneer master of cinematic storytelling who had one foot in nineteenth-century American thought and feeling and the other in the twentieth. Both men shared an interest in depicting American history and a penchant for sentimental humanism. Like D. W. Griffith, Ford balanced epic themes and intimate dramas in a personalization of the past, but Ford's films, unlike Griffith's, became increasingly self-conscious in their vision of an American past, representing it not as a pure celebration of myth, but exploring it as a constructed discourse summed up in an oft-repeated line from *The Man Who Shot Liberty Valance* (1962): "When the legend becomes fact, print the legend." Thus, Ford's work evidences a modern self-reflexivity in dealing with the relationship of history, myth, and national identity.

His films *The Iron Horse* (1924) and *3 Bad Men* (1926), both still extant, as well as more modestly scaled but equally interesting ones, like *Straight Shooting* (1917), demonstrate a quality that Ford's sound-era films would also possess: evidence of the painter's eye for depicting human enterprise against the landscape of the West. Equally significant, they achieve what would become a Ford trademark sustained throughout the sound era: the heart-rending contrast between the community-centered aspirations of settlers and the harsh and unforgiving qualities of the Western frontier.

Unfortunately, we cannot address Ford's silent films in depth in this volume, because our ability to reach any trustworthy conclusions about Ford's body of work in the Western during these years is compromised by the sparse number of extant films. This problem has changed little since Andrew Sarris eloquently remarked in 1975, "we possess infinitely more filmed evidence of D. W. Griffith's

A fragile community in a harsh landscape: Ethan Edwards greets his brother as he returns to the family homestead in *The Searchers* (1956). John Wayne and Walter Coy. Courtesy of The Lilly Library, Indiana University, Bloomington, Indiana.

career before 1915 than of Ford's before 1920."[10] But it is not just the amount of lost early work that causes Ford to seem to be primarily a director of *sound-era* Westerns. After *3 Bad Men,* Ford spent more than a decade away from the Western. His move was paralleled in the Hollywood film industry as a whole after the advent of talkies. The difficulties of sound recording initially discouraged the making of Westerns, and then public taste seemed to shift to more dialogue-bound, topical fare (such as gangster films) or escapist musicals, screwball comedies, and historical bio-pics. Although Westerns continued to be made throughout the thirties as B-pictures, and in much smaller numbers as major productions (such as Cecil B. DeMille's *The Plainsman* [1936]), Ford is commonly credited with almost singlehandedly reviving the genre's status as a form for serious storytelling with the release of *Stagecoach* (1939).

Stagecoach was praised by critic André Bazin as the epitome of classical perfection. Returning to the film now, one is struck less by its classicism than by its disturbing darkness, visually and thematically, and its "Popular Front" resonance with the class and social issues raised by the Great Depression. In this respect, Ford's *The Grapes of Wrath* (1940) and a Western such as *Stagecoach* are linked by their championing of the common citizen who is "under attack."

Ford's return to the Western with this Academy Award–nominated film was not just a passing nod to his cinematic roots: the form would dominate his work from the postwar period to the end of his career. At their release, his post–World

War II Westerns, *My Darling Clementine* (1946), *Fort Apache* (1948), *3 Godfathers* (1948), *She Wore a Yellow Ribbon* (1949), *Wagon Master* (1950), *Rio Grande* (1950), *The Searchers* (1956), *The Horse Soldiers* (1959), *Sergeant Rutledge* (1960), *Two Rode Together* (1961), *How the West Was Won* (1962), *The Man Who Shot Liberty Valance* (1962), and *Cheyenne Autumn* (1964), were not always favorably reviewed by critics or even taken seriously, although they were often praised for their visual beauty and their "poetry" of form and feeling. Ford himself admitted that the three films of the so-called cavalry trilogy (*Fort Apache, She Wore a Yellow Ribbon,* and *Rio Grande*) were made to recoup the financial losses of *The Fugitive* (1947), his arty adaptation of Graham Greene's *The Power and the Glory.* He shot them to build his resources so he might make films to which he felt personally committed without studio interference.[11]

Ford had contracted as a director with Fox in 1931, and as their "star" director in the 1930s he enjoyed an unusual amount of control over his projects. But because he had started his career in the 1910s, he had also enjoyed what might be regarded as Hollywood's glory days of directorial freedom.[12] That early experience, combined with his notoriously cantankerous personality, inevitably meant that he chafed against studio attempts to control both his everyday work process and the final film product. There is evidence that Darryl Zanuck actively—and intelligently—contributed to his films, such as *The Grapes of Wrath, How Green Was My Valley* (1941), and *My Darling Clementine,* but Ford was more comfortable working with an independent producer like Walter Wanger or at RKO, both of which were willing to give him carte blanche.[13]

Ford's urge toward independence was rewarded with differing degrees of autonomy during the war years. Ironically, he turned to Herbert J. Yates of Republic Pictures. John Ford at Republic Pictures was an incongruous collaboration (Hollywood's most honored director at a minor studio that had a reputation for turning out movies to make a buck, not an Oscar), but the perceived complexity and significance of Ford's "popcorn" Westerns of the nineteen-forties and early fifties have only grown over the years.

As this volume shows, Ford's apparent indifference to the artistic potential of the Western and to his status as a poet—as an artist—was belied by his self-conscious approach, not only to history, but to the Western as an art form—even when he was at lowly Republic Pictures. But the word "ambivalence" is also often used in relation to his sound-era Westerns. The Western past is often presented in Ford's films as compelling in its nostalgic appeal and visually luminous, but as many of our contributors point out with varying emphases, Ford's Westerns also present this past as a site of social restraints, human suffering, and emotional loss that make the notion of the Western as a celebration of frontier "freedom" ironic.[14]

Ford on location in Monument Valley shooting *Stagecoach* (1939), a film for an independent producer, not a controlling studio. Tim Holt on the right.
Courtesy of the Wisconsin Center for Film and Theater Research.

The pessimism of American films in the post–World War II period is convergent with the often-remarked darkening of the past in Ford's last quarter-century of Westerns. Here, the paradoxes or contradictions of Ford's style and ideological imperatives are foregrounded: the blending of expressionistic features in lighting with photographic realism, the elliptical quality of his "classical" narratives, his unique handling of film space and refusal to adhere to conventions of classical Hollywood screen direction. There is, as well, an intense emotionality to his films, achieved without reliance on melodramatic close-ups and eschewing camera movement.

By any standard, it might seem unnecessary or even perverse to have to argue for the greatness, the importance, the uniqueness of John Ford's oeuvre in general, and of his Westerns in particular. Anyone interested in Ford's work cannot help but wonder if, at this particular time, it is indeed necessary to return to John Ford and to Westerns. Or, as long-standing "pillars" of the pantheon of American cinema, are John Ford and his films in danger of becoming too familiar to us?[15] Is the return to Westerns branded by the credit "Directed by John Ford" nothing more than a return to another dead white male of an over-analyzed cinematic canon?

Over twenty years ago, in a special issue of *Wide Angle* devoted exclusively to the director, Peter Lehman felt compelled to exclaim, "John Ford? Again? Probably more has been written about John Ford than any other American director."[16] In 1978 that assessment was an accurate one. As well as countless articles and special issues of periodicals (both in the United States and abroad), a large number of books of criticism and bio-criticism of Ford were published under the title *John Ford* from the 1950s through the 1970s, including Jean Mitry's (1954), Philippe Haudiquet's (1966), Peter Bogdanovich's (1968), and Joseph McBride and Michael Wilmington's (1975). Finally breaking with titular tradition, Andrew Sarris's *The John Ford Movie Mystery* (1975) and J. A. Place's two volumes derived from her dissertation, *The Western Films of John Ford* (1974) and *The Non-Western Films of John Ford* (1979), appeared as major contributions to Ford scholarship.[17]

Much praise was the rule rather than the exception in considerations of Ford[18]—so much so that Andrew Sarris, whose admiration of Ford was deep enough for him to place the director in his "pantheon" of American film directors, took Peter Bogdanovich to task for "Fordolatry" that made "Ford the last and greatest monument of Monument Valley."[19] The same observation could be applied to a host of others who wrote on Ford during this period. Lindsay Anderson, a British film director and self-proclaimed "rabid fan," echoed many others in calling Ford "probably the greatest film director working in the world's richest film making tradition."[20] Even Sarris, in spite of his wish to curb the excesses of "Fordolatry," also found ample inspiration in Ford as a "poet" and a "painter."[21]

As insightful as it was, the impressionistic and highly personal mode of film criticism practiced by Anderson, Bogdanovich, and Sarris was in the process of falling out of fashion as academic film studies developed in the United States and Great Britain and took up approaches borrowed from anthropology, literary analysis, and psychoanalysis. Critically embracing directors as artists whose sensibility and personality could expressively dominate a film became passé as academic film scholarship moved toward an attempt to systematically account for the meaning of films as products of culture. In such an accounting, filmmakers could only be "subjects," cultural agents formed by historical and ideological circumstances; films were "texts" rather than "works" attributable to a single personality, and these texts produced "effects" over which directors had little conscious control.

In spite of structuralist and poststructuralist critical trends that renounced interest in individual author-filmmakers as visionary artists, attention to Ford's films remained a touchstone, a common reference of filmgoing experience, and a subject for discussion. Thus in 1969, when Peter Wollen offered a ground-breaking application of semiology and structuralism to film in *Signs and Meaning in the Cinema,* John Ford's films figured prominently; when, in that same year, the *Cahiers du cinéma* collective set about applying Lacanian psychoanalysis and Althusser-influenced structuralism to a film, they chose Ford's *Young Mr. Lincoln* (1939).[22] In the late 1970s and early 1980s, emerging young scholars such as Peter Lehman, Brian Henderson, Nick Browne, and Robert Ray continued to address Ford. "Fordolatry" was replaced by new, more academically oriented perspectives that emphasized ideological, narratalogical, signifying, and stylistic issues. In the 1980s and 1990s, other than biographies or reminiscences that provided accounts of working with Ford, Ford scholarship was confined primarily to the fringes of film studies, limited to valuable but iconoclastic scholars, such as Tag Gallagher and William Darby, who chose to approach Ford from perspectives that are implicitly or overtly hostile to modern theories of cinematic authorship or contemporary critical methodologies.[23]

Nevertheless, structuralist- and poststructuralist-influenced film scholars referenced Ford again and again, even when their critical projects were engaged with the theoretical trends that tended to de-center the director as the authorial source of a film's "effects."[24] The contributors to this volume share this fascination with Ford, whether seen as system, effect, or old-fashioned auteur, for his name still denotes a compelling, admirable set of texts.

By any standard, Ford remains one of a handful of the cinema's greatest artists in spite of, as well as because of, the critical evaluation and reevaluation(s) of his work that took place throughout and after his career. In an era of film criticism in which artistry is rarely discussed, ubiquitous lists of the "greatest" and "best" films provide confirmation that the notion of artistic standing, while reduced to a level of media consumerism, has not been forgotten.[25] In the list of three hundred and sixty film classics compiled by the British magazine *Sight and Sound* from the responses of filmmakers and critics worldwide, Ford emerges as the director most often named, with eleven films cited. These included his Westerns *My Darling Clementine, Fort Apache, She Wore a Yellow Ribbon, Rio Grande, Wagon Master, The Searchers,* and *The Man Who Shot Liberty Valance;* ironically, these films were often dismissed by critics on their original release.

While the value of compiling lists of the greatest films is always subject to argument, another measure of continued significance is Ford's influence on other directors. Ford's work has exerted a visible influence on Steven Spielberg, whose *ET* (1982) uses *The Quiet Man* (1952) to mark the defining moment when ET learns what it is to be human. Ford's *The Searchers* figures as an overt narrative influence on George Lucas's *Star Wars* (1977) as well as on modern captivity narratives, including Paul Schrader's *Hardcore* (1976) and Martin Scorsese's *Taxi Driver* (1976).

In spite of this, the passage of time and changing trends in popular culture, in filmmaking, and in film scholarship have all combined to eclipse Ford in the public consciousness. Alfred Hitchcock and, perhaps, Orson Welles are among the few directors from the classical period who remain well known to the general public and the subject of broad popular and scholarly inquiry. Although Hitchcock was not as honored a director in his lifetime as Ford, his films seem to speak more readily to a postmodern audience comfortable with an ironic, paranoid, sexually violent vision of the world. In such an era, how can we expect Ford's humanistic, nostalgic, sentimental films to fare? To contemporary viewers, Ford's films, most often characterized by a mixture of comedy and pathos, patriotic Americana and family-centered romanticism, might well seem as old-fashioned as anything that D. W. Griffith ever made.

Nevertheless, renewed scholarly interest in the history of the West as well as in the literary and cinematic Western suggests that it is time to return to the work of the most famous, if not the "greatest," director of Westerns in cinematic history.[26] We hope this book will provide the opportunity to return to these important (and subversively "enjoyable") films with new critical and theoretical perspectives. In focusing on a single director, the essays gathered here seek to situate the Ford Westerns as distinctively "Fordian," and any volume such as ours almost inevitably returns to the director as author-subject. The goal of this volume, then, is to provide perspectives on Ford's Westerns that evidence the range of theoretical and critical approaches found in modern film studies. The articles presented here also suggest the interest of contemporary film scholars in issues of race, gender, and economic relations, as well as in stylistic and narrative structures that relate to other art forms, such as painting, music, and literature.

We begin with Robin Wood's 1971 essay, "'*Shall* We Gather at the River?':
The Late Films of John Ford," which is actually a seminal examination of Ford's entire career. Wood eloquently argues that, with the exception of *The Man Who Shot Liberty Valance*, Ford's later films lack a passionate engagement in their material, and he mounts this argument by way of comparisons with earlier films such as *Stagecoach* and *My Darling Clementine*, as well as the cavalry trilogy. The later films are hollow, Wood argues, the work of an artist profoundly disillusioned with American society's failure to live up to its democratic and humane ideals. For the same reasons, Ford's later films also manifest a retreat to the exotic, the elegiac, and the nostalgic (a view Barry Grant seconds in his discussion of Ford's Westerns in relation to the novels of James Fenimore Cooper).

Written within an auteurist framework and as film studies as a discipline was beginning its life in the universities, Wood's essay also set the stage for Ford criticism to follow. Wood stresses Ford's paternalistic treatment of Native Americans and women. Native Americans in Ford's early films are a "pure archetype" of savagery, "a concept rather than characters"; paternalistic treatment, as in *Cheyenne Autumn,* is the best of what they receive at Ford's hands. Love relationships have at their core gallantry or heartiness, rather than sexual attraction; relationships in the films are important insofar as they lead to marriage and family, the continuity of tradition and the founding of civilization. In briefly examining these issues, Wood anticipates many of the concerns of subsequent Ford criticism and of the essays collected here—the troublesome question of how Ford's films come to represent gender and, particularly, ethnicity.

Gaylyn Studlar takes issue with longstanding critics who characterize Ford's treatment of women as traditional and even reactionary; at the same time, she disputes more recent commentaries on the Western (by Lee Clark Mitchell and Tompkins) that see it as a fundamental flight of masculinity from femininity. Instead, Studlar argues, Ford's Westerns feature a heretofore unrecognized "accommodation of masculinity to feminine values (Christianity, family-centered domesticity)" and a potentially feminizing sacrifice to ensure the birthright of future generations of Americans.

In Studlar's argument, Ford frequently complicates the genre's gender stereotypes even as he deploys them. Fallen women (Denver in *Wagon Master* and Dallas in *Stagecoach*) are shown to be isolated from the nurturing and humane values of family life, while schoolmarms and wives often embrace the hardships of frontier life (Lana in *Drums along the Mohawk* [1939], Mrs. Jorgensen in *The Searchers*) or the possibilities of romance (Philadelphia in *Fort Apache*). They do so not as civilized, refined Easterners, but as aggressive frontier women who startle their men. Studlar further recognizes the tenderness and civilizing values held by some Fordian male heroes (such as Sandy and Travis in *Wagon Master*, Gil in *Drums along the Mohawk*, and even Tom Doniphon in *The Man Who Shot Liberty Valance*). Ford's most admirable heroes also display a gentility and commitment to domesticity not typically associated with the genre. Following the logic of Victorian culture, men in Ford's Westerns who mourn dead wives and family (such as Nathan Brittles in *She Wore a Yellow Ribbon*) show a greater capacity to embrace the living and to make the world a better place. In this context, the repudiation of Ethan Edwards's harsh racism, destructiveness, and isolation in *The Searchers* takes on added resonance. Studlar's arguments stimulate us to consider the varied sources of sentiment in the Western as well as to view Ford's films in a new way.

Charles Ramírez Berg argues for a comparable rethinking of Ford's depiction of ethnicity in these Westerns. While there are many notoriously offensive moments in Ford's Westerns, Berg suggests that their cultural commentary is more complex, ambivalent, and interesting than that of a simply racist filmmaker. For example, Ford's use of Mexican film stars, who speak Spanish as well as interpret Native American languages, gives his Westerns a sense of cultural authenticity unprecedented in Hollywood cinema of the period.

Stressing Ford's Irish heritage as a basis for his sympathy for marginalized ethnics, Berg maps out a cultural poetics whereby Native Americans, Mexicans, African Americans, Swedes, Slavs, poor whites, and, of course, Irish-immigrant pioneers are pushed to the social margins by an oppressive "Yankee" Protestant mainstream that seeks to dominate both them and the landscape. Berg finds the former groups organized into a series of dualisms and dialectics, whereby Ford Westerns celebrate immigrant ethnics and question assimilation into the "heartless, oppressive, and intolerant" WASP mainstream. The new Americans of Ford's films "gather at the river of the Margin-frontier and show themselves to be . . . guileless and giving, raucous and lively, humorous and humane." This is evidenced through their brawling ("an oppositional carnival of ethnicity"), their singing and dancing (the creation of community or its interruption by mainstream values), and their marching and parading (military action or organization as a means for the marginalized to rise in social status). Yet even among the lovingly portrayed multicultural marginalized, villains sometimes arise (the Cleggs in *Wagon Master*) that test tolerance and justice across racial and ethnic boundaries. Again, this serves as testimony to the complexity of Ford's vision. Berg further distinguishes between the obvious dramatic narrative in Ford's Westerns, on the one hand, and a cultural narrative that is parallel to it (much

"We'll be the morals of decorum!"—spiked punch and the ethnic carnivalesque. The Irish sergeants (Victor McLaglen, Dick Foran, and Jack Pennick) with Sergeant Beaufort (Pedro Armendáriz) in *Fort Apache* (1948).
Courtesy of the Lilly Library, Indiana University, Bloomington, Indiana.

like the classical Hollywood cinema's conventional romantic subplot); each strand contains its own villain, climax, and resolution. From his perspective on narrative structure, Berg demonstrates again how central ethnicity is to the meaning of the Ford film and how complicated a presence it can be in his work.

Joan Dagle's article, "Linear Patterns and Ethnic Encounters in the Ford Western," also focuses on Ford's depiction of race and ethnicity, but does so more exclusively in relation to the narrative structure and narration of Ford's sound-era Westerns. Dagle contrasts the early, linear approach to storytelling of Ford's prewar *Stagecoach* with the more circular and episodic storylines of *Fort Apache* and *The Searchers*. This general shift is accompanied by simultaneous complications in Ford's rendering of Native Americans in the postwar films. *Stagecoach* simply opposes the diverse white passengers in the coach, who eventually become unified by their ordeal, to the distant, alien, and attacking Apache. An early skirmish with the Native Americans in *Fort Apache* seems to replicate the textual politics of *Stagecoach*, but the film subsequently complicates this scheme, as we learn the reasons for the Apache's departure from their reservation and see the fort commandant's obstinate refusal of a peaceful mediation. At the fort, a fairly harmonious white enclave has been disrupted by the arrival of the new commandant, Lieutenant Colonel Thursday, as much as by the Apache revolt led by Cochise. Similarly, *The Searchers* initially promises classical linearity with the reports of Comanche attacks; however, the ensuing search for the captive Debbie constitutes a series of criss-crossing travels within an ambiguous time scheme.

By subjecting sequences from these films to closer analysis, Dagle enables us to appreciate more fully the nuances and subtle techniques whereby Ford carefully guides spectator interpretation of and emotional engagement with dramatic action. She argues that "in the postwar period, ideological disturbances regarding notions of masculinity, nationhood, and race affect Ford, the genre, and the larger culture and 'erupt' in the films in interesting ways." Yet she carefully notes that these shifts in Ford's approach to narrative and narration do not occur gradually over time—the 1950 *Wagon Master* is as linear a film as any in the Ford canon, while *Stagecoach*'s quizzical geography and mismatched screen direction hint at the more significant dislocations to come in *The Searchers*.

Peter Lehman provides another example of fresh ideological analysis by examining in unprecedented detail the place of money and capitalism in Ford's Westerns. Lehman argues that the Westerns consistently fail to overtly acknowledge the central role capitalism played in civilizing the West. Instead, Ford's evil capitalists—the selfish banker in *Stagecoach*, the Indian trader Meacham in *Fort Apache*, the double-dealing fort sutler of *She Wore a Yellow Ribbon*, and Futterman, the duplicitous frontier entrepreneur in *The Searchers*—are excluded from and in opposition to the humane Fordian ideals represented by the families and communities tied to the land. Lehman traces the motif of money and its exchange through the body of Ford's work, noting its strong dramatization in *Young Mr. Lincoln*. As a store owner, Ford's Lincoln employs an exemplary barter system (law books for dry goods) and, as a lawyer, he settles disputes in a search for justice rather than for monetary gain. This concept of a capitalism that cannot be spoken characterizes nearly all of Ford's sound Westerns—perhaps most notably in the mystery surrounding the source of Ethan Edwards's freshly minted coins and his bequest of the Edwards family farm to Martin Pawley.

The next three essays consider Ford's Westerns in relation to other art forms. Ed Buscombe's essay, "Painting the Legend," written more than a decade after Robin Wood's, takes an entirely different approach to Ford and the Western by examining the "controlling influence which visual images had upon the formation of the idea of 'the West' and subsequently upon the Western as a cinematic genre." In this argument, illustrator-painter Frederic Remington holds a decisive place. For unlike ethnographic and romantic landscape painters (such as George Catlin among the former, and Albert Bierstadt and Thomas Moran among the latter) who took the American wilderness as a subject, Remington pursued an action-adventure aesthetic in which popular notions of the West "became overwhelmingly dominated by images of fierce struggles between man and man, and between man and nature." Buscombe also stresses that such images, more widely distributed than photographs at the time, were still influenced by photographic experiments of the late Victorian era (such as those recording animal motion).

Buscombe places painting and photographic conventions of rendering the American West—focusing on dramatic, violent subjects—within the historical and cultural framework of the Spanish-American War, which, with Teddy Roosevelt's help, decisively established a version of American virility at the frontier. Yet, Buscombe points out, Remington sustained a different vision of frontier masculinity, that of the itinerant cowboys, ragtag settlers, and "horse soldiers" who achieve victory in defeat. Buscombe suggestively links this vision to U.S. reluctance to recognize its imperialistic motives and actions against both Native Americans and Mexicans. Ford's films share much with Remington's perspective on Western expansion and the military exploits that supported it (and other imperialist moves, as on Cuba). "This is not to say that the cinema merely reproduced what already existed," Buscombe concludes, "only that by the time Western films began to be made a corpus of work was in existence which already predefined what 'the West' could be taken to mean." His observation takes on particular force if one recalls that Ford's first feature-length Western film, *Straight Shooting* (1917), was only eight years away from Remington's last depictions of Western subjects (1909).

Like Edward Buscombe's essay, Kathryn Kalinak's "'The Sound of Many Voices': Music in John Ford's Westerns" considers these films from the stand-

Ford's films share much with Remington's perspective on Western
expansion. *She Wore a Yellow Ribbon* (1949).
Courtesy of the Museum of Modern Art Film Stills Archive.

point of another art form: in this instance, music. Kalinak illuminates the variety and complexity of musical materials used in these films (and which Ford often personally selected), as part of their ideological project of "defining an American nation." Kalinak combines archival research into Hollywood production practices with close textual analysis to argue that in *My Darling Clementine* and *Stagecoach* Ford creates a sense of community by excluding Others (the Indian and Mexican characters, sexual and legal outlaws). She further asserts that the selection, placement, and performance of songs in all his sound Westerns construe ideological boundaries as legendary history.

Beyond the particular case of Ford Westerns, Kalinak broaches larger issues of classical Hollywood style and, even more broadly, the question of how "music operates in and through culture and what happens to music's function when it becomes channeled through a film score." In reference to classical Hollywood, Kalinak's answer to that question is that these films "harness music's expressivity" through cultural associations that make music "a kind of aural shorthand." Following the conclusions of film music scholar Caryl Flinn, Kalinak further asserts that music can have a "utopian function" that imbues its listeners with an aching nostalgia for more fulfilling, simpler times. In Ford's case, music serves to authenticate the director's construction of an idealized past on the Western frontier.

Barry Grant completes our trilogy of essays that situate Ford's Westerns in relation to other art forms. Grant makes a very specific and long overdue comparison of Ford's films with the proto-Westerns of James Fenimore Cooper and his novels, including *The Last of the Mohicans*, featuring Natty Bumppo. Grant finds that Ford and Cooper share a predilection for flaws in technique (Cooper's stilted prose and Ford's discontinuous screen action), while generating and sustaining powerful national myths, such as the opposition of community and individualist values. The striking parallels between Cooper and Ford are also evidenced in their similar deployment of landscape. In the stories of both, landscape serves to test their characters' moral ideals and especially their ability to embrace intuitive, democratic values free of European prejudices. For example, Natty Bumppo's knowledge and love of the terrain contrasts with the British officers' imperial distaste for this colonial frontier, just as the Ringo Kid in *Stagecoach* understands more readily than any other white character the skills necessary to survive, including deciphering the meaning of Native American smoke signals.

Finally, as Grant notes, both artists "moved from an initial optimism about America and democracy toward increasing doubt and disillusionment," to the extent that late in their careers, both Cooper and Ford created elegiac works with abstracted landscapes associated with island utopias (Cooper's *The Crater* and Ford's *Donovan's Reef* [1963]). In considering the utopian (and dystopian) impulses in Ford's late films, Grant elaborates on and extends one of Robin Wood's earlier observations. Grant finds, in the similar trajectories of these two artists, evidence of the cyclicality of the Western and of all popular genres. His essay thus clarifies in great detail Ford's relationship to Cooper's legacy as it also offers insights into the iconographic and narrative development of the entire genre.

This part of our volume concludes with Charles Maland's survey of Ford's public reputation. Maland argues that the director came to be identified chiefly with the Western rather late in his career. He traces Ford's image from the twenties and thirties, when he was seen as a pipe-smoking artiste and admirer of German director F. W. Murnau, through the thirties and forties, when he came to be imaged as a social realist with a strong commitment to his Irish roots as well as to making films, such as *The Informer* (1935), *The Grapes of Wrath*, and *How Green Was My Valley*, that are visually artful and emotionally moving in telling stories of common people who are tested by social and economic situations.

Maland discovers through examination of film reviews, trade publications, and popular press commentary that the image of Ford we typically hold today—the hard-nosed but inspiring artist—has its roots in screenwriter Frank Nugent's influential 1949 profile of the director for the *Saturday Evening Post,* "Hollywood's Favorite Rebel," as well as in film critic Lindsay Anderson's assessments of Ford in the early 1950s. While the *Cahiers du cinéma* critics in that decade long ignored Ford, in spite of the *politique des auteurs,* he was fully recognized as the consummate auteur director of Westerns in the early 1960s.

This recognition was simultaneous with the appearance of several of his Westerns (from *The Horse Soldiers* [1959] through *The Man Who Shot Liberty Valance*) and was also influenced by the writings of Peter Bogdanovich, Michael Barkun, and Andrew Sarris, American critics who acknowledged more readily than their French predecessors in auteurism Ford's achievements as a director working within a generic and stylistic context. "So," Maland concludes, "John Ford was, according to his public reputation at different points in his career, the aesthete, the Irish genius, the chronicler of the West, and Pappy. He was also, according to observers at various times, a realist, a master film stylist, a liberal, a conservative, a patriot, and more."

As Maland suggests, we can learn a great deal about Ford and his Westerns from the commentary of "observers at various times," and in the spirit of this remark, we have assembled in Part 2 of this volume a dossier of documents. These provide sample commentaries that reveal Ford's public figure as it was constructed over the decades, as well as illuminating the pattern of his own public comments on his career, critics, friends, and the Hollywood filmmaking system. The first of these documents, "John Ford: Fighting Irish," from a 1936 issue of *New Theater* magazine, portrays Ford as a gruff, Oscar-winning artist; Frank Nugent's highly influential "Hollywood's Favorite Rebel" follows as an important marker of a major shift in Ford's public reputation. We also include Ford's essay on John Wayne, previously unavailable in English, and originally published in the Italian journal *Hollywood* in March 1951. "The Old Wrangler Rides Again" provides a fascinating interview with Ford just before the release of *Cheyenne Autumn*. In this article, Ford makes a spirited defense of Westerns and argues that the genre offers the best possible subject for the movies. He also gives a "take-no-prisoners" assessment of the role of movie critics in constructing his reputation, and comments on the role of women and Native Americans in Westerns. Finally, we include the moving posthumous tribute to Ford published in the Directors Guild of America publication, *Action*, in 1973. While these pieces may be read as supplements to the academic essays that precede them, we believe that they stand on their own and hold enormous interest in and of themselves.

The more we study the works of John Ford, the more we appreciate the intricacies of their meanings. Obviously, different audiences in different places, times, and cultural circumstances produce differently nuanced interpretations, but even given this, ambiguities abound in Ford. Within a genre originated by Hollywood and renowned for its accessibility of meaning, for its simplicity if not for its simple-minded approach to everything from acculturation to violence, Ford's films challenge us with their complexity not only in individual films, but across films. In order to address that diachronic complexity in Ford, we asked each of our contributors for analyses that extend beyond a single film.

We believe that the essays in this volume have value in illuminating the strong appeal of Ford's work to contemporary scholars who are interested in ethnicity and gender, narrative and cinema as a syncretic form, as well as the relationship among cinema, myth, and the representation of history. At the same time, we know that further explorations into Ford's Westerns are required. Critics tend to gloss over Ford's "minor" or less "legendary" Westerns (*3 Godfathers, The Horse Soldiers*) in favor of exploring his better-known works. Among the former we would include his extant silent Westerns for the Universal and Fox studios as a high priority for future research. Moreover, while Charles Maland's essay broaches the issue of Ford's reputation in relation to particular films, full-scale studies of the reception of Ford's films and assessments of what his films meant to their immediate audiences would prove invaluable.

We expect film critics and scholars will continue to explore John Ford's Westerns as long as movies matter. Although the Western may only occasionally experience a muffled revival or may be involved in an ongoing transmutation into other genres, the evidence in this volume—and on the screen—continues to testify to the overwhelming richness and relevance of John Ford's Westerns.

NOTES

1. There are many different versions of this famous statement, and we have let those differences stand in this volume, in part because the circulation of more than one version resonates with the notions of history and myth that Ford pursues in so many of his Westerns. Also, it is virtually impossible to know which version is correct. In response to our inquiries, the Directors Guild told us that it has neither written minutes nor a recording of the proceedings (telephone conversations, October 1998). Most often, Ford is quoted as having said, "My name's John Ford. I make Westerns." Joseph L. Mankiewicz, who should have remembered (since the meeting was all about him!), quotes Ford as having said, "My name's John Ford. I am a director of Westerns" in Bogdanovich, *John Ford* (Berkeley: University of California Press, 1968), 19. However, the more formal construction of this version of the statement also makes it somehow less mythically Fordian, less fitting for a man whose persona was long associated with a scoffing at pretension.

2. See Bogdanovich, *John Ford*, 19; Robert Parrish, *Growing up in Hollywood* (New York: Harcourt, 1976), 201–210; and Tag Gallagher, *John Ford: The Man and His Films* (Berkeley: University of California Press, 1986), 340–341.

3. Ford's birth date is often listed as 1895, but the correct date is 1894, according to Gallagher, *John Ford*, 2, as well as Joseph McBride and Michael Wilmington, *John Ford* (New York: Da Capo Press, 1975), 1.

4. The citation, read by President Nixon, included the following: "In the annals of American film, no name shines more brightly than that of John Ford. . . . As an interpreter of the nation's heritage, he left his personal stamp indelibly printed on the

consciousness of whole generations both here and abroad. In his life and in his work, John Ford represents the best in American films and the best in America." An edited version of the award show has been available on laser disc as "The American Film Institute Life Achievement Awards: John Ford," Image Entertainment, Inc.

5. Quoted in McBride and Wilmington, *John Ford*, 18.

6. Bogdanovich, *John Ford*, 23.

7. See Ronald L. Davis, *John Ford: Hollywood's Old Master* (Norman: University of Oklahoma Press, 1995), 12.

8. Robin Wood, "John Ford," in *Cinema: A Critical Dictionary*, vol. 1, ed. Richard Roud (New York: Viking, 1980), 371.

9. See Gallagher, *John Ford*, 16, 503.

10. Andrew Sarris, *The John Ford Movie Mystery* (Bloomington: Indiana University Press, 1975), 16.

11. See Ford's interviews with Lindsay Anderson in Anderson, *About John Ford* (New York: McGraw-Hill, 1981), 16, 22, 26. Ford tells Anderson, "You do the best you can. . . . And remember that with all these pictures, I wasn't just working to pay off on *The Fugitive*, but to make enough for *The Quiet Man* as well" (22).

12. See Gallagher, *John Ford*, 457–469, on Ford's working methods.

13. See George Custen, *Twentieth Century's Fox: Darryl F. Zanuck and the Culture of Hollywood* (New York: Basic Books, 1997), 238–239, 253–254; on Ford's working with Wanger on *Stagecoach* and *The Long Voyage Home* (1940), see Matthew Bernstein, *Walter Wanger, Hollywood Independent* (Minneapolis: University of Minnesota Press, 2000), 146–150.

14. In 1971, Robin Wood observed that after *Stagecoach*, twenty-four of Ford's thirty-four feature films were set in the past, "and nowhere does he show either the inclination or the ability to confront the realities of contemporary American life in his work" (Robin Wood, "'Shall We Gather at the River?': The Late Films of John Ford," *Film Comment* 7, no. 3 [Fall 1971], 14, reprinted in this volume). Richard Slotkin's interpretation of Ford's cavalry trilogy in *Gunfighter Nation* takes issue with the view that Ford's films, at least in this specific case, were divorced from contemporary national political concerns. See Slotkin, *Gunfighter Nation: The Myth of the Frontier in Twentieth-Century America* (New York: Atheneum, 1992), 328–343, 347–365.

15. Andrew Sarris placed Ford within his "pantheon" of outstanding Hollywood directors in that bible of U.S.-style auteurism, *American Cinema: Directors and Directions* (New York: Dutton, 1966), 43–49.

16. Peter Lehman, "Editorial," *Wide Angle: Special John Ford Issue* 2, no. 4 (1978), 3.

17. Sarris describes Anderson's "John Ford" as "written in 1955 and finally published in the magazine *Cinema* in 1971." However, a part of Anderson's critical commentary on Ford's work was previously published in the United States as "John Ford," *Films in Review* 2, no. 2 (Feb. 1951), 5–16. See Sarris, *The John Ford Movie Mystery*, 9. Other works of the period include Jean Mitry's *John Ford* (Paris: Editions Universitaires, 1954), John Baxter's *The Cinema of John Ford* (New York: A. S. Barnes, 1971), Philippe Haudiquet's *John Ford* (Paris, Editions Seghers, 1966), McBride and Wilmington's *John Ford*, and Bogdanovich's *John Ford*. For noteworthy special issues devoted to Ford, see the selected bibliography at the end of this volume.

18. The striking exception to this rule is Michael Dempsey's "John Ford: A Reassessment," *Film Quarterly* 28, no. 4 (1975): 2–15.

19. Sarris, *The John Ford Movie Mystery,* 15.

20. Lindsay Anderson, *About John Ford* (London: Plexus Publishing, 1981), 9.

21. Sarris, *The John Ford Movie Mystery,* 24.

22. Peter Wollen, *Signs and Meaning in the Cinema* (Bloomington: Indiana University Press, 1969); *Cahiers du cinéma* Collective, "*Young Mr. Lincoln,*" in *Movies and Methods,* vol. 1, ed. Bill Nichols (Berkeley: University of California Press, 1976), 493–528.

23. William Darby is clear in his adherence to notions of the film director as a site of unified authorship: "My aim is not to place him [Ford] inside any theory of cinematic authorship or to filter his work through some current ideological sieve but rather to demonstrate the high degrees of thematic and artistic coherence in his western films" (Darby, *John Ford's Westerns: A Thematic Analysis with a Filmography* [Jefferson, N.C.: McFarland, 1996], 1). See also Tag Gallagher, who notes, "To propose that John Ford was as major an artist as ever produced by America is to invite ridicule, at least today" (*John Ford,* vii).

24. See, in particular, Brian Henderson, "*The Searchers:* An American Dilemma," *Film Quarterly* 34, no. 2 (Winter 1980–1981): 9–23, reprinted in *Movies and Methods: An Anthology,* vol. 2, ed. Bill Nichols (Berkeley: University of California Press, 1985), 429–449; Nick Browne, "The Spectator-in-the-Text: The Rhetoric of *Stagecoach,*" *Film Quarterly* 29, no. 2 (Winter 1975–1976), reprinted in Nichols, ed., *Movies and Methods,* vol. 2, 458–475; Robert Ray, *A Certain Tendency of the Hollywood Cinema* (Princeton, N.J.: Princeton University Press, 1985). For a more explicitly auteurist approach to Ford, see Peter Lehman, "An Absence Which Becomes a Legendary Presence: John Ford's Structured Use of Off-Screen Space," *Wide Angle* 2, no. 4 (1978), 36–42, and his "Looking at Luke's Missing Reverse Shot," *Wide Angle* 4, no. 4 (1981), 65–70.

25. On the level of popular discourse, Ford has not been overlooked, though he does not figure as prominently as one might expect. In the recently released American Film Institute list of "The 100 Best Films of 100 Years," two of Ford's sound-era Westerns appear (*Stagecoach* at no. 63 and *The Searchers* at no. 96). The AFI list is most obviously an industry promotion (and celebration) of its product in the last two decades.

26. In addition to Richard Slotkin's work, see Jane Tompkins, *West of Everything* (New York: Oxford University Press, 1992), and Lee Clark Mitchell, *Westerns: Making the Man in Fiction and Film* (Chicago: University of Chicago Press, 1996). For new perspectives on Western history, see William Cronon, George Miles, and Jay Gitlin, eds., *Under an Open Sky: Rethinking America's Western Past* (New York: W. W. Norton, 1992).

PART ONE
ESSAYS

1

"SHALL WE GATHER AT THE RIVER?"

THE LATE FILMS OF JOHN FORD

Robin Wood

The Man Who Shot Liberty Valance seems to me John Ford's last successful movie; yet most of Ford's admirers appear to place a very high value on the three features that followed it, finding sustained significance in *Donovan's Reef*, explaining away the weaknesses of *Cheyenne Autumn* in terms of studio interference, and acclaiming *Seven Women* as a masterpiece. Of these three films only *Cheyenne Autumn* strikes me as deserving any great effort of critical attention, the other two seeming thin and perfunctory; and I have yet to find any convincing case made out for them by their professed admirers—a case that doesn't simply take their value for granted and concentrate on the kind of peripheral felicities one can expect *any* Ford to offer. This article is at once an attempt to account for the failure of these films as I see it, and an open call for reasoned disagreement, for a demonstration of their substance or stature.

One way of defining the relationship of Ford's late films to his previous work would be to compare *The Man Who Shot Liberty Valance* with *My Darling Clementine*. One's immediate reaction to the juxtaposition may at first seem paradoxical: that the later is more complex but less rich. In fact, the sense that *Clementine* is the less complex work proves on reflection to be illusory: the impression derives simply from the fact that its complexities are experienced as resolvable in a constructive way, the different positive values embodied in East and West, in civilization and wilderness, felt to be ultimately reconcilable and mutually fertilizing. There is, it is true, as in all of Ford's Westerns a pervading note of nostalgia to be taken into account. But the tone of the opening and close of *Liberty Valance* is more than nostalgic: it is overtly elegiac.

It is, however, the long central section of *Liberty Valance* that most invites comparison with *Clementine*, and the difference of tone here is very marked. It is partly determined by the movement away from location shooting to studio work in the later film, and partly by the characterization: both tend strongly

"'*Shall* We Gather at the River?': The Late Films of John Ford," by Robin Wood, originally appeared in *Film Comment* 7, no. 3 (Fall 1971), pp. 8–23. Reprinted by permission.

toward stylization. The sense of community is certainly there in *Liberty Valance*—in the restaurant, the schoolroom scene, the political meeting—but it is sketched rather than lovingly created. It is not that there is an absence of detail; what is lacking in the later film and present in the earlier is something much less tangible, something perhaps only describable in loose terms such as "aura" but palpably *there* in *Clementine*. One sees this, I think, if one asks where in *Liberty Valance* there is an equivalent of the Sunday-morning sequence where Earp and Clementine join and dignify the dance on the newly dedicated floor of the unbuilt church. The schoolroom scene in *Liberty Valance,* though it has something of the same *thematic* value—the development of civilization within a primitive community—seems in itself relatively cursory, as if Ford were by now content with establishing what was necessary where earlier a major element in the creative impulse had been an outgoing love and tenderness for the thing itself. The characterization in the later film is very much broader, two-dimensional, verging in several cases on the comic-grotesque. Fonda's Wyatt is a far more detailed creation than either Stewart's or Wayne's performance in the later film. The grotesquerie of the minor parts is immediately striking if one compares Marvin's Valance with Walter Brennan's Clanton, or Edmond O'Brien's editor with Alan Mowbray's Shakespearean actor: this latter comparison offers the difference between an essentially straight character-part rendered into caricature by the performance and an inherently grotesque role given a naturalistic roundness and complexity. It is difficult to make these distinctions without suggesting that *Liberty Valance* is the inferior film, and this is not my aim (I think both reach a level of achievement where discriminations of the A-is-better-than-B kind become merely petty and academic). All I want is to establish here, as a starting point, are the different natures of the two films, and to suggest that there is more than one possible explanation: one could argue that Ford in his old age had the right to take his previous work for granted, that no one should ask him to do again what he did in *Clementine* when he wants, perhaps using *Clementine* as a reference point, to go on to do something quite different; or one could argue that something very important in his earlier work had been undermined or whittled away, leaving a gap the new developments, while very interesting in themselves, cannot fill. Far from being incompatible, these two explanations can co-exist, suggesting in their juxtaposition something of the complexity of the issues involved in confronting late Ford.

In fact, *Liberty Valance* makes perfect artistic sense. The main body of the film has something of the nature of the morality play, the characters conceived more in terms of their functions than in terms of naturalistic characterization: Ford had undoubtedly by then developed a much sharper consciousness of the thematic level of his work. Before one accuses Edmond O'Brien, Lee Marvin, or Andy Devine of overplaying or crudity, one should pause to consider the homogeneity of tone of which their histrionic hyperbole constitutes a major

Tom Doniphon presents a cactus rose to Hallie in
The Man Who Shot Liberty Valance. What characters lose will be defined
in concrete, dramatic terms. James Stewart, Woody Strode, Vera Miles,
John Wayne, John Qualen, and Jeanette Nolan.
Courtesy of The Lilly Library, Indiana University, Bloomington, Indiana.

element: it is above all what distinguishes the main body of the film from the framework, where this quality is totally absent. The distinction is most obvious in the playing of Devine, since (unlike Marvin and O'Brien) he appears in both framework and flashback: the Link Appleyard of the film's "present," though an entirely convincing development of the character, appears thoroughly subdued and demoralized beside the Link Appleyard of the film's past; he has become sadder and more sensitive, the inherent pathos has become manifest. In his development is epitomized the whole relationship between framework and flashback. The Old West, seen in retrospect from beside Tom Doniphon's coffin, is invested with an exaggerated, stylized vitality; in the film's "present" (still, of course, *our* past, but connected to our present, as it were, by the railroad that carries Senator Stoddard and Hallie away at the end) all real vitality has drained away, leaving only the shallow energy of the news-hounds, and a weary, elegiac feeling of loss. What is lost for the characters is defined in concrete, dramatic terms in the film—but there is beyond this a sense that the loss is also Ford's. What Ford had lost becomes steadily clearer, I think, through a close examination of the three post–*Liberty Valance* films; for the moment, suffice it to say that it is what was so abundantly and pervasively present in *Clementine:* in the texture and spirit of the film as much as its thematic structure.

Of Ford's nine feature films from *The Searchers* to *Liberty Valance* all but two (*The Rising of the Moon* and *Gideon of Scotland Yard*) are set in America and are concerned to varying degrees with episodes and epochs in American history; of the three made since, only *Cheyenne Autumn* is set in America, the other two in very remote parts of the world, and a fourth film started by Ford and abandoned because of illness (*Young Cassidy*) is set in Ireland. Coincidence, perhaps, but I find the simple fact in itself suggestive. The course of Ford's flight from his own country—I think it amounts to that—to the Pacific, to China, or back to Ireland, is interrupted only by his account of the desperate trek of the Cheyenne back to their native country. The relationship of *Cheyenne Autumn* to the cavalry trilogy (*Fort Apache, She Wore a Yellow Ribbon, Rio Grande*) parallels that of *Liberty Valance* to *Clementine* and is even more richly suggestive. The failure of *Cheyenne Autumn* as a work of art is due less to studio interference than to Ford's inability—after so many years working with Indians, and despite scrupulous care in research—to create a really convincing Cheyenne life: his actors may be going through all the correct motions but they remain wooden Indians. This failure of the imagination relates significantly to much else in Ford (indeed to many of his imaginative successes) and I shall return to it. The film becomes intensely moving only, I think, when one sees it in relation to the earlier cavalry films, and thinks of Ford rather than of his characters.

That Ford himself wanted us to be aware of a connection is suggested by a number of cross-references, some of which at least can hardly have been unconscious. *She Wore a Yellow Ribbon* was the first Ford film in which Ben Johnson appeared and the second in which Harry Carey Jr. appeared (the first was *3 Godfathers,* a year earlier). In it, Johnson is a sergeant and Carey a lieutenant. They are both cavalrymen again (though now mere troopers) in *Rio Grande,* having also appeared together in the intervening *Wagon Master. Cheyenne Autumn* not only reunites them as troopers but nostalgically gives to Johnson his two recurring catchphrases from *Yellow Ribbon:* "That ain't in my department," and "I don't get paid for thinking." What's more, Johnson did not appear in any of Ford's intervening films and had become largely overlooked in Hollywood movies, so his casting in *Cheyenne Autumn* constitutes one in the long line of Fordian "resurrections" of forgotten or passed-over actors; it is also a resurrection of the earlier character, though he now has a different name.

This reminder is sufficient to alert us to a number of specific reversals of motifs from the cavalry trilogy (especially *Yellow Ribbon*). In *Yellow Ribbon* the Indians' horses are stampeded by the cavalry; in *Cheyenne Autumn* the Indians stampede the cavalry horses. In *Yellow Ribbon* a solitary white man (Johnson, in fact) is pursued by a party of Cheyenne, and escapes by urging his horse over a chasm which the Indians' horses can't leap; in *Cheyenne Autumn* a solitary Cheyenne is pursued by a party of white men, and escapes in precisely the same manner (here, even the movement within the image is reversed, right to left in the earlier film, left to right in the later). One of the most touching and thematically central scenes in *Yellow Ribbon* is the nocturnal burial, with full honors, of General Clay, the Confederate general reenlisted as a trooper after the Civil War; one of the most visually impressive scenes in *Cheyenne Autumn* is the ceremonial burial of the Indian chief, in which the Cheyenne warriors move on horseback against the skyline in a way that strikingly recalls certain of Ford's favorite heroic cavalry images.

Such specific reversals point of course to far more general reversal-patterns in *Cheyenne Autumn*. There is a significant transference of Christian imagery. The best reference point here is the climax of *Rio Grande*. There, troopers Johnson and Carey (with Claude Jarman Jr.) protect the white children they have rescued from the Indians in a church. A little girl summons the cavalry by ringing the church bell, and the troopers actually shoot down Indians through a cross-shaped aperture in the church door. In *Cheyenne Autumn* it is shells from cavalry cannons that kill and injure Indian children who are under the protection of Quaker Deborah Wright (Carroll Baker), the film's chief representative of Christianity. What is striking is not merely the reversal but the weakening of the Christian imagery. Church, bell, and cross in *Rio Grande* are integrated in a climax of triumphant force and power; Deborah in *Cheyenne Autumn* is largely ineffectual, unable to do anything amid the chaos of the battlefield but wind a rag as a bandage around a child's injured leg without even removing the blood-soaked clothing already covering the wound.

Ford clearly made *Cheyenne Autumn* with the deliberate intention of righting the balance of sympathies and allegiances in the earlier cavalry Westerns, and the intention is partly realized in the reversal-patterns. At the end of *Fort Apache* John Wayne, having adopted Henry Fonda's dress, mannerisms, and persona, and having contributed to the whitewashing of his character, is about to depart, on the mission of herding the last rebel Indians back into the reservations. The film seems to me—quite astonishingly, in view of what has gone before—to be at that point solidly behind him. At least, it is extremely difficult to detect any irony in the tone of the last scene, Wayne's abrupt (as presented) capitulation to the kind of fascist policy and outlook the rest of the film seemed to have been criticizing being linked unequivocally with that continuity of tradition which Ford consistently endorses in his work: a complete analysis of the scene would reveal, I think, the intimate interconnection of its every detail, relating the attitude to the Indians to the naming of Shirley Temple's baby ("Michael Thursday York O'Rourke"). Those who see irony and ambiguity here must concede, I think, that they are arguing against the tone of the scene and trusting the tale, not the artist. Certainly, the ending does violence to the previous development of the Wayne character and to the whole drift of the preceding narrative. *Cheyenne Autumn* undoubtedly reverses Ford's decision there, at least as far as the Indians are concerned.

In fact, diverse pulls and impulses have always existed in Ford. At times they can give rise to a rich complexity (*My Darling Clementine*) or carefully defined ambivalence (*The Man Who Shot Liberty Valance*), at others to confusion and self-contradiction, as at the end of *Fort Apache*. An artist need not necessarily be a clear thinker, but Ford's self-contradictions can sometimes be very disconcerting. Peter Bogdanovich, questioning him as to whether the men should have obeyed Fonda in *Fort Apache* knowing that he was wrong, elicited the following forthright response: "Yes—he was the colonel, and what he says goes; whether they agree with it or not, it still pertains. In Vietnam today, probably a lot of guys don't agree with their leader, but they still go ahead and do the job."* The interview was done during the filming of *Cheyenne Autumn,* which contains, in the Karl Malden sequence, one of the most devastating attacks on blind obedience the cinema has given us. (It's not a pleasant thought, but I can't escape the feeling that the fact that Malden plays a foreigner—a sort of Prussian archetype—was crucial in enabling Ford to denounce the character and his reliance on orders unequivocally: he is somehow not quite the U.S. army, not quite "one of us.") This is not a marginal point: concepts such as duty and obedience are integral to the Fordian value-complex. In *She Wore a Yellow Ribbon*—greatest of the cavalry trilogy and one of Ford's most deeply satisfying— the conflicts inherent in his attitude to duty, to the "book of rules," are treated in a beautifully complex and flexible way. He is always at his greatest as an artist when he (or his material) can allow his central traditionalist values to be challenged without being radically undermined. The attempt to "tell it the other way" in *Cheyenne Autumn* is quite another matter. The rich and complex ethic of the cavalry trilogy is built on interlocking and interdependent concepts of civilization, of the Indians, and of the cavalry itself; its structure collapses in ruins if the values invested in those concepts are undermined or reversed.

Ford's Westerns have always implicitly acknowledged that American civilization was built on the subjugation of the Indians; it is his attitude to that fact that changes. It is obvious that Indians in Westerns are not just a people but a concept: they have a basic mythic meaning on which individual directors ring

---

John Ford, by Peter Bogdanovich. Movie Paperback, p. 86.

many changes but which remains an underlying constant. As savages, they represent the wild, the untamed, the disruptive, the vital forces that remain largely unassimilable into any civilization man has so far elaborated: in psychological terms, the forces of the Id. James Leahy has drawn a parallel (in *Movie* 14) between Major Dundee's fanatically dedicated campaign against the Indians in Peckinpah's film and Captain Ahab's mission to destroy the White Whale. The psychological attitudes of directors who have made Westerns can usually be found accurately epitomized by or implicit in their treatment of Indians, as one sees if one examines the role of Indians in, say, *The Big Sky, Run of the Arrow,* and *Little Big Man* and works outward from that to apply one's findings to the total oeuvres of Hawks, Fuller, and Penn. In Ford's Westerns of the late thirties and early forties, the role of the Indians is relatively simple and not far removed from this pure archetype. The presentations of the Indians in *Stagecoach* and *Drums along the Mohawk* is almost entirely untroubled by any sense of them as individual human beings. The allegorical overtones of the stagecoach journey in the former help define the Indians' role. There are three coach stations, each more primitive than its predecessor. At the first there are no Indians; at the second the supposedly friendly Indians defect in the middle of the night; the third has been burnt down. When the Indians at last attack, Ford produces that stunning visual effect of the coach suddenly emerging into the great arid sandy waste; it is stunning not only because of its visual power but because of the symbolic overtones, the association of the Apache with barren desert. In *Drums along the Mohawk* the Indians are again screaming, destructive savages, a concept rather than characters, but a new and very important component is added to this by way of modification: Ford's paternalism, which continues basically unchanged right through to *Cheyenne Autumn.* As well as supplying Henry Fonda and Claudette Colbert with a devoted Indian servant, the film culminates in a poetic vision of integration that invariably (and understandably) evokes jeers from contemporary audiences, but which is rather touching in its naiveté: Indian and Negro, accepted in their subservient roles, joining in the salutation of the American flag.

An Indian makes a brief but significant appearance in *Clementine:* "Indian Joe," shooting up the town in a drunken frenzy, disturbing Wyatt Earp's first "civilizing" visit to the barber's. Earp knocks him around a bit and wants to know why he's been let out of the reservation: in racial terms the scene is obviously very unpleasant, but in mythic terms very meaningful, civilization conceived as demanding the rigorous suppression of the untamed forces Indian Joe represents.

The paternalist attitude dominates the treatment of the Indians in the cavalry trilogy: the noble and dignified Cochise in *Fort Apache,* and John Wayne's old friend Pony That Walks in *Yellow Ribbon* (the scene of their conference is perhaps the best involving an individual Indian in all Ford's Westerns), are in terms of presentation but two sides of the same coin. As in *Drums along the Mohawk*, the contrariness of Indians is typically attributed (in differing ways and to differing degrees) to the influence or interference of evil white men; which is a way of at once excusing the Indians and condescending to them. The presentation of the Indians in *Fort Apache* reveals characteristic confusion (rather than complexity—for the divergent attitudes are not held in any meaningful balance): the loathsome Meacham, purveyor of bad liquor, refers to them cynically as "children" and we are clearly meant to find the remark offensive. But Ford's own attitude isn't altogether clearly distinguishable from its inherent paternalism—Meacham is a nasty father, Ford supports kind ones—and one is left reflecting that, after all, it is only the cynicism in the remark that is supposed to be offensive. But Ford is too intelligent, too honest, and too generous to be quite content with that; and he builds up Cochise into a figure of considerable dignity and moral weight (though he remains very much the "noble savage," with the implication that he would behave himself if the white men were nice to him). He is sufficiently a presence to lead us to question not only Colonel Thursday's obviously monstrous attitudes and errors, but the whole validity of building a civilization at his expense. It is already the problem of the Indians that constitutes a potential threat to the stability of the whole structure of values elaborated in the cavalry films.

Cochise as a figure of considerable dignity and
moral weight in *Fort Apache* (1948).
Pedro Armendáriz, John Wayne, and Miguel Inclán.
Courtesy of The Lilly Library,
Indiana University, Bloomington, Indiana.

Comparisons between Ford and Hawks are usually mutually illuminating, nowhere more so than in their treatment of Indians. In *Red River* the Indians merely fulfil a plot function and the presentation of them is conventional and non-personal; it is *The Big Sky* that provides the basis for comparison. Hawks is scarcely more successful than Ford in creating a convincing Indian life on the screen, but the implicit attitude is radically different from Ford's. When Ford's heroes move out into the wilderness, they carry the frontier with them, extending it, establishing civilization. The whole movement of *The Big Sky* is a movement beyond the frontier, into the uncultivated wilds, away from what Boone (Dewey Martin) succinctly describes as "stinking people." Boone ends up accepting his marriage with an Indian girl and at least partial integration in her tribe: a denouement unambiguously endorsed by the film and unimaginable in Ford (compare the treatment of Martin Pawley's Indian "marriage" in *The Searchers*!). Most striking of all, perhaps, is the famous scene of the finger amputation, one of Hawks's favorite examples of his fondness for using violence or pain as material for robust humor. Jim (Kirk Douglas) knows the Indian superstition that you can't enter heaven if you don't die physically complete; and so, riotously drunk on whisky, he crawls in the dust around the campfire with his friends, searching for the severed finger which has been casually tossed aside. The white man becomes an Indian (just as, earlier, in the town, he picked up and adopted a Negro dance step), quite unself-consciously and without the slightest hint of condescension: there is no suggestion in Hawks's treatment of the scene that Jim is debasing himself. Can one imagine such a sequence in Ford?

The corollary of this opposition lies in the two directors' responses to civilization. Hawks's work, in fact, offers very little by way of a constructive attitude to civilization: most typically, his movies tend to become celebrations of all that civilization can't contain. Metaphorically, his heroes are always moving outside the frontier, either (in the adventure films) to form their own primitive societies with their own strictly functional rules for survival, or (in the comedies) into an exhilarating and perilous chaos and anarchy. Ford, on the contrary, is the American cinema's great poet of civilization. Where Hawks's world is dominated by the Id, Ford's is dominated by the Superego—though, in the best films of both, the domination is not unchallenged.

The ambivalence of Ford's attitude to civilization that reaches full explicitness in *Liberty Valance* is implicit in all his work. It is already very clear in *Stagecoach*. There, at one extreme, are the Apache, like an incarnation of the spirit of the wilderness, savage and irreducible; but the opposite pole is represented by the Purity League ladies who are (according to Claire Trevor) worse than the Apache. Between the two unacceptable extremes come characters embodying partially conflicting values between which one feels Ford's allegiances to be divided. The luncheon scene at the first coach station, for example, sets the artificial Southern gallantry of the fallen gentleman Hatfield against the natural courtesy of the outlaw Ringo; and sets the "cultivated" sensibility of cavalry wife Lucy Mallory against the natural sensitivity of the fallen Dallas. At the end of the film, as Ringo and Dallas drive away to start a new life together, Doc Boone comments, "Well, they're saved from the blessings of civilization." But Ringo and Dallas are setting out to start a farm and raise a family: their proposed future embraces precisely the fundamentals on which civilization is built.

The values that are in conflict in *Stagecoach* are partly reconciled in *Clementine*, Ford's most harmonious vision of a primitive but developing civilization. When Wyatt Earp and Clementine dance together on the church floor, it is as if Ringo were united with Lucy Mallory (except that Earp is the new marshal and Clementine sweeter, and more generous and open, than Lucy): the union of the natural with the cultivated. At the end of the film Clementine—without the flowered bonnet that marks her out as the girl from the East, and wearing a simple dress of the kind becoming her environment—is planning to stay on as a schoolteacher, while Earp hopes to pass that way again sometime: it [the scene] is touchingly tentative rather than triumphant, but rich in a sense of potentiality.

My Darling Clementine (1946), Wyatt Earp and Clementine Carter as "the union of the natural with the cultivated." Cathy Downs and Henry Fonda.
Courtesy of Barry Grant.

The Girl from the East turns up again in *Fort Apache,* in the person of Shirley Temple, and adds a further problem to that dense but problematic film: if civilization is adequately embodied in Miss Temple, with her relentless dimpled affectations, is it really worth defending? Everyone in the film coos over her effusively, and there is little indication that Ford realized that we might not fall in line and do the same. The partial answer is that the film's dramatization of the concept of civilization does not depend exclusively on her: there is the deeply affectionate and detailed portrayal of the "civilization" of the fort: the cavalry itself, and their wives and homes. The role of the cavalry in Ford's value system is a complex one. It is the defender of civilization, but it also embodies within itself what are for Ford civilization's highest values—honor, chivalry, duty, the sense of tradition—so that it almost comes to stand for civilization itself. Yet, clearly, it can never quite do this: the cavalry life is in obvious respects too specialized, too much a thing apart, and what is basic to Ford's (and most other people's) concept of civilization—marriage, home, family—is necessarily marginal to it.

Central to Ford's work is the belief in the value of tradition. This is clearly what attracts him so much to the cavalry—his cavalry, for, despite the authenticity of material details of dress, ritual, etc., it is obviously a highly personal creation. In the trilogy, the cavalry becomes Ford's answer to mortality and transience. Individuals come and go, but the continuity of tradition is unbroken, the individual gaining a kind of immortality through the loss of his individuality and assimilation into the tradition. The emphasis is on continuity rather than development: indeed, the moral objection to the end of *Fort Apache* is that it deliberately and perversely eschews the possibility of development by insisting that nothing in the tradition may change. The civilized values embodied in the cavalry—honor and duty—are essentially superego values, through the ever-recurring rituals and ceremonies that continue without modification. This is the most important difference between the concepts of civilization enacted in the Tombstone of *Clementine* and the cavalry of the trilogy, and it perhaps explains why Ford, wishing to affirm a belief in the continuity of civilized values, in a world changing radically and with alarming rapidity, turned from a developing community to an unchanging military body for an embodiment of his ideals.

The treatment of love relationships in Ford forms an entirely consistent part of this pattern: one could easily relate it, in psychological terms, to the presentation of the Indians on the one hand and the cavalry values on the other. Suffice it to say here that Ford tends to sublimate sexual attraction into either gallantry or heartiness: the relationships positively presented are always strictly "wholesome" and honorable. Romance and courtship have their own rules and rituals, and sexual love is never regarded by Ford as a value in itself. It becomes one only when subordinated to the concept of marriage and family, conceived less as the relation of individual to individual than as the establishment of con-

In a world changing radically, Ford turned to an unchanging military for "an embodiment of his ideals." John Wayne in *Rio Grande* (1950).
Courtesy of The Lilly Library, Indiana University, Bloomington, Indiana.

tinuity within a civilized tradition. He never treats sensuality positively: he can only tolerate Chihuahua in *Clementine* when she is shot and dying, whereupon he promptly sentimentalizes her (the character is the film's one major weakness). It is symptomatic also that he is so ill at ease when forced to depict sexual abnormality: the rapist in *Sergeant Rutledge* is conceived and acted in the crudest, most conventional terms; and Ford's direction of Margaret Leighton's Agatha Andrews in *Seven Women* looks as if someone had explained to him what a lesbian was five minutes before shooting and he hadn't had time to recover from the shock. Again, Hawks provides an illuminating contrast. The incestuous relationship of Tony and Cesca in *Scarface* becomes, in the last scenes, the most positive force in the film: the catastrophe is provoked not by the "abnormal" feelings but by the characters' refusal to confront and accept them, acceptance coming as a triumphant (if short-lived) release—Hawks anticipating Bertolucci by over thirty years! Hawks's treatment of sexual relationships has, of course, its own inhibitions and oddities; with his "primitive" lack of interest in tradition goes—again in sharp opposition to Ford—an apparent lack of interest in marriage except in the most superficial sense of the term. Yet the positive relationships in his films can incorporate eroticism more easily than can those in Ford. The Wayne/Dickinson relationship in *Rio Bravo*, for example, has a strong, if muted, erotic charge: in the Doc Holliday/Chihuahua relationship in *Clementine* the eroticism (very crudely and untenderly handled) is seen merely as part of Holliday's degeneration, as against the purity offered by Clementine.

In Ford's presentation of a growing civilization in *Clementine* and a "permanent" civilization in the cavalry films, nostalgia plays a key role. It is a paradox of the cavalry films, in fact, that "the army" is regarded as at once unchanging and in the past—it isn't the modern army. Ford's respect for the past works on various levels, in his casting as much as in the lovingly detailed re-creation of time and place. In a profoundly characteristic scene of *Fort Apache*, Dick Foran is let out of the jailhouse to sing "Genevieve" to an audience that includes Guy Kibbee, George O'Brien, Anna Lee, and Shirley Temple (also in the film are Pedro Armendáriz, Ford's old friends Ward Bond and Victor McLaglen, and Mae Marsh). The scene is like an old stars' reunion. The words of the song beautifully evoke the spirit of the cavalry trilogy, with its intermingling of historical reality and deeply personal fantasy: "But still the hand of mem'ry weaves / The blissful dreams of long ago." Of Ford's thirty-four feature films since *Stagecoach*, at least twenty-four are set in the past, and nowhere does he show either the inclination or the ability to confront the realities of contemporary American life in his work.

It is easy to argue that, in *Clementine*, *Wagon Master*, and the cavalry trilogy, Ford is primarily concerned with constructing a value system, only secondarily with depicting various stages in American civilization. Yet the two impulses are so closely interwoven as to be really inseparable. For his vision to retain its vitality, it was necessary for him to feel at least a possible continuity between the civilization depicted in his films and that of contemporary America. Already in the forties this must have been difficult; by the sixties it had clearly become impossible. What can Ford possibly be expected to make of contemporary American society—whether one calls it disintegrating or permissive—where no values are certain or constant, all traditions questioned and most rejected, all continuity disrupted, and where the army is a dirty word? Yet how could he possibly remain unaffected by it, unless his art became finally petrified and sterile? What is lost in *Liberty Valance* that was triumphantly present in *Clementine* is faith; hence the film's elegiac tone, and the sad, and very saddening, lack of conviction in the subsequent films.

Returning at last to *Cheyenne Autumn*, we can now clearly see the effect on Ford's structure of values of the reversal-patterns: it is, quite simply, undermined, and falls in ruins. The change in Ford's attitude to American civilization can be vividly illuminated by juxtaposing his two Wyatt Earps and the communities for which they are spokesmen: Fonda in *Clementine*, James Stewart in *Cheyenne Autumn*. The very concept of civilization has dwindled from its rich and complex embodiment in the church-floor dance of *Clementine* to the later Earp's desire to be allowed to finish his poker game undisturbed. An obvious weakness in *Cheyenne Autumn* is Ford's failure to define a coherent response to Deborah (Carroll Baker). Part of the trouble may lie in the reported studio interference with the casting. Ford told Peter Bogdanovich, "I wanted to do it right. The woman who did go with the Indians was a middle-aged spinster who finally dropped out because she couldn't take it any more. But you couldn't do that—you have to have a young, beautiful girl." One can explain his failure with the character in terms of a clash between his original concept and the conventional noble heroine. The problem is that Deborah most of the time seems silly and ineffectual, with her ludicrous inculcation of the alphabet, but the spectator is never sure that she is meant to be, so that the foolishness comes to seem in Ford as much as in the character. Deborah's ineffectuality is the more disappointing in that there are signs near the beginning of the film that she was partly meant to embody values that would effectively challenge those invested in the cavalry, and especially the Fordian nostalgia: she tells Widmark in the schoolhouse scene that he thinks only about the past, but she thinks of the future. Nothing in the film really fulfills the promise of radical questioning implicit in that moment.

Centrally revealing in the film is the incident involving Sergeant Wichowsky (Mike Mazurki) and his decision not to reenlist. On the night his enlistment period expires, Wichowsky gets drunk in his tent, where he is confronted by Captain Archer (Widmark). He tells Archer that he is a Pole, and in his country the Poles are persecuted by Cossacks; this, he now sees, is what they are doing to the Cheyenne—the cavalry are Cossacks; he won't reenlist. Archer can give him no answer to this. The next morning, as the troop rides on to continue the persecution, Wichowsky is in his place once again. No reason is given for his change of mind: perhaps none is necessary: there is simply nothing else for the man to do. And this is precisely Ford's position. The cavalry values have become shallow and worn: nowhere in the film is the treatment of the cavalry warmed and enriched with the loving commitment that characterized the trilogy. Yet, although Ford sees this well enough, like Wichowsky he can only "rejoin" them. Faced with the dilemma of the Cheyenne's predicament, he can only come up with the old paternalist answer, in the old paternalist figure of Edward G. Robinson. There is no more poignant moment in Ford's work than that in which Robinson in his bewilderment looks at a portrait of Lincoln and asks, "What would you do, old man?" But the poignance derives more from our sense of Ford's identification with

With *Cheyenne Autumn* (1964), Ford "tries to place the Cheyenne at the center of his value-system but merely turns them into an alternative establishment."
Courtesy of The Lilly Library, Indiana University, Bloomington, Indiana.

the character at that point and from our knowledge of his past work (particularly, of course, *Young Mr. Lincoln*, in which Fonda's performance so beautifully and convincingly incarnates the essential Fordian values) than from any success of artistic realization within the context of the film itself. The technically poor backprojection in the scene of Robinson's meeting with the Cheyenne was a misfortune necessitated, one gathers, by Robinson's unfitness to travel. But in expressive terms it has a sad appropriateness, adding the dimension of visual phoniness to the scene's general lack of conviction.

Ford's values are not really reversed; they are just disastrously weakened. His commitment to the cavalry is a commitment to the establishment; when he tries to place the Cheyenne at the center of his value system, he merely turns them into an alternative establishment, but without the richness and complexity of the cavalry world of the earlier films. The conception remains obstinately paternalist, the Indians' stiff and boring nobility thinly concealing Ford's condescension. The Sal Mineo subplot seems designed to offset this; it is said to have been severely cut by Warner Brothers in the final editing, but on the evidence of what is left one doubts whether it would ever have carried much conviction. Only an anti-establishment artist could hope to succeed with the kind of reversals Ford attempts in *Cheyenne Autumn*—as one can see if one turns from that to *Little Big Man*. Penn comes nearer than any other director to creating an Indian life and culture of genuine vitality, and this is partly because his social and psychological attitudes themselves tend to be subversive, because he is fascinated by spontaneity, by uninhibited natural responses, by the Id impulses. His presentation of white civilization in *Little Big Man,* although its obvious source is in Thomas Berger's novel, may owe something to *Cheyenne Autumn*'s Dodge City sequences. But the Dodge City interlude remains just that: it is never satisfactorily assimilated into the overall tone of the film, there is no significant give-and-take relationship between the "civilization" shown there and the Cheyenne. *Cheyenne Autumn* is a film without any really convincing positive center that yet never quite dares take the plunge into despair.

For all its failures, *Cheyenne Autumn* is a sufficiently rich and substantial film for some sort of positive case to be made out for it, and the interested reader should be referred to the article by Victor Perkins in *Movie* 12. If I find it much harder to discuss *Donovan's Reef* and *Seven Women,* this is because I find both films so weak that I can't imagine what serious case could be argued in their defense. *Donovan's Reef* is, according to *Movie,* Ford's *Hatari!* Certainly, one can see resemblances: both films have an improvisatory feel about them, something of the loose, relaxed air of a prolonged family party; both depict what one might take for their creators' ideal societies, as imagined at that stage of their careers. *Hatari!* seems to me considerably below the level of Hawks's greatest work, but *Donovan's Reef* is sadly inferior to it. Both "ideal" societies show a disturbing tendency toward the infantile: neither, at least, appears to encourage the development of anything one might call full human maturity. What gives *Hatari!* its organic life and formal coherence is the recurrent motif of interrelationships between instinct and consciousness, animals and humans, the primitive and the sophisticated. *Donovan's Reef* is formally a mess: it quite lacks *Hatari!*'s relaxed but unifying rhythm. Its narrative line is hopelessly broken-backed, Amelia Dedham's capitulation to the Ailakaowa way of life being so rapid (and so perfunctorily charted) that by halfway through the film there seems absolutely no reason why she should not simply be Told All, and the resulting plot-maneuvers to eke out the narrative before the final denouement become tedious and irritating in the extreme. This may seem a superficial objection—an apparently weak narrative line, after all, may serve (as in *Hatari!*) merely as a pretext for a series of thematic variations. But there is a difference between the almost unnoticeable narrative of *Hatari!* and the positive annoyance of that in *Donovan's Reef,* and the slipshod impression the film makes on this level seems to me symptomatic of a more general slovenliness and unconcern.

The nearest I have found to a reasoned defense of the film lies in the few hints offered in Peter Wollen's *Signs and Meaning in the Cinema,* where we are told that "the *auteur* theory enables us to reveal a whole complex of meaning in films such as *Donovan's Reef.*" The "whole complex of meaning" Mr. Wollen has in mind is presumably outlined in this passage:

In many of Ford's late films—*The Quiet Man, Cheyenne Autumn, Donovan's Reef*—the accent is placed on traditional authority. The island of Ailakaowa, in *Donovan's Reef,* a kind of Valhalla for the homeless heroes of *The Man Who Shot Liberty Valance,* is actually a monarchy, though complete with the Boston girl, wooden church and saloon, made familiar by *My Darling Clementine.* In fact, the character of Chihuahua, Doc Holliday's girl in *My Darling Clementine,* is split into two: Miss Lafleur and Lelani, the native princess. One represents the saloon entertainer, the other the non-American, in opposition to the respectable Bostonians, Amelia Sarah Dedham and Clementine Carter. In a broad sense, this is a part of a general movement which can be detected in Ford's work to equate the Irish, Indians and Polynesians as traditional communities, set in the past, counterposed to the march forward to the American future, as it has turned out in reality, but assimilating the values of the American future as it was once dreamed.

The motifs to which Mr. Wollen alludes are certainly present, more or less, in *Donovan's Reef.* The question he fails to ask—and which the Structuralist heresy helps him to evade—is this: how are "the values of the American future as it was once dreamed" *realized* in *Donovan's Reef*? It seems to me that, if those values (as I take it) are equated with Ford's earlier ideals and aspirations, they are consistently and painfully debased, all under cover of the film's rowdy humor. The Boston girl no longer represents anything significant in the way of cultural refinement: the civilization she comes from is briefly and grotesquely caricatured (the Boston board meeting, which one would set beside the Dodge City sequences of *Cheyenne Autumn* as evidence of how Ford's faith had crumbled), and she herself brings nothing to Ailakaowa that it couldn't do without. The shift in courtship patterns from the gallant to the hearty-brutal is surely significant: Clementine wasn't subjected to crude horseplay or the ultimate indignity of a spanking to encourage her to submit to her man. The church provides the film's one good scene—the Christmas Eve celebrations—but again one finds a coarsening of the values it embodied in *Clementine.* Ford's religion has always been more social than metaphysical; when he attempts to be religious he becomes merely religiose and maudlin. The church floor in *Clementine* is, typically, the scene of a dance, not a service. Yet as a social hub it has a profoundly serious significance into which the scene's varied and delicately handled comic elements are easily assimilated without the least incongruity. The Christmas Eve sequence in *Donovan's Reef* is—in a film largely given over to the childish—touchingly childlike. But the farcical elements (Marcel Dalio's clumsy overplaying is symptomatic) are no longer safely contained within an overall seriousness of affect. The church is no longer the focal point for a society, but a place where wildly heterogeneous elements assemble for a brief lark. As for the splitting in two of poor Chihuahua, one can see well enough that Miss Lafleur is her descendant—the similarities are confirmed by the way both are unceremoniously deposited in water by the film's heroes, apparently with Ford's full approval. But Mr. Wollen would have to explain rather more fully what Chihuahua is supposed to have in common with Lelani, who, although she isn't a sufficient presence in the film to count for much, clearly has more in common with Clementine, both in personality and in the treatment accorded her, and might have provided Mr. Wollen with another of his "significant" structural reversals. The passage quoted is a good example of how the apparent "scientific" rigors of Structuralist criticism can conceal the most extraordinary looseness of argument. In fact, *Donovan's Reef* is only interesting if one ignores the film and concentrates on its abstractable motifs; it can be defended only by a method that precludes any close reading of what is actually on the screen.

The tiresome and protracted buffoonery of *Donovan's Reef*, far from embodying any acceptable system of values, merely conceals an old man's disillusionment at the failure of his ideals to find fulfillment. The sadness inherent in Ford's situation reaches partial expression in *Seven Women*, which is why that film is so much less irritating. One can produce quite a *frisson* by cutting, mentally, across twenty years, from the moment where Clementine and Wyatt Earp walk toward developing civilization (in the form of the church) accompanied by a stately and devout rendering of "Shall We Gather At the River?" to the moment where Sue Lyon leads the children out of collapsing civilization (in the form of the mission) with a panicky and perfunctory singing of the same hymn. But if the film is Ford's acknowledgment of the disintegration of everything he had believed in, it is all done at several removes. He has fled not only to the other end of the world but to (for him) eccentric and partly uncongenial subject matter. (It is surely significant that Mr. Wollen, in his structural analysis of Ford, nowhere refers to this film.) The result is at best an accomplished minor work, though that is perhaps a generous estimate of a film that only intermittently transcends the schematic conventionalities of its script. There are numerous incidental felicities of mise en scène, but of the kind that suggests an old master skillfully applying his "touches" rather than an artist passionately involved in his material. Anne Bancroft carries off the central role (the eighth woman?—I can never get the sum out right) with magnificent swagger and assurance, but I hardly think it will go down in film history as her subtlest or most rounded characterization. I get the impression that the actress, like the character she is playing, looked round, summed up the situation, and set her mind to doing the best she could and enjoying herself as much as possible under the somewhat discouraging circumstances.

My chief impression of *Seven Women* is of hollowness. The essence of the film is a thinly concealed nihilism. The lack of real religious feeling in Ford prevents him from finding any transcendent spiritual values in the missionaries and their work; any positive belief in the mission as a community, or as an epitome of civilization, is made nonsense of by its futility, by its inner tensions and outer ineffectuality. The only alternatives presented are barbarism and the "tough" bitterness of Anne Bancroft. Ford's barbarians are merely brutes: he can't conceive of them as possessing any natural fineness, and their vitality is presented as exclusively destructive. They are monstrous Id-figures rising up to take revenge on the worn and faded superego values of civilization. Ford's presentation of them is very crude and simplistic, quite adequately expressed through Mike Mazurki's pantomime-giant "Ho-ho-ho." There are moments of quiet and touching tenderness, such as Miss Argent's farewell and Bancroft's response to it; but on the whole Ford's sense of positive human value seems greatly enfeebled.

It would be ungenerous to end on such a note. My primary aim is not to offer gratuitous insult to the failed late works of one of the cinema's great masters, but to right an injustice; for it seems to me that sentimentally to hail films like *Donovan's Reef* and *Seven Women* as masterpieces is insulting to Ford's real achievement. That achievement depended on a commitment to ideals which the society Ford lives in has signally failed to fulfill. But that invalidates neither the ideals nor the films. One shouldn't expect Ford to be able to cope with the kind of radical reorientation the failure of those ideals within American society demanded. The late films, certainly, have their poignance, but it is the product of their failure, not of their strength.

2

SACRED DUTIES, POETIC PASSIONS

JOHN FORD AND THE ISSUE OF FEMININITY IN THE WESTERN

Gaylyn Studlar

Lindsay Anderson once remarked, "When one thinks of it, it's a sensitive idea—a marvelously poetic idea—to call a film about Wyatt Earp and the gunfight at the OK Corral *My Darling Clementine*."[1] However, the title *My Darling Clementine* (1946) is more than a poetic gesture or idea, for the film spends as much time and energy establishing the growing attraction between cattleman-turned-marshal Wyatt Earp (Henry Fonda) and nurse-from-the-East-turned-schoolmarm Clementine Carter (Cathy Downs) as it does motivating and showing the gunfight at the OK Corral.[2] *My Darling Clementine* is thus recognizable as a Ford Western: it is surprisingly evasive in fulfilling the logic of a genre often regarded as uninterested in women at best, overtly misogynist at worst. From a feminist perspective, the title, theme song, and film itself are by no means ideologically unproblematic: the male is placed as the apparent "speaking subject" and the female is the "object" of his affection. Nevertheless, *My Darling Clementine* stands as one indicator of how the sound Westerns of John Ford often focus, with unexpected "poetic" intensity, on women and on "femininity" in ways that run counter both to recent assertions and to more long-standing critical expectations for the Western as a cinematic and literary form.

In its traditional manifestations, the Western is obviously male-centered storytelling. Over the years, some commentators have considered the genre childish, grounded in male adolescent adventure fantasies, and with little of note to say about women, gender, or sexuality.[3] Taking a somewhat different perspective, Leslie Fiedler's *Love and Death in the American Novel* considers the childishness of the Western quite important to matters of gender, for it makes the Western a highly visible example of the model American story. This story embraces "juvenile and regressive" themes and posits the woman as a "feared and forbidden other."[4] Westerns, says Fiedler, separate their heroes "from the women they preserve," a "taboo" evident in everything from Cooper's Leatherstocking Tales to Hemingway's novels.[5] Fiedler considers such "classic works" of American fiction one with the pop culture narratives "in which the cowhand and his side-kick ride in silent communion through a wilderness of sagebrush, rocks, and tumbleweed."[6] "Isolation," remarks Fiedler, "is the key, the non-presence of the customary. . . . And what 'he' [the hero] especially does not want is *women!*"[7]

In *West of Everything* literary scholar Jane Tompkins extends Fiedler's thesis to assert that the Western's power over audiences resides largely in the anxious flight of masculinity from femininity.[8] Tompkins argues that what men flee in the Western is not merely the cluttered Victorian interior but, more emphatically, "the domestic dramas that go on in that setting."[9] In recognizing that women in Westerns are assigned roles representing civilization as something to escape, she echoes not only Fiedler's analysis, but Robert Warshow in his seminal essay on the genre as a specifically cinematic form.

In "Movie Chronicle: The Westerner," Warshow argues that the great cinematic attraction of Westerns arises from the innate seriousness of the genre's moral order and the implications its preferred style of masculinity embodies for that order. For Warshow, the hero represents first and foremost a concept of honor, so that he is placed "constantly in situations where love is at best an irrelevance."[10] Warshow explains: "If there is a woman he loves, she is usually unable to understand his motives," and because she is from the East, "her failure to understand represents a clash of cultures."[11] Love for this "virtuous woman" will ultimately compel the Westerner to forsake "a way of life."[12]

While Warshow recognizes the stereotyped division of gender functions in the Western as part of a melodramatic moral order, Tompkins goes much further than Warshow to posit these differences as immutably opposite in an ideology of "sexual politics." She asserts that in the Western, women's Eastern ways continually threaten the masculine enterprise of taming the land, which provides the defining qualities of masculinity that the Western seeks to validate. As a result, says Tompkins, a hostility to women, to their ways, and to their words permeates Western narratives, landscapes, and characters. The Western "hates" the language of women because it reminds men "of their own interiority; women's talk evokes a whole network of familial and social relationships and their corollaries in the emotional circuitry."[13]

Unlike Warshow, Tompkins believes the Western's fundamental ontology depends upon constructing the West as a site of masculine retreat where emotion must be repressed, femininity dismissed, and domesticity denigrated. As "the Western struggles and strains to cast out everything feminine," claims Tompkins, its heroes strive "to be the opposite of women. They can't read or dance or look at pictures. They can't play. . . . They can't look at flowers . . . or carry on a conversation."[14] These hard, silent heroes must assert their gender-specific domination over land, self, and Other through sadomasochistic activity directed against animals, women, and other men (often Native American "Others").[15]

One might assume that, in seeking to prove her generalizations, Tompkins would refer at length to the work of John Ford, classical Hollywood's acknowledged master of the Western. However, she virtually ignores his films, confining references to brief citations of a character, a scene, or an exchange of dialogue. For example, she refers to the "Quaker woman" in *Cheyenne Autumn* (1964) as an example of a character who "belongs to the Christian world view the Western is at pains to eradicate."[16] In her only extended analysis of Ford's work, she approaches *Wagon Master* (1950) as an exemplar of a "conscious registering" of "the lack of fit between the way characters in Westerns treat horses and the salient, dynamic presence of the animals themselves."[17]

Why does Ford figure so obliquely (and so oddly) in Tompkins's claims? One reason, I believe, is that with more extended analysis, it is obvious that Ford's films do not fit her notion of the Western, especially when it comes to the inscription of gender, even as they also complicate the claims of Fiedler and Warshow. Women in Ford Westerns typically are not the enemy of all that the hero represents. Female protagonists such as Philadelphia Thursday in *Fort Apache* (1948), Hallie in *The Man Who Shot Liberty Valance* (1962), and Deborah Wright (the "Quaker woman") in *Cheyenne Autumn* create subtle as well as obvious challenges to the East/West ideological divide as a predictable aspect of Western gender as well as geographical stereotype. In spite of female characters' stereotyped origins, their narrative function is often complex rather than simple, as are the qualities they represent in relation to expected generic norms of sexual difference. At the same time, Ford's male heroes do, indeed, play and dance, look at flowers—and sometimes even grow them; they are not shut down into "a pitiably narrow range of activities" in seeking to banish the "feminine," and do not adhere to Tompkins's tautological model of masculine behavior.[18]

Although Tompkins's generalizing conclusions about the Western are deeply flawed, her work is valuable for its attempt to treat masculinity and femininity in the Western in relation rather than as separable entities, and I will follow that strategy here, if to very different ends.[19] I will argue that Ford's sound-era Westerns impress us with the need to return to the question of gender in the genre. Not only do they assume a particular critical resonance when one considers their status in Hollywood, but they constitute a body of canonical texts unrivaled in the genre for critical acclaim, cinematic influence, and longevity of development (from the 1910s through the 1960s).

A number of film scholars writing in the 1970s and 1980s, including Andrew Sarris, Robin Wood, and Tag Gallagher, have alluded to the importance of gender in relation to familiar Fordian themes such as duty.[20] Michael Dempsey, perhaps the harshest critic of Ford in these years, declared in 1975 that he was seeking to demolish "the myth of Ford's great artistry"; in reference to the director's portrayals of women, he argued:

> The vast majority of Ford's women are as mired in stereotypes as his non-whites; they exist only in relation to men, whom they mother, feed, comfort, and bury. . . . their glorification effectively removes them from "masculine" areas of life. . . . for the most part, his are simply "waiting women" whether they are wives, mothers, daughters, or prostitutes.[21]

Dempsey is neither the first nor the last to observe that Ford makes generous use of many of the Western's instantly recognizable "impoverished stereotypes" for female characters. These fall into two main categories: woman as sexual object (i.e., the saloon hostess, female bandit, "Indian squaw," or prostitute) and woman as wife and mother, or prospective wife (the "schoolmarm," the rancher's daughter).[22] But contrary to Dempsey's dismissal of Ford's films as conventionally chauvinistic, Tag Gallagher has noticed that in them, "Traditional male-female roles are constantly exchanged."[23] This observation is intriguing, but Gallagher does not develop it, and he does not remark on how this might be reconciled with his other observation (echoing Dempsey) that Ford's females "exist for the warrior's repose."[24]

I wish to show that not only do Ford's films complicate many contemporary critical discussions of the flight of male protagonists from the feminine, but that some of his films also go so far as to break down gender polarities to suggest the accommodation of masculinity to feminine values (Christianity, family-centered domesticity). I will argue that his Westerns provide the basis for questioning Tompkins and other scholars who adhere to the commonly held view that, in the words of Martin Pumphrey, "the [Western] genre makes an absolute and value-laden division between the masculine and feminine spheres."[25] Nevertheless, I will not be offering an apologia that seeks to redeem Ford from charges that his work is repressive to women. Nor will I be arguing that in the Fordian system women can escape the order of sexual difference. Ford's Westerns do not liberate women from their limited handful of traditional Western film roles.

There is no denying that Ford's Westerns offer a conservative view of the genre's commonly available, historically grounded social roles based on gender. Admittedly, Ford never seems to think of disrupting the basic social terms of the nineteenth-century patriarchal order or of reconceiving women outside of roles constructed in relation to and corollary to the man's, such as entertainer-prostitute or, in the domain of the domestic, mother, daughter, or sweetheart. In this regard, we should probably remind ourselves that Ford, like so many "pantheon" directors (such as Jean Renoir and Ernst Lubitsch), was a product of the nineteenth as well as the twentieth century.

Ford's Westerns do ask the audience to recognize something of their female characters' full humanity and their equality in opposition to their function as sexual fantasy fulfillment for men. Moreover, they undercut the Western's expected denigration of domesticity and expulsion of Eastern, "feminine" values in favor of the lone hero. As Andrew Sarris has noted in reference to *My Darling Clementine,* "What is odd . . . is how little regret Ford shows for the doomed anarchic spirit of the Wild West."[26] Thus, the gender politics of Ford's Westerns may not be of the sort to be called progressive, but they resist certain key assumptions recently attributed monolithically to the Western. In this respect my argument shares a critical basis with Charles Ramírez Berg's article in this volume, which attends to the complexity of the inscription of race and ethnicity in Ford's sound-era Westerns.

Ford's Westerns present themselves as a mythic discourse on the epic forging of national identity. They present this experience in visual and narrative terms that adhere to Virginia Wright Wexman's description of the Western landscape "less as a challenging obstacle to be overcome than as an overarching force capable of crushing all human aspiration."[27] In Ford's vision of the frontier, Westerners—male and female—must submit themselves to the Christian sacrifice necessary to secure their communal (and national) identity. That sacrifice entails the burdens of isolation and loneliness, the submission to physical hardship, and the unpredictable loss of friends and family to nature or to human-inflicted violence.

The self-consciousness of Ford's approach to this pioneer ethos is illustrated in *The Searchers* (1956) when Mr. Jorgensen (John Qualen) blames "this country" for killing his son. In response to his outburst, Mrs. Jorgensen (Olive Carey) gives a stirring speech that sums up essential Fordian values of resiliency, courage, and sacrifice on behalf of the nation:

> Now Lars, we just happen to be Texicans. A Texican is nothing but a human man way out on a limb, this year and next, maybe for a hundred more, but I don't think it'll be forever. Someday this country's going to be a fine, good place to be. Maybe it needs our bones in the ground before that time can come.

Mr. Jorgensen explains the impromptu speech—"My wife was a schoolteacher"—but Fordian humor does not undermine Mrs. Jorgensen's point. In fact, Ford is rather like Mrs. Jorgensen, the former schoolteacher: his films are eloquent statements of the need for sacrifice in sustaining a community that must find meaning beyond (and for) present hardship. Sacrifice is demanded at civilization's outpost—"way out on a limb"—whether that precarious location is an isolated ranch in West Texas, a nascent town called Tombstone, Arizona, or a far-flung military outpost, Fort Apache, New Mexico Territory.

Mrs. Jorgensen's statement blurs gender when she speaks of herself and her husband as "Texicans" and defines a Texican as a "human man." Her reference to the "human man" might be read as privileging the male experience at the frontier, but within a landscape inhospitable to human enterprise, masculinity and femininity share in—and are equalized by—the pioneer experience. At the micro level, this phenomenon may appear almost offhandedly, as in *Wagon Master* when Fleuretty Phyffee (Ruth Clifford) climbs aboard the wagon that her longtime companion, Doctor Hall (Alan Mowbray), has volunteered to take over a dangerous path. "You big ham," she mutters, looking at him with concern (as well as disdain) even as she risks her life to remain with him. Thus, a quietly shared humanity rather than a "clash of cultures" often governs the relations between men and women in Ford's West.

While depending upon established generic conventions of character construction, Ford's films frequently defy the boundaries of the received critical model, in which the good woman, as the genre's primary embodiment of Eastern civilization, functions as a "threat to masculine independence and as the negative against which individual masculinities are tested."[28] For example, in *My Darling Clementine*, Bostonian Clementine Carter successfully adapts to the West, more so than the man, Doc Holliday (Victor Mature), she has traveled thousands of miles to find.[29] In spite of his gunfighting and gambling talents, Holliday exhibits the moral and physical weakness often associated with corrupted Eastern elitism (as opposed to Western democracy). Dissipated by

"What kind of a person am I?" The Eastern woman successfully adapts to the West in *My Darling Clementine* (1946). Clementine (Cathy Downs) and Doc Holliday (Victor Mature).
Courtesy of the Museum of Modern Art Film Stills Archive.

drink and illness, he is burned out morally, physically, and emotionally. Although he is in the West, he remains apart from it, psychologically bound to the past and to his professional failures. For him, Clementine represents the East and its refinements: "This is no place for your kind of person," he tells her, but she pointedly responds, "What kind of a person am I, John?"

Contrary to Holliday's assessment, Arizona is a suitable environment for Clementine; she quickly becomes a part of the emergent frontier community of Tombstone. When bells ring to celebrate a church dance, an assertive Clementine asks Wyatt Earp (Henry Fonda) to accompany her to the festivities. This moment could be read as one in which her Eastern influence works to civilize the Westerner, but it also signals her agency in becoming a part of the Western community and discarding a hopeless romantic attachment that symbolizes her link to a moribund East. After the dance, Clementine and Wyatt are observed in the crowded hotel dining room in the midst of a relaxed and slightly raucous mealtime celebration that offers one of the film's most persuasive images of the formation of the ideal couple within the emergent frontier community.

This scene is among the many in Ford's Westerns that support J. A. Place's observation that "women are vital in unifying the Fordian community . . . and they have their own place in the structure of any society."[30] Expressing a similar perspective, Richard Slotkin has remarked of *Fort Apache* that

> the female or matriarchal side is assigned a moral weight equal to the authority vested in Thursday. The women are entrusted with the preservation of the fundamental rituals that bind Ford society together; they are identified with the principles of democratic egalitarianism.[31]

As these critics have noted, women do have an important place in the Fordian order. However, that place is paradoxical, affirming the importance of women in the culture of a mythic West and yet often defining female characters' social roles by the performance of activities that fit the nineteenth-century notion of women's "sacred duties."

Those duties and the film's attitude toward them conform to the norms articulated by Catherine Beecher and Harriet Beecher Stowe in 1869:

> Women's profession embraces the care and nursing of the body in the critical periods of infancy and sickness, the training of the human mind in the most impressible period of childhood, the instruction and control of servants, and most of the government and economics of the family state. These duties of woman are as sacred and important as any ordained to man.[32]

In fulfilling the "sacred duties" of nineteenth-century womanhood, women in Ford's West cannot escape upholding traditional "feminine" values (home and family, marriage and parenthood, religion and altruistic sacrifice, etc.).[33]

Thus, in *She Wore a Yellow Ribbon* (1949), Mrs. Allshard (Mildred Natwick), the commandant's wife, tends wounded soldiers, comforts children orphaned by a massacre, and sews a Confederate flag to adorn the coffin of a former Southern general who dies as "Private John Smith" in a skirmish with Indians.

Although the narrowness of their social duties might seem to force such women characters into a predictable civilizing role, Ford's Westerns frequently present us with women characters who meet the demands of frontier life in unexpected ways. These include Lana Martin (Claudette Colbert) and Mrs. McKlennan (Edna Mae Oliver) in *Drums along the Mohawk* (1939). The latter is striking in her plainspoken independence and assertion of military-like authority ("I'm used to having my orders obeyed"). In *3 Godfathers* (1948), Miss Florie (Jane Darwell) cheerfully runs the Apache Wells station by herself, and Mrs. Jorgensen in *The Searchers* is not beyond taking her fan and slapping the rump of the Captain Reverend Samuel Clayton (Ward Bond) when he teases her about throwing a wedding party for her daughter Laurie without the wedding. These women demonstrate a good-humored accommodation to harsh circumstances and embody the pioneering spirit in "masculine" ways that blur the Western's conventionally inscribed gender difference.

Nevertheless, like Mrs. Allshard in *She Wore a Yellow Ribbon,* women in Ford's Westerns often fall within familiar categories that adhere to the genre's conventional gendered social structure. Even when this is true, without closer analysis we have little idea of what Ford's films do with these stereotypes. Expectations created by generic conventions may be apparently fulfilled in the beginning of many Ford films, only to be undermined later. Of particular interest in this regard is the treatment of the entertainer-prostitute, the sexual woman. In *My Darling Clementine*, Chihuahua (Linda Darnell), the saloon girl who loves Doc Holliday, is a classic example of a one-dimensional stereotype, but more often Ford's narratives slowly reveal how such stereotypical characters embody both the strongest qualities and the most poignant vulnerabilities of his female protagonists.

For example, in *Wagon Master,* a Mormon wagon train heads west. The two hired wagon masters, Travis (Ben Johnson) and Sandy (Harry Carey Jr.) hear music in the desert. They investigate the apparent source, a solitary medicine-show wagon. Perched on it is a young woman. Her unrefined, overtly sexual pose and her entertainer's costume, cut low in cheap shiny fabric, serve to mark her as a "loose woman." She appears to be drunk, and she utters a familiar barroom line: "You might offer a lady a drink." Travis assumes that Denver (Joanne Dru) is asking for alcohol. He picks up a whiskey bottle from the ground and hands it to her, but she bats it away. "Water," she whispers, "just a drink of water." We learn that the troupe was forced to drink their "light'ning elixir" because they had run out of water.

As is typical of Ford Westerns, *Wagon Master* offers little dialogue to explain Denver or her past, but her attitude and actions continue to reveal that she is far more complex than the stereotype of the entertainer-prostitute she initially seems to embody. Along the trail, Denver experiences a growing, if exceedingly wary, attachment to "that rube," Travis. Numerous close-ups emphasize her looking at him with a steady gaze that reverses the expected alignment of the male with sexual looking. Yet when Travis steps in to defend her from a lecherous visitor she does not respond with gratitude, but admonishes him: "Look, you don't have to protect me. I can take care of myself. I'm used to it." When he says he is "sorry," she interrupts, "—and I don't need any sympathy either." She goes on to defiantly assert, "I've done nothing I need be ashamed of, no matter what you and your friends say."

It is Denver's face that we see almost exclusively in this exchange, and it is clear from her wary self-protectiveness that she has not led an easy life. Travis brings her sturdy shoes (appropriate for walking a thousand miles behind a wagon) to replace her flimsy ones, and Denver seems shocked at his thoughtfulness. Later, when he suddenly rides up and proposes to her as the medicine-show wagon pulls away to take another route, she is even more startled. Denver literally runs away after uttering an emotion-filled but oddly impersonal "Good-bye, fella," a line that reminds us of a prostitute or a saloon hostess saying adieu to her nameless customer.

Denver in *Wagon Master* (1950): unrefined and overtly sexual, but more complex than the stereotype leads us to expect. Joanne Dru.
Courtesy of The Lilly Library, Indiana University, Bloomington, Indiana.

The woman who has not led an easy life and
the man who wants to marry her: Denver (Joanne Dru)
runs away from Travis (Ben Johnson) in *Wagon Master* (1950).
Courtesy of The Lilly Library, Indiana University, Bloomington, Indiana.

Although this is not overtly stated, Denver appears to be one in the long line of Fordian orphans—often female—who are most poignantly represented by Dallas (Claire Trevor), the prostitute heroine of *Stagecoach* (1939). *Stagecoach*, arguably Ford's most famous Western, expands upon a motif already given emphasis in the director's silent film *3 Bad Men* (1926): the sexual and economic vulnerability of the girl or woman who is without a family. In the earlier film, Millie (Priscilla Bonner) is lost to her brother, Bull Stanley (Tom Santschi), when she runs off with Sheriff Layne Hunter (Louis Tellegen). She believes Hunter will marry her. Instead, he attempts to prostitute her.

Bull, a notorious outlaw, is a man willing to shoot a robbery victim in cold blood, but when he finds his sister dying, he tenderly rocks her back and forth as she rests on his lap.[34] This is not a sudden or momentary transformation, but has occurred because of the humanizing influence of yet another Fordian orphan, Lee Carlton (Olive Borden). During an attempt to steal horses on the trail, Bull levels his pistol at a buckskin-clad figure crouched over a dead man. He prepares to pull the trigger, but the figure takes off a wide-brimmed hat. "By golly—he's a woman!" declares Spade Allen (Frank Campeau), one of Bull's two companions in banditry. Unaware that Bull was preparing to shoot her in the head, Lee stands and then leans against his chest, immobilized by grief over her father's death. The camera refuses to cut away, but centers on an extended scene of Bull almost imperceptibly responding to her presence until he slowly places his arm around Lee to comfort her. In an ironic turn of fate, he and his two compatriots become Lee's protectors. She calls them "my three bad men," and Bull, apparently the baddest of the bad, experiences an emotional reawakening through his unspoken love for the much younger Lee.

No matter what their gender, Fordian characters like Bull and Millie often face the emotional, economic, and social consequences of their lack of family, but *Stagecoach* suggests that these consequences can be particularly devastating for a woman. Along the stagecoach journey to Lordsburg, Dallas walks in the moonlight outside the stage stop. The Ringo Kid (John Wayne) follows her. He warns her that "strays" get picked off by Apache. "I guess you don't know how it feels to lose your own folks," he says as he attempts to explain why he must go to Lordsburg to shoot it out with the Plumbers, who killed his father and brother. Dallas recounts how she lost her parents "in a massacre in the Superstition Mountains." "That's tough, especially on a girl," he responds. The sexually innocent Ringo, imprisoned since age sixteen, does not recognize that Dallas is a prostitute. In this scene, only the film audience is privileged to appreciate the melancholy resignation expressed in Claire Trevor's delivery of Dallas's next line: "You have to live, no matter what happens."

Dallas's revelation of the massacre that left her an orphan alerts the audience to the circumstances that have led her to prostitution. Her status as a social pariah is established early on when we see her marched out of a town by its Law and Order League. Along the journey, she is quietly shunned by other, more respectable passengers, including the soldier's wife, Mrs. Mallory (Louise Pratt), and the gambler, Mr. Hatfield (John Carradine). Her nervousness, embarrassment, and wounded defiance serve to communicate that she is sexually transgressive because of economic necessity rather than personal predilection.

Yet circumstances also force Dallas to assume the role of nurse for Mrs. Mallory's baby, born on the journey. It is the madonnaesque image of Dallas showing off the newborn in her arms that solidifies Ringo's romantic interest: the film cuts to a telling close-up of him intently watching her. Pam Cook has rightly observed that the "shots of her [Dallas] cradling Lucy's baby . . . are quite transgressive, since prostitutes are outside the family and the law."[35] To Ringo, who can only judge Dallas by what he observes, she is "the kind of girl a man wants to marry" and the film confirms his judgment of her rather than society's.

As is well known, Ford's sympathy is with outcasts, no matter what their gender, and *Stagecoach* is not the first or the last Ford Western to accord that sympathy to women who, because of their lack of "sexual purity," are judged harshly by other characters. In spite of Ford's inscription of sexual idealism and his oft-noted "reverence for motherhood and family," sexually and socially transgressive women like Dallas can become "sweethearts" and wives in Ford's Westerns, as they do in *Wagon Master* and *Two Rode Together* (1961) as well as in *Stagecoach*.[36]

Most daringly, that sympathy is also extended to sexually tainted captives of the Comanche in *The Searchers* and *Two Rode Together,* and to the sexual hostage of a Mongolian warrior in Ford's last film, *Seven Women* (1965), which has been called a geographically displaced Western.[37] All three of these late Ford films centralize the role of the woman within one of the oldest forms of American frontier literature, the captivity narrative.[38] While the last film is significant for its shift to the perspective of the female hostage, Marty Roth argues that *The Searchers* is one of Ford's most interesting films because, in having its narrative work through the daughter rather than through the son, it lays bare the fact that "what is at stake in the genre is female purity."[39]

Roth's comment foregrounds woman's role in Westerns as a symbol of racial identity. In a patriarchal world where white "civilization" confronts the danger of red "savagery," the white woman's sexuality attains ultimate symbolic value. Yet *The Searchers* goes so far as to deconstruct the binarism of racial and sexual difference to reveal the violent, racist ideas of a masculinist discourse that infects women as well as men. Martin Pawley (Jeffrey Hunter) and Ethan Edwards (John Wayne) search for years for Debbie Edwards (Natalie Wood), Ethan's niece, who was stolen at age nine in a Comanche raid. Martin wants to rescue Debbie from captivity even though she has adapted to Comanche life and is now the wife of Chief Scar (Henry Brandon), the man who killed her family.

Westerns normally are expected to assert the good woman's role in bringing civilization to the frontier and maintaining it there. Typically, women do this through being the primary devotees of education, family, religion, and nonviolence. After years of separation, Laurie Jorgensen (Vera Miles) insists that Martin Pawley, her love interest, cannot continue his quest. It is too late to continue searching for Debbie because "she's a woman growed . . . with savage brats of her own." She insists that Debbie's own mother would want Ethan "to put a bullet in her brain." Ironically, Laurie's bloodthirsty speech is delivered while she sits in her white wedding dress. By making the sexually innocent Laurie the voice for patriarchal sexual norms and for violence against the sexually transgressive captive woman, Ford throws the opposition between civilization and savagery into confusion and the role of the woman in maintaining that opposition into relief.

Just as many of Ford's female characters blur the boundary between "good" woman and "bad," other female characters, like Laurie in *The Searchers,* break down the expected division between femininity as Eastern, passive, and bound to nonviolence, and masculinity as Western, active, and liberating in its love of violence. While Laurie represents the "cruelty for cruelty" position that Tompkins associates with the hard Western hero, Marty Pawley becomes the representative of compassion, forgiveness, and tolerance. He rescues Debbie in spite of opposition from everyone in the community except Laurie's mother, Mrs.

Mrs. Jorgensen and Martin Pawley establish "feminized" values of forgiveness
and love across the boundaries of gender. Olive Carey, Jeffrey Hunter,
and Vera Miles in *The Searchers* (1956).
Courtesy of The Lilly Library, Indiana University, Bloomington, Indiana.

Jorgensen (Olive Carey), who continues to refer to Debbie as "our little girl."[40] As a result, *The Searchers* may be used to challenge current claims that the spheres of masculinity and femininity are polarized in the Western, for Mrs. Jorgensen and Martin Pawley establish a constellation of "feminized" values—Christian forgiveness, love, and tolerance—across the boundaries of gender.

In opposition to the views of Tompkins and Fiedler, who emphasize the isolation of the Western hero, Virginia Wright Wexman has called attention to "the central role played by the romantic couple in creating the Western's ideological meaning." She argues that "the couple forms the cornerstone of the genre's image of the family on the land," and identifies "the family farm as the goal toward which the story moves."[41] Throughout Ford's Westerns, the emphasis on romance and on the formation of the couple speaks to Ford's almost obsessional foregrounding of the family as the source of all good in securing the future of the nation. Indeed, almost all of Ford's Westerns, including *The Iron Horse* (1924), *Stagecoach, Drums along the Mohawk, My Darling Clementine, Fort Apache, She Wore a Yellow Ribbon, Rio Grande* (1950),

Sergeant Rutledge (1960), and *Two Rode Together,* give extended attention to the love match that leads to marriage.

One of Ford's most mature depictions of romance and marriage between equals is *Drums along the Mohawk,* which provides an emotionally moving articulation of Wexman's model of the Western as a story of "the family on the land."[42] Contrary to Tompkins's claim that Westerns are stories that "pay practically no attention to women's experience," this film provides a pronounced shift to the woman's perspective as well as to her experience.[43] Indeed, the film opens with a close-up on the bridal bouquet of Magdalena Borst (Claudette Colbert), an upper-class girl in colonial New York who marries Gil Martin (Henry Fonda), a farmer. Immediately after "Lana" and Gil are married, they set out on Gil's wagon (with cow in tow) for the Western frontier, the Mohawk Valley.

On her first night at their cabin, Lana is so frightened that she breaks down in tears and vows to go home to her mother in Albany. Soon, however, she stops "being scared." She happily works side by side with her husband in the fields doing the same hard physical labor. Gil does not dominate Lana; on the contrary, they seem full partners, and as the film progresses, he seems more dependent on her emotionally than she on him. When their house is burned down by Indians, it is Lana who calmly presents the solution and tells her husband how they will live: they will sign on to serve as hired hand and seamstress to a wealthy widow. Gil is shocked and protests in a shrill, hysterical voice, "No, Lana, a girl like you can't hire out." Perhaps out of embarrassment that he has not provided for her adequately, Gil, not Lana, clings to the aura of his wife's "Eastern" ways and her genteel origins. Lana has shed the pretenses of class to become a true frontier woman. She will do what has to be done to make sure she and her family survive, including donning a soldier's uniform and taking up a musket to defend the fort from attack.[44]

Michael Dempsey claims that Ford projects "a distrust of 'feminine' emotions" that limits his films to registering "the macho male's queasiness about intimacy and equality with women."[45] Certainly lines such as "Do you like me as much as your old farm?" might not suggest a film of great erotic nuance, but tender feeling, sexual expressivity, and domestic satisfaction are realized in *Drums along the Mohawk* with the "delicacy of emotion" that Andrew Sarris attributes to Ford's best work.[46] On Gil and Lana's wedding night, a simple walk up the narrow stairway is imbued with poetry as Lana leads the way to their "honeymoon" chambers, then slowly turns the corner after moving close to Gil and asking, "Do you love me as much as I love you?"[47] Later, on the farm, Gil's adoration of Lana is inscribed in the utter panic in his voice when he fears losing her after she miscarries.

Scholarship on the Western frequently asserts that women characters can function only in relation to men within the form's generic terrain.[48] But just as common stereotypes in the Western are opened up to uncommon complications in Ford's films, so too does the relational definition of women like Lana (who function as mother, wife, sister, or sweetheart to men) acquire unexpected narrative and symbolic dimensions. As well as illustrating the central importance of the formation of the romantic couple, *Fort Apache* provides an extended example of the narrative foregrounding of women's experience and their values in Ford's imagined frontier social order.

Philadelphia Thursday (Shirley Temple) and her father, Lieutenant Colonel Owen Thursday (Henry Fonda), ride in a stagecoach bound for Fort Apache and Colonel Thursday's new, unwelcome assignment as commandant at what he dismisses as a "ten-penny post." Philadelphia comes from the East but she is not marked as irrevocably Eastern. She immediately adopts the words and ways of this "classless" Western territory. With youthful exuberance, she imitates the stage hands who irreverently call her father "soldier boy," and when she enters a stage stop, she bonds with the isolated wife of the stationmaster. "Ma" (Mary Gordon) inquires about the origins of Philadelphia's stylish hat: "St. Louis?" "No, Boston." Without dropping a beat, Philadelphia whisks it off her head to give to the plump Scottish-brogued woman to try on. In a long shot, her father looks on with a grim expression as his daughter erases the differences of class and breeding that he maintains at every opportunity. By way of contrast, Philadelphia quickly comes to stand for the egalitarian values of the West that figure prominently in the utopian Fordian universe; those values, paradoxically, are often represented by women and enlisted men, those at the margin or bottom of the hierarchical military structure.

At the fort, Philadelphia experiences a homecoming to a family she never had. She has lived as a virtual orphan: her mother is dead, her father left her in schools while he was stationed in Europe. The Thursdays' arrival interrupts a George Washington's Birthday dance. Philadelphia is whirled away to dance by an eager Captain York (John Wayne). The next morning, she appears on the back porch of their quarters to greet Michael O'Rourke (John Agar), the handsome lieutenant she met en route to the fort. She is disappointed to learn that he comes not to see her, but to leave his card for his new commanding officer. He sits. She stares at him, and forgets both her station and the fact that she is in her "nightie" until Captain York teasingly reminds her. Her friendly manner and lack of pretense cut through the formality of rank and the isolation of frontier life to immediately make her part of the Fort Apache community. When Philadelphia discovers that the quarters she shares with her father are unlivable, she wastes no time in seeking help from her mother's best friend, Mrs. Collingwood (Anna Lee), who enlists the aid of Mrs. O'Rourke (Irene Rich).

The presence of these women asserts the centrality of family life in the fort, and the film accords them respect as a vital part of the community of army professionals. Even though they become "waiting women" when their men are called into military action, they also play an active role as partners in the professional lives of their husbands. Mrs. Collingwood's husband, Sam (George O'Brien), served with Colonel Thursday in the Civil War. He was involved in some misstep (perhaps alcohol-related) that causes Thursday to refuse to shake his hand on meeting him again at Fort Apache. When the troop pulls out on a mission, Mrs. Collingwood receives notice of her husband's much longed-for transfer to the military academy. The other women insist that she have him called back. She refuses after musing to herself, "Sam's no coward . . . never was." She then seems to have a premonition of the impending military disaster ("I can't see him. All I can see is the flags," she says as she stares into space). Mrs. Collingwood's action seals her husband's fate (he will die), but the film affirms rather than questions her decision, for she is motivated by the desire to redeem her husband from his lingering sense of inferiority, articulated by him at the dinner scene at the Collingwood home, as well as by Thursday's disrespectful treatment of his former colleague.[49]

While the women of the fort are important as a collective in establishing the film's "feminized," family-centered values, Philadelphia Thursday's desire for Michael O'Rourke fuels a key plot line in *Fort Apache*. She could be viewed as a mere appendage to Colonel Thursday, one of his "*fe*male relations" (as Captain Brittles refers, in comic frustration, to Mrs. Allshard and her niece, Miss Dandridge, in *She Wore a Yellow Ribbon*), but it is Philadelphia's desire that provides a positive contrast to her father's self-aggrandizing desire to be "the man who brought Cochise back."

Mrs. Collingwood's decision will redeem her husband, but also seal his fate. Shirley Temple, Anna Lee, and Irene Rich in *Fort Apache* (1948).

Courtesy of The Lilly Library, Indiana University, Bloomington, Indiana.

Philadelphia is not waiting to be objectified by a man's desires. She falls in love at her first sight of Michael O'Rourke, the son of an Irish sergeant major. Like Laurie Jorgensen in *The Searchers*, Philadelphia is a Fordian ingenue who straightforwardly asserts her desire. In the film's opening sequence, she accidentally breaks in on Michael as he bends over a basin to wash. With a mixture of admiration, amusement, and pleasure on her face, she openly stares at the barechested young man. She hands him a towel, and when he stands up and sees that she is not the stationmaster's wife, he fumbles in embarrassment and exits with much apologizing. Unembarrassed, she continues to follow him with her eyes. Later, as Michael rides behind the coach, Philadelphia surreptitiously watches him in a mirror while pretending that she is removing something from her eye. At the fort, Mrs. Collingwood asks Michael's mother how her son looks. Philadelphia blurts out, "Oh, he looks wonderful!" Her father forbids Michael to see her, because he regards the match as unsuitable because of differences of class and ethnic origin. Nonetheless, Philadelphia shows up at the O'Rourkes' home. Although Michael's father says she must leave, Mrs. O'Rourke has the last word: Philadelphia will stay. Mrs. O'Rourke (like the film viewer) recognizes that the girl's desire is indicative of Ford's highest values (the formation of the couple, and therefore the family), unlike her father's, which is portrayed as inhumanely destructive.

Colonel Thursday appears to be interested only in getting out of Fort Apache and furthering his career. Captain Collingwood tells him, "This isn't a country for glory," but Thursday ignores his advice and gets his command massacred. But even in his narcissistic folly, Thursday's actions reveal one moment of family love and loyalty. When he dismisses a rebellious Captain York to go to safety with the supply train, without explanation he abruptly adds, "And take O'Rourke with you."[50] His only possible motivation is that he cannot bring

Love at the woman's first sight of the man. John Agar and Shirley Temple in *Fort Apache* (1948).
Courtesy of The Lilly Library, Indiana University, Bloomington, Indiana.

himself to sacrifice his daughter's future marital happiness. Later, as he rejoins his men, who are hopelessly besieged in a box canyon, he apologizes for being late to Michael's father (Ward Bond), who retorts, "Save the apologies for our grandchildren."[51]

In this scene, the film most poignantly brings the two lines of action (Philadelphia's desire for Michael, her father's desire for glory) together to register the familial promise of the former's love and the cost in lives of the latter's ambition. Saving Michael from certain death redeems Colonel Thursday from imposing the most heartrending emotional toll on his daughter. Nevertheless, the ending is bittersweet. Most commentators on Ford have talked extensively about Captain York's apparent reversal (from individualism to regimentation), but another eloquent aspect of the ending has been largely overlooked. In the final scene, Philadelphia is a solemn-faced wife and mother who faces an uncertain future. Her girlish enthusiasm is gone as her husband, Michael, prepares to do his duty as an officer. The two related plot lines contrasting the values of two members of the same family continue to be intertwined, for Philadelphia is still affected by her father's foolish decision to force a military confrontation with the Apache: Michael leaves with the regiment on a campaign that would have been unnecessary had Colonel Thursday not insisted on leading a charge against Cochise's men.

Rather than attempt to dominate the land or escape from society, male characters in Westerns such as *Fort Apache* and *Drums along the Mohawk* convey the sense that on the frontier, settlers cling to human companionship and to the hope of happy domesticity. Gallagher has asserted that feeling, not logic, governs Ford's films, but perhaps it is more appropriate to say that in Ford's work, and especially in his depiction of life on the frontier, feeling is logic, it is the only logic for making meaning out of survival, and at its healthiest manifestation it has to find a communal voice.[52]

Although Ford's protagonists may be isolated on remote homesteads or in far-flung towns and outposts, his love stories are enacted against a repertoire of community rituals: dances, serenades, marriages, births, and burials. These female-identified rituals are so important in Ford that the man who interrupts them is inevitably marked as marginal and dangerous. For example, in *The Searchers*, Ethan Edwards's impatience with his own family's funeral service ("Put an amen to it," he yells while stomping away) marks him as dangerously flawed. Similarly, in *Fort Apache,* Owen Thursday interrupts one dance, calls a halt to another one, and violates the sanctity of the O'Rourke home. Such males may be capable of becoming legendary figures, but their behavior and values put the nascent frontier community in danger—from within and without.

Will Wright has described typical Western heroes as "saddle tramps, outlaws, or hired gunfighters . . . fighting just to enter a society."[53] Ford is not very much interested in lone cowboys, gunmen, or drifters. When such men do appear in Ford's films (as with Bull Stanley in *3 Bad Men*) they are always brought into uneasy relationship with the norms of the family and the value of their individualism is questioned rather than mythically affirmed. Lone males at the edge of society, independent of social norms and free of emotional ties to family, are not heroes in the Fordian universe. Either these men are transformed, or they remain immutably transgressive and inevitably marginalized.

As a consequence, Ford's protagonists do not bear out Tompkins's claim that the Western's typical hero is willing to return "cruelty for cruelty." The one notable exception is Ethan Edwards in *The Searchers*. While the character accrues considerable mythical qualities due to the casting of John Wayne, Ford immediately establishes that this hard, silent wanderer cannot be redeemed for normal family life, in spite of his unrequited love for his sister-in-law. His presence at his brother's dinner table turns a relaxed family meal into a tension-filled encounter with racist intolerance and just plain meanness. He growls at Martin Pawley, his nephew by adoption, "A fella could mistake you for a half-breed."

Tompkins claims that men like Ethan are valorized as the norm for masculinity in the Western even though "Silence, the will to dominate, and unacknowledged suffering aren't a good recipe for happiness or companionability."[54] But *The Searchers* emerges very unmistakably as a major critique—rather than an advocacy—of what Tompkins claims is the genre's standard model of masculinity. Ford's film undermines Edwards's ability to function as a Western hero, even in the hero's traditional manly ability to get a job done. In keeping with the expected physical prowess and frontier skills of the Western hero, Edwards presents himself as an experienced frontiersman, but at major junctions in the search for his niece, a captive of the Comanche, it is the "soft" juvenile lead, Martin Pawley (Jeffrey Hunter), rather than Edwards, who provides the knowledge and understanding that allow the captive Debbie to be returned home.[55]

If Ethan Edwards is the exception, then Martin Pawley is the rule in Ford, for many of the director's heroes are "soft" males, and masculinity is very much centered around family or institutionally bound community (such as the military).[56] The many communal and notably gentle heroes in Ford's Westerns undermine the claims of critics such as Tompkins and Lee Clark Mitchell who regard hard, silent, violent heroes as the norm. In reference to one of Ford's most acclaimed non-Westerns, *The Quiet Man* (1952), William Pechter has noted, "it is the hero who presses the claims of civilization and the heroine who is brought from wildness into domesticity."[57] Guided by his mother's nostalgic stories of the Ireland they left while he was still a child, Sean Thornton (John Wayne) gives up boxing, leaves the United States, and returns to the land of his birth. When he marries, he plants roses and longs for children, but the social contract of the community demands that he fight to keep his wife, who mistakes his gentleness for cowardice.

While women like Lana in *Drums along the Mohawk* reveal surprising "masculine" strengths, Ford's male heroes, even the physically strongest, like Sean Thornton, inevitably reveal an unexpected "feminine" vulnerability and nuanced emotional core. For example, in *Wagon Master,* Travis's relaxed and gentle manner strikes an immediate contrast with his profession as a casually unscrupulous horse trader. At first, he rejects the entreaties of Elder Wiggs (Ward Bond), the plain-spoken leader of a group of Mormons, who wants Travis and his partner Sandy to guide his people through difficult terrain to the San Juan Valley. Travis and Sandy watch the wagons depart, albeit with a twinge of regret:

> Sandy: Gosh, all those women and children.
> Travis: Yeah, and that redheaded gal.
> Sandy: What's gonna happen when they reach that desert?
> Travis: Oh, I don't know. We warned 'em, didn't we?

In the Fordian universe, Travis's justification rings hollow because he is avoiding the most important responsibility: the duty to protect women and children as the foundation of the family and, therefore, the future. Travis and Sandy change their minds in what must be the sweetest and most unusual register of a decision in the entire genre: Travis begins to sing "I left my gal in old Virginie" and, smiling, Sandy responds with the refrain of the song.

This scene might be dismissed as evidence of sentimental paternalism, but *Wagon Master* focuses on how these two men's "natural" gentleness finds a home amongst the peace-loving Mormons. Over the course of the journey, their stake in the future becomes bound up with a religious community and with women (Sandy with Prudence, the red-headed gal; Travis with Denver). Late in his career, Ford himself articulated his preferred approach to history in words that resonate with *Wagon Master:* "I like to make my pictures about the little people, who begin to feel the thirst for self-respect growing within themselves, who become aware of their belonging to a community."[58]

As several critics have noted, Ford Westerns often center on male protagonists who are integrated into communities from the outset. This is particularly evident in the cavalry trilogy (*Fort Apache, She Wore a Yellow Ribbon,* and *Rio Grande*). In *Wagon Master* and *Drums along the Mohawk,* as in many of Ford's Westerns, the West is not positively articulated for the audience as the last free place where a man can (and must) display "cruelty in return for cruelty."[59] On the contrary, in Ford's West there are family men (such as Martin Pawley in *The Searchers,* Gil Martin in *Drums along the Mohawk,* Nathan Brittles and Colonel Allshard in *She Wore a Yellow Ribbon*); potential family men (such as Travis in *Wagon Master,* Jim Gary in *Cheyenne Autumn,* and Bob Hightower in *3 Godfathers*); and cold-blooded killers (such as Ethan Edwards).

Ford's films value men who have the potential to become fathers and husbands, the "soft" men who avoid killing.[60] Gil Martin joins the militia to defend the Mohawk Valley from Indians. When Lana finds him, barely alive, he describes the carnage of a battle and recounts, with dismay, how he watched his friend Adam (Ward Bond) killing Indians: "... he was grinning ... I thought, he's having a good time. He likes this." Rather than hardness and independence, tenderness and tolerance are valorized in the mature male protagonist. In *Wagon Master,* Travis appears calm, confident, and virtually unflappable, but he is no killer. He is forced by circumstance to shoot the Cleggs, a perverse "family" of outlaws, to prevent them from taking the grain upon which the Mormon settlement depends for survival.[61] Afterward, in a gesture registering frustration and despair at having to kill human beings, even ones so evil, he hurls the gun into the brush.

In Ford's West, wanton killers do not become patriarchs. This is illustrated in one of Ford's most complex statements on this issue, *The Man Who Shot Liberty Valance.* Tom Doniphon (John Wayne) kills the outlaw Liberty Valance in cold blood. His killing of Valance echoes a thousand other Westerns in which the hero rids the town of the villain and "gets the girl," but Doniphon gives up his girl, Hallie (Vera Miles), and fades into obscurity rather than attaining mythic transcendence. How can this be? Tom first appears to fit the stereotype of the ideal Westerner as described by Lee Clark Mitchell. Mitchell argues that Western heroes are dichotomous creatures in whom manhood is identified "in characteristic ways with the terrain: as hard but gentle, generous yet unforgiving, inexpressive if nonetheless capable of being read, and so on."[62]

As one of the most taciturn and tough of Ford's heroes, Tom Doniphon may appear to fit this model, but he turns out to be much "softer" than expected. He kills Valance at the prompting of Hallie, who wants to save Ranse Stoddard. After Tom discovers Ranse in Hallie's arms, he does not respond to this romantic loss in the manner of the typical Western hero who stoically withstands the hardships of his marginal social position. Instead, he drunkenly burns his house in what has to be interpreted as an attempted suicide.[63] Tom survives only because his hired man and friend, Pompey (Woody Strode), pulls him from the flames. In an expression of feeling uncharacteristic of a Western hero as described by Mitchell or Tompkins, Tom regrets his sacrificial act and says so. He tells Ranse that he shot Valance, and adds bitterly, "I wish I hadn't." Rather than being a transcendent hero who mediates between the past and the future, wilderness and civilization, by defying the woman's civilizing influence, Tom Doniphon acts (violently) on the wishes of the woman he loves and, in doing so, destroys his own future.[64]

This is in complete contrast to the model of the Western hero presented in Owen Wister's *The Virginian,* a text much cited by contemporary scholars of the genre. This novel is regarded as archetypal in offering up the Western hero as one who displays a "cool art of self-preservation" and a commitment to do what he must ("A man's gotta do what a man's gotta do")—in spite of the opposition of the good woman.[65] Mitchell also uses the novel to support his claim that Westerns obsessively narrate the attainment of manhood in a celebration of individualism, physical dexterity, and masculine independence that centers on "proving the male body."[66]

Admittedly, there are Ford films that may adhere to this model of attaining manhood (such as *The Iron Horse*), but masculinity in Ford's Westerns is rarely achieved through physical performance in a manner that conforms to the model of *The Virginian*. Ford's Westerns are typically more interested in psychological and emotional revelation than in asserting the meaning of manliness through raw physicality and a "celebration of the male physique."[67] Countering much-cited archetypes of the genre like *The Virginian, Rio Grande* foregrounds the emotional growth of a middle-aged male protagonist. Like *My Darling Clementine, Rio Grande* demands to be read as a poetic gesture: in this case, one that turns an episode of the Indian Wars and the heroics of a historical figure (General George Crook) into the story of a man and a woman reclaiming domestic love and emotional balance.[68]

Rio Grande demonstrates the emotional transformation of Kirby Yorke (John Wayne) from a man rigidly invested in a man's duty to his profession into one who confronts the loneliness of his life and decides to change. It is also the story of his wife, Kathleen Yorke (Maureen O'Hara), and her reconciliation to the duties of an army wife as a necessary part of her romantic reconciliation with Kirby. Both Kathleen and Kirby must confront and resolve the tension between the demands of duty and the love of family.

Both women and men require the emotional balance to weigh love and duty.
Kathleen and Kirby Yorke (Maureen O'Hara and John Wayne) in *Rio Grande* (1950).
Courtesy of the Museum of Modern Art Film Stills Archive.

Kathleen Yorke comes to the fort in search of their son, who has enlisted as a private after failing math at West Point. Kirby is stopped dead in his tracks by the first gaze he has exchanged with Kathleen in fifteen years. Carrying out orders during the Civil War, he torched Kathleen's family home. She has never forgiven him. Their son, Jeff (Claude Jarman Jr.), asks, "What kind of man is he, mother?" Kathleen replies, "A lonely man, a very lonely man." The film visually confirms her statement: as Kirby walks alone by the river, a telling close-up reveals his haggard sadness. Neither is Kathleen immune to the effects of their separation. Kathleen has displaced her eroticism onto her relationship with her son. When she sees Jeff, she kisses him all over his face and then on the mouth in a gesture that recalls Lana kissing Gil in *Drums along the Mohawk*.

Tompkins claims that the Western hero, "always subjected to duress, is forbidden to register his pain."[69] In *Rio Grande*, Kirby Yorke is candid about his suffering, but initially his revelation suggests a kind of macho bravado, a dare to his son to take it like a man: "You've chosen my way of life . . . hope that you have the guts to endure it . . . it's a life of suffering and hardship and uncompromising devotion to your oath and your duty." Nevertheless, manly duty is not upheld unconditionally, for *Rio Grande* suggests that men need more than guts to endure frontier life; they require the comfort of a family, and the emotional balance to weigh duty and love.[70]

In addition to his macho assertions, Kirby bears a Civil War nickname, "Ramrod, Wreckage, and Ruin." It seems ill-suited to a man who has kept a music box that plays "I'll Take You Home Again, Kathleen." Kirby courts his estranged wife with flowers and serenades by the regimental singers. Kathleen can see that he's "grown more thoughtful," but Kirby's stubborn refusal to think beyond a narrow framework of duty for their son drives her to stony silence. When she attempts to negotiate with him to release Jeff from service, he declares, "He must learn that a man's word to anything, even his own destruction, must be honored."

The depth of Kirby's commitment to her and to his family is not made clear until he is willing to violate protocol—and duty—in an act that recalls Colonel Thursday's saving of Michael O'Rourke. To keep Jeff from the prospect of seeing action against the Apache, Kirby assigns him to an escort for a wagon train of the fort's women and children. Kathleen responds to Kirby's showing favoritism to protect Jeff:

> Kathleen: He'll think that . . .
> Kirby: He's my son—our son. He's too young to . . .
> Kathleen: He'll still hate it, Kirby—but I love you for it.

Of course, in the Fordian universe, such gestures often have more emotional than practical value.[71] Kirby and Kathleen cannot foresee that the Apache will attack the convoy to which Jeff has been assigned to keep him out of harm's way.

Just as Kirby must learn to relinquish perfect adherence to professional duty in order to be a father and a husband, Kathleen must be reconciled to her duty as an army wife. This reconciliation occurs gradually, telegraphed in scenes such as the one where she joins the other women to do their husbands' washing. However, the difficulty of her social role and the emotional suffering that will be attached to her decision are communicated most forcefully in the scene in which the regiment returns from rescuing captive children. She anxiously looks for Jeff, and when she finds him safe, she runs to him, takes his arm, and walks in step beside him. In front of them, a wounded Kirby rests on a horse-drawn travois. Realizing it is he, Kathleen looks down at him, and in a gesture of ritual acceptance rather than spontaneous emotion, she silently leaves her place beside Jeff and takes Kirby's hand to walk beside him.

If Fordian heroes like Kirby Yorke openly register the "unmanly" pain that is supposedly banished from the Western, Kathleen Yorke's experience supports the observation that Ford's Westerns often present melancholy portraits of women's economic, emotional, physical, and sexual vulnerability in the West. As Joseph McBride and Michael Wilmington have remarked, "If there is one characteristic common to all Ford's heroines, it is this: they suffer. Their children leave home, their husbands are killed, their homes are burned."[72] Ford's female characters, like Kathleen Yorke and Lana Martin, Mrs. Jorgensen and Mrs. McKlennan, face harsh situations that take a tremendous emotional toll, but we can now appreciate that all Fordian protagonists, whether male or female, do so.

In fact, suffering brought on by a sense of loss is one of the key emotions in the Fordian West, and it is one shared by most of Ford's protagonists, male and female (Dallas and Ringo in *Stagecoach,* Clementine and Wyatt in *My Darling Clementine,* Hallie and Tom in *The Man Who Shot Liberty Valance*). Sometimes loss is expressed through direct if understated means, as in the presence of numerous orphans in Ford's Westerns. However, Michael Dempsey sees loss in Ford's Westerns as linked to gender in a more specific and pernicious way. He argues that Ford's female characters are often relegated to the status of "dead wives [who have] vanished before the movies begin, the better to serve as a remote icon whose earthly virtues we are expected to take on faith."[73]

Dempsey fails to recognize that Ford's films ascribe a specifically Christian, feminine, and nineteenth-century meaning to the expressive ritual of mourning as a response to the loss of the loved one(s). In this cultural practice, the perfection of the loved one was not at issue, but the gentility of the mourner was. Associated with a religious experience in which the survivor's heart would be softened, mourning was credited with preparing the bereaved "to receive divine grace."[74]

This nineteenth-century, sentimental view of death informs Ford's Westerns, with the process of mourning typically depicted through the funeral ceremony or graveyard visitation. Such scenes are ubiquitous in the Ford oeuvre and are to be found in *The Iron Horse, Young Mr. Lincoln* (1939), *She Wore a Yellow Ribbon, The Searchers, The Man Who Shot Liberty Valance,* and *How the West Was Won* (1962). In *My Darling Clementine,* Wyatt's trip to visit his brother James's grave establishes that he is not a raw frontiersman opposed to civilization, but is basically genteel, thoughtful, and loving.[75] The part of *How the West Was Won* directed by Ford focuses on a gentle young man, Zeb Rawlings (George Peppard), who naively goes off to the Civil War as an excuse for adventure. After his service, he returns to the family farm in Ohio to discover that his beloved "Ma" (Carroll Baker) has died in his absence and is buried in the family plot where she often went to talk to her dead father. It is Zeb's realization of the loss of his mother (his father has died in the war) that prompts him to set out for the West and a new life.

As Karen Halttunen has noted, within the nineteenth-century sentimental view of death, the loved one was irreplaceable. Mourning was a Christian lesson in loving one another, for "the bonds of love that stretched across the great divide of death were thus believed stronger than those ties that bound families together in life."[76] In nineteenth-century America, the process of mourning was believed to hold the promise of wider benefits to society. As Halttunen notes, "Mourning was regarded as the most sacred of social feelings because the heart softened by affliction turned with greater love not only to the departed loved one, but to all living members of the family, and finally to all mankind."[77] Thus, in *My Darling Clementine,* Wyatt tells his dead brother, killed by rustlers, that he hopes that he will be able to make the country "safe for kids like you."

This emphasis on the emotional rather than the physical means that many of his characters (most often men, but on occasion women) are obsessed with memory and with the past.[78] In *She Wore a Yellow Ribbon,* Captain Nathan Brittles is devoted to the memory of his wife, Mary, and their daughters, who apparently died in an Indian attack. Brittles tends their graves, talks to Mary, and, in the final scene of the film, accepts flowers from Miss Dandridge (Joanne Dru) to "report" to Mary about his appointment to Chief of Scouts. These scenes suggest that the bonds of domestic love can be so powerful for the male protagonist that they cannot be severed by death.[79]

Such gestures are also significant in establishing Fordian manhood as being attached to feminine values of domesticity, Christianity, and emotional expressivity. Ford sentimentalizes death through a strategy that suggests that in the sentimental, "feminized" culture of his fictional nineteenth-century West, human beings express their deepest feelings most transparently in mourning for the dead. However, this is not a confirmation of the view that Westerns are death-obsessed.[80] Instead, such scenes of mourning reveal the fundamental gentility of Fordian protagonists—whether male or female—and their adherence to a cult of domesticity. These moments also suggest the emotional toll of the loss of human companionship on the frontier. In Ford's Westerns, violence has a price that is paid across the years in the tender of loneliness and regret. Contrary to the declaration of a character in *Two Rode Together*, in Ford's vision of the nineteenth-century West, one can never expect that "the past can bury the past."

Ford's sound-era Westerns challenge the claims of contemporary film scholarship regarding the expected meaning of gender in the genre by being more interested in reconciliation than revenge, hard-won domesticity than domination over the land, the formation of families than the legitimation of violent "legendary" masculinities. Even though Ford's female characters reside in worlds that attempt to assert the hierarchical division of gender (as well as race and class), these films frequently undermine Western conventions and complicate expectations attached to gender by unsettling the genre's female stereotypes. In discussing the representation of history, Douglas Pye has noted that Ford's films "expose very clearly a number of the conflicts, even contradictions, which are inherent in the genre but are normally suppressed."[81] Pye's remarks can also be applied to the complex inscription of gender in Ford Westerns, one which demands that we look beyond current critical boundaries.

Ford's Westerns also challenge the notion that the genre rests on a fundamental opposition between masculinity, standing for the wild freedom of the frontier, and a femininity that must be rejected as the symbolic representation of an emasculating civilization. Thus, these canonical texts complicate more generalized claims that the genre symbolically silences and expels women as well as that its male protagonists flee everything feminine. Indeed, as I have attempted to show, many of Ford's most memorable female characters, including Denver, Dallas, Kathleen Yorke, Philadelphia Thursday, Lana Martin, and Mrs. McKlennan, display behaviors traditionally coded as masculine within the genre (such as gallantry, heroism, adherence to duty, and sexual assertiveness). At the same time, Ford again and again reaffirms the "softer" feminine values (including devotion to happy domesticity, displays of romantic love and sentimental affection, and commitment to principles of forgiveness and nonviolence) and attaches them to normative masculinity through characters such as Gil Martin in *Drums along the Mohawk*, Martin Pawley in *The Searchers*, Captain Brittles in *She Wore a Yellow Ribbon*, and Sandy and Travis in *Wagon Master*. The displacement of such "feminized" values onto men demonstrates that women are not the only icons for civilization in Ford's Westerns, even if the duties Ford's male protagonists often perform in support of these values remain gender-differentiated according to nineteenth-century social norms.

As a consequence, Ford's Westerns integrate femininity in complex, plural, and contingent ways that do not adhere to received notions of the Western that emphasize the genre's focus on a violent masculinity that celebrates individualism and isolation. In fact, if Ford can be faulted for anything, it is that his Westerns reveal more of the emotional sensitivity of men than of women, and his films display a greater interest in men and their embracing of "feminine" values than in women and their negotiation of a restrictive social order and accommodation to a harsh land.

In showing how Ford's films offer a very different picture of the gendering of the Western than Tompkins and other scholars currently maintain, we can only conclude that the subtle nature of Ford's films, their unusual complexity, and their depth of feeling in representing emotionally laden values that cut across presumed gender differences have not been sufficiently appreciated. Also, their relative neglect in recent criticism means that a salient question remains unanswered: Are Ford's films exceptional or do they signal that film and literary scholars need to see the entire genre with fresh and more open eyes? This question raises the possibility that not only is Ford a more subtle filmmaker than critics such as Tompkins acknowledge, but the Western, in its construction of gender, is a more plural and interesting cinematic genre than they have assumed.

Certainly, we must be careful not to regard Ford's work—or the genre as a whole—as an ahistorical, nostalgia-driven repetition of a single narrative, immune to changes in the development of the Western, to shifts in cultural or industrial trends, or to alterations in directorial approach.[82] This said, Ford's oeuvre offers the promise of the Western as an emotionally challenging—even poetic—form. That fact alone makes it imperative to move beyond current scholarship and continue to address these films as exemplars of the Western as popular storytelling in one of its most satisfying forms.

NOTES

1. Interview with Henry Fonda in Lindsay Anderson, *About John Ford* (London: Plexus, 1981), 222.

2. Andrew Sarris has also suggested Ford's propensity to detour from expected generic norms: "Ford's Westerns never depended excessively on the machismo matchups of quick draws, but rather on the normally neglected intervals between the gunshots when men received haircuts, courted their sweethearts, and even partook of fragments of frontier culture" (Sarris, *The John Ford Movie Mystery* [Bloomington: Indiana University Press, 1975], 117).

3. In his seminal work first published in 1950, *Virgin Land*, Henry Nash Smith says that by 1889, the Western "had sunk to the near-juvenile level it was to occupy with virtually no change down to our own day" (120). Smith deals at length with the sensationalistic literary devices used to construct the dime novel heroine. In particular, see chapter 10 of *Virgin Land: The American West as Symbol and Myth* (Cambridge, Mass.: Harvard University Press, [1950] 1978), 112–120. Richard Maltby also notes that the Western is "several things at once—a myth of origin, an adolescent male fantasy, an account of the individual's relation to society, and more." See Maltby, "A Better Sense of History: John Ford and the Indians," in *The Book of Westerns*, ed. Ian Cameron and Douglas Pye (New York: Continuum, 1996), 43.

4. Leslie Fiedler, *Love and Death in the American Novel,* revised edition (New York: Stein and Day Publishers, 1975 [1960]), 348–349.

5. Fiedler, *Love and Death,* 347.

6. Fiedler, *Love and Death,* 355.

7. Fiedler, *Love and Death,* 355, emphasis in original.

8. Jane Tompkins, *West of Everything: The Inner Life of Westerns* (New York: Oxford University Press, 1992), 81.

9. Tompkins, *West of Everything,* 66.

10. Robert Warshow, "Movie Chronicle: The Westerner," rpt. in *Film Theory and Criticism,* ed. Gerald Mast and Marshall Cohen, second edition (New York: Oxford University Press, 1979), 474, 471.

11. Warshow, "Movie Chronicle," 471.

12. Warshow, "Movie Chronicle," 471.

13. Tompkins, *West of Everything,* 66.

14. Tompkins, *West of Everything,* 127.

15. Tompkins, *West of Everything,* 41, 63–64, 73, 81.

16. Tompkins, *West of Everything,* 41. Although not citing Ford by name, she supports her claim that the Western genre presents "an ongoing guerrilla war against the church as an institution" with an obvious allusion to his films when she says that the "only trace" of Christian congregations is "the sound of a hymn—always 'Shall We Gather at the River?' to which the answer is implicitly no" (35).

17. Tompkins, *West of Everything,* 40–41, 54–55, 68–69, 90–92.

18. Tompkins, *West of Everything,* 128. She argues, "The free, wild prairie promises liberation from stuffy interiors and bad family scenarios . . . but the type of heroism it seems to legitimize doesn't produce a very viable person, a person who enjoys living with himself and other people." Ford's flower-tending males tend to prefer roses and include Buck Sweet (Ward Bond) in *3 Godfathers* (1948), Captain Nathan Brittles in *She Wore a Yellow Ribbon* (1949), Tom Doniphon in *The Man Who Shot Liberty Valance,* and, in a non-Western context, Sean Thornton in *The Quiet Man* (1952). Tompkins inadvertently alludes to the possibility of another mode of masculinity in the Western when she remarks on a photograph of a young John Wayne (in cowboy garb) and his expression as being "pure and sweet; shy, really, and demure" (65).

19. For an insightful review of Tompkins's book, see Edward Buscombe, "Book Reviews," *Journal of Film and Video* 47, nos. 1–3 (Spring–Fall 1995), 128–130.

20. Robin Wood, "'Shall We Gather at the River?': The Late Films of John Ford," *Film Comment* 7, no. 3 (Fall 1971), 8–17 (reprinted in this volume); Sarris, *The John Ford Movie Mystery,* especially 126, 156–158, 188; Tag Gallagher, *John Ford: The Man and His Films* (Berkeley: University of California Press, 1986), especially 260.

21. Michael Dempsey, "John Ford: A Reassessment," *Film Quarterly* 28, no. 4 (1975), 2, 4, 7.

22. See, for example, Pam Cook, "Women," in *The BFI Companion to the Western,* ed. Edward Buscombe (London: Andre Deutsch/British Film Institute, 1988), 240–241. Cook acknowledges Ford's interesting treatment of gender in noting that his films "produced some significant reverberations" in their exploration of the "inherent tensions" in the Western's expected depictions of women.

23. Gallagher, *John Ford,* 174.

24. Gallagher, *John Ford,* 260.

25. Martin Pumphrey, "Masculinity," in Buscombe, ed., *The BFI Companion,* 181.

J. A. Place notes the "respect for each sphere" that Ford shows. See J. A. Place, *The Western Films of John Ford* (Secaucus: Citadel Press, 1974), 82.

26. Sarris, *The John Ford Movie Mystery,* 119.

27. Virginia Wright Wexman, "The Family on the Land," in *The Birth of Whiteness,* ed. Daniel Bernardi (New Brunswick, N.J.: Rutgers University Press, 1996), 162, 142, 147. Ed Buscombe's observation in reference to silent films applies also to Ford's Westerns: "Those who assume that the Western hero traditionally preferred horses to women may be unprepared for the frequency with which romantic love turns the mechanism of the plot in these early films" (Buscombe, *The BFI Companion,* 26). Tompkins asserts that the Western celebrates masculine suppression of feeling because its heroes "are trying to get away from other people and themselves" and "want to dominate the land" (*West of Everything,* 6–7). It could be argued that Ford's choice of Monument Valley as the impossibly rugged and inhospitable site of so many of his Westerns (including the Edwards's homestead in *The Searchers*) forces the audience to realize (at some level) the utter impossibility of dominating this land, as well as the extremely fragile nature of the pioneers' enterprise.

28. Pumphrey, "Masculinity," 181.

29. Tag Gallagher describes Clementine as "willful, pushy . . . [a woman who has] crossed a continent all alone" (Gallagher, *John Ford,* 233).

30. Place, *The Western Films,* 81.

31. Richard Slotkin, *Gunfighter Nation: The Myth of the Frontier in Twentieth-Century America* (New York: Harper Perennial, [1992] 1993), 338. He also says that in the film, "women's values stand equal to men's" (35).

32. Catherine E. Beecher and Harriet Beecher Stowe, from *The American Woman's Home* (1869), quoted in Norton Juster, *A Woman's Place: Yesterday's Women in Rural America* (Golden, Co.: Fulcrum Publishing, 1996), 231.

33. See also François Truffaut's remarks: "For a long time, I criticized his view of women—which I found too 19th century. Then I realized that, thanks to John Ford, a splendid actress like Maureen O'Hara has been able to play some of the best women's roles of the American cinema between 1941 and 1957" ("About John Ford," *Action* 8, no. 8 [Nov.–Dec. 1973], 5, reprinted in this volume).

34. The need for the male to forgive and protect his sexually errant sister is also given voice in *Rio Grande* (1950) through the character of Tyree (Ben Johnson). Texas Rangers have a warrant for his arrest. Tyree tells his Army pals how he shot a man who could ruin his sister's reputation, and he will satisfy the law only when he knows she is safe from scandal, i.e., in California with her new husband.

35. Cook, "Women," 241.

36. Cook, "Women," 241.

37. Richard Combs, "At Play in the Fields of John Ford," *Sight and Sound* 51, no. 2 (1982), 126. Combs argues that *Seven Women,* set in China, "is in essence a Western with its isolated mission/fort and its band of marauding savages."

38. For a helpful compilation of early captivity narratives by both men and women, see Alden T. Vaughan and Edward W. Clark, *Puritans among the Indians: Accounts of Captivity and Redemption 1676–1724* (Cambridge, Mass.: Harvard University Press, Belknap Press, 1981).

39. Marty Roth, "'Yes, My Darling Daughter': Gender, Miscegenation and Generation in John Ford's *The Searchers*," *New Orleans Review* 18, no. 4 (Winter 1991), 70.

40. Other than Martin Pawley, Mrs. Jorgensen seems to be the only person who

never wavers from the idea that Debbie must be rescued. In the end, Debbie's rescue and reinsertion into white society seem predicated on her reversion to childhood, both at the moment that Ethan decides not to kill her (he lifts her over his head as he did when she was a girl) and when she enters the Jorgensen house accompanied by Mrs. Jorgensen. Richard Maltby has called attention to the contradictions in Ford's presentation of the woman as captive of the racial Other. See Maltby, "A Better Sense," 34–49.

41. Wexman, "The Family on the Land," 162–163, 142.

42. J. A. Place discusses *Drums along the Mohawk* as a Western in *The Western Films,* 44, as does the "Colonial Period" entry by Edward Countryman in Buscombe, ed., *The BFI Companion,* 93.

43. Tompkins, *West of Everything,* 41.

44. It is Lana, not Gil, whom the camera follows in key moments: the departure of the citizen army from the valley to fight, the death of General Herkimer (Roger Imhof), and the final attack on the fort. Women take up weapons to fight off "savage" attacks in *The Iron Horse* as well.

45. Dempsey, "John Ford," 11, 9. Dempsey dismisses Ford's love stories as "insipid" and refers to the director's love matches as featuring "saintly tintypes mated to Ford's stolid heroes" (8–9).

46. Sarris, *The John Ford Movie Mystery,* 172.

47. Marty Roth claims that it is a "commonplace" that "in his films John Ford elides sexuality" (Roth, "'Yes, My Darling Daughter,'" 8).

48. Cook, "Women," 240–241.

49. Gallagher is an astute commentator on Ford's work, but I believe he misreads Mrs. Collingwood's actions when he states that they uphold "glory . . . [as] an acceptable goal in the system" (*John Ford,* 250).

50. William Darby reads this order as Thursday's sending Sergeant Major O'Rourke back, which is then purposefully misinterpreted by York so he can save the younger O'Rourke instead. However, I believe the pattern the film sets up of Thursday's behavior in the scene in the O'Rourke home is followed here too. In both scenes, Thursday's aggression is followed by what amounts to a softening of attitude or an apology. See Darby, *John Ford's Westerns: A Thematic Analysis with a Filmography* (Jefferson, N.C.: McFarland, 1996), 104.

51. Slotkin claims that a shot registers Thursday's dismay at the prospect of sharing grandchildren with Sergeant Major O'Rourke. There is no such shot, and no reason for one. After all, this is a prospect that Thursday himself has engineered by sending Michael to safety. See Slotkin, *Gunfighter Nation,* 341. I also must disagree with his reading of Thursday's disastrous "last stand" as "a potentially redemptive or regenerative act of violence" that "purges the worst elements from the army by killing Thursday . . . and by leaving York in command" (241). The irony is that Thursday's death doesn't end his influence. In the final scene, York's uneasy defense of Thursday's Custer-like legend and his preparing for action against the Apache indicate that both he and the cavalry are still trapped into carrying out Thursday's death-dealing policies. The viewer knows that peace could have been secured with negotiation, but for Thursday's arrogance and outright stupidity.

52. Gallagher, *John Ford,* 199.

53. Will Wright, *Sixguns and Society: A Structural Study of the Western* (Berkeley: University of California Press, 1975), 151–152.

54. Tompkins, *West of Everything,* 128.

55. A Proppian analysis would no doubt reveal that the narrative of *The Searchers* constructs Marty as the "hero" in mythic structural terms. Martin is the first to recognize that there is "something funny" with the Comanche trail leading them away from the real object of the "murder raid"—the Edwards's ranch. Late in the film, Mose Harper (Hank Worden) refuses to give the location of Chief Scar's camp to Ethan. He will give it only to Marty ("five fingers, Marty, five fingers"). Marty, not Ethan, translates this cryptic message into the place where rivers meet. Marty kills Scar, rescues Debbie, and is reunited with Laurie. For an examination of how Ford's many ad hoc changes to the script of *The Searchers* increased Ethan's antisocial characteristics as well as radically separated him from the community and the family, see Arthur M. Eckstein, "Darkening Ethan: John Ford's *The Searchers* (1956) from Novel to Screenplay to Screen," *Cinema Journal* 38, no. 1 (Fall 1998), 3–24.

56. As an illustration of "soft" masculinity in Ford's Westerns, the regular appearance of loquacious and sentimental Irishmen, often named Sergeant Quincannon or Mulcahy (most often played by Victor McLagen), deserves attention.

57. William Pechter, *Twenty-Four Times a Second: Films and Film-Makers* (New York: Harper & Row, 1971), 239.

58. Eric Leguèbe, *Le Cinéma Americain par ses auteurs* (Paris: Guy Authier, 1977), 77, quoted in Gallagher, *John Ford,* 435.

59. Tompkins, *West of Everything,* 65.

60. With remarkable frequency, Ford's protagonists are men who often desperately attempt to use words to keep from fighting. In *Fort Apache,* York attempts to negotiate peace with Cochise. Similarly, Nathan Brittles (John Wayne) in *She Wore a Yellow Ribbon* tries to prevent war by going to talk to the old chief, Pony That Walks.

61. Families without women are suspect, and Ford almost inevitably presents them as perverse and destructive: the Clantons in *My Darling Clementine,* the Cleggs in *Wagon Master,* and the other Cleggs in *Two Rode Together.*

62. Lee Clark Mitchell, *Westerns: Making the Man in Fiction and Film* (Chicago: University of Chicago Press, 1996), 185.

63. Richard Maltby offers a different interpretation. He says that Tom is "too tainted by the wilderness to resist the descent into anarchic violence and alcoholic degeneracy on the loss of his girl." See Maltby, "A Better Sense," 38.

64. The very qualities that make Tom such an awesome figure also seem to impede his relationship with Hallie. She seems at ease with Ranse as an equal (in spite of his education), but she appears somewhat emotionally distanced from Tom and hesitant in his presence. The scene in which she watches him from the doorway as he walks away in the darkness registers the complexity of their relationship from her perspective. Michael Dempsey argues that women in Ford's films are "reverentially dominated by men" ("John Ford," 9). In the case of Tom and Hallie, he may be correct—but Ford seems to realize it too.

65. Owen Wister, *The Virginian* (1902), quoted in Mitchell, *Westerns,* p. 101. See Tompkins, *West of Everything,* 4, 7, 30, 62–66, 69, 72, 131–155, 157, and Mitchell, *Westerns,* 94–119.

66. Mitchell, *Westerns,* 119. On masculinity achieved through physical performance, see 151–159.

67. Mitchell, *Westerns,* 169.

68. General George Crook (1829–1890) was famous for his service in the Indian Wars. He fought against the Chiricahua Apache and Geronimo and, like Kirby Yorke, pursued his Apache adversaries into Mexico.

69. Tompkins, *West of Everything*, 126.

70. Tag Gallagher argues that in Ford's work "Love and sexuality are transformed into duty" (*John Ford*, 169), but *Rio Grande* suggests that this is not always the case.

71. Another memorable example of the emotionally fulsome but futile gesture occurs in *Stagecoach*. Doc Boone (Thomas Mitchell) risks his life by confronting Luke Plummer in the saloon and threatening him with murder charges if he takes a shotgun into his fight with Ringo. Plummer backs down, but outside, unbeknownst to Doc, Luke's girlfriend tosses him another shotgun from her place on the balcony.

72. Joseph McBride and Michael Wilmington, *John Ford* (New York: Da Capo Press, 1975), 199.

73. Dempsey, "John Ford," 8. It should be noted that due to numerous diseases, including dysentery, typhus, cholera, malaria, childbed fever, and depression, women suffered from a higher mortality rate than men in Western states during much of the nineteenth century, while death rates in Eastern states stayed at the same level for women and men. See Cathy Luchetti and Carol Olwell, *Women of the West* (St. George, Utah: Antelope Island Press, 1982), 27.

74. Karen Halttunen, *Confidence Men and Painted Women: A Study of Middle-Class Culture in America, 1830–1870* (New Haven: Yale University Press, 1982), 130.

75. This impression is also solidified by a scene played for comedy in which Wyatt first sees Clementine alight from the stage. He is struck virtually speechless by the sight of her and proceeds to act as hotel porter. Somewhat unexpectedly, he seems to know exactly what a "lady" would need: he asks the hotel to prepare a bath for her and give her the necessities so she can "freshen up."

76. Halttunen, *Confidence Men and Painted Women*, 130.

77. Halttunen, *Confidence Men and Painted Women*, 132.

78. Comparing Ford to Hawks, Andrew Sarris remarks, "John Ford's characters remain confined within old memories and old allegiances. . . . Fordian cinema is the cinema of reminiscence" (Sarris, *The John Ford Movie Mystery*, 158).

79. Halttunen, *Confidence Men and Painted Women*, 130. For a different perspective on this subject, see Ann Douglas, "The Domestication of Death," in *The Feminization of American Culture* (New York: Doubleday, [1977] 1988), 200–226.

80. Tompkins, *West of Everything*, 31. Tompkins states that Westerns are death-obsessed because they dwell on the moment in which "risking your life becomes the supreme form of heroism" rather than on the mundane, everyday Christian struggle with sin. As Sarris observes, Ford has a "penchant for directing away from the obligatory action climaxes" (*The John Ford Movie Mystery*, 119).

81. Douglas Pye, "Genre and History: *Fort Apache* and *The Man Who Shot Liberty Valance*," *Movie* 25, no. 1 (Fall 1974), 1.

82. As William Pechter has observed, "the effect of [Ford's postwar films] . . . remains not one of repetition but rather of incessant variation and diversity" (Pechter, *Twenty-Four Times a Second*, 239).

3

THE MARGIN AS CENTER

THE MULTICULTURAL DYNAMICS OF
JOHN FORD'S WESTERNS

Charles Ramírez Berg

John Ford's depiction of people of color is the most distressing feature of his
body of work. It has prompted a number of critics to take him to task for his
insensitive portrayals of ethnic minorities. An early attack came from Robin
Wood, who in 1971 noted (in "'*Shall* We Gather at the River?': The Late Films
of John Ford," reprinted in this anthology) the director's abstraction of Native
Americans into savage threats to civilization as well as Ford's paternalistic attitude toward them, which "continued basically unchanged" from *Drums along
the Mohawk* (1939) "right through to *Cheyenne Autumn*" (1964).[1] This paternalistic streak was elaborated on a few years later by Michael Dempsey, who
challenged Ford's automatic appointment to the auteur pantheon.[2] Since then,
many disparaging analyses of Ford's treatment of ethnic and minority groups
have appeared.[3]

To be sure, Ford's paternalism and his condescension toward and stereotyping of people of color are incontestable. Still, for all that, this essay will contend
that it is a mistake to dismiss Ford too hastily as one more racist filmmaker. It
will propose that the films of John Ford cannot be fully appreciated without
taking into account his Irish heritage. Remembering that he was the son of Irish
immigrants, surely something he never forgot, one begins to appreciate the fact
that his films emanate from the position of that oppressed ethnic minority and
that his stories typically focused on marginalized outcasts. This made his cinema far different from most Hollywood films, which centered on the WASP
Mainstream as a matter of course and looked uncritically at assimilation. Thus,
counterbalancing Ford's stereotyping is a richly textured multicultural vision
that is nuanced in comparison with the broad strokes that characterized much
of classical Hollywood's ethnic representation.

This multiculturalism is evident, I believe, in the majority of Ford's films,
but it is especially pronounced in his Westerns. His frontier communities are
filled with ethnics, in the more general sense that Ella Shohat speaks of ethnicity,
namely as a means of describing a wide range of disenfranchised outsiders, "a
spectrum of identities and differences, all ultimately involving questions of in-

equalities of power."[4] Furthermore, within Ford's pluralistic multiculturalism, ethnicity includes not just the Irish, who are—understandably enough—Ford's Ur-ethnics, but also a host of socially (and geographically) marginalized Others, among them various tribes of Native Americans, Mexicans and Mexican Americans, women and African Americans, Slavs and Poles, Frenchmen and Italians, Swedes and Germans, poor whites and Southerners.

Ford's culturalism is multiple not only because numerous ethnicities are sympathetically represented, but because Ford shows ethnicity to be a hybrid property. Take, for example, the layered cultural identities and multiple affiliations of the kind Ford routinely portrayed with his Native Americans, who speak English, Spanish, and their Indian language and move freely across a permeable U.S.-Mexican border. Or consider the collective ethnicities of Elena de la Madriaga (Linda Cristal) in *Two Rode Together* (1961), who is born an aristocrat in Mexico, then, as a captive of the Comanche, lives as the wife of a warrior, is later "rescued" and sent to a U.S. cavalry fort, and finally, to escape the racism there, moves to California. Such depictions indicate that Ford regarded cultures not as autonomous, static, or fixed states, but rather as fluid, evolving, and organic ones that were inextricably intertwined.

Ford's films have a multicultural world view rooted in the fact that, for him, ethnicity is the most important human attribute. It is the wellspring from which Ford's two cornerstone values, justice and tolerance, flow. Because, in his view, all that was good in the American experience originated from ethnicity, Ford was extremely suspicious of assimilation. He regarded it as an insidious trade-off involving the enforced erasure of one's cultural identity, as well as the adoption of the Mainstream's rigid, intolerant, and merciless value system. Ford's skepticism about assimilation was part of his generally contradictory attitude toward America, which led him to critique the American Mainstream even as he patriotically celebrated the nation as a whole. This conflicted perspective, I would argue, comes from the fact that John Ford, as the son of immigrants, found himself culturally suspended between Ireland's potato famine and the American Dream. Not surprisingly, a consistent theme in his Westerns is the tension between ethnics, who have been exiled to the social and geographical Margin, and the elite WASP Mainstream who drove them there.

This essay, then, is a multicultural examination of Ford's conflicted Westerns that privileges the fact that he was an Irish American filmmaker who had one foot in each culture, Mainstream American and ethnic Irish.[5] This multicultural perspective, which positions Ford as an Irish American filmmaker who made ethnic films within the Hollywood studio system, brings at least three important aspects of Ford's Westerns into bold relief. First, several familiar Fordian motifs—the drunken brawling, the singing and dancing, the militarism—can be appreciated as expressions of ethnicity, rather than being dismissed solely as embarrassing directorial "touches." Second, Ford revealed his multi-

Sergeant Rutledge (1960): the Western as a site of tension between ethnics, who have been exiled to the social and geographical margin, and the elite WASP Mainstream. Jeffrey Hunter, Woody Strode, and Carleton Young.
Courtesy of the Museum of Modern Art Film Stills Archive.

ethnic sympathies, especially for Native Americans, Mexicans, and Mexican Americans, in subversive ways. Most significant are his subtle but effective manipulations of cinematic elements such as casting, characterization, music, and sound effects. Third, his consistent ethnic sensibility manifested itself in the form of a well-defined cultural narrative that ran just below the surface of a film's dramatic narrative. Within this cultural subplot Ford investigated the nature of ethnicity in America. But before getting to a discussion of all this, let me situate Ford as an ethnic filmmaker, look at the social position of the Irish in this country during Ford's formative years, and outline the ways in which his films are culturally distinct from most Hollywood movies of his time.

FORD AS ETHNIC FILMMAKER

Understanding Ford as a minority artist requires recalling the sociohistorical context from which he sprang, particularly the terrible discrimination the Irish endured during the director's formative years. Born to Irish immigrant parents in a farmhouse near Portland, Maine, in 1894, Ford grew up in a time when Irish immigrants were reviled in America. As the wholesale denigration of Irish immigrants retreats in time, it may be difficult to appreciate just how despised they were. But sociologist and novelist Andrew Greeley reminds us what it meant to be Irish in the last half of the nineteenth century and the first half of the twentieth:

> While the psychological degradation of the Irish was certainly no worse than that to which blacks have been subjected, it must also be said that from 1850 to 1950 there were no dissenting voices being raised on the subject of the American Irish; no one praised any aspect of their culture, no one suggested that Irish might be beautiful, no one argued that their treatment was both unjust and bigoted.[6]

This hostile social climate notwithstanding, John Ford entered the social Mainstream, and found success there as one of the top Hollywood directors of the classical era.[7] Nevertheless, I would argue that his were minority-focused films. First, because they were made by a member of a denigrated minority group. Second, because their treatment of ethnics was unlike that of most classical studio cinema, in that they explicitly endorsed ethnicity, particularly immigrant ethnicity; they celebrated immigrant ethnics and their Marginalized communities; they questioned assimilation into the WASP Mainstream; and they sometimes valorized Native American, Mexican American, and African American ethnicities.

This focus on minorities and minority perspectives was at odds with Hollywood's ideological *raison d'être,* namely the promotion of the WASP Mainstream. As a result, a built-in friction between Hollywood's "mainstreaming project" and Ford's counter-hegemonic immigrant sensibilities is evident throughout his cinema. Hollywood's "America" was constructed to conform to the majority's utopian view of itself—white (from Western European stock), well-to-do, Protestant, and English-speaking.[8] Of course, Hollywood's attempts to present this coherent, upbeat America were never wholly successful—the socially repressed continually returned to knock on Main Street doors. Still, a generally positive—and exculpatory—portrayal of the WASP Mainstream and a consistently derogatory—and disparaging—attitude toward various forms of Otherness did emerge. In contrast, Ford's films centered not on the dominant Mainstream but on the immigrant, working-class, socially and geographically isolated Margin.[9] And just as most Hollywood cinema used people of color to prop up its WASP self, Ford's films—especially his Westerns—used them to promote immigrant ethnicity over the eastern Anglo elite.

FORD AS NARRATIVE ETHNOGRAPHER

Ford's fictional American frontier, like the historical one, is a territory up for grabs, "a region," in the words of Gregory H. Nobles, "in which no culture, group or government can claim effective control or hegemony over others."[10] Consequently, it is in perpetual disequilibrium. The struggle to control it in Ford's films—as in American history—is a contest between the Mainstream

Table 3.1

Mainstream	Margin	Native
WASP establishment elite; represented in the West by colonizers and assimilated Westerners	European immigrants, especially the Irish (pioneers, settlers, soldiers) at the frontier	Native Americans

WASP establishment and the Native Americans (see Table 3.1). Squeezed between them at the Margin frontier are the pioneer ethnics (the soldier-agents of the Mainstream, who carry out its colonizing project, as well as the immigrant and working-class settlers).[11]

Let us examine each of these three main groups.

The WASP Mainstream

For Ford this is the white Yankee elite, centered in the urban northeast. Rigid, hypocritical, and intolerant, they are self-righteously convinced of their social, moral, and racial superiority. This Mainstream is typically represented at the frontier by a handful of arrogant colonizers, among whom Henry Fonda's Lieutenant Colonel Thursday in *Fort Apache* (1948) is the archetypal example. They may also be social-climbing frontier folk who have adopted the Mainstream's hard-hearted value system: for example, the self-righteous ladies of the Law and Order League who drive the prostitute heroine out of town at the beginning of *Stagecoach* (1939), and the similarly narrow-minded army officers and their wives at the fort in *Two Rode Together*, who insensitively query Elena about her sexual experiences as the woman of a Comanche warrior.

The money, power, and influence of the Mainstream are corrupting forces rather than civilizing ones. That corruption is exemplified by the crooked banker Gatewood (whose wife is a leading member of the Law and Order League) in *Stagecoach*. Another example is Guthrie McCabe (James Stewart), the cynical, egotistical, and mercenary marshal in *Two Rode Together*. To enhance his salary he takes 10% of the profits of every business in Tascosa, showing that he has sold out to the capitalist cultural Mainstream. Without a connection to their root culture, those in the assimilated Mainstream have, according to Ford, no moral core. In its place they substitute self-serving capitalist traits (greed, materialism, careerism, legalistic rigidity, intolerance).[12] In short, if ethnics and minorities are sometimes stereotyped in Ford's films, the WASP Mainstream *always* is, with its members consistently depicted as heartless, oppressive, and intolerant.

The Ethnic Margin: Betwixt and Between

Implicit in Ford's Westerns is a social caste system, enforced by the intolerant Mainstream, that marginalizes immigrant ethnics and banishes them to the frontier. As Joseph McBride puts it, Ford's "characters are typically refugees from constricting societies (Europe, urbanized America) in which once vital traditions have hardened into inflexible dogmas."[13] The Mormons' exile to the desert wilderness in *Wagon Master* (1950) is emblematic of the way Ford's ethnics were cast out from the Mainstream. He even illustrates their expulsion from the town by the sheriff and his armed deputies near the beginning of the film, a scene that echoes a similar one in *Stagecoach* in which Doc Boone (Thomas Mitchell) and the prostitute, Dallas (Claire Trevor), are exiled. A variation on this theme is Elena's self-exile in *Two Rode Together,* when she decides to go west rather than withstand the rampant racism at the army fort. Besides escaping intolerance, Ford's Margin ethnics leave the cultural center for two other reasons. First, to increase their opportunities. Second, to find a space where they can openly practice their ethnicity, which is impossible within the tightly constrained, ethnically cleansed Mainstream. So they gather at the river of the Margin-frontier and show themselves to be in the main guileless and giving, raucous and lively, humorous and humane.

The Native: The Great Unknown

Often regarded as enigmatic racial Others, Native Americans in Ford's Westerns primarily serve to define the ethnics at the Margin. Ford accomplishes this in two ways. The first is by using the treatment of peaceable Native Americans as a test of Margin characters' sense of justice and tolerance. Those who treat them humanely—(Captain Kirby York [John Wayne] in *Fort Apache* and Captain Nathan Brittles [John Wayne] in *She Wore a Yellow Ribbon* [1949], the Mormons in *Wagon Master,* Lieutenant Jim Gary [Richard Widmark] in *Two Rode Together,* and the missionary Deborah Wright [Carroll Baker] and Captain Thomas Archer [Richard Widmark] in *Cheyenne Autumn*), or who can count a token Native American among their friends (Gil [Henry Fonda] in *Drums along the Mohawk*)—are Ford's heroes. Conversely, negative treatment of innocent Native Americans signifies villainy (Reese Clegg's [Fred Libby] violation of the Navajo woman [Movita Castaneda] in *Wagon Master,* the duplicitous Indian agents in *Fort Apache* and *She Wore a Yellow Ribbon,* the U.S. cavalry's killing of the innocent Look [Beulah Archuletta] in *The Searchers* [1956]).

A second function of Native Americans in Ford's Westerns is to serve as the social and racial boundary for immigrant ethnics at the frontier: the impenetrable racial-cultural "hard place," if you will, against which the immigrant pioneers are pressed by the Mainstream "rock" of assimilation. In this sense, Native Americans in Ford's films serve to fix the cultural limits for Margin ethnics. If the Mainstream represents Ford's fear of what the Margin ethnics will likely become via assimilation, the Native American is what they *can't* become—

The violation of a Navajo woman tests the Mormons' sense of justice and tolerance in *Wagon Master* (1950). Ward Bond and Movita Castaneda.
Courtesy of the Museum of Modern Art Film Stills Archive.

another race. Ford's settlers are therefore sandwiched between the ever-advancing colonizing Mainstream and the Native American's inscrutable Otherness. Though they struggle to maintain an ethnic identity separate from both, Ford's immigrant pioneers discover that the effort is hopeless. Eventually they must choose between assimilation into the Mainstream or life among the Native Americans, both of which are viewed as cultural deaths. Being caught between the devil of the intolerant Mainstream and the deep blue sea of Native American Otherness is the subject of *Two Rode Together,* and the film graphically demonstrates the Margin's fear of both. At the Mainstream end of the spectrum, there is Elena's cruel treatment by whites at the army fort, a form of social death. A white woman (Mae Marsh) illustrates the cultural death at the Native American end for Ford's pioneer ethnics. Long thought to be dead, she is discovered living as a Comanche captive. But she requests that the investigating army officer, Lieutenant Gary, not change her record. "You'd rather be listed as dead?" he asks. "I am dead," she replies.

Yet, perhaps in appreciation of their ethnicity, there is a positive side to Ford's depiction of Native Americans. ("My sympathy," Ford once said, "was always with the Indians."[14]) Accordingly, Ford's Native Americans are culturally cohesive and, like the immigrant ethnics, struggling to maintain their culture in the face of the Mainstream's genocidal onslaught. As such, they are a mirror image of the ethnics at the Margin. Probably the best rendering of this cultural equivalence comes in *Wagon Master,* when the Mormons and the Native Americans each confront and tolerate the mysterious other, locking arms and circling a flickering campfire in a Navajo dance.

Alongside Ford's three major social groups can be found two more Others who play an interesting, if minor, part in his Westerns: African Americans, and Mexicans and Mexican Americans.

African Americans: The Marginalized of the Margin

Rare in Ford's West, though more numerous than in classical Hollywood's West, African Americans exist at the racially segregated outskirts of Margin society. Other than the grateful Blacks seen in *The Horse Soldiers* (1959) and what looks to be a lone Black cowpoke in the saloon in *Stagecoach* (who speaks Spanish!), they usually appear as faithful African American servants: Woody Strode's Pompey in *The Man Who Shot Liberty Valance* (1962), Daisy (Beulah Hall Jones) in *Drums along the Mohawk,* and Lukey (Althea Gibson) in *The Horse Soldiers.* Their narrative function is, like the Native Americans', to make explicit the tolerance—and thus for Ford, the heroic righteousness—of the ethnic margin. The exception that proves the rule, of course, is *Sergeant Rutledge* (1960), where Ford tries to make amends for this pattern of a marginalized depiction of African Americans.

Mexicans and Mexican Americans: The Hybrid Race

Mexicans and Mexican Americans straddle the line between the Margin and the Native in an interesting way for Ford. Mexicans in Mexico are typically light-skinned, upper-class, and well educated (the Mexican army officer [Alberto Morin] in *Rio Grande* [1950]; Emilio Fernández y Figueroa[15] [Antonio Moreno] in *The Searchers*). Mexicans in the United States and Mexican Americans, however, are usually darker-skinned inhabitants of the Margin's fringes (Chris [Chris Pin Martin], the station master at Apache Wells in *Stagecoach;* the Mexican Americans on the streets of Tombstone in *My Darling Clementine* [1946] or in the cantina in Shinbone in *Liberty Valance;* Link's [Andy Devine] wife and children in *Liberty Valance*). As they approach the narrative's center stage, and particularly if they are female, they are frequently stereotyped as sneaky and untrustworthy (for example, Chris's wife Yakeema [Elvira Rios], who assists the *vaqueros* in taking the spare horses in *Stagecoach,* and the wily Chihuahua [Linda Darnell] in *My Darling Clementine,* who helps the tinhorn gambler cheat Wyatt Earp in a poker game). Occasionally, however, Ford allows them to step out of the background and break out of the stereotype (Pedro Armendáriz's characters in *3 Godfathers* [1948] and *Fort Apache*, Elena in *Two Rode Together*).

Interestingly, they are often conflated with Native Americans. This racial equation occurs both at the narrative level (with, for example, Yakeema in *Stagecoach*, the Thursdays' maid [Movita Castaneda] in *Fort Apache*, the Navajo woman [Movita Castaneda] in *Wagon Master*, and Chihuahua [whom Wyatt threatens to send "back to the reservation"]) and in his casting choices, when Ford cast Mexican actors as Native Americans (Movita Castaneda in several films, Miguel Inclán in *Fort Apache*, Dolores Del Río, Ricardo Montalban, and Gilbert Roland in *Cheyenne Autumn*). This could be seen as racial confusion or, as I will argue about the casting in *Fort Apache*, a fairly accurate rendering, since most Mexicans are *mestizos,* of both Spanish and *indio* blood.

FORD'S MARGIN MOTIFS

Thinking of Ford's films as emanating from the ethnic Margin sheds considerable light on several of his recurrent motifs that, when regarded solely as auteurist penchants, are at best quaint directorial tropes and at worst tiresome and repetitive self-indulgence. Let me focus on three of them—brawling and carousing, singing and dancing, marching and parading—to tease out their expressions of ethnicity.

Brawling and Carousing

In Ford's West, the Marginals' ethnicity gives them ready access to emotional and sentimental human expression, which is certainly exemplified by the many instances of their drinking and fighting. These scenes of ethnic exuberance mark a major fault line between Ford's supporters and his detractors. True, the steady—some would say endless—stream of protracted boozing and fisticuffs can be tedious in the extreme and has been seen as stereotyping of the Irish.[16] But that is when it is seen from a Mainstream point of view. From the Margin's perspective, these actions are an oppositional carnival of ethnicity meant to disrupt Mainstream sensibilities (in the narrative and in the audience too). For example, in *Stagecoach* the bombastic banker Gatewood (Berton Churchill) attempts to shame the drunken Doc Boone. "You're drunk, sir!" Gatewood tells him. But in a John Ford film drunks are never shamed. "I'm happy, Gatewood," Doc Boone replies cheerfully. "Boo!" These antics illustrate the free-wheeling joy of being alive, which for Ford is another positive attribute that flows directly from ethnicity. Drunken revelry represents unabashed cultural contestation from the Margin, a cinematic St. Patrick's Day festival that Ford employs as if to say, "We are Irish and proud of it, this is how we choose to act, and what are you going to do about it?" Moreover, these passages are Ford's litmus tests of assimilated conformity: characters (and, presumably, viewers) who show their impatience with them only reveal the degree to which they have sold out to the Mainstream. Ford's characters' carousing, therefore, presents a cultural polemic: the ethnic-less Mainstream is inhibited and dull, the ethnic Margin is loose and fun.

Singing and Dancing

Ubiquitous in Ford's Westerns, communal music serves multiple functions. First, of course, these occasions draw the ethnic community together and celebrate it as vital, unified, and uninhibited. For instance, right after the good citizens of Tombstone dedicate their unnamed church in My Darling Clementine, they immediately strike up the band and have "a dad-blasted good dance." Second, these parties are used to contrast the ethnics' unbridled self-expression with the WASPs' humorless reserve.[17] In Fort Apache, for example, there is Sergeant Mulcahy's (Victor McLaglen) playful attempt to spike the punch at the noncommissioned officers' ball, and his earnest—and therefore comical— efforts to "act respectable" ("We'll be the morals of decorum," he promises his master sergeant). Compare this with the unmistakable disgust on Lieutenant Colonel Thursday's face at having to dance to the barroom tune "Golden Slippers" with a noncommissioned officer's wife. Finally, Ford will use a dance to indicate the intrusion of insidious Mainstream values into the frontier. Thus Lincoln's (Henry Fonda) unease at the upscale ball in Young Mr. Lincoln (1939), where he is told that he dances in "the worst way," contrasts with Mary Todd's (Marjorie Weaver) comfortable familiarity with high-society customs. In like manner, Ford uses the army officers' dance in Two Rode Together to proclaim the second coming of the Law and Order League. Indeed, one sign of the infiltration of mean-spirited Mainstream values is the classical music that is played in the scene—the Blue Danube waltz has replaced the common reels, popular tunes, and saloon songs typically heard at Ford's ethnic dances.

Militarism: Marching and Parading

How can we reconcile Ford's distrust of dominant power structures with his rampant militarism, symbolized by his fondness for scenes of men marching in parades? From the perspective of the Margin, such seeming contradictions find at least a partial explanation. First of all, there is a long tradition of ethnic militias and police and fire brigades in American history, stretching back to before the Civil War.[18] Thus it is important to note that in the experience of nineteenth-century immigrant groups, parading in uniform was a socially sanctioned way of expressing ethnic pride.

Second, military service has always been a viable way for America's disenfranchised to improve their lot. For many members of the underclass, the military is an opportunity: a good, steady job that pays a decent wage and raises one above dead-end alternatives such as poverty, crime, and exploitive manual labor. Before and during the Civil War it was common for military recruiters to meet boatloads of Irish immigrants just as they disembarked onto American soil.[19] "I stepped right off a boat and right into uniform," the military doctor (Sean McClory) says in *Cheyenne Autumn,* "and I had the good sense to stay there." Moreover, the military uniform is a sign of upward social mobility. The dignity with which Sergeant Major O'Rourke (Ward Bond) holds himself in *Fort Apache,* and his beaming pride in his West Point–educated son, Lieutenant Michael O'Rourke (John Agar), capture this well.

Third, the service can enhance an ethnic's self-image by leveling race, class, and ethnic differences. The reason two young officers from opposite ends of the social spectrum are able to vie for Olivia's (Joanne Dru) attentions in *She Wore a Yellow Ribbon* is that they are on more equal footing in the army than they would be in civilian life. (And in the end, it is the "commoner," Lieutenant Cohill [John Agar], not the WASP swell from the East [Harry Carey Jr.], who wins her affections.)[20] The first row of dancers in *Fort Apache*'s Grand March sequence is a prime example of military pluralism: the haughty Colonel Thursday links arms with the wife of the Irish sergeant major, and the sergeant major (Ward Bond) with Thursday's daughter (Shirley Temple). (There are real limits to this pluralism, which Ford probes in *Sergeant Rutledge.*)

Finally, military service implies patriotism, and it is an effective way for members of the underclass to demonstrate their love of country to a prejudiced Mainstream. Unquestioning patriotism understandably becomes a core characteristic of Ford's soldiers' ethos, and they are devoted to a tradition that expands social and economic horizons for them and those like them. Much of the pride that the African American "buffalo soldiers" possess in *Sergeant Rutledge* derives from the loyalty they have for the institution that gave them a chance. "The Ninth Cavalry is my home," declares Sergeant Rutledge (Woody Strode) on the witness stand, "my real freedom, and my self-respect." Similarly, Sergeants Mulcahy (Victor McLaglen) and Quincannon (Dick Foran) gallantly lead their men in Colonel Thursday's suicidal attack on Cochise.

From this perspective, it is understandable why a second-generation Irish American director would celebrate militarism with a long cinematic parade of soldiers. The perspective also helps unravel one of the biggest mysteries in Ford's cinema, the transformation of Captain York (John Wayne) at the end of *Fort Apache.* Not only does York adopt the uniform, the manner, and, we suppose, the values of Lieutenant Colonel Thursday, a superior officer he was at odds with, but, as Robin Wood has noted, the film seems to endorse York's metamorphosis. But throughout the film, Captain York is portrayed as a professional soldier who obeys orders, regardless of how much he may disagree with them or dislike Thursday. York's transformation is consistent with his (and Ford's)

The Grand March in *Fort Apache* (1948) provides a prime example of military pluralism. Shirley Temple, Ward Bond, Irene Rich, and Henry Fonda.
Courtesy of The Lilly Library, Indiana University, Bloomington, Indiana.

loyalty to the institution, which ultimately prevails over any misgivings he may have had about his superior's judgment.[21]

Even so, and in keeping with Ford's conflicted attitude, there is a critique of the Mainstream embedded within that ostensibly conformist conclusion. A happy ending for *Fort Apache*, which might have shown Captain York opposing and changing the system, would falsify the workings of American assimilation as Ford understood them. Instead, Ford demonstrates the cultural and ideological co-optation of a decent man. It is a painful and disappointing ending—and that is precisely Ford's point. As Joseph McBride has written, with *Fort Apache* Ford shows "that an insane system may be perpetuated by noble men, and indeed, that it *needs* noble and dedicated men to perpetuate itself. . . . It is comforting to think that evil is done by beasts, monsters or 'pigs,' but profoundly disturbing to realize that it is done by human beings."[22] From a multicultural perspective, what we witness at the end of *Fort Apache* is the disturbing sight of Captain York's assimilation and his resulting complicity with the Mainstream's program of genocide. As the son of immigrants, Ford may have been sympathetic to the military,[23] but he was not blind to its failings, nor to its dual role as the settlers' protector on the one hand and the Mainstream's imperialist enforcer on the other. One of the more powerful aspects of Ford's cinema, consequently, is its ability to capture the double-edged sword of assimilation in America—opportunity and exploitation.[24]

MULTICULTURAL SUBVERSIONS AND THE CHICANO AT FORT APACHE

Ford's stereotyping of Others conformed to Hollywood's representational poetics—then and now. As a result, it is hardly surprising that Ford's American Indians were handy antagonists and that he often stereotyped them. What *is* surprising is the number of times he either represented them respectfully or undermined the stereotype altogether. A modest example of the former is the narrator in *She Wore a Yellow Ribbon* complimenting the Indian warriors as "the finest light cavalry in the world." Furthermore, Ford's Indians are generally understood as victims of, at best, white America's shameless exploitation, and at worst, in Ford's words, genocide.[25] And Ford empathizes with them, to the point of occasionally seeing the winning of the West from their perspective. In *Wagon Master*, for example, the Navajo chief says he considers all white men thieves. This includes Travis (Ben Johnson), one of the film's heroes, who, though he denies it, is the man who once cheated the tribe in a horse trade. Another example is the Apache in *Fort Apache* who are led by Cochise out of the reservation in order to keep their dignity in the face of demeaning treatment by the corrupt Indian agent, Meacham (Grant Withers).

These cases are obvious, and some have been discussed before. But there are more subtle and more telling examples of Ford's cultural subversions, especially in *Fort Apache*. I want to comment on how Ford cleverly uses basic cinematic components—casting, language, character development, music, and sound effects—to demonstrate his cultural sensitivity to Native and Mexican Americans.

In *Fort Apache*'s retelling of the defeat at the Little Bighorn, the Custer character is commanding officer Lieutenant Colonel Owen Thursday, who is not only arrogant and aloof, but stubborn, stupid, and bigoted into the bargain. The film contrasts Thursday with Cochise (Miguel Inclán), who behaves with dignity and honor. For this role, Ford broke Hollywood's unwritten law about the casting of people of color (people of color who figure importantly in the narrative are played by whites; actors of color are allowed to play ethnic characters as long as they stay within the established stereotype).[26] Opposing or ignoring these rules, Ford cast the dark-skinned *mestizo* (Mexican *indio*) performer Miguel Inclán, one of the most distinguished character actors of the Mexican cinema, to play the non-stereotypical Cochise.[27] One final authentic touch in *Fort Apache* is Cochise's speaking historically correct Spanish (in addition to his Native American language), rather than broken "Hollywood Indian" English. Granted, these are small details, but there are enough of them to signal Ford's bucking Hollywood's stereotypical paradigm, and, more importantly, these choices endow Cochise and his tribe with a cultural specificity seldom seen in a classical Hollywood film.

Cochise's Spanish is interpreted by an army sergeant named Beaufort, played by Pedro Armendáriz—another top Mexican film star.[28] Ford gives us Sergeant Beaufort's cultural dossier piecemeal, so fixing his ethnicity is not easy. We see that he is accepted as an equal by the Irish sergeants (Dick Foran, Jack Pennick, and Victor McLaglen) at the fort, and that he partakes in the sergeants' shenanigans (at one point their drinking gets them busted and jailed). Clearly, he knows the "army way" as well as any soldier. We subsequently find out that he was a major in the Confederacy (his nickname is "Johnny Reb") and served as an aide to Jeb Stuart. When he is hand-picked by Captain York to accompany him into Mexico in search of Cochise, we discover he is fluent in Spanish. Still later, we learn that Sergeant Beaufort is Mexican American. When he and Captain York pause at the Rio Bravo before entering Mexico, York offers him a drink of whisky. Before taking a swig, Beaufort raises the bottle with a respectful glance toward Mexico and says, *"Por la tierra de mi madre"* ("For the land of my mother").

Sergeant Beaufort's cultural hybridity makes him one of the richest of all of Ford's secondary characters and arguably the most interesting and finely drawn Chicano in classical Hollywood cinema. To fully appreciate this, it must be remembered how much Hollywood's classical cinema abhors ambiguity in plot or characterization. Clarity is paramount, and since the paradigm has little time to explain minor characters, the more simply they are presented, the better. Going by the strict rules of the paradigm, Sergeant Beaufort's rich ethnic background should have been greatly simplified or just dropped (and the part recast to eliminate any chance of viewer confusion). But by letting his elaborate ethnicity unfold as it did (and as it would in American life), Ford acknowledges—and illustrates—the multilayered cultural complexity of the American experience. It is sociologically honest filmmaking seldom seen in Hollywood cinema, before or since.

One last example from *Fort Apache* will illustrate how Ford undercuts conventional stereotyping to level differences between groups. It comes at the end of the film, when Lieutenant Colonel Thursday foolishly orders the cavalry into battle against Cochise. In preliminary skirmishes, Ford depicts the Indian warriors in stereotypical Hollywood fashion: their attacks are accompanied by high-pitched yelping on the soundtrack, the standard auditory sign denoting the barbarity of the Native American.[29] Here, as in most Westerns, this is contrasted with the U.S. cavalry's riding into battle as the bugler sounds the charge. Grandiloquent soundtrack music typically completes the genre's coded depiction of the cavalry's "correct"—and heroic—way of doing battle.

Pedro Armendáriz as Sergeant Beaufort, the most finely drawn
Chicano in classical Hollywood cinema, with Miguel Inclán
as Cochise, in *Fort Apache* (1948).
Courtesy of The Lilly Library, Indiana University, Bloomington, Indiana.

Ford begins this way, but gradually peels away the cavalry's "civilized" features, together with Richard Hageman's triumphant movie music. First an officer's (George O'Brien) hat flies off his head. Then in quick succession, the bugler is killed, silencing the sounding charge, the regimental flag falls, and the music completely drops from the soundtrack (the rest of the battle is played without a note of either diegetic or non-diegetic music). Stripped of the magisterial signs of superiority, the horse soldiers yip and yelp just as the Native Americans do. By demonstrating that high-pitched war cries are not culturally specific to Native Americans, but simply the sounds made by warriors rousing themselves to enter battle, Ford dismantles a core stereotypical sign of Otherness in the Western, one that even he had used in *Stagecoach*.

DRAMATIC VS. CULTURAL NARRATIVES

The third major aspect of Ford's ethnic sensibilities is evidenced in two different narrative strands that are distinguished in the director's films: the obvious dramatic narrative (the main plot, typically focusing on, say, rescue, revenge, or survival) and a parallel cultural narrative (Ford's persistent subplot, primarily concerning the interaction between Mainstream and Marginal cultures). Ford usually embeds the cultural narrative within Hollywood's requisite romantic subplot, so that the romance often contains a cultural dimension. Each narrative comes to its own resolution. As with most Hollywood films, the dramatic narrative is resolved first, and often satisfactorily, providing the obligatory Hollywood happy ending. Like the romantic subplot on which it is based, Ford's cultural climax comes last, and it qualifies the happy ending. The qualification is sometimes positive, idealizing the surviving community as having realized Ford's vision of multicultural harmony (for example, the similar endings of *Drums along the Mohawk* and *Rio Grande,* in which ethnics and Native Americans are joined together beneath the American flag). At other times the cultural resolution casts a disturbing shadow over the conclusion (as with Captain York's troubling assimilation into the Mainstream in *Fort Apache,* or the end of *The Searchers,* which I'll discuss momentarily).

Sometimes (in *Fort Apache, 3 Godfathers, She Wore a Yellow Ribbon,* and *The Searchers*), Ford's subplot is strictly cultural and not romantic at all. In *The Searchers,* for example, Ethan's bringing Debbie back from the Native concludes the dramatic narrative, and his exclusion from the Margin in the film's famous last shot ends the cultural one.[30] One difference between the two narratives is that while the dramatic one always has an overt villain (Scar in *The Searchers*), the cultural subplot raises a cultural question. Because of the way morality stems from ethnicity for Ford, these cultural questions are moral ones as well. In *The Searchers,* the cultural question is, Can Ethan, the heroic representative of the Margin, overcome his racism? To the extent that he doesn't kill his niece but brings her back to the Margin community, he can. But with Ethan's scalping Scar it is highly doubtful that his racial tolerance extends beyond his family. In the end, Ethan is isolated from the rest of the Margin ethnics because the uncontrollable ferocity of his hatred of Native Americans threatens the Margin's tenuous moral equilibrium, which is based on justice and tolerance.

Table 3.2 will help to distinguish between the dramatic and cultural narratives by giving the resolution of each. In addition, the table specifies the main cultural dilemma(s) that Ford poses in each film. Besides outlining the outcomes of the twin narratives in Ford's sound Westerns, it illustrates how skillfully Ford embroidered his cultural message onto fairly standard genre formulas.

By viewing the films in such a schematic fashion, we can see clearly that, except for *Cheyenne Autumn* and *Sergeant Rutledge,* Ford's cultural focus is mainly on "his" (western European) Margin-ethnics. Even the films ostensibly about people of color, *Cheyenne Autumn* and *Sergeant Rutledge,* follow this pattern. Particularly troublesome in both are the white romantic subplots that end them. The tired predictability of these films' conclusions suggests that one of the things that makes Ford's other Westerns special is their final cultural commentary, which is absent in both of these cases. Instead, these two films end by simply reverting to the standard Hollywood romantic subplot, which disappointingly shifts their focus to what should be secondary white characters. Because the final resolution in Hollywood cinema is so powerful ideologically,

Table 3.2

	Dramatic Resolution	Cultural Dilemma	Cultural Resolution
Stagecoach	Ringo confronts and kills the Plummers	Is there a place at the Margin frontier for outsiders now that Mainstream intolerance has infected the Margin?	No. Ringo and Dallas escape into Mexico
Young Mr. Lincoln	Cass is exposed as the murderer	Should Lincoln stay in the Margin or follow his ambition—and Mary Todd—into the Mainstream?	Ignoring the devotion of Carrie Sue, Lincoln opts for Mary Todd and Mainstream success
Drums along the Mohawk	Colonists are victorious over the British and the Native Americans	Can Mainstream Lana learn to accept the Margin?	Yes. Lana becomes a frontier woman; multicultural harmony is established
My Darling Clementine	The Clantons are killed	Can Mainstream Clementine learn to accept the Margin?	Yes. Clementine accepts the Margin, and will become the new schoolmarm
Fort Apache	Mainstream imperialist arrogance leads to the massacre of the soldiers	Should Captain York loyally obey orders or his (more tolerant) ethnic conscience?	York obeys orders, survives, but then assimilates into the Mainstream
3 Godfathers	Bob saves the baby	Can Bob redeem himself after his attack on the ethnic Margin community?	Yes. Bob redeems his robbery transgression against Margin by assuming fatherhood and going to prison
She Wore a Yellow Ribbon	Captain Brittles avoids war with Native Americans. ("No casualties, no Indian war, no court martial.")	Can Brittles serve two masters—the U.S. Army and his ethnic conscience—and avoid an Indian war?	Yes. Moreover, Brittles receives a scout's commission and returns to the Margin's fold; multicultural harmony is established
Wagon Master	The Cleggs are killed	Can the untolerated Mormons tolerate non-Mormon cowboys and a prostitute?	Yes. The cowboys and prostitute are integrated into the Mormon Margin community; peaceful coexistence with Native Americans and multicultural harmony are established

(Table continues on next page)

Table 3.2 (Continued)

	Dramatic Resolution	Cultural Dilemma	Cultural Resolution
Rio Grande	Children are rescued, and Trooper Yorke proves his manhood	Can Mainstream Mrs. Yorke learn to accept the Margin?	Yes. Mrs. Yorke adapts to the frontier; multicultural harmony is established
The Searchers	Debbie's return to the Margin	Can Ethan overcome his racism?	No. Ethan is separated from the Margin
The Horse Soldiers	The Union strike force successfully completes its mission	Can Marlowe serve two masters—the U.S. Army and his ethnic conscience—and carry out his raid on the South?	? Unclear. The love of northern Colonel Marlowe and a Southern belle transcends cultural differences
Sergeant Rutledge	The dramatic conclusion is the cultural one: Hubble is exposed as a rapist-murderer, Rutledge is exonerated	Can a Mainstream institution, the U.S. Army, overcome its racism and give an African American a fair trial?	Yes, but qualified by a romantic, not cultural, subplot: white romance rekindled
Two Rode Together	Romantic conclusion: Guthrie McCabe joins Elena on the stage for California	1) Can McCabe overcome his racism? 2) Is there a place at the Margin frontier for outsiders now that Mainstream intolerance has infected the Margin?	1) Yes. Romance transcends racism: McCabe rejects the fort's and the town's Mainstream values, commits to Elena, and flees with her 2) No. Elena flees farther west, to the new frontier of California
The Man Who Shot Liberty Valance	Ranse reveals the truth about who killed Liberty Valance, but it is rejected in favor of "the legend"	1) Will Hallie choose Tom, the defender of the Margin, or Ranse, the representative of the Mainstream? 2) Can Tom be a cold-blooded killer and the defender of the Margin?	1) Hallie, like Lincoln, chooses the Mainstream; but at the end, she and Ranse resolve to return to Shinbone 2) Like Ethan, Tom is separated from the Margin community
Cheyenne Autumn	The dramatic conclusion is the cultural one: The Cheyenne arrive at their ancient homeland, and negotiate to remain there	Can the Mainstream overcome its racism?	For the moment, yes. Romantic, not cultural, subplot: white romance rekindled

Are Ford's true protagonists inevitably the whites, even in a film about people of color? Carroll Baker as Deborah Wright in *Cheyenne Autumn* (1964). Courtesy of the Museum of Modern Art Film Stills Archive.

these two films' ultimate cultural commentary is made by what comes last—the white romantic happy ending. These conclusions imply that the films' true protagonists were the white characters all along. Ironically, though they were meant to expose American racism, *Sergeant Rutledge* and *Cheyenne Autumn* lack the cultural resonance that so many of Ford's other Westerns have. And this suggests a paradoxical corollary: Ford's films comment on race and culture most profoundly—and most progressively—when their main plot is about something else.

CULTURAL PLOT FORMATIONS

In the remaining Westerns, Ford's cultural interest is mainly in the Margin and its relationship to the Mainstream. Based on the cultural dilemmas, their plots cluster around five discrete plot formulas:

1. *The Conversion-to-the-Margin Plot.* This is usually the story of a woman from the Eastern Mainstream who adjusts to frontier life and adopts tolerant ethnic-Margin values: Lana (Claudette Colbert) in *Drums along the Mohawk,* Clementine (Cathy Downs) in *My Darling Clementine,* Mrs. Yorke (Maureen O'Hara) in *Rio Grande.* The lone male is Guthrie McCabe in *Two Rode Together.* Lana's transformation is the most fully elaborated and therefore the most emblematic of the three. A prim and proper woman from the Eastern establishment, she leaves her comfortable home and heads into the wilderness with

her new husband, Gil. But on her first night in her husband's log cabin, she is startled at the sight of Blue Black (Chief Big Tree), a friendly Native American. She breaks down and begs to go back. "I'm going home," she cries. "I'm no frontier woman!" But she stays by her husband's side, perseveres, has a baby, and slowly adjusts to life on the frontier. The scene in which she tells Gil that they're expecting a second child marks her conversion to the Margin. "I feel," she says, "as if I'd just begun to live all over again." And for Ford, by converting to the Margin, she has.

2. *The Assimilation-to-the-Mainstream Plot.* In this story, a character succumbs to the lures of the Mainstream (Lincoln in *Young Mr. Lincoln,* Hallie in *The Man Who Shot Liberty Valance*) or fails to straddle the line between Margin and Mainstream successfully (Captain York in *Fort Apache*). In these films, Ford reveals his tragic view of assimilation. Though probably unavoidable for Euroethnics, and though it may mean material success and maybe even improving the Mainstream, assimilation always exacts a heavy price from Ford's characters. As I have discussed, it is made most disturbingly explicit at the conclusion of *Fort Apache,* when Captain York emulates Lieutenant Colonel Thursday. But the price of assimilation casts a pall over the ending of *Young Mr. Lincoln* as well.

In it, Lincoln's Margin/Mainstream cultural dilemma is cast as the tension between ambition and modesty, and it is made explicit in his speech at Ann's grave. "I don't know," he says. "I'd feel such a fool, settin' myself up as a-knowin' so much." Still, by the end of *Young Mr. Lincoln* he's well on the road toward Mainstream success, which Ford sees as inextricably tied to assimilation and his tragic fate. The film's bittersweet ending arises out of the tension between the conflicting resolutions of its two narratives. The dramatic narrative concludes neatly with a triumphant celebration of American values: success is achieved by the talented lawyer from the Margin, the real murderer is caught, and the American system of justice prevails.

But the cultural subplot is busy responding to the questions posed by Lincoln's dead mother in Rosemary Benet's poem quoted in the film's prologue ("What's happened to Abe? / What's he done? / . . . Did he grow tall? / Did he have fun? / Did he learn to read? / Did he get to town? / Do you know his name? / Did he get on?"). Ford's film replies that he "got to town" and did indeed "get on"—he entered the Mainstream and achieved success there. In the process, however, he forsook the Margin ideal, represented by Ann Rutledge (and perhaps by Carrie Sue), and replaced it with the snooty representative of the Mainstream, Mary Todd. Yes, Lincoln succeeds in the Mainstream, positively affecting American history in the process, but he pays dearly for assimilating. For Ford, the life of Lincoln spells out the exacting terms of the American Dream's cultural bargain: Mainstream success requires assimilation; assimilation means cultural, and sometimes actual, death.[31]

3. *The Cultural Balancing Act.* Two soldiers, Captain Nathan Brittles (John Wayne) in *She Wore a Yellow Ribbon* and Colonel John Marlowe (John Wayne) in *The Horse Soldiers,* are caught between allegiances to their ethnic values and to the military institution. In focusing on these soldiers' plights, Ford highlights the messy cultural politics of American imperialism, in which immigrant ethnics—in a test of their loyalty—are required to fight and kill first each other (in the Civil War), then, on the Western front, the Natives. From this perspective, the disconcerting story of Colonel Marlowe in *The Horse Soldiers* (who helps destroy the South in order to preserve the Union) becomes a sobering correction to the fantasy heroics of Captain Nathan Brittles, who so deftly, heroically, but improbably manages to serve two cultural masters at once in *She Wore a Yellow Ribbon.*

4. *The Contamination-of-the-Margin Plot.* This story focuses on the Margin society to chart the results of its "infection" by the virus of Mainstream gentility. In order to escape the encroaching hypocritical Victorian value system, the protagonists of *Stagecoach, Wagon Master,* and *Two Rode Together* are forced to retreat to a culturally healthier frontier. There are several implications of this, none of them favorable for Margin-ethnics. The first is that the infection is irreversible. Mainstream values, once introduced to the frontier, mean the beginning of "civilization" and the end of tolerance, as we see in the treatment of Dallas, the Mormons, and Elena, and the reversion to the letter rather than the spirit of the law, as we see in the treatment of the Ringo Kid. The second is that Mainstream assimilation is practically inescapable. It can be delayed, but we know what Elena and Guthrie may not: mainstream assimilation will eventually come to California too. The only way to save oneself from, in Doc Boone's ironic phrase, "the blessings of civilization" is to do what Ringo and Dallas do, seek refuge "across the border," outside the United States.[32]

5. *The Cultural Redemption Plot.* Three protagonists, Robert Hightower (John Wayne) in *3 Godfathers,* Tom Doniphon in *The Man Who Shot Liberty Valance,* and Ethan Edwards in *The Searchers,* "sin" against the Margin by acting against Ford's cardinal values, justice and tolerance. These stories ask if they can be redeemed. Bob Hightower can, even though he robbed the Welcome town bank. Culturally and legally he is redeemed by rescuing a baby from a dying woman, saving the child at the price of his freedom, refusing to relinquish custody of the child, and serving jail time for his transgression. Tom Doniphon's crime, murder, is more grievous, and on top of that, he never seeks redemption. His punishment is to be excluded from the Margin, like Ethan. If Tom's ostracism is less poignant than Ethan's, it is probably because it happens off-screen.
Ethan's cultural "sins" are the worst of all: his adherence to vigilante violence and vengeance, culminating in his scalping of Scar, and his racial intoler-

ance. Having rejected the Mainstream and loathing the Native, when he is expelled by the Margin at the end of *The Searchers* Ethan becomes Ford's most tragic character. Without a cultural home, he is like the dead Indian warrior whose eyes he shoots out—doomed to "wander forever between the winds." In the character of Ethan, Ford crystallizes the triumph and tragedy of American history. Ford correctly sees—and shows—that settling the West required courage as well as savagery. In insisting that westward expansion involved both bravery and barbarity, the cultural conclusion of *The Searchers* is among the most emotionally unsettling and ideologically clear-sighted moments in American cinema.

I have endeavored to show that, as an Irish American, John Ford was an ethnic filmmaker. His films centered on the ethnics he knew best, the Irish and other first- and second-generation European Americans who, a century ago when Ford was growing up, were among the most socially stigmatized and marginalized groups in America. Because he depicted the fluidity and hybridity of cultures, his films were impressive, sometimes progressive—and sometimes even groundbreaking—examples of multiculturalism.

The progressiveness of Ford's cinema came from consistently taking the side of the oppressed against the Mainstream. The problem in Ford's Westerns from a multiculturalist's standpoint is that for him, the oppressed at the Margin were principally Euro-ethnics. Ford's overarching project was to elevate Irish and European ethnics above WASP elites, not to put people of color down. Unfortunately, in trying to accomplish the former he often ended up doing the latter. Since his first allegiance was to Euro-ethnics, Ford's multiculturalism never completely overcame his white ethnocentrism. At its worst, this resulted in his insensitive treatment of people of color, the oft-mentioned stereotyping and paternalism.

But Ford's multiculturalism was driven too by an obsession with justice and tolerance, which, at its best, offset his ethnocentrism. In his Westerns, this resulted in such counter-hegemonic elements as his persistent critique of the Mainstream and his ubiquitous cultural subplot. Moreover, as his career progressed, the cultural focus of Ford's films widened beyond class and ethnic discrimination to include racial prejudice. Paradoxically, though, his most direct attacks on prejudice, in *Sergeant Rutledge* and *Cheyenne Autumn*, were the least satisfying culturally and aesthetically. His multiculturalism and his ideological critique of dominant ideology were most powerful in his other Westerns, where he could play with and subvert familiar genre formulas. Because of his ethnic background, his cultural formation, and his adherence to justice and tolerance, Ford's Westerns were never "just" Westerns. Beneath the grandeur of their sweeping dramatic narratives, Ford's cultural subplots were busy asking the most fundamental American question: Could America ever achieve its inclusive ideal—malice toward none, justice and liberty for all?

Racial intolerance dooms Ethan Edwards to "wander forever between the winds" in *The Searchers* (1956). Ken Curtis, Harry Carey Jr., Ward Bond, Bill Steele, Jeffrey Hunter, and John Wayne.
Courtesy of The Lilly Library, Indiana University, Bloomington, Indiana.

NOTES

I was supported during the writing of this article by a Faculty Research Fellowship generously awarded by the University of Texas at Austin.

I would like to thank George Lellis, Gaylyn Studlar, and Matthew Bernstein for the illuminating comments they made on earlier drafts of this article.

1. Robin Wood, "'*Shall* We Gather at the River?': The Late Films of John Ford," *Film Comment* 7, no. 3 (Fall 1971), 12.

2. Michael Dempsey, "Ford: A Reassessment," *Film Quarterly* 28, no. 4 (Summer 1975), 5–9. Ford's stereotyping, Dempsey felt, was a major flaw in his oeuvre that could be neither ignored nor explained away. Though Ford "wants to 'do right,'" wrote Dempsey, "he cannot escape his own innate condescension" toward Native Americans, Asians, and African Americans, who are trivialized and stereotyped in film after film (7).

3. See also Brian Henderson's "*The Searchers:* An American Dilemma," *Film Quarterly* 34, no. 2 (Winter 1980–1981): 9–23, rpt. in *Movies and Methods: An Anthology*, vol. 2, ed. Bill Nichols (Berkeley: University of California Press, 1985), 429–449; Angela Aleiss, "A Race Divided: The Indian Westerns of John Ford," *American Indian Culture and Research Journal* 18, no. 3 (Summer 1994): 167–186; Jim Weigert, "John Ford and the Indians," *Media Educators Association Journal* (1979): 10–13; Kirk Ellis, "On the Warpath: John Ford and the Indians," *Journal of Popular Film and Television* 8, no. 2 (Spring 1980): 34–41.

See Lee Lourdeaux's *Italian and Irish Filmmakers in America: Ford, Capra, Coppola, and Scorsese* (Philadelphia: Temple University Press, 1990) for a treatment of the Irishness of Ford's cinema. See also Joseph McBride's "Half Genius, Half Irish," in *John Ford*, ed. Joseph McBride and Michael Wilmington (London: Seeker & Warburg, 1974) for a nice analysis of the cultural duality in Ford. On Ford's depiction of Irish male drinking, see Stephanie Demetrakopoulos, "John Ford's Irish Drinking Ethos and Its Influence on Stereotypes of American Male Drunks," *Midwest Quarterly* 32, no. 2 (Winter 1991): 224–234. On the religious aspect of Ford's films, see Paul Giles, "The Cinema of Catholicism: John Ford and Robert Altman," in *Unspeakable Images: Ethnicity and the American Cinema*, ed. Lester D. Friedman (Urbana: University of Illinois Press, 1991), 140–166.

Finally, Tag Gallagher's thorough study, *John Ford: The Man and His Films* (Berkeley: University of California Press, 1986), deals with Ford's portrayals of Native Americans and defends Ford's films against charges of racism and intolerance.

4. Ella Shohat, "Ethnicities-in-Relation: Toward a Multicultural Reading of American Cinema," in Friedman, ed., *Unspeakable Images*, 216.

5. In the main, I will employ a critical method pioneered by Ella Shohat, Robert Stam, Hamid Naficy, Teshome H. Gabriel, and other multicultural film critics. See Shohat's "Ethnicities-in-Relation" and her "Gender and Culture of Empire: Toward a Feminist Ethnography of the Cinema," in *Otherness and the Media: The Ethnography of the Imagined and the Imaged*, ed. Hamid Naficy and Teshome H. Gabriel (Langhorne, Penn.: Harwood Academic Publishers, 1993), 45–84; and Ella Shohat and Robert Stam, *Unthinking Eurocentrism: Multiculturalism and the Media* (New York: Routledge, 1994).

For more examples of this type of criticism, see, for example, the other articles in the anthologies mentioned above, as well in Chon A. Noriega, ed., *Chicanos and Film: Representation and Resistance* (Minneapolis: University of Minnesota Press, 1992); Chon A. Noriega and Ana M. López, eds., *The Ethnic Eye: Latino Media Arts* (Minneapolis: University of Minnesota Press, 1996); bell hooks, *Black Looks: Race and Representation* (Boston: South End Press, 1992) and *Reel to Real: Race, Sex and Class at the Movies* (New York: Routledge, 1996); and Mark Winokur, *American Laughter: Immigrants, Ethnicity, and 1930s Hollywood Film Comedy* (New York: St. Martin's Press, 1996).

6. Andrew M. Greeley, *That Most Distressful Nation: The Taming of the American Irish* (Chicago: Quadrangle Books, 1972), 120.

7. See Charles Maland's chapter in this volume.

8. Or, in Neal Gabler's view, Hollywood's America was the Jewish moguls' *conception* of the American mainstream's utopian view of itself. It was driven, according to Gabler, by a desire to assimilate "so ruthless and complete that they cut their lives to the pattern of American respectability as they interpreted it." See Gabler, *An Empire of Their Own: How the Jews Invented Hollywood* (New York: Anchor Books, 1988), 4.

9. John Ford was not the only Hollywood filmmaker close to his immigrant roots. Many first- and second-generation Americans rose to top creative positions during the studio era. Frank Capra (born in Sicily) and Elia Kazan (born in Turkey of Greek parents) both came to the United States as children. Many other directors, among them F. W. Murnau, Ernst Lubitsch, Fritz Lang, Billy Wilder, Fred Zinnemann, Erich Von Stroheim, Charles Vidor, Rex Ingram, Alfred Hitchcock, and Charlie Chaplin, emigrated

here from Europe. Most of the heads of the major studios—Carl Laemmle, Adolph Zukor, William Fox, Louis B. Mayer, Harry Warner—arrived in the United States in their youth. (Warner's three younger brothers, Albert, Sam, and Jack, were born in the United States after their parents emigrated from Poland. See Gabler, *Empire*, 120–127.)

But much of the cinema these filmmakers produced was "naturalized," in both the ideological (dominant ideas made invisible as common sense) and culturally transformative (an alien made into a citizen) meanings of the term. Of this group, Chaplin's cinema is probably the most culturally ambiguous (his Tramp was upwardly mobile, though Chaplin's films criticized a dehumanizing system) and thus the most like Ford's. And though it is true that some of these directors contested the status quo (Lang, Hitchcock, and Wilder, especially), their films tended to elide ethnicity from their critique. As a result, many of the characters in their films seemingly possessed no ethnicity at all. Thus, for Capra it was Mr. Smith who went to Washington; for Wilder, the ethnically nondescript Joe Gillis who made the fateful turn into the driveway on Sunset Boulevard; and for Lang, the culturally neutral Eddie Taylor who ran for his life in *You Only Live Once* (1937). In contrast, Ford's characters were, as Tag Gallagher says, "always distinctly characterized as representative of a specific culture. There is no confusing a Boston Wasp with an Irish-American or Swede" (Gallagher, *John Ford*, 478).

10. Gregory H. Nobles, *American Frontiers: Cultural Encounters and Continental Conquest* (New York: Hill & Wang, 1997), xii.

11. A distinctive element of Ford's Westerns is that he takes pains to distinguish between the segregated white ethnics and the assimilated mainstream, and shows the built-in antagonism between the two groups. When depicted in most other Westerns, this animosity plays out as a class battle that pits the sod-busters against the large ranchers. In Ford, as I have said, immigrant ethnicity is almost always foregrounded.

12. Of course, some of Hollywood's classical-era cinema was similarly suspicious, and sometimes explicitly critical, of the mainstream's dominant ideology—the cinema of Orson Welles (*Citizen Kane* [1941], *The Magnificent Ambersons* [1942]) and Fritz Lang (*Fury* [1936], *You Only Live Once* [1937]) provides powerful examples. But Welles's and Lang's characters were generally class rather than ethnic Others. Ford's outsiders were defined by more than one marginalizing marker—class *and* ethnicity at a minimum, and sometimes race or gender as well. See also Peter Lehman's article, "How the West Wasn't Won," in this volume.

13. McBride, "Half Genius," 21.

14. Quoted in Gallagher, *John Ford*, 254.

15. The character's name is Ford's homage to Mexican director Emilio Fernández and Mexican cinematographer Gabriel Figueroa, both of whom assisted him in the making of *The Fugitive* (1947). Fernández was his assistant producer, Figueroa his cinematographer.

16. Demetrakopoulos, "John Ford's Irish Drinking Ethos." See also Lane Roth, "Ritual Brawls in John Ford's Films," *Film Criticism* 7, no. 3 (1983): 38–46.

17. As Dr. Kersaint (Thomas Mitchell) asks the sullen governor (Raymond Massey) in *The Hurricane* (1937), "Is there any law against dancing and singing when your heart is happy?"

18. See Carl Witke, "Militia, Fireman, and Police," chapter 6 in *The Irish in America* (Baton Rouge: Louisiana State University Press, 1956).

19. Witke, "Militia, Fireman, and Police," 136; see also the documentary *The Irish in America* (1997), produced by Rhys Thomas for A&E Productions. Myles Keogh,

mentioned in *She Wore a Yellow Ribbon* as a friend of Nathan Brittles, serves as a historical example of the Irish immigrant who signs up to be a U.S. soldier. As in the film, the real Myles Keogh died with Custer at the Little Bighorn.

20. In Ford's *The Hurricane* (1937), the importance of a uniform is made explicit when Terangi (Jon Hall) remarks to his wife (Dorothy Lamour), "What a difference a cap makes! In Tahiti . . . I'm just the same as a white man." In this regard, the point of *The Hurricane* is to illustrate how violently the colonizers respond to the perceived threat of a native presuming to act as an equal.

21. In Peter Bogdanovich's *John Ford* (Berkeley: University of California Press, 1968), 86, there is the following exchange:

In Fort Apache, *do you feel the men were right in obeying Fonda [Lieutenant Colonel Thursday] even though it was obvious he is wrong and they were killed because of his error?*

Yes—he was the Colonel, and what he says—goes; whether they agree with it or not—it still pertains. In Vietnam today, probably a lot of guys don't agree with their leader, but they still go ahead and do the job.

22. McBride, "Half Genius," 109. Tag Gallagher echoes the sentiment; see *John Ford*, 253–254.

23. Ford sought military service twice. As a young man, he applied to the Naval Academy but was rejected. Later, when the United States entered World War I, he volunteered for naval duty. This time, bad eyesight caused his rejection.

24. A point that is superbly demonstrated in *The Long Gray Line* (1955), which celebrates the military even as it criticizes it for shutting out and ignoring Marty Maher (Tyrone Power), who is clearly shown by the film to be not only a good soldier but a better man than many who attended West Point.

25. "My sympathy was always with the Indians," said John Ford. "Do you consider the invasion of the Black and Tan into Ireland a blot on English history? It's the same thing, all countries do the same thing. There's the British doing it, Hitler doing it, there's Stalin. Genocide seems to be a commonplace in our lives" (Gallagher, *John Ford*, 254).

26. As Jane Tompkins puts it, "An Indian in a Western who is supposed to be a real person has to be played by a white man" (*West of Everything: The Inner Life of Westerns* [New York: Oxford University Press, 1992], 9). Michael Wood noted a similar pattern in the portrayal of Blacks by whites in the movies. "There is obviously some murky principle at work that says that we can recognize dignity in blacks only when white folks dress up and lend a bit of dignity to them" (Michael Wood, *America in the Movies* [New York: Basic Books, 1975], 133–134).

In his films, Ford further revised the ethnic casting rule so that when an Indian character is singled out, the peaceable and humane ones tend to be portrayed by Native Americans (Chief Big Tree in *Drums along the Mohawk* and *She Wore a Yellow Ribbon*, Inclán in *Fort Apache*, Jim Thorpe in *Wagon Master*), the savage and violent ones by whites (Henry Brandon in *The Searchers* and *Two Rode Together*). Woody Strode's playing a Native American in *Two Rode Together* and a Mongolian warrior in *Seven Women* (1965) is an instance of Ford's adhering to Hollywood's minorities-can-play-any-ethnicity rule (and doing something he did throughout his career—giving an old friend some work).

27. Among many other roles, Miguel Inclán played, for example, the villain in the film that made Dolores Del Río a star upon her return to Mexican cinema from Hollywood, *María Candelaria* (1943), then played the heroic cop-on-the-beat in the urban

melodrama *Salón México* (1948). (Both films were directed by Emilio Fernández.) Inclán was also featured in the role of the blind man in Luis Buñuel's *Los Olvidados* (1950).

28. Armendáriz, who began working in Mexican films in 1935, was one of the best-known and most popular Mexican leading men. He gained fame by teaming with Dolores Del Río in several films directed by Emilio Fernández. In 1945 he won the Mexican film industry's Best Actor Award (for his performance in *La Perla*, Fernández's adaptation of John Steinbeck's *The Pearl*), and won another in 1953.

29. What Tompkins calls "That yipping sound on the sound tracks that accompanies Indian attacks" (*West of Everything*, 9).

30. I am reading the ending of *The Searchers* as Ethan's exclusion because, while it is true that he does stop short of entering the Jorgensen's house, it is also true that he is not invited in. Furthermore, the door closes on him as he walks away. This interpretation is different from those of scholars who, like Brian Henderson, see the ending as Ethan's "self-exclusion" (Henderson, *"The Searchers,"* 447). Maybe it is a mutual isolation.

31. One can see how Ford would be attracted to the cultural assimilation plot of Sinclair Lewis's novel *Arrowsmith*, which he filmed in 1931. The in-or-out cultural plot of *Arrowsmith* is similar to *Young Mr. Lincoln*'s, but it concludes with Dr. Arrowsmith (Ronald Colman) doing exactly the opposite of Lincoln. Arrowsmith must decide between fame, wealth, and recognition as a scientist at an elite research institute, or service as a physician to the needy (immigrant Italians in the urban East, Swedes at the Margin, and the Black Natives in the West Indies). Like Lincoln, he also loses a woman (his wife, played by Helen Hayes) who serves as the Margin's conscience. But Arrowsmith is able in the end to do what Lincoln could not: reject the Mainstream's definition of success and the comely temptress (Myrna Loy) who comes with it. *Arrowsmith* allows Ford to rewrite Lincoln's story, only with a more palatable cultural resolution. In this revised version, a Marginal protagonist achieves (actually, redefines) Mainstream success without assimilating and without compromising his ethnic values.

32. There are other Ford characters who withdraw from America. Sean Thornton (John Wayne), in *The Quiet Man* (1952), leaves the United States in search of his ethnic roots. So do Donovan (again Wayne) and company in *Donovan's Reef* (1963), a wonderfully multicultural (and countercultural) film that discloses Ford's continuing loss of faith in the American Mainstream, to the point that a far-flung retreat seems the only viable ethnic alternative.

4

LINEAR PATTERNS AND ETHNIC ENCOUNTERS IN THE FORD WESTERN

Joan Dagle

"My name is John Ford. I am a director of Westerns."

"Sorta like round about: man says he's going one place, means to go t'other."

—Ethan Edwards

John Ford's Westerns, like all films in the genre, are informed by a paradigmatic American narrative: the story of the settlers' movement from East to West.[1] The irreducibly linear trajectory of the historical movement of "civilization" across the continent constitutes the meta-narrative of the Western genre, with each film's own story either a fragment or a microcosmic version of that linear meta-narrative. As examples of classical Hollywood narrative, traditional Westerns also reflect principles of linearity in the way their narration constructs and presents the stories.[2] Ford's Westerns embody these principles and practices of linearity, but they also challenge them, doing so increasingly in the postwar period. To compare, for example, the "classical" *Stagecoach* (1939) with the "revisionist" *The Searchers* (1956)[3] reveals the extent to which the relentless linearity of the former, with its journey from the Easternized Tonto through the desert landscape to the frontier town of Lordsburg, has given way in the latter to an elliptical pattern and penchant for wandering, in both the diegesis, which is filled with characters moving back and forth, circling over the same ground for years, and in the narration, which "loosens" the linear plot structure to incorporate both "digressions" and temporal disjunctions.

In the Ford Western, this movement away from linearity in the postwar period is coincident with an increasingly complex investigation of the racial implications of the Western's meta-narrative.[4] For example, in *Stagecoach*, the Indians are remote, alien figures, projections of white fears of the "savage land" they seek to settle; in *The Searchers*, the direct confrontation between Ethan and Scar, racial and cultural antagonists, turns the Western narrative inside out to reveal its racism. The conjunction of increasing non-linearity and complex investigations of race is an intriguing aspect of Ford's postwar Westerns.[5] Although some feminist theory has argued that linear narrative is inherently patriarchal (and white and masculinist) and therefore any textual challenge to dominant racial or gender codes necessarily involves ruptures in linearity, that position seems needlessly reductionist and any causal connection between these two impulses can only be speculative.[6] However, in the 1940s, Hollywood film narrative does become more complex (influenced, according to many critics, by *Citizen Kane* and most evident in the case of film noir), and we can surmise that in the postwar period, ideological disturbances regarding notions of masculinity, nationhood, and race affect Ford, the genre, and the larger culture and "erupt" in the films in interesting ways. Impossible issues of causality aside, the more pronounced emphasis on non-linear patterns and the more complex investigation of racial and ethnic encounters work together in Ford's postwar films, often in mutually constitutive ways, and their conjunction reshapes the Ford Western.

"My name is John Ford. I am a director of Westerns."[7] So Ford introduced himself when, at a meeting of the Screen Directors Guild in 1950, he spoke against Cecil B. DeMille's attempt to oust Joseph Mankiewicz as guild president because of Mankiewicz's alleged Communist sympathies. It is intriguing that in a moment of ideological crisis within the industry and American society in general, Ford, whose career had oscillated (in his own eyes as well as in the view of the press) between "prestige" films and Westerns, would choose to identify himself for the record—and thus claim the right to speak—by positioning himself in relation to his work in the Western genre. It is as if his work in the Western gives him the authority not only to speak but to resolve the crisis. (His counterproposal that the guild support Mankiewicz was accepted.) This anecdote seems to confirm an intuitive sense of the centrality of the Western within American popular culture and within the American film industry, an assessment often echoed in film criticism. Ford began directing Westerns in 1917[8] and he is a central figure in the development both of the genre and of the classical Hollywood narrative mode. What the episode illustrates is the ease with which "John Ford," "the Western," and "classical Hollywood cinema" can collapse into almost interchangeable terms. André Bazin, for example, claims that "The Western is the only genre whose origins are almost identical with those of cinema itself" and he frequently uses Ford's *Stagecoach* as an example of "the ripeness of classical art"—and even as "the ideal example of the maturity of a style brought to classical perfection."[9]

The Western film evolved within the development of classical Hollywood cinema, the mode of filmmaking dominating the American industry. The conventions governing the narrative structure of classical Hollywood cinema emphasize strong linear patterns.[10] As a product of classical Hollywood cinema, the Western incorporates these general features of linearity while its own specific story matter reflects the genre's meta-narrative, which retells the American "linear" myth of westward expansion. The Western thus encodes a powerful convergence of linear patterns, making it, arguably, the genre most tied to linearity.

Ford's prewar *Stagecoach* can be seen as a virtual textbook illustration of the linear construction of the classical Hollywood Western. On the level of story, *Stagecoach*'s narrative is about a group of characters who embark on a journey across difficult and dangerous terrain in order to get from one point to another. The story is thus framed by the logic of a linear journey: the story begins when the group assembles and starts out and it ends (almost) when the group reaches its destination. Most of the characters (an escaped convict, a prostitute, a cavalry officer's wife, a gambler, a whiskey salesman, a drunken doctor, a dishonest banker, a sheriff, and the driver) live on the frontier, the edges of the perpetually shifting boundary of white civilization, and their journey is from a (relatively) "Easternized" town (which considers the prostitute, the doctor, and the gambler undesirable) to a rougher, more "primitive" Western town. The journey from one to the other involves crossing a "wilderness" landscape where Apache Indians under Geronimo are attacking ranchers. The specific journey from Tonto to Lordsburg, along with its implicit metonymic recapitulation of the Western meta-narrative, provides the linear structure of the story.

On the level of narration, *Stagecoach* presents the story in linear, chronological order with clearly defined sequences that segment the journey into alternating parts: sequences depicting the stagecoach's movement and sequences depicting the stops along the way. Each segment is causally motivated and each works to "hook" into the next one, producing a linear plot design. Each "step" of the journey and each segment of the narration bring the stagecoach closer not only to Lordsburg but also to the final threat, the attack by the Apache. The attack functions as the anticipated-and-deferred narrative climax, and its outcome will determine whether or not the journey is successfully completed. In both story and narration, then, *Stagecoach* relies on strong, relentless linear paradigms.

Stagecoach's linearity traces the trajectory of the white passengers, who are on a collision course with the Apache. The landscape and the Indians who inhabit it are set in clear opposition to the coach and its inhabitants, as the narrative relies on an underlying inside/outside binary symbolic structure.[11] Outside the stagecoach are the hostile forces that would destroy the fragile community: the attacking Apache warriors and, metonymically, the landscape, the West, the place without the values of white civilization. "Whiteness," then, is constructed in opposition to what lies "outside." Within this inside/outside logic, the Apache function as purely alien figures, as the racial Other to the white community and against which the white community constructs its identity. The Apache appear to materialize out of the landscape in the famous shot that begins as an elevated, extreme long shot of the stagecoach moving across the terrain and then pans quickly left to reveal the Apache gathered on a cliff top. There are three closer shots of the silent warriors and then another shot of the stagecoach that, again, pans to the Apache as they descend from the cliff to begin the attack. Through these five shots and the myriad long shots during the attack, the film constructs the Apache only as impenetrable surface, as unknowable. Dallas's aside, "There's worse things than Apaches," said in response to the women of the Law and Order League, who with their smug faces and contemptuous stares are running her out of town, is not corroborated by any textual evidence.

With each stage of the journey, the passengers become more vulnerable to Apache violation of the barrier between inside and outside. During the first stage, from Tonto to Dry Fork, the coach is accompanied by a cavalry troop. Along the way, Ringo boards the coach and tells Curley that he has seen a ranch burning, evidence that Geronimo's group is nearby. At the first stop, Dry Fork station, run by the Picketts, a white couple, the passengers learn that the cavalry troop must change course; the passengers vote to continue on, unescorted. During the second stage, the troop and coach separate on the trail and the coach continues to Apache Wells, unprotected by anything "outside." With the second stop at Apache Wells, the passengers have moved beyond the "borders" of white space and white civilization. This station is operated by a Mexican, Chris, and his Apache wife, Yakeema, and the four hands are Mexican. When the four *vaqueros* run off, followed shortly after by Yakeema, there is speculation that one or all may be going to alert Geronimo, and Apache signals are seen in the nearby hills.

From this "transitional" space where the white community encounters, briefly, traces of Apache culture mediated through the Mexican characters, the coach sets out on the third stage, the tense run to Lee's Ferry. All that remains of this third station are the signs of the Apache's intrusion into and destruction of white space: smoldering ruins and the half-naked body of a white woman. Hatfield, the Southern gambler, covers her body with his cloak, registering the sexual violation. The racially charged fear of sexual attack by the Apache (invasion "into" the white female body) is now incorporated into the threat facing the passengers (and will motivate Hatfield's intention to shoot Lucy with his last bullet when it looks as if the Apache will overtake the stage). They hasten to cross the river and begin the fourth stage of their journey, the final leg to the safety of Lordsburg. Almost immediately, an arrow penetrates the compartment and the attack begins, an extremely violent clash between two radically and racially opposed forces, one made inevitable by the progressive logic of the encounters.

Stagecoach reveals the dynamics by which the white community constructs its identity (as a human and humane community) through racial opposition. The projection "outward" of fears of violence, including sexual violence, allows the passengers to control their own divisions and hostilities inside both

"Signs of the Apache's intrusion into and destruction of white space": Hatfield covers the "half-naked" body of a violated woman with his coat in *Stagecoach*. Frame enlargement.

the stagecoach and the way stations. During each segment up to the stop at Lee's Ferry, tensions within the group erupt and are resolved or suppressed. *Stagecoach* uses two types of "inside" spaces: the coach compartment and the interior shelters of Dry Fork and Apache Wells. Ford establishes the space of the coach compartment—and the places of the passengers within it—through cutting, specifically through eyeline matches. Almost all shots taken from inside the compartment are one-shots or two-shots, with a few three-shots. Many of the tensions (for example, between Doc Boone and Hatfield, or Dallas and Lucy Mallory) and even alliances (for example, between Dallas and Ringo) are established through cutting; only rarely, as in the case of Doc Boone and the whiskey salesman Peacock, who sit next to each other and are repeatedly framed in two-shots, is a relationship articulated otherwise. A sense of separateness and conflict is thus constantly constructed inside a very intimate and communal space, capturing the ambivalent nature of this "community."

The interiors of the way stations are also ambivalent spaces: framing emphasizes the low ceilings and the doorways of the mise en scène, suggesting the idea of enclosure and, metaphorically, the safety that these spaces represent. Yet the tensions of the group erupt here also, beginning with the oft-remarked table scene at Dry Fork where Lucy and Hatfield pointedly snub Dallas.[12] But these interiors are also spaces in which the group forges its sense of unity, most notably in the votes they take to determine whether or not they will go on and in the emotional bonds (excluding only Gatewood, the banker) forged by the birth of "little Coyote," Lucy's baby. When they reach Lee's Ferry—where the interior space has been destroyed by the Apache raid—they have neither the opportunity nor the need for further unity-building. The imminent threat of the Apache provides the final impetus they need: they are united as the pursued, fleeing the hostility of the savage attack. And they now "deserve" their last-minute rescue by the miraculously reappearing cavalry troop.

There is, also, a third space associated with the white community: the "outside" of the stagecoach, where Buck and Curley (and later Ringo) sit, framed in two-shots. Although it is a "transitional" space between outside and inside, it "belongs" clearly to the inside half of the opposition. Buck and Curley are the ostensible authority figures, responsible for the others, and they function as part of the group during the stops and the attack. Their own interaction—tension based on Buck's initial misunderstanding of Curley's motive for taking Ringo into custody, cleared up along the way—mirrors the dynamics of the passengers inside the coach.

Although they share a common goal, the characters' histories provide them with widely differing motives for wanting to reach Lordsburg and are also the source of their conflicts with each other. The disgraced ex-Confederate aristocrat-turned-frontier-gambler in uneasy alliance with "a great lady" trying to reach her cavalry officer husband, the prostitute run out of town, the drunken doctor evicted from his lodgings, the outlaw bent on revenge for the deaths of his family, the banker absconding with stolen funds, the whiskey salesman trying to get home, the driver completing a run, the sheriff trying to keep his friend's son from being killed—almost all find their stories resolved through the Apache attack and the arrival at Lordsburg. With the loss of Hatfield, who dies in the attack, and Gatewood, who is arrested in Lordsburg, the group appears to have succeeded in defining itself as a community, as signaled by Mrs. Mallory's and the wounded Peacock's reaching out to Dallas. The one storyline that continues past the completion of the journey is Ringo's. Ringo is the central character,

"Fleeing the hostility of the savage attack" unites the stagecoach's diverse passengers: the climactic Apache attack in *Stagecoach*. Frame enlargement.

but for the duration of the journey the trajectory of his storyline blends into the common goal. Once the journey is over, his classically constructed storyline, dually articulated in a "revenge plot" (his search for Luke Plummer) and a "romance plot" (his relationship with Dallas), resolves itself in the film's final section. It is the privileging of his storyline beyond the common "end" that confirms his function as *Stagecoach*'s central character, the Western hero.

At the Apache Wells station, Dallas asks Ringo to choose between revenge and love. He chooses love and, with her help, prepares to escape from Curley and go to his ranch in Mexico, but the Apache signals stop him from riding away. In effect, the (impending) confrontation with the Apache means that Ringo no longer has to choose: he cannot abandon the other passengers and so he will get to Lordsburg and Luke Plummer. Curiously, Dallas and Curley both now accept, as if it were inevitable, Ringo's pursuit of revenge. Dallas no longer tries to talk him out of confronting Luke, and Curley lets him go off with Dallas in Lordsburg, surely knowing he will seek out Luke. By some unexamined narrative logic, the violent clash between white hero and the alien Apache allows Ringo to reconcile the conflicting desires in his character and "connect" the two parts of his storyline. When Curley and Doc Boone "save" Ringo and Dallas from "the blessings of civilization" by sending the buckboard off into the desert (to Ringo's Mexican ranch instead of to jail), *Stagecoach* constructs Ringo as the classically "balanced" Western hero, poised between "garden and wilderness," "civilization and savagery."[13] The linear trajectory of *Stagecoach*'s narrative is now complete.

However, in spite of its overall linearity, *Stagecoach* contains some implicit, subtle, or (more tenuously) "potential" violations of linearity. Numerous critics, and Ford himself,[14] have commented on the violations of the 180° rule (the principle of continuity editing that keeps screen direction "coherent" and linear) during the attack sequence. In fact, *Stagecoach* violates screen direction repeatedly in virtually every sequence involving exterior shots of the moving coach. One particularly blatant example occurs when the stagecoach and the cavalry troop part company. Outside of Dry Fork, a long shot frames both the troop and the stagecoach at the split in the trail; the stagecoach is traveling diagonally across the screen from lower left toward upper right and the troop is moving from center toward upper left. The next shot is of the troop column moving diagonally from lower right toward upper left and it is followed by a shot of the stagecoach moving diagonally from lower center toward upper left. Both troop column and stagecoach appear to reverse direction in the sequence. Similarly, during the sequences depicting the stagecoach's journey between stops, Ford repeatedly cuts from a long shot of the stagecoach moving in one direction across the Monument Valley landscape to a shot of Buck and Curley facing the opposite way.

Ford's comment that in the attack sequence the violations of the 180° rule are irrelevant—"It didn't matter a damn in this case"[15]—is true enough in that the viewer is never confused about what is happening. However, the repeated and pronounced "confusion" of screen direction during the journey is not so insignificant. The apparently linear journey of the diegesis, from one point to another, is in fact constituted by "multi-directional" fragments that do not add up to a coherent space. (That viewers do not in fact experience the journey as "incoherent" is testimony to the power of the linear paradigms invoked by the film.) It is impossible to figure out the "geography" mapped by these shots.

Other features of this impossible geography have been pointed out by Edward Buscombe. In arguing that "Though a real place, Monument Valley functions in *Stagecoach* as imaginary geography," Buscombe points out three imaginary features of the film's construction of space: although the journey takes two days, the coach never leaves the thirty miles of Monument Valley; "Sometimes virtually the same shot is used at widely separate parts of the narrative"; and, although "one naturally supposes, given that the stagecoach is leaving an area of settlement and striking out across hostile Indian-occupied territory, that its progress is westward . . . this is not in fact the case," since the coach travels from Bisbee, Arizona, to Tonto, to Lordsburg, New Mexico, a southwest to northeast route.[16] (We also know that Lordsburg is a stop on Peacock's eastward trip from Tonto to Kansas City, Kansas.) There is, therefore, a pretext of linearity, but "in reality" the journey retraces its steps, moves chaotically around an enclosed space, and travels "away" from the Western frontier. Of course, nothing of the kind is acknowledged within the diegesis, but the potential for exploiting non-linear structures is clearly present in this text.

Similarly, *Stagecoach* contains the space where something other than hostile, violent confrontation between the white passengers and the Indians could occur: Apache Wells, where the disparate cultures of the West have merged. The Spanish-speaking Mexican figures are themselves signs of cultural intermingling, and the marriage of Chris and Yakeema signifies a further racial merger. In her brief appearance, Yakeema is heavily coded to suggest bicultural duality: she is an Apache woman who sings in Spanish, her costume has both Mexican and Indian elements (the blanket over her shoulder, her jewelry), and a Mexican actress plays an Indian character. Here, as in Ford's later Westerns, Spanish is the West's language of cultural mediation and exchange, and Yakeema, Chris, and Ringo (who calls out in Spanish to Chris when Dallas asks him for hot water) all speak it. On the one hand, the film accurately portrays the cultural pluralism and intermingling of the West, in Mexican-Indian relationships (Chris, Yakeema, and the *vaqueros* at Apache Wells) and Mexican-white relationships (Luke Plummer has a Mexican "retainer," Buck has a Mexican wife, and Mexican characters are among the "background" characters in both towns).

On the other hand, the film often adopts racist stereotypes and perspectives on non-white cultures and characters.[17] What is most significant is that although Ringo, the hero, speaks Spanish and is able to quickly "read" the distant Apache signals, neither he nor any of the other passengers speak (or share the frame) with Yakeema. Their only interaction with her occurs when she first appears in the interior space, and her presence serves to reinscribe the barrier between Indian and white as Peacock gasps, "She's savage!" In fact, what the Apache Wells episode illustrates is the failure of cultural mediation and of Chris and Yakeema as a couple. Once the stagecoach leaves this place, it encounters the effects of racial hatred—the carnage at Lee's Ferry and the Apache attack—and the film's underlying inside/outside dichotomy remains intact. At the film's conclusion, Ringo and Dallas, the white romantic couple, implicitly stand in opposition to Chris and Yakeema, even as they head for the Mexican border.

If *Stagecoach* adheres to linearity by "absorbing" or masking its non-linear elements and if it raises the possibility of cultural and racial mediation or exchange only to reject it in favor of the unquestioned ideology of "white conquest" of the West, Ford's postwar films tend to chart a different course. However, while it is tempting to create a Fordian "progression" from *Stagecoach* to the later films, such constructions are all too easily revealed as oversimplified impositions on a body of work that itself loops backward and forward with respect to structural patterns, style, and ideology. There are postwar films (e.g., *My Darling Clementine* [1946] and *Rio Grande* [1950]) in which racial hierarchies remain in place and "whiteness" is constructed to include the assumption of cultural superiority,[18] and there are postwar films (e.g., *Wagon Master* [1950]) to which Frank Nugent's comment about *Stagecoach* is applicable: "He [Ford] hews to the straight narrative line with the well-reasoned confidence of a man who has seen that narrative succeed before."[19] And yet, the white male protagonists of the postwar Ford Westerns do more often than not find themselves on a "detour" from the linear trajectory of the Western myth that places them in increasingly complex relationships with their racial "opposites."

The shift from prewar to postwar paradigms first occurs in *Fort Apache* (1948). As Peter Lehman notes, "*Fort Apache* marks the beginning of Ford's development of the Indians as a culture, rather than a mere physical threat to whites. White treatment of the Indians in *Fort Apache* is frequently unjust and, even at its best, threatens Indian cultural integrity."[20] What is most significant about *Fort Apache*'s "take" on the Western meta-narrative of white conquest is that the violent confrontation between the cavalry under Colonel Owen Thursday, a transplanted Easterner, and the Apache under Cochise that is the narrative's climax occurs only because a clearly articulated alternative—the first in a Ford Western—fails. Captain Kirby York works out an agreement with Cochise that would have the two nations cease the killing and live in peace. Thursday's refusal to honor York's promises and negotiate in good faith causes the climactic battle. And his racist refusal to acknowledge that Cochise is an excellent military strategist causes the battle (based on that of the Little Bighorn) to turn into a massacre in which he and many members of the regiment are killed.

Fort Apache can be read as a "transitional text" in the Ford Western, in which the linear paradigms of the Western narrative are temporarily displaced and the narrative presents a "detour" that takes the hero from racial confrontation to mediation. This complex film is about the regiment as a community, its internal divisions overcome in the face of the battle; the conflict between the Eastern Thursday and the Western York; and the historical process itself, which has "rewritten" the story of "Thursday's Last Charge" as a glorious and heroic event, a distortion that at the end of the film York, now Fort Apache's commanding officer, helps perpetuate.[21] It is also about the meetings between the two cultures: two violent encounters that bracket two attempts at mediation, the first when York journeys to meet with Cochise and the second when Thursday has lured Cochise to come to him. Through visual construction and use of dialogue, these places in the text construct a perspective not present in *Stagecoach*: one "inside" the world of the Other.

Fort Apache is the first film of the Seventh Cavalry trilogy, and its narrative, like those of the other two, *She Wore a Yellow Ribbon* (1949) and *Rio Grande* (1950), is centered on the regiment as both an "outpost" of the white push to settle the West and a type of frontier community. (Since white women function in Ford's Westerns as the "sign" and repository of domesticity and civilization, their presence in Western settings—whether town, ranch, or fort—signifies the possibility of that place becoming the site of community; the regiment inside Fort Apache functions symbolically as a community precisely because it is articulated as both a domestic and a military entity through the often foregrounded presence of the female characters and their stories.) The rituals of the regiment and the rigors of life in a frontier fort hold the group together until the simultaneous arrivals of Colonel Thursday, accompanied by his daughter Philadelphia, and young Lieutenant Michael O'Rourke, newly graduated from West Point and son of the fort's sergeant major, cause the group's sense of cohesiveness to fragment. Thursday criticizes the lax Western standards of conduct and dress at Fort Apache ("The uniform, gentlemen, is not a subject for individual, whimsical expression"), and he strenuously objects to the romantic relationship developing between Philadelphia and Michael O'Rourke as "not suitable or proper" because of the army's adherence to the "class barrier." Indeed, Thursday objects to being this far west at all, calling Fort Apache "godforsaken" and "the end of the rainbow," and he is bitter at the army's exiling him to a place in which he cannot advance his career. He makes his initial appearance at the fort as a literally and figuratively disruptive force, when his unexpected arrival stops a regimental dance. Thursday's snobbery and rigid adherence to army regulations threaten to pull the community apart. With his contempt for the Apache, he embodies an arrogant white imperialism, an attitude that leads to massacre.

The first appearance of the Apache in the film occurs just before the halfway point, and the narrative logic governing their representation and function echoes that of *Stagecoach*. Their appearance is set up by the discovery of the tortured corpses of the troopers sent out to repair cut telegraph lines. The Apache threat has been revealed in a progressive series of signs of their presence: news that they have been seen off the reservation, cut telegraph lines, dead soldiers. The teleological thrust of the narrative leads directly to the expectation of violent confrontation; and the expected scene does occur, engineered by Thursday.

Thursday sends out a detail, headed by Lieutenant O'Rourke, to recover the bodies, but he is using the detail as bait; he has a troop of soldiers trailing behind waiting for the Apache to attack. The attack sequence begins with a bullet whistling past the lieutenant's body, the first indication that the Apache are present. The wagon and its escort begin a furious retreat, racing across the desert. An extreme long shot of the soldiers incorporates a pan right to reveal Diablo's band of Mescalero Apache on a cliff top, echoing (with the direction of the pan reversed) the first shot of the Apache in *Stagecoach*.

The construction of the chase sequence violates screen direction repeatedly in its two dozen shots, but, as in *Stagecoach*, those "violations" are narratively unproblematic and, along with the truck-mounted moving camera that keeps pace with the racing horses, serve to make the sequence visually dynamic and exciting. The sequence concludes with a long shot of Thursday's troop riding into the frame to meet the distant, oncoming detail and engage the pursuing Indians, again echoing *Stagecoach*'s construction. However, this encounter between whites and Apache, which seems to be worked out in accordance with the narrative paradigms of *Stagecoach*, is only the first of several encounters in *Fort Apache* and is immediately followed by a sequence that begins to undo the trajectory of violent confrontation.

After a fade-out, the narrative resumes with the troop's arrival at the Indian agent's place. The narrative ellipsis signaled by the fade is more than a spatial and temporal gap; in effect, it marks a refusal to "complete" the linear trajectory of the narrative that began with the construction of the Apache as hostile savages, alien, unknowable, inhuman. From this point on, the narrative will work to provide an alternative trajectory, a "detour" from the binary logic of white/Indian as mutually exclusive terms with "white" as the superior.

The sequence at Meacham's is designed precisely to educate Thursday about the corrupt history of the government's treatment of the Apache. Although Thursday insists that York treat Meacham with "due respect" because he is a representative of the United States government, even he comes to condemn the man as "a blackguard, a liar, a hypocrite, and a stench in the nostrils of honest men" after he listens to Meacham's insincere pieties about his "wayward children" and discovers the illegal whiskey and rifles he sells them and the rigged scales for weighing government beef.

The crux of the sequence occurs, however, in York's speech about Cochise. Framed in a three-shot, with York on the left, Meacham slightly crouched in the middle, and Thursday on the right, York tells Thursday that the government signed a treaty with Cochise five years ago, and as a result his Chiracahua Apache and other Apache groups came to the reservation to live in peace. They did so for two years, until "the dirtiest, most corrupt political group in our history," the Indian Affairs bureaucrats, sent Meacham. "Then it began: whiskey but no beef; trinkets instead of blankets; the women degraded, the children sickly, and the men turned into drunken animals. So Cochise did the only thing a decent man could do. He left, took most of his people, and crossed the Rio Bravo into Mexico." And when Meacham appeals to Thursday with "He broke his treaty," York quickly replies, "Yes, rather than see his people wiped out." York here "speaks for" the Apache. His words reclaim Cochise as "a decent man," not an alien savage; they also suggest not only the indecency of Meacham and those setting government policy, but, implicitly, the regiment's (and his own) complicity in that indecency as an enforcer of that policy. The static nature of the shot forces the spectator to assume Thursday's position as attentive listener.

As the rest of the film reveals, however, York's words do not cause Thursday to reformulate his relation to the Apache. The next sequence, a staff meeting at Fort Apache, sets up York's journey to Mexico to meet with Cochise. When Thursday asks York if Cochise would listen to and believe him, and York replies, "Cochise knows me, sir. I've never lied to him," it seems that Thursday has been persuaded to work for a peaceful settlement that includes a guarantee of decent conditions on the reservation. The exchange also reveals that York's knowledge of Apache customs and of Cochise's history comes from direct contact. What the sequence disguises, however, is that securing peace and establishing a decent life for the Apache are not Thursday's reasons for sending York to bargain with Cochise. When Thursday murmurs "The man who brought Cochise back," he indicates that he sees this as an unexpected chance to win glory in the Eastern press; that consideration, and not concern for the Apache, will govern his actions.

The next section of *Fort Apache* consists of four segments: the first part of York and Sergeant Beaufort's journey to Mexico; Thursday's confrontation with the O'Rourkes over his daughter; the completion of York's journey and his arrival at Cochise's camp; and the noncommissioned officers' dance, which ends as York and Beaufort return from their trip. Each segment is about moving into another's space, crossing an inside/outside barrier, and the narration's deliberate alternation between and juxtaposition of the segments sets up contrasts.

York's journey, depicted in the first and third segments, is a journey "out," away from Fort Apache, away from the white community. The narration "interrupts" the journey with the second and fourth segments and places it "against" these two segments, which depict the "inside" space of Fort Apache where the regiment's internal divisions are played out. York travels, under a truce flag, into Cochise's world; Thursday barges into the O'Rourkes' quarters; and the officers attend the noncommissioned officers' dance. Overall, then, because it is framed by York's journey, this section of *Fort Apache* is constructed along the Western's inside/outside symbolic axis of opposition between white community and savage wilderness, while each sequence negotiates the inside/outside barrier governing its specific space. The significance of York's meeting with Cochise is thus located within an elaborate convergence of "meetings." York's crossing of the barrier, his entry into Cochise's world, seeks to reverse the logic of crossing the barrier in *Stagecoach*, where Apache entry into the white world can only be imaged as violent.

The sequence depicting York and Beaufort's journey is visually spectacular and narratively "excessive," filled with extraordinary cinematography, powerful editing, and dramatic music, but conveying very little "information." As in the case of the journey in *Stagecoach*, the geography is "imaginary" and screen direction is not consistent. The first half of the sequence (nine shots, prior to the dissolve to the shot of the O'Rourke quarters) emphasizes the landscape itself and the act of moving through its vast and "alien" spaces. The sequence emphasizes York's movement away from the constraints of Thursday's command and, along with his "solitary" life (that is, with no wife or children), positions him as a Western figure comfortably "at home" in the open wilderness. Significantly, one of the shots looks far down on an awesomely huge circular rock and then pans right to unexpectedly reveal York and Beaufort on a cliff top—recapitulating the earlier shot of the Apache. York's movement away from the white community both literally and symbolically distances him from an identity based on that community's idea of "whiteness." Screen direction in these nine shots establishes a strong left-to-right pattern that, as Buscombe said of the direction of *Stagecoach*'s journey, seems to violate the logic that would have a right-to-left screen direction indicate movement "further" into the wilderness (as if the screen were a map). Here, however, the "wrong" direction seems to serve a specific function. Precisely because York's search for Cochise constitutes an ideological "detour" from the trajectory of the white narrative of westward expansion and conquest, it is fitting that the narrative logic figures that search "against" the east-to-west implications of right-to-left screen direction.

After the first nine shots, the narration suspends the journey and presents the sequence in the O'Rourke quarters. In the confrontation between Thursday and Sergeant Major O'Rourke over the relationship between their children, this sequence foregrounds the internal divisions of class, (white) ethnicity, and military caste that threaten the regiment.

At the end of this encounter, the narration returns to York's journey and the arrival at Cochise's camp in Mexico. In the third shot of this sequence, York and Beaufort see the first Apache signal that tells them they have been spotted. Beginning with the ninth shot, Ford places the camera among the rocks of the cliffs above York and Beaufort. The tenth shot is an extreme long shot looking down from the rocks to their distant figures. The eleventh shot is of two Apache standing among the rocks, slightly above camera level; the camera then pans up and frames another Apache. The camera is now "inside" the Apache space and perspective, and in the next four shots, as York and Beaufort ride into Cochise's canyon, dismount, and walk up to Cochise, Ford continues to place the camera in a variety of positions clearly within the Apache perspective.

Not only are York and Beaufort figured as "outsiders" in these shots; perhaps even more significantly, the spectator is positioned within Apache space, "as" Apache. In effect, the formal textual strategies of camera placement and framing have prefigured the ideological work of the sequence: York's "undoing" of the white/Indian binary opposition.

"Inside the Apache space": *Fort Apache*'s narration shifts as Captain Kirby York (John Wayne) and Sergeant Beaufort (Pedro Armendáriz) arrive in Cochise's camp.
Still courtesy of The Lilly Library, Indiana University, Bloomington, Indiana.

The rest of the segment uses a shot/reverse shot pattern (seven shots) as York and Beaufort face Cochise and Geronimo, followed by two final shots that include all four characters. The dynamics of cultural mediation and exchange are expressed in four brief lines of Spanish dialogue[22] and in ritual gestures. Beaufort has come with York to act as translator because he and Cochise speak Spanish while York's Apache "has its limits." Beaufort greets Cochise ("Buenas tardes, illustres Jefe"); Cochise returns the greeting ("Buenas tardes"); Beaufort introduces York, who salutes; York extends his arms; Cochise reaches one arm out to touch York's hands; York greets Cochise ("Buenas tardes, Jefe"); Cochise returns the greeting ("Buenas tardes"); the two drop their arms; York smiles, and the shot fades out. In the next-to-last shot (shot twenty-three), Beaufort and York are on the left side of the frame and Cochise and Geronimo are on the right as York and Cochise touch hands. In the next and final shot, the camera is directly behind Cochise and Geronimo, who are placed on opposite sides of the frame, with York and Beaufort framed between them, facing the camera. Again, the camera's position is aligned with Apache space. (Interestingly, because of the framing, the rifle that Geronimo holds appears to be pointed directly at Cochise's head and York and Beaufort appear to be standing directly under it, suggesting an ominous undercurrent to the scene and to Geronimo's character.[23]) Optical point-of-view in *Stagecoach* has its complexities; as Nick Browne has shown in the dinner sequence at Dry Fork, spectator identification is split between optical point-of-view (aligned with Lucy, the "insider") and empathetic response (aligned with Dallas, the "outsider").[24] This split allows the spectator to "cross" the inside/outside barrier within the white community, but not that between the white and Indian cultures. In *Fort Apache,* however, the narrative has constructed not only the diegetic space in which York and Cochise can mediate cultural opposition, but also a subject position for the spectator that structures identification with the Apache, an "unsettling" perspective that will become an uncomfortable one when it is repeated later in the film during the massacre.

The fourth segment returns to Fort Apache for the noncommissioned officers' dance, where the regiment's internal tensions are again on display. Trapped by his own respect for rules and protocol, Thursday must partner Mrs. O'Rourke in the Grand March. Ford films the Grand March as an aesthetic interpretation of military movements, with "marchers" arranged in columns and rows. In its pattern of linking-and-splitting, it also symbolically enacts the tension between division and community that characterizes the regiment. Although the March forces Thursday, Mrs. O'Rourke, Sergeant Major O'Rourke, and Philadelphia to link arms, the two men look grim and uncomfortable throughout, indicating the artificiality of the March and of the image of "mediation" between the ranks (and white ethnicities and classes) that it represents.

The two narrative lines that make up this section of *Fort Apache*, York's journey to find Cochise and the activities inside the fort, come together at the end of this sequence with the sudden appearance of York and Beaufort, just returned from Mexico. An angry confrontation then occurs between York, who has persuaded Cochise to come back to U.S. territory with all of his people in order to negotiate with Thursday, and Thursday, who reveals that he has no intention of honoring York's words to an "illiterate, uncivilized murderer and treaty-breaker," a "breech-clouted savage," and instead plans to confront Cochise with military force. Thursday's racist contempt for Cochise prevents him from thinking in terms other than those of exclusion ("There's no question of honor, sir, between an American officer and Cochise"). He orders O'Rourke to cancel the dance and he orders York to submit (yet again) to his authority, disrupting the processes of mediation and setting in motion the chain of events that will lead to the massacre.[25]

Ironically, Thursday's actions also bring the regiment together as a unified force, defined precisely by its opposition to the Indians. The white community transcends its ethnic and class divisions by setting its communal "whiteness" against the alien force, just as the passengers did in *Stagecoach*. Thursday's

"Thursday refuses to enter the space of cultural mediation that is opened one last time": the failed negotiation in *Fort Apache*. The Indian agent Silas Meacham (Grant Withers), Sergeant Mulcahy (Victor McLaglen), Captain York (John Wayne), Lieutenant Colonel Thursday (Henry Fonda), Captain Collingwood (George O'Brien), and Sergeant Beaufort (Pedro Armendáriz) meet with Cochise (Miguel Inclán) before the final massacre. Still courtesy of the Museum of Modern Art Film Stills Archive.

actions, then, "redirect" *Fort Apache*'s narrative toward the linear paradigm of the Western that figures encounters between whites and Indians as hostile and violent, and away from the exploration of "mediation" in the previous four-part section of the film. However, although Thursday rejects York's alternative trajectory, the "detour" that places him in dialogic relation with Cochise, the narrative briefly reopens the space of cultural mediation in the sequence that contains Cochise's speech.

If the narrative logic of *Stagecoach* leads toward an inevitably hostile confrontation between the white community and the Indians, *Fort Apache* has a double-sided narrative logic that on the one hand leads toward the massacre and on the other leads toward the moment when Cochise speaks, albeit through the mediation of Spanish and Beaufort's translation. After the attack by Diablo's band, York "speaks for" Cochise; when York journeys to Mexico, Cochise enters the narrative, but he speaks only the words of greeting; finally, in a meeting with Thursday, Cochise's voice is heard telling his version of the history of white/Indian relations, and he and his voice command the attention of Thursday and the spectator. To some extent, his speech is powerful because the narrative has been both anticipating and deferring it.

Unlike Thursday, who is openly dismissive and contemptuous during the meeting, Cochise strives for reconciliation and mediation. He recapitulates the history of the move to the reservation and the destructiveness of Meacham that York had recited, and then he delivers his terms for peace: "We looked to the great white father for protection. He gave us slow death. We will not return to the reservation while that man is there or anyone like him. Send him away and we will speak of peace. If you do not send him away, there will be war. And for each one of us that you kill, ten white men will die." Thursday is furious at both the threat and Cochise's assumption that he is an equal partner in the negotiation. He calls Cochise a "recalcitrant swine," orders Beaufort to insult him ("Tell him I find him without honor"), and says he will attack unless the Apache return to the reservation. Because Thursday refuses to enter the space of cultural mediation that is opened one last time, the narrative resumes the trajectory leading to violent confrontation.

The sequence of the massacre is constructed so as to evoke conflicting responses. Camera placement positions the spectator first with Thursday and the regiment as he leads the charge straight into a dead end, a box canyon; then with York, who watches from a nearby ridge; then with the Apache as they wait in the rocks and prepare to attack. The multiplicity of literal perspectives corresponds to the "confusion" of ideological perspectives in the sequence: Thursday is condemned and redeemed by his actions, and he both fails as a leader and embodies the highest standard of leadership (when he returns to die with his men); the regiment is finally unified, and it is destroyed; the Apache are guilty of appalling slaughter, and there seems to be a grim justice in their actions. The linear narrative paradigm may be reinscribed by this violent confrontation, the "detour" recuperated, but the double-sided narrative logic of *Fort Apache* undermines a sense of resolution.

In the final sequence York, now a colonel, talks with visiting Eastern reporters. When he confirms the well-publicized but false account of "Thursday's Last Charge" that has now become legendary, he both lies ("Correct in every detail") and tells an ironic truth ("No man died more gallantly, nor won more honor for his regiment"). The jarring reversal of the facts is matched by an apparent reversal of character. York himself is an embodiment of the sequence's ambiguities and uncertainties, for not only in his rank but also in his dress and manner he appears to have taken on something of Thursday's public persona. These unsettling reversals and the ambiguities concerning history and truth that are raised through them need to be understood as a continuation of the uneasy narrative resolution provided by the massacre in the previous sequence. It is as if the only way York—and at least to some extent Ford—can resolve the contradictions that the narrative has raised is by refusing to consider them and, instead, substituting for the anxieties of history a glorification of the regiment as an entity unto itself. (Hence the presence of Philadelphia and Michael's baby, Michael Thursday York O'Rourke, embodiment of the "resolution" of the regiment's disparate elements.) Dedication to this image of the regiment allows York to "forget" the massacre; it also allows him to continue to avoid questioning the very idea of westward expansion and his role in that project.[26] However, that neither the massacre sequence nor the final epilogue can provide the type of "settled" resolution of, for example, *Stagecoach* is an indication of *Fort Apache*'s distance from the linear paradigms of the classical Western.

It is in Ford's later postwar Westerns that the narrative "detours" are most pronounced and the encounters and confrontations between white protagonists and racial "others" are most complex.[27] Characters trace increasingly pronounced circular or "looping" patterns through space (e.g., *3 Godfathers* [1948]), the narration incorporates temporal dislocations (e.g., *The Man Who Shot Liberty Valance* [1962]), and, at times, the white hero is dislodged as the focus of the narrative (e.g., *Cheyenne Autumn* [1964]). Of all the postwar Westerns, however, it is *The Searchers* (1956) that most powerfully combines non-linear structures of story and narration with a complex investigation of the white hero's relation to race, racial Others, and his own racism. The Western's classical linearity is disrupted on the level of story by the five-year circular wanderings of Ethan and Marty, and on the level of narration by the elaborate "flashback" sequence of Laurie's reading Marty's letter. And at the center of the narrative, in the place of the Western hero, is the problematic figure of Ethan Edwards, alienated, sadistic, bent on vengeance, filled with racial hatred. As it foregrounds the issue of Ethan's and the white community's racism, and reveals racism as a structuring element of the Western meta-narrative, *The Searchers* seems to push the classical Western paradigms to their limit and even to the point of collapse.

When Ethan Edwards arrives at his brother's ranch at the start of *The Searchers,* he sets in motion a narrative that initially appears to follow the trajectory of the classical linear paradigms of story and narration. First there is news the following morning of a raid on a neighbor's livestock; then the pursuit by a group of Texas Rangers and volunteers; next the murder raid by the band of Comanche who used the livestock raid as a decoy; then the Rangers' location of the Comanche; and finally the battle at the river. This pattern of escalating violence between white settlers and Indians in the first part of *The Searchers* follows the linear model of *Stagecoach,* and within this pattern, as in the earlier film, the Indians are constructed as an utterly alien force. Before the battle, they seem to materialize out of the landscape, poised on top of the cliffs, and their savagery and alienness are stressed throughout the section.

The sequence in which the Comanche attack the Edwards ranch, killing Aaron, Martha, and their son, Ben, and abducting Lucy and Debbie, their daughters, not only reinforces the construction of the Indians as alien and Other, but also explicitly constructs the threat as sexual. The attack itself is not represented. However, two moments convey the nature of the events. Inside the house, Aaron and Martha prepare for a possible attack. When she realizes the significance of her parents' actions, Lucy reacts. The camera tracks straight in to a close-up of her terrified face as she screams. The tracking in to a close shot of Lucy's hysterical outburst is jarring, particularly because this type of intrusive shot is uncharacteristic of Ford's Westerns. It occurs once again in *The Searchers,* when the camera tracks straight in to a close shot of Ethan's face as he and Marty leave the fort after questioning the "insane" white women recaptured from the Indians. Ethan's face registers his "insane" hatred as one of the women (echoing Lucy) screams offscreen. This camera technique clearly conveys not only the absolute opposition between Indian and white settler, but also the underlying fear and threat of sexual violation and attendant madness. (In contrast, another of Ford's rare uses of this kind of shot occurs in *Stagecoach* when Ringo is first seen. The uniqueness and power of that shot, however, serve to underscore Ringo's function as the hero.) The second moment occurs at the end of the sequence in which Debbie escapes to the family cemetery. As she crouches by her grandmother's grave, a shadow falls across her body. She looks up and the reverse shot dramatically reveals Chief Scar, bare-chested, with war paint, jewelry, and feathers—an exotic and erotically charged body. In a gesture celebrating his obvious "phallic power," Scar raises an animal horn to his lips and blows as the shot fades. At the beginning, then, *The Searchers* foregrounds the question of white fears of sexual violation and miscegenation, issues only hinted at in *Stagecoach.*

However, although *The Searchers* begins by echoing the pattern of the classical Western narrative, the film changes course, as virtually all Ford scholars have noted. The narrative loses its sense of linear development; events seem to start and stop and start over again, just as Ethan and Martin leave, return, leave, return, leave, and return again, seemingly caught in a repetitive loop.[28] The repetitiveness is stressed in the sequence in which Ethan and Martin return to the Jorgensen ranch the year after Brad's death. As the Jorgensens come out to meet them, the editing, mise en scène, camera positions, and music echo those of the opening sequence, when Martha and then the other members of the Edwards family emerged from their house to greet Ethan as he materialized out of the desert landscape. The contrast between the domestic space and the landscape, between inside and outside, between those who stay and those who wander—all the familiar oppositions of the classical Western narrative—are again reinscribed through this series of shot/reverse shot images. The sequence is one of the numerous "internal rhymes" or parallelisms with which *The Searchers* is filled, and its deliberate evocation of the opening implies circularity and possibly even closure. And indeed, the first part of *The Searchers,* with its classical trajectory, is over. At this point, as the text appears to begin again, it constructs an alternative narrative based on Ethan's obsessive pursuit of Scar and Debbie, a pursuit that continually doubles back on itself as Ethan traces and retraces his steps for five years.

Instead of the relentless linearity of the classical Western narrative, *The Searchers,* like *Fort Apache* but in an extended way, disrupts the pattern by constructing a spatial-geographical "detour" as Ethan and Martin crisscross the landscape. Temporal as well as spatial markers are vague, and we cannot map their movements with any certainty. The peculiarities of this section of *The Searchers,* which constitutes the main portion of the narrative, include indeterminacies of time and space, the seeming futility of the pursuit, and the repetitious nature of events (setting out, returning, setting out, etc.). These, along with the focus on Ethan's maniacal persistence and on his racist hatred not only of Scar but also of his "contaminated" niece, have led numerous Ford scholars to agree that *The Searchers* is a "psychological epic" or that it depicts an "inward journey"—in short, that it is a revisionist Western intent on examining the racist underpinnings of the ideology of manifest destiny.[29]

The Searchers is arguably Ford's most complex and even contradictory Western. The classical paradigm is problematized, its ideological foundation under scrutiny, and its narrative structure loosened and complicated. The narrative also incorporates a dizzying number of echoes, mirrorings, and parodies, and it is both an examination of the central and familiar conventions of a popular genre and the vehicle for numerous personal gestures, including the powerful textual and extratextual father/son trope that is inscribed throughout the film.[30] But at the center of the text's meaning is the Ethan/Scar pairing, the vehicle for

Ford's reexamination of the dynamics of westward expansion and the meaning of whiteness.

Ethan and Scar have often been read as if they were "mythic" figures, ideological mirrors of each other's racial hatred seeking only bloody vengeance, Scar for the sons murdered by white men, Ethan for his brother's family murdered by Scar's Comanche.[31] Critics have also seen Scar as a manifestation of Ethan's repressed desires. The opening sequence of the film makes clear that Ethan loves Martha and that his unexpected arrival disrupts the domestic world. It is thus easy to read Scar's violent attack on the family (including the implied rape of Martha) as the displaced eruption of Ethan's desires and to read Ethan's subsequent pathological behavior as the result of guilt.[32] The "imaginary geography" of Monument Valley, then, becomes the space of cultural confrontation (between Scar and Ethan as the racial antagonists of the Western paradigm) and the landscape of a psychological journey (in which Ethan faces his own hatred and fears, imaged through Scar as his "double"). Seen in this way, Ethan becomes a "darker" version of York, that is, a Western hero whose racism is not displaced onto another character. The confrontation with Scar, which has been both anticipated and deferred, becomes the goal of the journey (since finding Debbie— the ostensible goal—requires some sort of encounter with Scar), and the narrative logic makes this confrontation increasingly desirable as Ethan and Marty repeatedly find his trail only to lose it again. When Scar and Ethan do finally meet, two-thirds of the way through the film, the complex of racial and sexual fears that underlie the narrative comes to the surface.

Ethan's knowledge of Indian culture, including Comanche culture, is extensive and enables him to stay on Scar's trail. More interesting, however, is his identification with Indian culture, an identification which complicates the reading of Scar and Ethan as racial antagonists. Ethan's clothing reflects the disparate segments of his character.[33] His Confederate coat, in which he says he wrapped Lucy's body for burial, indicates both his outsider's allegiance to a lost cause and his alienation from the contemporary social world; it also links him to Southern racism and fears of miscegenation, especially as his account of the discovery and burial of Lucy recalls Hatfield's gesture of covering the woman's body at Apache Wells with his cloak in *Stagecoach*. Ethan also wears the hat, shirt, scarf, jeans, and suspenders of the Western hero. At one point, he wears a calico shirt, identifying him with Debbie (her apron) and the white captives he sees at the cavalry fort, even though he repudiates them. His rifle is encased in a buckskin sheath with long fringe, suggestive of the frontiersman but also of Indian influence. These disparate elements make it impossible to "fix" his identity. His intimate knowledge of Indian beliefs is similarly hard to account for. How does he come to know so much, including religious beliefs, about a people he hates?[34] The question of Ethan's relation to Indian culture is pointedly raised in his first confrontation with Scar.

When Ethan and Scar meet, through the mediation of Emilio Figueroa, the multicultural dynamics of colonization in the West are foregrounded, as in *Fort Apache*. The space of mediation is again identified with Mexico. It is ironic that despite his knowledge and skills, Ethan is powerless, here and throughout his search, to find Scar on his own. At this point, it is Figueroa and Mose Harper (inexplicably echoing Ethan and conducting his own search for Scar and Debbie in the desert) who have located the chief called Cicatriz—"Mexican for Scar," as Ethan explains to Martin.

The sequence depicting the meeting with Scar begins with long shots as Ethan, Marty, Figueroa, and his men ride into the Comanche camp. However, after they dismount and Scar emerges from his teepee, Ford underscores the climactic nature of this moment through the editing. Through shot/reverse shot cutting, the sequence alternates a series of four shots of Scar, Ethan, Scar, and Martin, punctuated by dramatic music. This wordless "confrontation" is followed by a longer shot as Figueroa steps between Ethan and Scar to begin his translation-mediation. However, Ethan interrupts, walks up close to Scar, and addresses him, insultingly, in English ("Scar, eh? Plain to see how you got your

Ethan Edwards's taunting challenge to Scar: "You speak good American for a Comanch'; someone teach ya?" Emilio Figueroa (Antonio Moreno), Martin Pawley (Jeffrey Hunter), Ethan Edwards (John Wayne), and Chief Scar (Henry Brandon) when Ethan and Martin "come to trade" in *The Searchers*.
Frame enlargement.

name"). When Scar replies in English ("You, Big Shoulders; young one, He Who Follows"), Ethan, still face-to-face with Scar in the frame, issues his taunting challenge: "You speak good American for a Comanch'; someone teach ya?" The accusation is clear: Scar learned English from his white (female, sexual) captive, Debbie. A few moments later, after Ethan has revealed that he understands some of the Comanche Scar speaks to Figueroa, Scar returns the taunt. As the two men move to enter Scar's teepee, in another two-shot, Scar pauses, turns to Ethan, and says: "You speak good Comanche; someone teach you?" Given the logic of the text's "rhyming patterns" and the "mirroring" of Scar and Ethan (and even the unexplained source of Ethan's knowledge of Comanche culture), the reciprocal nature of the insult is clear and stunning. Scar is accusing Ethan of having learned Comanche through intimacy with a Comanche woman. This confrontation, then, is about the "exchange" of racial and sexual desires or transgressions as the two men mirror each other's taunts. The "double standard" of white attitudes toward interracial sexual conduct—that it is acceptable for white men to have sexual contact with non-white women, but unacceptable for non-white men to have sexual contact with white women—is exposed, and the Western's racialist discourse is turned inside out.[35]

This challenge to the racism and fear of miscegenation that underlie the narrative of white imperialist westward expansion is repeated throughout *The Searchers,* most pointedly through Laurie Jorgensen (in love with Martin) and the depiction of the cavalry. Just as Ethan's intimacy with Indian culture is echoed in the "crazy" Mose Harper's parodic "war whoops" and dances, his "insane" desire to kill Debbie because she has had sexual contact with Scar is echoed by Laurie Jorgensen. When Ethan and Martin return after having found Scar and Debbie, and after Ethan's attempt to kill her, they interrupt Laurie's wedding. Dressed in a white wedding gown (which signifies not only a virgin bride but also in this context the racially "uncontaminated" white woman), Laurie argues with Marty, telling him Ethan is right: "Fetch *what* home? The leavings of a Comanche buck . . . with savage brats of her own? . . . [Ethan will] put a bullet in her brain. I tell you Martha would want him to." Laurie embodies the socially accepted racism of the white community, the legitimacy behind Ethan's "insanity." In addition to exposing Ethan's and Laurie's racism, *The Searchers* demystifies the role of the cavalry in securing the West for white settlement. They are seen "herding" their Indian captives in a freezing winter landscape, and Ethan and Martin discover the bodies of Indian women and children they have killed. Ethan's wandering, looping journey takes him and Martin away from the white community's assumptions until he confronts Scar and his own hatred and until he and Marty confront the cavalry's institutionally sanctioned slaughter.

The other object they encounter is, of course, Debbie. *The Searchers* constructs several symbolic bodies, each coded in racial terms. Ethan and Scar are

Debbie is "constructed as the 'assimilated' body: she looks Indian, speaks Comanche, and tells Marty that 'These are my people. Go.'" Martin (Jeffrey Hunter) and Debbie (Natalie Wood) in *The Searchers.*
Frame enlargement.

racial opposites who have transgressed the boundaries that separate them; Laurie is the "intact" white female body. Interestingly, however, Debbie does not represent Laurie's opposite, the grotesque, "violated" body of Ethan's and Laurie's expectations. It is the unseen—and indeed *absent*—bodies of Martha and Lucy that fill that role. (Significantly, it is Ethan but not Martin who sees these bodies.) Debbie is instead constructed as the "assimilated" body; she looks Indian, speaks Comanche, and tells Marty that "These are my people. Go." Her symbolic counterpart is, then, not Laurie but Marty.[36] As the orphan who is one "eighth Cherokee and the rest Welsh and English," he is completely absorbed into white culture and treated as "kin" by everyone except Ethan. It is Marty's "hybridity" that allows him to resist Ethan's and Laurie's characterization of Debbie and that prevents him from desiring revenge even when Ethan tells him that his mother's scalp hangs from Scar's spear ("That don't change nothing," he replies). Debbie and Marty, then, stand opposed to the ideology of "racial purity" implied by the other symbolic bodies of the text.

However, if *The Searchers'* challenge to the Western paradigm makes it one of Ford's most brilliant and complex investigations of the genre, it also makes the film a somewhat problematic text, bordering on incoherence at times. It is as if the "detour" undermines the structure to such an extent that recuperation is impossible. The linearity of story and narration collapses in the sequence in which Laurie reads Marty's letter aloud. As critics have noted, this section, which occurs halfway through the film, is the most extreme instance of fragmentation and ellipticality in a text marked by those tendencies.[37] There are gaps and discontinuities in the diegesis and in the construction—places where it is impossible to understand the connections between shots—and numerous shifts in narration (Laurie's voice-over; Marty's voice-over; suppression of diegetic sound; "objective" rendering of image and sound). This is also the section that seems to contain contradictory ideological messages: the revelation of the savagery of the cavalry versus the racism of the "comic" portrayal of Look, the Indian "wife" Marty acquires in trade. Critics have tried to excuse this section in various ways, but it is impossible to ignore Peter Lehman's conclusion that "Despite all [its] critiques of racism, the fact remains that the film contains disturbing moments of racism."[38] *The Searchers* is a powerful text because it confronts the racism underlying the Western paradigm, but it is also a text that cannot completely resolve the issues it raises.

Like *Fort Apache, The Searchers* attempts to resume the linear trajectory of the classic Western narrative in its final section. When Ethan and Marty return to the Jorgensens after their encounter with Scar and Debbie, it is Mose Harper who again tells them where to find Scar. The Rangers, along with Ethan and Marty, go out to attack Scar's camp. Captain Reverend Samuel Johnson Clayton, one of the text's father figures, is both the local preacher conducting funerals and weddings and the head of the Texas Ranger company policing the territory. In his name and duties, he represents the twin forces of white imperialism—the Bible and the gun—and he articulates the colonizer's view of the colonized, referring to the Indians as "murderers" and "childish savages." After the many years of "delay," Sam Clayton resumes the pursuit of Scar's band that had been suspended when Ethan and Marty struck out on their own. The resolution of the narrative centers on Clayton's orchestration of the final violent clash of white and Indian cultures, in which the Rangers, joined by the cavalry, are victorious. It seems as if *The Searchers* reasserts and completes the linear paradigm after all—"correcting" itself after the long, elliptical, fragmented middle.

And yet, the resolution does not quite hold together. Scar is killed, but by Marty (who merely reacts in instinctive self-defense) rather than Ethan. Ethan rides into Scar's teepee and emerges with his scalp, looking shocked. Ethan then chases Debbie, but at the last minute, with her raised in his arms, an echo of a moment from the beginning of the film when she was a child, he embraces her instead of killing her. Debbie and Martin are both taken into the Jorgensen house in the final shot, reabsorbed into the Western family, as Ethan remains outside and turns his back to them, facing the desert. With the closing of the door, the final sequence mirrors, in reverse, the opening sequence. By ending where it (the journey, the film) began, linearity gives way to circularity. But the significance of all of these markers of closure is not clear. How are we to understand Ethan's motivation? What does it mean that he scalps Scar? Why does he suddenly lose his hatred for Debbie and what she represents? Has he "purged" the Indian "contamination" from his world? Or has he abandoned the ideology of racial "purity"? How are we to read the "new" Western family that includes the assimilated, or recovered, or hybrid bodies of Marty and Debbie? *The Searchers* leaves these questions unanswered and unanswerable. Indeed, as Lehman has argued, *The Searchers* seems to center on missing or suppressed knowledge, from literal questions of identity (as in the first word of the text, "Ethan?") to startling gaps in the story.[39] The most striking of these gaps occurs when Ethan says to Marty in the Jorgensen bunkhouse, "There's something I want you to know." Marty interrupts him, and Ethan never finishes the sentence. What is the missing information? Would it explain Ethan's relationship to Marty and why it was Ethan who "just happened" to find Marty and bring him to Aaron and Martha after the Indian raid that killed his parents? Or is it, along with the other unanswered questions, part of a textual incoherence, signifying precisely the inability of *The Searchers* to answer the questions it raises?

Although *The Searchers* is the product of Ford's longstanding preoccupations with the Western's racial and structural patterns, it is also possible to read the film in the context of the postwar civil rights movement, as a displacement of the black/white tensions of 1956 onto the Western's conventions of the Indian/white settler conflict.[40] Like other postwar "revisionist" Westerns, *The Searchers* rewrites the genre in response to the ideological currents of the fifties. That *The Searchers* should raise questions about race and "kinship" that it cannot resolve suggests that the issues indeed resonate beyond the ostensible historical material.

According to Virginia Wright Wexman, the Western hero "has affinities with the communities of racial others that populate Western films" but at "a deeper level . . . his affiliation with the cause of the European homesteaders is far more compelling than his ties to racial others."[41] In some ways, this description fits Ethan as well as York and Ringo, although the complex racial terrain of *The Searchers* makes the question of allegiance at the end somewhat ambiguous. It is possible to see the "recovery of Debbie" as the reestablishing of a racist ideology, as Brian Henderson does, since her acceptance back into white society implies the continuation of the negation of "Indian law and Indian society."[42] But it is also possible to read the ending as a rejection of (another aspect of) racist ideology in Ethan's (and the white community's) acceptance of "kinship" based on adoption and affiliation rather than on blood or race, an acceptance that begins with Ethan's movement away from his repudiation of Marty ("I ain't your uncle") and of Marty's claim of kinship with Debbie ("She's your nothing") and culminates in his designation of Marty as his heir and acceptance of Debbie as his niece. That both readings are possible suggests a deep structuring ambivalence about race at work in the film.

In the fifties and especially the sixties, Ford and Ford's Westerns came under attack as racist. Ford defended himself by arguing production issues (for example, that he was the first—and virtually the only—Hollywood filmmaker to pay Native American and African American actors and extras wages equal to those of white personnel), by arguing that he had made films whose theme was racial tolerance and that his films represented racial others with dignity, and by arguing that as an Irishman he was able to understand both the Indians and the cavalry.[43] His defense, however, does not absolve the films from the charge of a different kind of racism: their complicity in racist structures of representation. The representation of racial groups as alien, as Other, through stereotyping, idealization, or denial of subjectivity, constitutes a kind of racism Ford did not, perhaps could not, acknowledge. Ford's anger at his critics (whom he called "mad, insane"[44]) is in some sense justified, but it is his bewilderment that is more telling. Postwar racial politics were something neither Ford nor the Ford Western—nor the larger culture—was able to think through, to resolve. Precisely because it raises the questions it cannot answer, *The Searchers* is the central text marking that dilemma.

Scar is a member of the Nawyaki Comanche. At one point in their journey, Ethan explains the name "Nawyaki" to Marty as meaning "Sorta like round about: man says he's going one place, means to go t'other." That description, of course, applies to Ethan's own journey, since he sets out meaning to track and kill Debbie, but instead takes her home; it also applies to the narrative structure of *The Searchers*, which begins with and then departs from the Western's traditional linearity. And it also applies to Ford's Westerns seen as a whole over time, beginning with the classical paradigms of *Stagecoach* but ending with the increasingly complex and disruptive patterns of the texts of Ford's postwar period.

NOTES

1. The "frontier thesis" as a defining American myth, formulated influentially by Frederick Jackson Turner in 1893, is discussed in Peter Stowell, *John Ford* (Boston: G. K. Hall, 1986), 15–53. On the significance of cinema in relation to this myth, see Thomas Schatz, *Hollywood Genres: Formula, Filmmaking, and the Studio System* (New York: Random House, 1981), 45–46.

2. Theories of narrative typically rely on a distinction between story (the characters and events, the "matter") and discourse (the presentation of the story material, the "how"). See Seymour Chatman, *Story and Discourse: Narrative Structure in Fiction and Film* (Ithaca: Cornell University Press, 1978). Some theories rely on a three-part model (as does David Bordwell in his analyses of classical Hollywood narrative; see below) based on story (what the reader has to deduce or reconstruct from the text), plot (the arrangement of the events as presented by the text), and narration (the act of telling). This essay follows the practice of some recent theorists who, like Steven Cohan and Linda Shires in their *Telling Stories: A Theoretical Analysis of Narrative Fiction* (New York: Routledge, 1988), have opted for "clarity and simplicity" (178 n) by adopting two terms: story and narration. Story refers to the material that is narrated; narration refers to the narrating of the material. The ordering or arranging of the story events is thus a function of the narration.

3. In chapter 6, "Narrative Structure: *Stagecoach* and *The Searchers*" (*John Ford*, 123–140), Stowell provides a detailed narrative breakdown of the two films, sequence by sequence, and an interesting comparison of the two narrative structures that analyzes what remains constant and what changes from the earlier to the later film.

4. Substantive discussions of race and racism in Ford can be found in J. A. Place, *The Non-Western Films of John Ford* (Secaucus, N.J.: Citadel Press, 1977), especially 242–243; in Peter Lehman's work on Ford in the first half of William Luhr and Peter Lehman, *Authorship and Narrative in the Cinema* (New York: Putnam's, 1977) and in Peter Lehman, "Texas 1868/America 1956: *The Searchers*," in *Close Viewings: An Anthology of New Film Criticism*, ed. Peter Lehman (Tallahassee: The Florida State University Press, 1990): 387–415; and in Brian Henderson, "*The Searchers*: An American Dilemma," rpt. in *Movies and Methods: An Anthology*, vol. 2, ed. Bill Nichols (Berkeley: University of California Press, 1985), 429–449. Most recently, Virginia Wright Wexman's work on the Western has offered important new interpretations of the genre's racial discourse that are of great significance for Ford's texts: "The Family on the Land: Race and Nationhood in Silent Westerns," in *The Birth of Whiteness: Race and the Emergence of the U.S. Cinema*, ed. Daniel Bernard (New Brunswick: Rutgers University Press, 1996), 129–169, and "Star and Genre: John Wayne, the Western, and the American Dream of the Family on the Land" in her *Creating the Couple: Love, Marriage, and Hollywood Performance* (Princeton: Princeton University Press, 1993).

5. Issues of linearity and race in Ford are not of course confined to his Westerns, although they are played out in specific ways in specific genres. See, for example, Matthew Bernstein, "Hollywood's 'Arty Cinema': John Ford's *The Long Voyage Home*" (*Wide Angle* 10, no. 1 [1988]: 30–45), which analyzes that film's "flouting" of Hollywood norms, including linearity. And see Place, *The Non-Western Films*, for discussion of Ford's treatment of race in other genres.

6. For a discussion of feminist and minority writers' responses to arguments about narrative linearity, see Margaret Homans, "Feminist Fictions and Feminist Theories of Narrative," *Narrative* 2, no. 1 (1994): 3–16.

7. The story of Ford's remarks to the Screen Directors Guild is told in Tag Gallagher, *John Ford: The Man and His Films* (Berkeley: University of California Press, 1986), 340–341. Mankiewicz's memory of the event is included in Peter Bogdanovich, *John Ford*, rev. ed. (Berkeley: University of California Press, 1978), 18–19.

8. See the Ford filmography in Gallagher, *John Ford*. J. A. Place, in *The Western Films of John Ford* (Secaucus, N.J.: Citadel Press, 1974), shows how the early silent Westerns set up many of the motifs of the later films.

9. The references are from the following essays by Bazin: "The Western: Or the American Film Par Excellence," in *What Is Cinema?*, vol. 2, trans. Hugh Gray (Berkeley: University of California Press, 1971), 140; "The Evolution of the Language of Cinema," in *What Is Cinema?*, vol. 1, trans. Hugh Gray (Berkeley: University of California Press, 1967), 29; and "The Evolution of the Western," in *What Is Cinema?*, vol. 2, 149. The first two remarks are frequently cited in discussions of *Stagecoach*.

10. Classical Hollywood narrative has been analyzed most thoroughly by David Bordwell. See Bordwell, "Classical Hollywood Cinema: Narrational Principles and Procedures," in *Narration, Apparatus, Ideology: A Film Theory Reader*, ed. Philip Rosen (New York: Columbia University Press, 1986), 17–34; and Bordwell, *Narration and the Fiction Film* (Madison: University of Wisconsin Press, 1985), 156–166. See also David Bordwell, Janet Staiger, and Kristin Thompson, *The Classical Hollywood Cinema* (New York: Columbia University Press, 1985), 3–11.

11. Roland Barthes argues for the structuring role of binary oppositions in forming the "symbolic code" of classical narrative in *S/Z*, trans. Richard Miller (New York: Farrar, Strauss & Giroux, 1974).

12. See, for example, Nick Browne, "The Spectator-in-the-Text: The Rhetoric of *Stagecoach,*" *Film Quarterly* 29, no. 2 (Winter 1975–1976): 26–38, rpt. in Rosen, *Narration, Apparatus, Ideology,* 102–119.

13. There are several well-known studies of the Western that analyze the genre's structural polarities between East and West, garden and wilderness, civilization and savagery, law and anarchy, etc., and that analyze the Western hero as a "mediating" figure who encompasses or reconciles those opposing concepts. For studies that specifically relate Ford's work to these terms, see Peter Wollen, *Signs and Meaning in the Cinema* (Bloomington: Indiana University Press, 1970); and Schatz, *Hollywood Genres.*

14. When asked why there were shots of the horses from "the wrong side," Ford replied, "You mean going right to left instead of left to right? I did that because it was getting late and, if I had stayed on the correct side, the horses would have been back-lit." He added, "I usually break the conventional rules—sometimes deliberately" (Bogdanovich, *John Ford,* 70).

15. Bogdanovich, *John Ford,* 70.

16. Edward Buscombe, *Stagecoach* (London: British Film Institute, 1992), 45–46. Compare John Baxter's comment that Monument Valley is "an area with little relation to the conventional geography of the West, a patchwork of natural features lending itself to subjective interpretation" in *The Cinema of John Ford* (New York: A. S. Barnes, 1971), 70; and also Joseph McBride and Michael Wilmington, *John Ford* (New York: Da Capo Press, 1975), 36–37: "Monument Valley is more than a real place to Ford. It is a state of mind."

17. Buscombe discusses the presence of Hispanic elements in *Stagecoach* and points out both the racism in its portrayal of Hispanic characters and the moments when the text seems to undercut racist discourse in the comic interchange between Peacock and Chris over Yakeema as "savage" (*Stagecoach,* 51–54).

18. On the cultural construction of "whiteness" in Ford's Westerns, see Lehman, *Authorship and Narrative,* 149–150; on the "return" to racial hierarchies, see J. A. Place on *Rio Grande* in *The Western Films,* 157.

19. From Nugent's review of *Stagecoach* in the *New York Times* (3 March 1939), quoted in Buscombe, *Stagecoach,* 81.

20. Lehman, *Authorship and Narrative,* 150.

21. The extent to which this ending is, can be, or should be read as ironic has been the subject of much critical debate. For an excellent analysis of the issues involved in the ending and for an intriguing reading of just how complex the film's idea of history is, see Leland Poague, "'All I Can See Is the Flags': *Fort Apache* and the Visibility of History," *Cinema Journal* 27, no. 2 (Winter 1988): 8–26.

22. Poague ("All I Can See," 13–14) and Baxter (*The Cinema of John Ford,* 85) read the use of Spanish differently, as a sign of Cochise's acquisition of "high culture." In Ford's Westerns, however, Spanish "stands for" Mexico, never Spain or Europe.

23. Geronimo is mentioned as York's antagonist at the end of *Fort Apache,* and it is Geronimo who attacks in *Stagecoach.*

24. See Browne, "The Spectator-in-the-Text."

25. Poague makes the point that, for all his rebel status, York never disobeys an order ("All I Can See," 16).

26. For a compelling reading of "the question of manifest destiny as specified in the explicitly detailed apparatus of political-military control imposed upon the Indian population" as the one "'unresolved contradiction'" of the film, see Poague ("All I Can

See," 24). His discussion of the ending partly differs from mine in that he places the Thursday/York and Thursday/Cochise relationships at the center of his analysis, whereas this essay argues that it is possible to place the York/Cochise relationship at the center of analysis.

27. It is also in the later period that Ford attempts, with mixed results, narratives centered on non-white protagonists: *Cheyenne Autumn* (1964) and *Sergeant Rutledge* (1960).

28. Stowell's chart (*John Ford,* 126–129) is useful here in illustrating the elliptical and circular story structure. Lehman (*Authorship and Narrative,* 85–95) has an extended discussion of the film's non-linear patterns.

29. See, for example, Stowell (*John Ford,* 136–137), Place (*The Western Films,* 208), and McBride and Wilmington, who quote Ford himself describing the film as "'a kind of psychological epic'" (*John Ford,* 153).

30. For example: Aaron, Ethan, Jorgensen, and Colonel Greenhill are fathers or surrogate fathers to the younger generation of Ben, Martin, Brad, and Lieutenant Greenhill; Scar is father to two murdered sons; Sam Clayton is a "father figure" in general and in relation to Ethan, with whom he repeatedly "battles" for authority; the film features John Wayne's son Pat and Harry Carey Jr., the son of the actor who worked extensively with Ford in silent Westerns as the cowboy hero; and John Wayne famously echoes Harry Carey Sr. in the final shot.

31. See, for example, Schatz (*Hollywood Genres,* 74–75), Gallagher (*John Ford,* 332), McBride and Wilmington (*John Ford,* 149).

32. See, for example, Place (*The Western Films,* 163–164), Lehman ("Texas 1868," 397), McBride and Wilmington (*John Ford,* 152).

33. Virginia Wright Wexman's analysis of silent Westerns includes discussion of the ideological significance of the disparate elements of the cowboy hero's costume. See "The Family on the Land," 133.

34. Indeed, some critics have read the episode in which Ethan shoots the eyes of the Comanche corpse as indicating that he shares the religious beliefs of the Comanche. See McBride and Wilmington, *John Ford,* 151–152.

35. Wexman describes *The Searchers* as "Perhaps the most revealing film in the entire Western canon in terms of miscegenation" ("Star and Genre," 114).

36. See Lehman ("Texas 1868," 405–411) for a discussion of the relationship between the body of Look and the absent bodies of Lucy and Martha; Place (*The Western Films,* 164) for a discussion of Marty and Debbie as "interracial"; and Henderson, *"The Searchers,"* for an intriguing analysis of kinship issues in the film.

37. Lehman is especially good at analyzing the discontinuities of this section; see "Texas 1868," 393–394.

38. Lehman, "Texas 1868," 404.

39. Lehman, "Texas 1868," 387–389.

40. See Henderson, *"The Searchers,"* and Lehman, "Texas 1868."

41. Wexman, "Star and Genre," 93.

42. Henderson, *"The Searchers,"* 435.

43. See, for example, Gallagher, *John Ford,* 341–343.

44. Gallagher (quoting Bertrand Tavernier), *John Ford,* 342.

5

HOW THE WEST WASN'T WON

THE REPRESSION OF CAPITALISM IN
JOHN FORD'S WESTERNS

Peter Lehman

"Gold *always* interests me," Uncle Shiloh Clegg, the outlaw leader, says ominously in *Wagon Master* (1950). Such an emphasis on money and trading is present in many of Ford's sound Westerns. In *Stagecoach* (1939) Gatewood, a corrupt banker, flees with his bank's money; in *Fort Apache* (1948) an Indian agent mistreats the Indians and contributes to an Indian war; in *She Wore a Yellow Ribbon* (1949), a fort sutler sells rifles to the Indians; in *Wagon Master*, bank robbers terrorize Mormon settlers; in *The Searchers* (1956) a trader sells information and then attempts to murder the men who paid for it so that he can rob them; in *Two Rode Together* (1961) a marshal seeks to rescue whites captured by Indians for purely monetary reasons; and in *Cheyenne Autumn* (1964) Wyatt Earp takes a cut from Tombstone's gambling.

Although *Young Mr. Lincoln* (1939) is technically a historical bio-pic rather than a Western, it is useful to group it with Ford's Westerns to consider how it and they look at money and trading. Set in Illinois prior to the Civil War, the film shares with the Westerns an emphasis on the historical settling of the West. The plot is set in motion by a family of settlers in a covered wagon. Furthermore, the film is centrally concerned with the tension between law and the "Wild West." Lincoln's mediating role bears comparison with that of Captain Reverend Samuel Clayton in *The Searchers* and with Ransom Stoddard's in *The Man Who Shot Liberty Valance* (1962). *Young Mr. Lincoln* is also much preoccupied with money and trading: Lincoln trades with the poor homesteaders; later when he is paid for a law case, he warily bites a coin, testing for counterfeit money. Interestingly, the famous *Cahiers du cinéma* collective analysis of *Young Mr. Lincoln* supplies the only significant discussion of the representation of money and trading in the Ford oeuvre; as we shall see, Ford scholars have been remarkably silent on this aspect of his Westerns.

In this essay, I examine Ford's use of money, trading, and capitalism in his sound-era films, but my intention is not to add yet another theme to the Fordian canon. Though at times Ford does thematize money—by, for example, relating it to greed—my interest lies in the ideology underlying his preoccupation with money and trading. Specifically, I will investigate the relationship of money and trading to Ford's representation of the West and American history, for it is only by considering this link that we can fully grasp the significance of the much celebrated and analyzed ideal Fordian community. I contend that it is only by repressing the role of money, trading, and capitalism in the West that Ford can represent his ideal communities and families, whether these are literal nuclear families or the symbolic family of the Seventh Cavalry. Ford's ideal families figuratively wash their hands of money, leaving it to those who threaten the very cohesion of the family and community. Ford's Westerns do not represent the evils of capitalism; instead they represent evil capitalists living at the margins of families, military units, and communities that are tied to the land in ways that do not seem to be economic. Only in *Cheyenne Autumn* is this benign vision seriously questioned, and then only obliquely.

Most books written on Ford's films either are silent on the subject of money, capitalism, and trading or only briefly mention it. Neither Joseph McBride and Michael Wilmington in *John Ford*, Tag Gallagher in *John Ford: The Man and His Films*, J. A. Place in *The Western Films of John Ford*, Andrew Sarris in *The*

Ford can represent the ideal family (symbolized by the Seventh Cavalry) only through the repression of capitalism. A scene from *Fort Apache* (1948) with John Wayne, Shirley Temple, Anna Lee, George O'Brien, and John Agar.
Courtesy of the Museum of Modern Art Film Stills Archive.

John Ford Movie Mystery, nor Lindsay Anderson in *About John Ford* discuss those issues. Nor did I give any significant attention to these matters either in my Ph.D. dissertation, "John Ford and the Auteur Theory," or in the versions of dissertation chapters published in *Authorship and Narrative in the Cinema.* It was not until my 1990 essay "Texas 1868/America 1956: *The Searchers*" that I turned my attention to them.[1]

My point here is not to be critical of the important work done by the first wave of Ford scholars; they opened the door and laid the groundwork for much of the later work, including my own. John Baxter's *The Cinema of John Ford* does raise these issues. Speaking of *Fort Apache* and *She Wore a Yellow Ribbon,* Baxter notes "the shadows of encroaching urban values, suggested . . . in both films by the crooked 'sutlers' whose capitalism destroys the balance of power on which the cavalry depends."[2] Of *Stagecoach,* he observes, "The 'town' characters are associated throughout with self-seeking and a lack of community spirit, to Ford twin aspects of capitalism" to which Baxter relates "Gatewood's theft, significantly of community funds."[3] Of *The Searchers,* he asks, "Is there any more American film than *The Searchers,* any work that more concisely sums up the dichotomy in American consciousness between the pioneer and the businessman, the soldier and the farmer?"[4]

Although he does not analyze the function of money, "crooked sutlers," or traders in the films, Peter Stowell also supplies a helpful context for doing so in *John Ford.* In a chapter devoted to the myth of American agrarianism in *The Grapes of Wrath* (1940) and *Tobacco Road* (1941), he notes, "That agrarianism became the credo of a major president and author of the Declaration of Independence gave it the stamp of political power and philosophical credibility. And that this credo became locked in a deadly battle with capitalistic mercantilism endowed it with the energy born of tension."[5] Stowell's remarks relate directly to Ford's idealized Western communities. Whether composed of homesteaders or the cavalry, they are associated with the land: a greedy trader like Jerem Futterman in *The Searchers* is to the Jorgensens and the Edwardses as a corrupt Indian agent like Meacham is to Captain York in *Fort Apache* or a gun-dealing sutler like Rynders is to Nathan Brittles in *She Wore a Yellow Ribbon.*

Although Stowell is not alone, French and British scholars have taken a greater interest in capitalism, money, and trading in Ford's films than have American scholars. The celebrated and somewhat notorious *Cahiers du cinéma* analysis of *Young Mr. Lincoln* is the most important example.[6] The *Cahiers* editors note how Lincoln (Henry Fonda), the shopkeeper, is called away to help a family of farmers who want to buy some things but have no money. He offers them credit but the mother is embarrassed to accept it, so they trade instead. It is via this trade that Lincoln comes into possession of a law book. The *Cahiers* editors draw two important conclusions from this. First, they note that Lincoln gives a speech in favor of credit in a film made and released during a recession that required the economic stimulus of consumption. Second, they write, "The fact that Law is acquired by barter introduces a circuit of debt and repayments which is to run through the film."[7]

The film's depiction of Lincoln's first case in Springfield motivates the *Cahiers* editors to once again return to the subject of money. A farmer owes another money. When the lender beats up the borrower, the latter files for damages amounting to almost the amount of the debt. Lincoln resolves the case by informing them that the difference between their respective debts is precisely the amount of his legal fee. "The farmers agree to pay him, and one of them tries to give him a fake coin. Lincoln first notices this by the sound it produces, then by biting the coin, and the scene ends on Lincoln's very insistent stare fixed on the forger."[8] Lincoln's solution, according to the *Cahiers* editors, functions in part to contribute to the myth of the great unifier. The film solves the problem without Lincoln having to choose between the two, much as, in a later scene, the film elides showing him choosing between pies at a Fourth of July baking contest. Most importantly, he will not choose between the two brothers who will be tried for murder. They also note, "Lincoln knows about money; he is not interested in its origins (credit, exchange, and debt form a circle) but it has a ring, a consistency, a value. It is precisely about a money swindle that Lincoln's *castrating power* . . . is manifested for the first time, as an empty, icy, terrifying stare."[9]

This insistence on the importance of the recurring role of money offers a profound insight, one that undoubtedly derives precisely from the Marxist perspective of the writers. Ironically, however, the *Cahiers* editors miss discussing one of the most important elements in *Young Mr. Lincoln:* the film's representation of capitalism and of Lincoln as a capitalist. Rushing to make their forced point about the function of credit in America in 1939, they simply gloss over the fact that Lincoln is a shop owner.

However, Lincoln is a very odd capitalist: he shows little or no interest in *making* money. His offer of credit to the pioneer family seems to spring from the goodness of his heart; he wants to help more than he wants to make money. When he offers credit, he doesn't seem to really even expect to be paid back. Contrary to the *Cahiers* suggestion, his offer of credit is in the spirit, not of a good businessman stimulating the economy, but of a humanitarian who seems to have forgotten that he is in business. It is precisely this pattern that recurs in the scene with the litigating farmers and, once again, the *Cahiers* editors overlook it. Lincoln has just set himself up in business as a new attorney in Springfield, yet his legal fee is based not upon what he could or should make from the case but, rather, upon what is expedient for his clients. Much as he offers credit and then trades for law books when credit is refused, he sacrifices his fee out of a desire to help the men. The fee amount is a simple strategy to unify the disputants. Even if one reads this solution as a jocular moment similar to Lincoln's apparent refusal to choose between pies during a pie-baking contest, the fact remains that he charges the farmers not out of any desire to make money for himself but out of a humanitarian impulse to bring them together. Finally, the same thing happens again in the main dramatic plot of the film when Lincoln decides to represent two brothers accused of murder by offering his services to the homesteading family (the same one he traded with) even though they cannot afford to pay.

A shop owner who gives away his goods and a lawyer who determines his fee (if any) for the good of his clients suggest what the *Cahiers* editors fail to notice—that Lincoln is a man who does not care about money! His glowering test of the farmer's coin is not because he has almost lost money but indicates, rather, his upset that someone has tried to deceive him. It reflects a moral and political disillusionment, not a self-interested one. The manner in which Ford cuts Lincoln off from the "dirty" reality of owning a small business or law practice is necessary for the heroic figure he creates. In so doing, Ford sets the pattern that he will develop in his sound-era Westerns.

Strange as it sounds, what the Marxist editors of *Cahiers* miss is the manner in which Ford represses the role of money in his representation of capitalism. Ford's ideal figures have little or no relation to money and none to profit.

Abe Lincoln (Henry Fonda) gives credit for law books
in *Young Mr. Lincoln* (1939).
Courtesy of the Museum of Modern Art Film Stills Archive.

The other side of the coin (pun intended) is that those who seek to trade and sell for profit in Ford's films are always represented as sleazy, repulsive, marginalized; they are characters who stand in stark contrast to the decent members of the Fordian community. Ford's vision of capitalism has no place for profit. Ford's good shopkeepers literally give things away while his evil ones are incessantly and solely driven by profit. Or perhaps, to put it more accurately, Ford begrudgingly recognizes the necessary function of profit in capitalism by displacing it onto unsavory characters. This displacement, as we shall see, is so persistent throughout his Westerns that it amounts to a near disavowal of the central characteristic of capitalism.

Images of money and trading play a more central role in *The Searchers* than in any of the other Westerns. Money enters the film near the beginning, when Ethan Edwards (John Wayne) throws his brother Aaron (Walter Coy) a bag of money and offers to pay his way. This action throws attention away from his emotionally charged relationship with his brother's wife, Martha (Dorothy Jordan). John Baxter perceptively notes of Ethan, "His characteristic way of tossing down bags of gold, to pay Aaron, and to bribe the Mexican who leads them to Scar's camp, suggests a cavalier contempt for money contrasting with Aaron's careful storage of the gold in a hollow chair, thus underlining the self-interest that, to Ford, justifies the latter's death in the Indian attack."[10] Baxter correctly notes Ethan's cavalier attitude toward money, though I think he goes too far in stating that Aaron's interest in it justifies his death. Aaron's death is essential to the plot, since it enables Ethan to undertake the quest to revenge Martha's death without Aaron's presence and even, perhaps, to symbolically take his place as an avenging lover-husband. Ethan's relationship to money is complex. His cavalier attitude toward it is reminiscent of Lincoln and is part of what positions him to be the film's hero, albeit a very strange one.

Baxter neglects to mention another feature of the money in *The Searchers*: its origins. In his analysis of *Sarrazine*, Roland Barthes distinguishes between money-based capitalism (a "sign") and a feudal system centered on land ownership (an "index").[11] Money of unknown origin is suspicious, and upsets the orderly patriarchal control of land in which property is passed on from generation to generation. Not only do we know where the latter type of wealth comes from, but also the mark of the wealth and its actual value are closely linked through the indexical relationship of the two. A hundred acres with cattle and crops, for example, don't just arbitrarily indicate wealth but produce the food we eat. Money, on the other hand, is an empty signifier of wealth. In and of itself it is worth little or nothing; its worth comes from representing exchange value. Not only, in other words, do we not know where it comes from, but it is in some sense false and valueless.

Much is made of the fact that we do not know the source of Ethan's money. The film hints at bank robbery several times, and the strange manner in which

Aaron notes that the gold is freshly minted, along with Ethan's dismissive response, increases our suspicions. Ethan's gold of dubious origins contrasts sharply with the value of Aaron's homestead within Ford's vision of the ideal community. After Aaron, Martha, and two of their children are killed and as Debbie (Natalie Wood) is held captive by the Comanche, Ethan introduces chaos into the supposedly orderly transition of the land under patriarchy. At one point in the film, after being wounded, he orders Marty Pawley (Jeffrey Hunter) to take down his dictated will. When he leaves the Edwards estate to Marty, the adopted son of the Edwards family, Marty flies into a rage, declaring Debbie to be Ethan's blood kin and the true heir to the land.[12] The manner in which Ethan acts here relates in a complex way to the film's separation of capitalism from ownership of the land. On the one hand, Ethan presumes his ownership of the land when he bequeaths it in his will but, on the other hand, his presumption of that ownership does not mark him as mercenary or greedy. He shows no interest in it for himself, except in determining who will inherit it.

If Ethan is cavalier about money, at the opposite end of the spectrum we find Jerem Futterman, a greedy trader who responds to a promise of a thousand-dollar reward in exchange for information about Debbie's whereabouts. Futterman's manner shows he cares nothing about the human drama of the kidnapped girl whose dress he has in his possession. He has no real desire to help Ethan find his niece. He only wants the reward money and drives a hard bargain, making Ethan pay in gold for his expenses and time in sending him a letter. When the deal is completed, he tries to get Ethan and Marty to spend the night so that they can spend more money. He offers cards and a jug and seems about to mention women when Ethan brusquely cuts him off and leaves. As Ethan leaves, Futterman greedily reminds him, "Don't forget my thousand dollars."

To clarify his significance in relation to capitalism, Futterman, who has been all but ignored in the critical literature, can be usefully compared not just with Ethan but with a number of other characters as well. Like Ethan, he is unmarried and in his own way poses a threat to the family model of the Edwardses, the Jorgensens, and other homesteaders. The Jorgensens are the family par excellence, even extending themselves to include Marty and, in the end, Debbie. When Ethan and Marty return home after the Jorgensens' son Brad has been killed in the search for Debbie and her sister Lucy, the conversation once again turns to the land. Lars, Brad's father, blames "this country" for his son's death, but Mrs. Jorgensen says the country is not evil. She sees their circumstances as part of a developing, historical process in which progress may require their "bones in the ground."

The Edwards and Jorgensen families are both idealized. Each is comprised of loving, hard-working parents and obedient children. The decency of these family members stands in stark contrast to Futterman's greedy, shady, and ultimately depraved behavior. Ownership of the land for the purpose of farming is associated with virtue and family values, and trading and money with greedy individualism and immorality. Baxter's claim that Aaron Edwards's death is justified because of the manner in which he hoards Ethan's money would be better applied to Futterman. Futterman literally dies because of his greedy association with money: he and his men die in an effort to ambush and rob Ethan and Marty. When Ethan takes his gold coins from Futterman's body, he does so not out of greed but out of a sense of justice. Aaron is more properly located between Ethan and Futterman in a ranking of contamination by association with money. On the one hand, as Baxter notes, he hoards the money Ethan throws at him, but, on the other hand, he is a hard-working, decent family man and homesteader. Ethan quite literally throws money at both Aaron and Futterman and both greedily accept it, but Aaron is not entirely adrift in the world of money and trading. Nor does his greed extend to murder.

Both gold coins and trading circulate throughout *The Searchers*. The potential treachery of trading is highlighted in a comic vein when Marty, thinking he is trading with the Comanche for trinkets, unknowingly acquires a wife. Near the end of the film, Ethan and Marty encounter a Mexican, Emilio Figueroa (Antonio Moreno), who, like Futterman, has information on Debbie's whereabouts. When they offer to pay him for his information, he, in contrast to Futterman, refuses the "blood money" they offer.

Ethan's coins appear five times: first when he throws them to Aaron, second when he throws them to Futterman, then when he reclaims them from Futterman's body, later when he offers to pay Figueroa for information, and finally when Reverend Captain Clayton tosses one in front of Ethan while trying to arrest him for robbing and murdering Futterman. As Ethan tosses Aaron the money, he says, "I expect to pay my way." Ethan's expectation that he pays for his brother's hospitality just as he must pay for Futterman's information marks him off from those truly tied to the land, who seem to live in a world without money. That Ethan's money returns to haunt him (when Clayton is about to arrest him) is a sign of its treachery. His money, whose origin is now in question, marks him as Futterman's murderer. We know he killed Futterman in self-defense and took back his own money. But money, unlike land, cannot be marked as being Ethan's; he "pays" his way in more ways than one by living in the world of circulating money rather than tying himself to the land. His oft-remarked inability to enter the home and join the family at the end of the film relates to this: Ethan wanders the way money circulates.

Homesteading the land is, of course, also associated with danger, as we see at the beginning of the film when the Edwards family is devastated by a Comanche attack. But this is danger of a different kind from that which comes with the circulation of money. The dangers associated with the land do not corrupt; they strengthen and ennoble the spirit and bind people together within a community. For urban Americans living in a money-based economy at the

Ethan Edwards attempts to buy information about the captive Debbie in
The Searchers (1956). Hank Worden, John Wayne, and Antonio Moreno.
Courtesy of The Lilly Library, Indiana University, Bloomington, Indiana.

time of the film's release, such a land/money opposition creates a nostalgic long-
ing for a mythic Western past.

Paradoxically, this tension between money and community runs throughout Ford's sound Westerns. Although the expanding Western communities he
celebrates were historically part of a capitalist economy, Ford marks money and
capitalism as distasteful at best and treacherous at worst. In *Stagecoach*, Ford's
first sound Western, this is made explicit. The banker, Gatewood (Berton
Churchill), is the evil figure inevitably associated with money. A banker absconding with his community's savings is the ideal figure to embody Ford's paradoxical
notion of capitalism. Critics have often noted that nearly everyone in *Stagecoach*
has some redeeming qualities, even such generally unsympathetic figures as Lucy
(Louise Platt) and Hatfield (John Carradine). Gatewood is the exception. Place
notes, "Gatewood, the banker, is the 'bad' character who constantly reminds
us how human the others are."[13] Stowell declares, "His [Gatewood's] entire being
is the antithesis of Ford's values."[14] These critical responses to Gatewood are,
I think, correct, and are evidence of just how much Ford despises characters
associated with money. Clutching his money bag to himself, Gatewood is indeed one-dimensionally villainous. Although he is living proof to the contrary,
he even pompously declares that what's good for business is good for America.

Noting that Gatewood is one of two characters that were added to the story upon which the film is based, Edward Buscombe places Gatewood within the historical and political context of the Great Depression, somewhat as the *Cahiers* editors do with Lincoln. He also notes, "Bankers are rarely accorded much respect in Westerns."[15] And while this is undoubtedly true, the fact is that Gatewood's villainy is linked to something more specifically Fordian and less historical—an abiding contempt for money that, I will argue, goes well beyond either the historical context of the Roosevelt administration or the usual Western genre treatment of bankers. Ford's suspicion of those associated with money is part of a pattern common both in the Western and in Hollywood cinema in general, though he inflects and develops it in a complex and sometimes unique manner. Ford's hostility toward money links Gatewood to the sutlers in *Fort Apache* and *She Wore a Yellow Ribbon*, Uncle Shiloh Clegg in *Wagon Master*, and Futterman in *The Searchers*.[16] These films were made over a number of years and do not reference a specific historical economic context such as the Great Depression.

In *Fort Apache*, Meacham (Grant Withers), an unscrupulous Indian agent, is at the center of one major scene. When the cavalry arrive at his store, the U.S. flag is not properly displayed. The dwelling is such a low structure that it appears that Meacham lives in a hole in the ground, like an animal. When Lieutenant Colonel Thursday (Henry Fonda) and his officers and men enter, it is

Capitalism at its most vile: the Indian agent Meacham answers to Captain York and Colonel Thursday in *Fort Apache* (1948). John Wayne, Grant Withers, and Henry Fonda.

Courtesy of The Lilly Library, Indiana University, Bloomington, Indiana.

dark and dank. Instead of beef, Meacham sells the Apache rot-gut whiskey, useless trinkets, and rifles. Even the scale used for weighing beef is rigged to cheat his customers. His mistreatment of the Indians justifies their leaving the reservation and leads to the massacre of Thursday's troops. The manner in which Colonel Thursday addresses Meacham sums up just how vile his character is: "Mr. Meacham, you're a blackguard, a liar, a hypocrite, and a stench in the nostrils of honest men. If it were in my power, I'd hang you from the nearest tree, leave your carcass for the buzzards."

Meacham is a minor character who is not even essential to the plot; all we need to know is that the Apache have been mistreated and are on the warpath. The scene with Meacham, however, etches details of his depravity in the viewer's mind. Seeing him and the filthy conditions in which he lives personifies his greedy evil. Associated with a corrupt "Indian ring," he embodies the group to which he belongs. His greed is the cause of the problems in the film. Indeed, he is so distasteful that something very interesting happens to Colonel Thursday in the scene—he becomes a "good" character. Throughout much of *Fort Apache*, Thursday is an unpleasant character. He is contrasted with the highly likable Captain York (John Wayne), with whom he is frequently at odds. Meacham is so despicable, however, that here Thursday emerges as an admirable figure with whom we identify. At this moment, he and York are in full agreement about Meacham's character.

In *She Wore a Yellow Ribbon*, Karl Rynders (Harry Woods), the fort sutler, sells rifles to the Indians. He has an extremely small role and is seen in only two scenes. Near the beginning of the film, we see him and a companion suspiciously prepare to leave the fort in a wagon. We only see them for a few seconds and they do not speak. They reappear in the scene when Captain Brittles (John Wayne), Lieutenant Pennell (Harry Carey Jr.) and Sergeant Tyree (Ben Johnson) watch from a distance as Rynders tries to sell rifles to the Indians. When his translator tells him that Red Shirt (Noble Johnson) says fifty dollars is too much to pay for a rifle, Rynders speaks his only lines in the film: "Too much, huh? Tell that grandson of a horse thief that I know he's got the money from the paymaster's box. Tell him I know he killed Major Cheadle. And tell him it's fifty dollars or no rifles." We then see him shot with an arrow. His companion, after being wounded, is thrown onto a fire alive. Their graphic deaths seem like just punishment for their heinous capitalist crimes.

The brief Rynders subplot bears comparison with the Meacham subplot in *Fort Apache*. From a strictly dramatic point of view, Rynders is not essential to the plot either. The film could once again simply present the Indians as armed and ready for warfare. How they got their arms or who in particular sold them their guns is not central. The fact that Rynders speaks only one line is evidence of his marginality within the film's dramatic structure. Ideologically, however, Rynders is crucial. His economic greed, like Meacham's, is a displacement onto a peripheral character of the fort's entire place within a larger capitalist economy. By making Rynders and Meacham so despicable, Ford situates the rest of the cavalry outside of capitalism.

As is typical of Ford, there is a moment in the comic subplot of *She Wore a Yellow Ribbon* that relates to money. When the troop presents Brittles with his retirement watch, he is told, "They all put in the hat for it, sir. Even Sergeant Hochbauer." What lightens the moment, of course, is precisely that Hochbauer (Michael Dugan) did contribute, for once placing community above self-interest. Red Shirt, the young Indian leader who prepares for war, is also associated with money. He robs the stage at the beginning and uses the stolen money to buy the rifles from Rynders. Money once again, then, not only circulates but does so in a purely destructive manner.

Wagon Master is another film filled with the negative circulation of money and trading. Indeed, the beginning of the film offers little else. We first see the Clegg family when they rob a bank and kill a man in the process. When we first meet Sandy (Harry Carey Jr.) and Travis (Ben Johnson), the two horse traders who will later lead the wagon train on its journey, Travis tries to talk a town marshal into a horse trade. Later, when Sandy and Travis enter town, their conversation deals with the price they will get for the horses and the amount of their profit. Later still, when Elder Wiggs (Ward Bond), the leader of the Mormons, tries to buy their horses, Travis ups the price. When Wiggs offers to meet their price and pay them extra if Travis will become wagon master, he turns the offer down, declaring the mission too dangerous and announcing that he and Sandy have been planning on playing cards.

Initially, then, Sandy and Travis are associated with trading and money in a manner usually reserved for Ford villains. Travis has even cheated the Indians. What saves Sandy and Travis is precisely the manner in which they give up that association to link themselves instead with the Mormon homesteaders. They do not join the wagon train out of mercenary motives but, rather, out of humanitarian ones. They see Wiggs leading his group in the wrong direction, where there is no water. Although they maintain the pretense of a business deal, they act out of genuine concern for the homesteaders. As it does for Lincoln, a commitment to community and homesteaders overrides their strict self-interest. They want to stay in town and play cards, but instead they leave with the wagon train. The journey totally transforms them, and the last image we see of them has each driving a wagon, seated next to a woman with whom he is romantically paired. They have abandoned trading and gambling for family, farming, and the land.

The Cleggs, on the other hand, continually act only on the basis of the most intense, immoral self-interest, of which robbing a bank and killing a man are only the beginning. Uncle Shiloh Clegg (Charles Kemper), the leader of the outlaw family, always puts his clan's self-interest above that of the larger group. When one of his sons is caught forcing himself upon an Indian woman, he prefers

Uncle Shiloh Clegg covets gold, while the Mormons are interested only in grain.
Ward Bond, Charles Kemper, and Hank Worden in *Wagon Master* (1950).
Courtesy of The Lilly Library, Indiana University, Bloomington, Indiana.

a fight to the peaceful solution of having his son whipped as just punishment
for his behavior.

In a scene that sums up much of this, Travis informs Wiggs that he doesn't
think the Mormons' grain wagon can survive the rugged trail ahead. Wiggs
replies, "That grain is more valuable to us than gold itself." He is interrupted
by the ominous entrance of Uncle Shiloh, who remarks, "Did I hear somebody
mention gold? Gold always interests me. You got gold in this wagon train,
Elder?" The manner in which he covets money rather than the seed associated
with the land pits him directly against Wiggs and makes him one of the most
explicitly capitalist characters within this Fordian dichotomy. Like Futterman,
he is totally without scruples, even attempting to murder Travis while pretending to mourn the death of his sons in a gunfight.

All of these characters tied to money, then, are despicable and immoral, even
to the point of disregarding the lives of others or directly causing their deaths.
Gatewood demands that the stagecoach continue its perilous journey without
regard to anyone's well-being (including, ironically, his own), his sole motivation being that, should they return to Tonto, he will be arrested for theft; the
sutler in *Fort Apache* mistreats the Apache in a manner that leads them to break
the treaty; Rynders attempts to sell guns to the Apache, who will then use those
guns to kill the soldiers of the fort community of which he is a member; Uncle
Shiloh Clegg puts his greed above the entire party of homesteaders and even
kills one of them in cold blood. His behavior is typical of those in Ford's films
who trade in money rather than tie themselves to the land and community.

In *She Wore a Yellow Ribbon*, Mrs. Abbey Allshard (Mildred Natwick), the wife of the post commander, remarks on the many gardens she has planted while in the cavalry. She has always had to move on before they have grown to fruition. Ford critics have often remarked on the desert/garden antinomy in Ford's Westerns, and while that antinomy does function in relation to the theme of civilizing the Western landscape, at times it has an additional function: gardeners are tied to the land. Mrs. Allshard's gardens show that even the cavalry community has a special relationship to the land. Although forced to move on, they desire to root themselves. Brittles's daily visits to his wife's grave, where he waters the flowers, similarly tie him to the land in spirit.

In opposition to the evil characters associated with money (Meacham, Rynders, Uncle Shiloh Clegg, Futterman) are Peter and Nora Ericson (John Qualen and Jeanette Nolan), the owners of Peter's Place restaurant in *The Man Who Shot Liberty Valance*. In what appears to be nothing but a typical bit of Fordian comic business, a running gag throughout the film has them giving Link Appleyard, the marshal, steaks on credit. A blackboard full of Xs shows how many steaks the Ericsons have given Appleyard on credit. Clearly the Ericsons will never be paid; they are, for all practical purposes, giving the steaks away, and they are giving them away to a marshal who does not even protect them! As such, they are reminiscent of Abe Lincoln the shopkeeper in *Young Mr. Lincoln*. They give credit not because it is good business (any fool can see that Appleyard is simply eating himself further and further into debt, as it were), but because they care about people. Indeed, their business is less of a real business than a home. It is an extended family unit that includes Hallie, the waitress, who is more of a daughter figure; Ransom Stoddard, whom they virtually adopt; and townspeople such as Tom Doniphon and Appleyard, as well as Peabody, the newspaper editor. Doniphon regularly enters through the back door, and scenes of him and Stoddard with the Ericsons create a sense that this is more a family gathered in the family kitchen than a business. It is within this context that the free steaks for Appleyard are crucial, for in Ford's world the only good capitalist is one who shows no concern for money and virtually gives things away. In other words, Ford presents a fantasy of capitalism where the very profit motive that drives it is absent, replaced by an idealistic sense of family and community.

In writing of *Fort Apache*, Gallagher observes, "A Kubrick applies placeboes to our consciences, showing us that evil, warped men cause evil; but Ford makes us uncomfortable, showing us that fine, noble people cause evil."[17] This may be true of Captain York and Lieutenant Colonel Thursday, fundamentally decent men whose sense of duty leads them to perform questionable actions. It is, however, the opposite as regards capitalists—Ford's films relentlessly and almost obsessively represent the evils of capitalism as resulting solely from evil, one-dimensional men. There is nothing "fine" about Gatewood, Silas Meacham,

Karl Rynders, Uncle Shiloh Clegg, or Jerem Futterman. They are quite literally the scum of the earth, and it is here, in regard to representing money and capitalism, that Ford's ideology breaks the veneer of complexity that, as Gallagher quite rightly points out, governs other aspects of his films. I cannot think of one complex figure of capitalism in all of Ford's Westerns. In the real world, the good capitalists like Lincoln and the Ericsons would be out of business in no time. All the greedy, corrupt sutlers, Indian agents, traders, and bank robbers personify evil itself, leaving no need or even room to represent the institution of capitalism. If York, for example, is a complex figure torn between duty and personal beliefs in *Fort Apache,* Meacham is as simple as they come. The same holds true for Brittles in comparison to Rynders and Ethan Edwards in comparison to Futterman. Where capitalism is concerned, Ford does indeed want us to believe that all its evils are caused by evil men. Any and all of them could speak Uncle Shiloh's line: "Gold *always* interests me."

As I noted above, Edward Buscombe observes that bankers in general are not respected in Westerns. His observation points to the need to pay more attention to this aspect of the entire genre. Not just bankers but railroad tycoons and businessmen are frequently portrayed in a negative light as greedy, immoral people lacking decent human values such as compassion, honesty, and loyalty. Some Westerns simply use money as a motivating plot device by means of bank robberies or stagecoach and train hold-ups. *The Great Train Robbery* (1903) fits and may initiate this pattern. Nevertheless, such important Western directors as Anthony Mann and Howard Hawks adhere to this conventional aspect of the Western genre in quite distinctive ways. Ford's concern with money differs from those of both Hawks and Mann and the differences are illustrative of the ideology of capitalism in Ford's Westerns.

Anthony Mann's *Bend of the River* (1952) provides an interesting example, since in some ways it resembles *Wagon Master.* A businessman strikes a deal with homesteaders to use his boat to help them reach their destination, promising that supplies he has sold them will follow before winter. Even though the homesteaders pay for the goods and their survival in the wilderness is contingent on them, the supplies never arrive. The homesteaders learn that the businessman refuses to release their supplies because gold has been discovered. The goods he sold the homesteaders are now worth much more if he resells them to prospectors so they can hunt gold. This development leads to many plot complications, including the death of the businessman. When he is killed, fighting a group of homesteaders for the supplies, a gunfighter (Arthur Kennedy) cynically remarks, "It's too bad. He seemed like a real nice fella." Jeremy Vale, the leader of the homesteaders (Jay C. Flippen), replies, "He was, until they found gold."

Later, miners try to buy the supplies from the homesteaders en route to the settlement. Jeremy Vale tells the miners, "I'm afraid our food is not for sale."

"Why not?" asks one of the miners. "Because it's more important than money. It means a new life for one hundred people. I don't suppose you can understand me but I can't take money for people's lives." The gunfighter, who has temporarily sided with the homesteaders, tempts the central character of the film (James Stewart) by asking him, "What would you rather have, a hundred thousand dollars or a thank you somebody'll take back in a few weeks?" Not surprisingly, shortly after that the gunfighter treacherously turns on the homesteaders. He plans to profit off their goods in the gold camp.

Clearly, this film opposes the decency of the homesteaders associated with family and the land to the treachery of those associated with money. Nevertheless, money functions quite differently in the film than it does in *Wagon Master*. Mann is much more interested in the psychological drama that the money precipitates than he is in the role money or capitalism plays in the communities settling the West. In this film, the temptation of money turns good men (like the businessman) into evil men and reformed men with a past (like the gunfighter) into villains, while enabling the hero, another reformed outlaw, to prove that men can change. Money also becomes the pretext for staging scenes of Western action. In fact, in this film most of the action sequences grow out of fights over money or the value of goods. This combination of psychological intensity and Western action supplies the focus of *Bend of the River*.

The situation is nearly reversed in *Wagon Master*. Ford's primary interest is in the homesteaders and their quest to settle the land. Although money leads to a short fight scene, it is not the cause of extensive action. In fact, money seldom functions primarily as a pretext for action in Ford's Westerns. Nor is he particularly interested in the psychological aspects of monetary temptation. For Ford, money is a necessary evil that enables him to purge his heroes and their communities of association with it. For example, his 1948 film *3 Godfathers* begins with a bank robbery that does supply a scene of brief Western action. Three central characters, including John Wayne, rob a bank. Shortly after making their getaway, they encounter a woman abandoned in the desert. After helping her give birth, the men promise the dying mother that they will be godfathers to her child. The rest of the film focuses on their selfless devotion to their godson as they attempt to deliver him to safety. They instantly forget the money they have stolen. In fact, the money almost inexplicably disappears from the film. At one point, their horses escape and we can surmise that the stolen money was in a saddlebag, but no one says a word about it. Indeed, the only reference in the film to the money is a brief image of one of the men tossing a bag to another as they flee the bank. The men themselves are never identified with money, let alone greed. In this regard they are identical to the heroes in *Wagon Master* who totally commit themselves to community and abandon their initial identification with and desire for money.

If money functions primarily within a psychological context and as a pretext for male action within Mann's Westerns, it functions primarily within the dynamics of the male group and male action in Howard Hawks's Westerns. The entire elaborate opening action sequence of *Rio Lobo* (1970), for example, is structured around robbing a gold shipment on a train. For my present purposes, however, *Red River* (1948) probably serves as the best Hawks Western to compare with Ford's work, since it narrates a story of the role of cattle ranching in settling the West. Furthermore, the screenplay was co-written by Borden Chase and based on his story "The Chisolm Trail"; Chase also wrote the screenplay for Mann's *Bend of the River.* Thomas Dunson (John Wayne) takes land in Texas away from its Mexican owner because, in the words of another character, it's too much land for one man to own. Dunson builds an empire on this land, only to find years later that his cattle are worthless. In the aftermath of the Civil War there is no money left in Texas, so Dunson decides to take the cattle on a dangerous journey to Missouri, where there is a market for the beef.

For three bank robbers, selfless devotion purges a desire for money. John Wayne, Pedro Armendáriz, and Harry Carey Jr. in *3 Godfathers* (1948).
Courtesy of The Lilly Library, Indiana University, Bloomington, Indiana.

Once again, cattle ranching and money are somewhat opposed. We're told that Dunson can't deal well with the situation because there is no person he can fight who embodies the evil—there simply isn't money. As before, money is the problem. Furthermore, far from making him appear like a selfish businessman, the film glorifies the manner in which Dunson appropriates the land. Still, if Mann's interest is in the psychological intensity precipitated by the situation, Hawks's interest is in the male bonding among the central characters, who are isolated by the long cattle drive. This bonding includes a father/son drama enacted by Dunson and the young man Matthew Garth (Montgomery Clift) he "adopted" as a boy years earlier, and a relationship of rivalry fraught with homoerotic overtones between Garth and "Cherry," a young, unproven gun-fighter (John Ireland) on the drive.

Even when Hawks's films seem to have a social-historical context—as do *Scarface* (1932), set in the Great Depression, and *Red River,* set during the settling of the West—that context is so minimized that it becomes little more than a pretext for examining the dynamics of the male group and the place of women in it. The cattle drive in *Red River* is very close to the fog that isolates the char-acters in *Only Angels Have Wings* (1939) and the economic depression in *Scarface* that does little more than isolate the gangsters as a criminal subcul-ture. Even the Civil War and its aftermath in *Rio Lobo* are only of interest in-sofar as they relate to the dynamics of male bonding and the awkward place of a woman who joins a group of war veterans on a mission.

It is important, then, to situate Ford's representation of money and capital-ism within a larger context. On the one hand, his ideology of money and capi-talism is quite ordinary both within the classical Hollywood cinema in general and in the Western genre in particular. Neither Hollywood nor Westerns are known for depicting wonderful bankers. On the other hand, as even this brief comparison with Hawks and Mann indicates, different directors use and in-flect these stock figures and elements of the Western in quite different ways. Ford is interested in money and its relationship to the ideal community in a way that Mann and Hawks aren't. Furthermore, in a film like *The Searchers,* as we have seen, he elaborately develops it, along with such related things as trading. In this case, it occupies a central place within his film, and is far more than a pre-text for scenes of Western action. We need to examine the role of money and capitalism in Westerns more carefully, moving beyond generalizations about character types.

Even when Ford reverses himself in *Cheyenne Autumn* and acknowledges the role of money and capitalism in the West, he does so in a brief, flat, one-dimensional manner.[18] The Wyatt Earp (James Stewart) of *Cheyenne Autumn* appears in only one sequence and has no more complexity than Gatewood, Meacham, Rynders, or Futterman. As many critics have noted, he is a simple inverse of the mythic, legendary Western figure and the hero of Ford's own *My*

Darling Clementine (1946). In that film, Ford even represses the fact that, as Paula Marks has shown, the Earps came to Tombstone as businessmen trying to make money.[19]

William Luhr has situated Ford's shifting representation of Earp between 1946 and 1961 within a larger pattern that relates both to the history of the genre and to historical social and cultural changes within the United States.[20] Not surprisingly within this context, Ford's Wyatt in *Cheyenne Autumn* is corrupt; he is on the take and gets a share of all of Tombstone's gambling business. *Cheyenne Autumn* is Ford's last Western, and in making Wyatt Earp the greedy figure associated with money, Ford at least implicitly acknowledges that money and greed lie not at the margins but, rather, at the center of the building of the American West. Who could be more central to that West than the legendary Wyatt Earp? Whereas Ethan showed no interest in playing cards at Futterman's, Earp shows no interest in anything *but* playing cards. Unlike Sandy and Travis in *Wagon Master* and even Hatfield in *Stagecoach,* he is irritated by anything that interrupts gambling and diminishes his winnings.

In a sense John Ford's West recapitulates a central element of the rise of capitalism in Europe and the western world. With the rise of a money-based economy and the belief that a camel had a better chance of passing through the eye of a needle than a rich man had of going to heaven, European Christians distanced themselves from this new form of wealth. Ford's corrupt sutlers, traders, and bankers are the very epitome of this kind of reasoning: Ford, for example, creates the category "corrupt sutler" so that the cherished Seventh Cavalry remains untainted by the evils of money. We learn from Lieutenant Cohill (John Agar) in *She Wore a Yellow Ribbon* that, unlike Pennell, who was born with a silver spoon in his mouth, the cavalry regulars have to draw their meager pay just to survive. Too much wealth is a sign of the dreaded evils of money. No one should ever care about money; they should care about the ideals of family and community, as embodied, for example, in the cavalry.

Ford needs to create a category of money handlers, the very existence of which helps purify the rest of the society.[21] Predictably, the heroes within that society, from the mythic Lincoln to the all-too-human and troubled Ethan Edwards, care little for money. For Ford the West is won by families who care not for money but for the land, and by the cavalry that selflessly fights to protect those settlers on the land. The families and the cavalry are all noble and without greed. Unfortunately, or perhaps fortunately for this ideology, the selfless nobility of the settlers and the cavalry is marred by the Futtermans, Cleggs, Meachams, and Rynders of the world, who represent the role of money, greed, and capitalism in the settling of the West that is otherwise totally repressed and lost in this account.[22] To redeploy the cliché about the vanishing West in the Western genre, it could be said that it is not only the West that vanishes in Ford's films, but also the true nature of capitalism.

NOTES

I would like to thank Matthew Bernstein, Gaylyn Studlar, William Luhr, and Melanie Magisos for their many insightful suggestions for revision.

1. Lindsay Anderson, *About John Ford* (London: Plexus, 1981); Tag Gallagher, *John Ford: The Man and His Films* (Berkeley: University of California Press, 1986); Peter Lehman, "Texas 1868/America 1956: *The Searchers*," in *Close Viewings: An Anthology of New Film Criticism*, ed. Peter Lehman (Tallahassee: Florida State University Press, 1990): 387–415; Peter Lehman, "John Ford and the Auteur Theory" (Ph.D. diss., University of Wisconsin, Madison, 1978); William Luhr and Peter Lehman, *Authorship and Narrative in the Cinema: Issues in Contemporary Aesthetics and Criticism* (New York: G. P. Putnam's Sons, 1977); Joseph McBride and Michael Wilmington, *John Ford* (New York: Da Capo Press, 1975); J. A. Place, *The Western Films of John Ford* (Secaucus: Citadel Press, 1974); and Andrew Sarris, *The John Ford Movie Mystery* (Bloomington: Indiana University Press, 1975).

2. John Baxter, *The Cinema of John Ford* (New York: A. S. Barnes, 1971), 79–80.

3. Baxter, *The Cinema of John Ford*, 81.

4. Baxter, *The Cinema of John Ford*, 44.

5. Peter Stowell, *John Ford* (Boston: Twayne, 1986), 55.

6. It is worth noting the reception of the *Cahiers* analysis in Gallagher's and Stowell's books. Gallagher focuses on the manner in which the *Cahiers* critics see Lincoln as a Republican and as more of a monster than a man, made inhuman by the Law he imposes on himself and others. Gallagher notes "the tendency of Frenchmen to oversimplify America" and vehemently rejects the "*Cahiers*' psycho-Marxist ideology [that] particularly misses the dialectical complexities of the Lincoln myth" (*John Ford*, 171). Gallagher then explicates that myth, but—not surprisingly—in so doing he never takes up the issues of trading and money.

Stowell's response is more complex. Like Gallagher, Stowell rejects the *Cahiers* notion that the film is part of a Republican campaign to get rid of President Franklin Roosevelt. Stowell does praise the *Cahiers* essay as "monumental and stimulating" and calls it "one of the landmarks of semiotic *explication du texte*" (*John Ford*, 35). Stowell's essay is commendable for not throwing the baby out with the bath water; however, Stowell notes, "What these French, Marxist-oriented editors failed to see is that the film's ideology is rooted in democracy, not capitalism, nor even republicanism" (35). Even if this is true (I'm not sure what it means to say a film's ideology is "rooted" in something), it misses an important corollary: there *is* an ideology of capitalism in Ford's films, and that ideology should be analyzed. Both Gallagher and Stowell overtly characterize the *Cahiers* editors as being foreign and Marxist, implying that for these reasons they miss something quintessentially American about the film that U.S. critics (such as themselves) are more likely to understand. I am not comfortable with such a dichotomy, and it may be no coincidence that French Marxists initiated major attention to the role of money, trading, and capitalism in Ford's films while American critics have ignored or minimized it.

7. Editors of *Cahiers du cinéma*, "John Ford's *Young Mr. Lincoln*," rpt. in *Narrative, Apparatus, Ideology: A Film Theory Reader*, ed. Philip Rosen (New York: Columbia University Press, 1986), 459.

8. Editors of *Cahiers du cinéma*, "John Ford's *Young Mr. Lincoln*," 462.

9. Editors of *Cahiers du cinéma*, "John Ford's *Young Mr. Lincoln*," 462.

10. Baxter, *The Cinema of John Ford,* 151.

11. Roland Barthes, *S/Z,* trans. Richard Miller (New York: Hill and Wang, 1974), 39–40.

12. Ethan may challenge the orderly patriarchal inheritance of land in an even more fundamental manner. As I have argued elsewhere ("Texas 1868"), *The Searchers* leaves many central narrative questions unanswered, such as whether Ethan is or is not a bank robber. For my students year after year, chief among those unanswered questions is the paternity of both Debbie and Marty. Ethan's past romantic relationship with Martha, combined with the fact that he was present around the time of Debbie's birth, all imply that he could be their father. Indeed, his obsession with Debbie could further foster such a reading. But he is also oddly obsessed with Marty. First, he downplays Martha's account of how Ethan saved Marty as a little boy. Perhaps protesting too much, Ethan declares that it just happened to be him, that he came along at the right time, and that nothing should be made of it. Even more oddly, later in the film Ethan informs Marty that he recognized Marty's mother's scalp among Scar's war trophies. If he just happened along and had no particular relationship with Marty's mother, why should he instantly recognize her scalp many years later? Could his desire to leave the land to Marty mean he is Marty's father?

While there are no clear answers to any of these questions, one thing is clear: Ethan brings disorder into the patriarchal passing on of land. Obviously, if he has fathered either Debbie or Marty, he is guilty of such disruption, but even if he has not fathered either of them, he is still guilty in leaving the land to Marty rather than acknowledging that it is the property of Aaron's and Martha's living, albeit now Comanche, daughter, Debbie.

13. Place, *The Western Films,* 33.

14. Stowell, *John Ford,* 29.

15. Edward Buscombe, *Stagecoach* (London: British Film Institute, 1992), 29.

16. In *Sergeant Rutledge* (1960), a black cavalry officer is falsely accused of rape and murder. The villain, however, turns out to be the fort sutler.

17. Gallagher, *John Ford,* 253.

18. Ford had previously introduced a corrupt marshal in the James Stewart character in *Two Rode Together,* but that film conforms to the patterns of the previous Westerns in two significant ways. Although he starts out interested in money, the marshal mends his ways and falls in love, a transformation that is marked as complete when he literally throws money away and leaves town on a stagecoach with his wife-to-be. The marshal's cynical greed helps the viewer idealize the cavalry. Richard Widmark's character, a career officer, is constantly marked as pure, idealistic, and poor—he acts out of noble motives and enthusiastically embraces his life of little money or material wealth. Furthermore, Widmark's commanding officer condemns the marshal's mercenary motives. The cavalry is untouched by capitalist greed and is glorified, in contrast to its depiction in *Cheyenne Autumn.*

19. Paula Mitchell Marks, *And Die in the West: The Story of the O.K. Corral Gunfight* (New York: Touchstone, 1989).

20. William Luhr, "Reception, Representation, and the O K Corral: Shifting Images of Wyatt Earp," in *Authority and Transgression in Literature and Film,* ed. Bonnie Braendlin and Hans Braendlin (Gainesville: University Presses of Florida, 1996).

21. Although historically Jews fulfilled that function, Ford's films are not anti-Semitic and his greedy capitalists are generally not marked or identified as Jewish.

22. Not surprisingly, Ford's most direct treatment of the evils of capitalism as an institution occurs not in a Western but, rather, in *The Grapes of Wrath*. *The Grapes of Wrath* reverses the ideal communities of the Westerns—the problem is precisely that there are no evil individuals to hold responsible for the farmers' losing their land. A frustrated man whose land has been repossessed by the bank desperately asks who he should shoot and is dismayed to learn that no one is responsible—the bankers, along with everyone else, are just doing their jobs. *The Grapes of Wrath*, in other words, lacks a character like Gatewood in *Stagecoach* who is the literal embodiment of evil. The film refuses to embody evil and so holds the larger system responsible.

If America in 1940 supplies Ford with a capitalist dystopia of community in relationship to money and the land, the seemingly timeless, precapitalist Ireland of *The Quiet Man* (1952) supplies him with a utopia. The relationship of the representation of capitalism in Ford's Westerns to that in his non-Westerns is beyond the scope of this essay, but it is illuminating to briefly consider *The Quiet Man*, another Ford film in which money plays a central role. In many ways the Ireland of *The Quiet Man* resembles Ford's idealized West—it is a precapitalist, feudal society with wealth tied not to money but to the land. John Wayne plays an American seeking refuge in this seemingly idyllic land after killing a man for money in the boxing ring. He fails, however, to understand the role of money, especially as a marriage dowry, in such a culture, misinterpreting marriage customs through a capitalist prism. At one point, like a typical Fordian Western hero, he purges himself of any association with money, greed, and capitalism. He hurls the dowry "fortune" into a fire.

6

PAINTING THE LEGEND

FREDERIC REMINGTON AND THE WESTERN

Edward Buscombe

At the end of John Ford's *Fort Apache* there is a scene in which Captain York (John Wayne) is discussing with a group of newspapermen the death of Colonel Thursday (Henry Fonda). "Of course you're familiar with the famous painting of Thursday's charge, sir," says the first newspaperman. "Yes, I saw it when last in Washington," replies York. "That was a magnificent work," says a second reporter. "There were these massed columns of Apaches in their warpaint and feathered bonnets. And here was Thursday, leading his men in that heroic charge." "Correct in every detail," confirms York. Though he knows the truth of Thursday's foolhardy action, York preserves the myth which the painting embodies: when the legend becomes fact, print the legend.

Despite the location of *Fort Apache* in Monument Valley, actually some six hundred miles as the crow flies from the Little Bighorn, the parallels between the fate of Colonel Thursday and that of General George Armstrong Custer are made explicit enough,[1] and in the scene just quoted we may assume that the scriptwriters have in mind the many versions of Custer's Last Stand which were painted in the wake of that traumatic event. Several of these pictures were reproduced in lithograph, and some 150,000 copies of that by Cassilly Adams are known to have been distributed. The dissemination of such works must have played a major part in the construction of one of the West's enduring legends.[2]

The history of the West has always been closely bound up with the forms of its representation—and misrepresentation; some of them, such as the myths of El Dorado and the Northwest Passage, so powerful that they determined the actual course of Western exploration. But in the later nineteenth century the construction of national mythologies became, in America as elsewhere, a major preoccupation.[3] The volume of material increased vastly under the pressures of massive expansion westward and the development of new means for the production and distribution of visual and written matter. The growth of mod-

ern communications, in the twin senses of railroads and newspapers, telescoped
the time gap between the occurrence of an event and its description, and magnified the tendency toward mythicization—to the extent that many of the most
famous figures became agents of their own publicity machine. Wild Bill Hickok
posed for his portrait in 1874 and in the same year Custer took an official
photographer along on his Black Hills expedition.[4]

In this process painting played a key role. Yet there has been little recognition of the controlling influence which visual images had upon the formation
of the idea of "the West" and subsequently upon the Western as a cinematic
genre. While due note has been taken of the importance of dime novels, plays,
and such extravaganzas as Buffalo Bill's Wild West Show, the place of painting
remains to be investigated.[5] Frederic Remington (1861–1909), probably the best
known of all painters of Western subjects, himself did a version of Custer's Last
Stand. Interestingly enough, a point to which we shall return, the mood of
Remington's picture is rather Fordian, stoicism and dignity in defeat contrasting with the frenzied heroics favored by other artists. John Ford is on record as

"The Last Stand" by Frederic Remington.
Originally published in *Harper's Weekly,* 10 January 1891.
Courtesy of the Woolaroc Museum, Bartlesville, Oklahoma.

having acknowledged Remington's influence. In his interview with Peter Bogdanovich, Ford remarks, "I like *She Wore a Yellow Ribbon*. I tried to copy the Remington style there—you can't copy him one hundred percent—but at least I tried to get in his color and movement, and I think I succeeded partly."[6] And according to McBride and Wilmington in their book on Ford, James Warner Bellah, the scriptwriter of *Sergeant Rutledge* and also the author of the stories on which Ford's cavalry trilogy is based, got the idea for a film about black cavalrymen from a Remington painting.[7]

But the relationships between Remington and the Western film genre are more far-reaching than a study of his direct and acknowledged effect upon its greatest exponent would reveal.[8] Remington in fact was to be closely involved in some of the decisive moments at which the image of "the West" became progressively focused. In order to understand the distinctive contribution which Remington made, however, we need briefly to unravel the three main strands which may be discerned within the extensive canvas of paintings of the West.

George Catlin is generally recognized as the first artist to devote himself seriously and single-mindedly to a visual record of life in the western territories. Catlin's motivation was primarily ethnographic, within the terms of a Rousseauesque conception of the nobility of the uncivilized. As he expressed it, "Black and blue cloth and civilization are destined, not only to veil, but to obliterate the grace and beauty of Nature. Man, in the simplicity and loftiness of his nature, unrestrained and unfettered by the disguises of art, is surely the most beautiful model for the painter—and the country from which he hails is unquestionably the best study or school of the arts in the world: such I am sure, from the models I have seen, is the wilderness of North America."[9] Catlin, who was self-taught, certainly had no other school, and his pictures document, in a primitive style, scenes of the material, cultural, and spiritual life of the Native Americans he encountered on his travels west of the Missouri in the 1830s. They enjoyed a considerable success as a traveling exhibition and Catlin later supplemented them with a collection of artifacts and some of his live subjects in authentic costume. This early precursor of the Wild West Show was taken by Catlin to Europe, and in 1845 Eugène Delacroix visited the display in Paris, accompanied by George Sand, and made some sketches.

Yet even before this date Europeans had begun to paint the West. Of the next two important painters after Catlin, one, Karl Bodmer, was a Swiss and later a member of the Barbizon school of French painting, while the other, Alfred Jacob Miller, though American, had trained in Paris, where he had become an admirer of Delacroix. Both these artists were hired as official painters on expeditions financed by wealthy Europeans in the 1830s, and in their work the pure and naive spirit of Catlin's ethnographic impulse mingles with the tourist's eye for the curious, the charming, and the unusual. Their pictures are an instance of what Jean-Louis Comolli has called the nineteenth century's "geographical extension of the field of the visible,"[10] as illustrators from Europe journeyed to record the discoveries of the explorers; partly in the interests of science, but partly to satisfy popular demand for artistic representations of the marvelous (science, art, and public entertainment being often aspects of the same thing at the time). Delacroix had himself produced a notable series of paintings following a trip to Morocco.[11] With Bodmer and Miller we have instead of the sensuality of the Orient the innocence of the West, but in each case it is the lure of the exotic which draws the artists.

The ethnographic impulse was never entirely effaced from Western painting (it is most strikingly embodied in the work of Seth Eastman for the first major achievement of American ethnography, Schoolcraft's *Indian Tribes of the United States, 1851–7*). Traces of it can be found in Remington and indeed in Western films. By the middle of the century, however, the scientific urge to document an authentic American culture, prominent in Catlin, more attenuated in Bodmer and Miller, had largely given way to a European-inspired rage for "Nature." A remarkably high proportion of the artists painting Western scenes in the 1850s and 1860s had studied in Düsseldorf, the center of German romantic art. Among them were Albert Bierstadt, Worthington Wittredge, George Caleb Bingham, Karl Wimar, and Emanuel Leutze, who painted the archetypal "Westward the Course of Empire Takes Its Way." Others, such as Thomas Moran, had trained elsewhere in Europe and fallen under the influence of Turner and Claude. Bierstadt and Moran especially gloried forth the sublime qualities of the Rockies and the desert landscapes, a panorama where the inhabitants figured, if at all, as tiny dots in the vastness of nature, which they subjected to European canons of taste. Bierstadt wrote back, "The mountains are very fine; as seen from the plains they resemble very much the Bernese Alps; they are of granite formation, the same as the Swiss mountains . . . the colors are like those of Italy."[12] At the top of Moran's painting "Glory of the Canyon" there is a rock formation which seems to be trying to turn itself into a ruined castle.

This admiration for a scene whose very attraction lay in its emptiness of the humanity which Catlin, Bodmer, and Miller had in their various ways depicted was in its turn to be overshadowed by a third regime in the last quarter of the century. Though Bierstadt achieved his greatest popularity during the 1860s, and continued working until 1900, by the end of this decade it was not the uplifting spectacle of natural grandeur, still less the sober documentation of vanishing cultures, which dictated the production of pictures. Instead, a new, far more popularly based taste, whose economic power was founded on the rise of mass circulation publications such as *Harper's Weekly* (begun in 1857), sent out a call for scenes portraying the excitement and immediacy of thrilling action. This was of course not entirely a nineteenth-century innovation; artists since the sixteenth century had viewed America as a land of violent confrontations. But in the last quarter of the nineteenth century, pictorial representations of "the

West" became overwhelmingly dominated by images of fierce struggles between man and man, and between man and nature.

Foremost among the artists who both catered to and produced this new taste was Frederic Remington, who in the less than thirty years of his active life from the early 1880s turned out over three thousand pictures, almost all of Western subjects. Remington and others like him, such as Charles Schreyvogel and Charles Russell, shifted the center of interest toward the drama and conflict which they perceived as the essence of frontier life. Remington claimed that his purpose was in a sense ethnographic: to document a way of life that was already in retreat. "I knew the railroad was coming. I saw men already swarming into the land. I knew the derby hat, the smoking chimneys, the cord-binder and the thirty-day note were upon us in a restless surge. I knew the wild riders and vacant land were about to vanish forever."[13] But though some of his pictures depict such subjects as "The Indian Game of Polo" and "Indian Method of Breaking a Pony," what he chiefly chose to record was the life of hard riding and hard fighting. The focus in his work is on the moment of action frozen at the point of its maximum impact. There is a marked tendency in Remington and his contemporaries toward the narrativization of painting; not surprisingly in view of the fact that so much of their work illustrated magazine stories and reportage about the West. Narrative in art may be nothing new, even in paintings of the West; some of Miller's work shows battles and chases. But even Remington's quieter compositions are founded on tension and suspense, while the most dramatic communicate a sense of action proceeding through time and irresistibly invite us to supply the story up to the moment the picture was "taken" or continue it afterward.

For such paintings the description "cinematic" seems not inappropriate, and Schreyvogel exploits this technique to the full. Indeed, he goes further: whereas Remington's figures characteristically proceed across the frame in long diagonals, Schreyvogel's frequently rush full tilt at the spectator, threatening to jump right out of the frame, and the trick of firing straight at the viewer anticipates the famous shot at the end of *The Great Train Robbery*.

Yet the relationship to cinematography is even closer than this suggests. Remington's first real success came in 1886 when he was commissioned by *Outing* magazine to illustrate an account of the so-called Apache War against Geronimo. It was just at this time that the experiments of Eadweard Muybridge in photographically recording the movements of animals were becoming widely known among painters. Muybridge's book *Animal Locomotion,* a milestone along the road to the cinema, was published in 1887 and among its subscribers were such eminent artists as Alma-Tadema, Millais, Rodin, Whistler, and Messonier, the painter of battle scenes. Messonier's picture of Napoleon on the field of battle, "Friedland 1807," was apparently modified by him in the light of Muybridge's revelations about the movement of the horse (that central icon

"A Misdeal" by Frederic Remington. Published in *Drawings,* 1897.
Photo Courtesy of Gerald Peters Gallery, Inc., Santa Fe, New Mexico.

of the Western scene) and Remington was greatly impressed by the result. Up until this point horses in full gallop had been represented with both front and back legs stretched full out. The success of the camera in recording what the naked eye could not perceive was capitalized on by Remington to impart a new realism to his work; he was reported to have "foresworn conventions and to (have) accepted the statement of the camera as his guide in the future."[14]

Received wisdom has it that the invention of photography shifted painting irrevocably onto the path which led to modernism. Once painting's function as a record of the visible world had been displaced by photography's superior claims to accuracy, so the argument runs, it was free to pursue formal experiment for its own sake.[15] But, even if this is so, "Western" painting chose the other path. Remington and others, breaking decisively with the European high art tradition which had dominated in the works of Bierstadt and Moran, developed a technique which, borrowing as it did from photography, was entirely at the service of making their subjects as "lifelike" as possible.[16] The implications of this for the cinema are suggestive. When Bazin calls the Western "the American cinema par excellence"[17] and when Godard says it is "the most cinematographic genre in the cinema"[18] each recognizes the centrality in dominant cinema, that is Hollywood, of action, of physical movement. It has been claimed that the Western, the first home-grown and successful genre in American cinema, affected the whole course of Hollywood, which might not otherwise have

"Downing the Nigh Leader" by Frederic Remington.
Originally published in *Collier's,* 20 April 1903.
Photo courtesy of the Buffalo Bill Historical Museum.

developed so rapidly and completely toward a form which privileged action above all else and hence, perhaps, secured its popularity.[19] However this may be, there can be little doubt that the photographically inspired realism with which paintings of the West in the period immediately prior to the invention of the cinema portrayed physical movement helped precipitate the Western as a popular cinema genre.

The case for the importance of painting in shaping the popular conception of the West is strengthened when one considers the rather different role played by photography. The invention of the cinema has conventionally been conceived as a development out of the chemical and technical discoveries of photography, even if more recent work has emphasized the contribution of machines for the production of visible movement, such as the phenakistoscope. Though it is true that painting could not actually reproduce movement, Remington's absorption of the lessons of Muybridge notwithstanding, in the provision of images of exciting action capable of capturing the popular imagination, images which would feed directly into the cinema, painting had several inestimable advantages over photography. In the first place, although some kinds of photographs of the West did achieve popularity (from the 1850s landscape photographs, especially in the form of stereoscopes, sold well to the middle classes), landscapes and portraiture were the only genres which photography could readily handle at this time.[20] The wet-plate collodion process, introduced in the 1850s, was capable of giving images of startling clarity, but it suffered from a crippling handicap: the equipment was unbelievably cumbersome. W. H. Jackson, the great landscape photographer of the 1870s, required a whole mule train to transport his camera, plates, and chemicals. It took him half an hour to set up for a single picture. Exposure times too were long. Despite the achievements during the 1880s of Muybridge and Marey (curiously in the present context Marey's photographic gun was based on the Colt revolver), the invention of the dry plate in the early 1880s and the genuinely portable camera at the end of this decade (Eastman's Kodak was patented in 1888), it was to be a long time before photography was both mobile and fast enough to capture action in the field.[21] Even by the end of the century, as Remington's own career demonstrates, newspapers still relied on sketch artists when a clear record of a battle was required.[22] If visual representations of stirring scenes of action were needed, only painting could supply them—until the invention of the cinema, in which were married both the summation of new techniques for photographing movement and the concept of restaging either real or imagined events.

The other great advantage which painting held over photography was that it could be mass-produced to a very high standard. Mention has already been made of chromolithography, which reached America in the 1840s and soon became a considerable industry, with literally millions of prints distributed in the years up to the end of the century.[23] Chromos, with Western scenes a particular favorite, were the only forms of visual art to hang in the homes of ordinary people and in their places of entertainment. Photographs, by contrast, were much more restricted in circulation. Daguerrotypes could not be reproduced at all. Even with the introduction of the wet-plate process, which made it possible to make more than a single print from a photograph, prints could not be used to illustrate books and newspapers. When *Harper's Weekly* began in 1857 it published photographs, but they had first to be transformed into woodcuts before they could be printed. By this date techniques for the faithful rendering of line drawings were well established and chromolithography in full swing. Not until the late 1880s was the modern half-tone process employed by *Harper's* to provide an accurate reproduction of photographs, and the process was not in general use for books and newspapers until nearly the end of the century. And still there was no equivalent to the vivid colors of the chromos.

By 1900, then, just at the moment when the cinema was ready to gather up into itself so many of the era's popular forms of entertainment, a whole plethora of ways of seeing and feeling, painting had created a taste for dramatic narrative and highly charged scenes of physical action, portrayed in a style whose realism was well adapted to the technical inheritance and popularly based social location of the new medium. But in so doing it narrowed the focus of what constituted "the West." Out of the vast potential range of heterogeneous material which western expansion had thrown up, painting helped construct a highly specific and distinctive articulation which henceforth became synonymous with the West. Painting, together with popular fiction, and commercial spectacles such as the Wild West Show, provided for the cinema an ample repertoire of stock types and narrative situations, but at the cost of limiting the scope. Certain geographical areas, certain types of people and situations became privileged, since these were the ones most adaptable to the exploitation of drama and conflict. One example will have to suffice. There are hardly any women at all in the paintings of Remington, Schreyvogel, and Russell. Where physical action became the center of the narrative, woman, defined by the nineteenth century as frail and passive, could not figure.[24] That women played a crucial, and at times strictly equal, role in the history of the West is attested in scores of documentary accounts.[25] That they were excluded from Western painting is an indication of how it selected and suppressed as it elaborated its field of discourse. In the cinema the inheritance of popular fiction and drama dictated that a place be found for women, yet of all film genres the Western is the one where women have the most marginal position.

A key moment in this process of distillation can be observed if we return to the career of Frederic Remington. There is a scene in *Citizen Kane* which takes place just prior to the beginning of the Spanish-American War in 1898. Bernstein reads out a cable which has just been received at the offices of the *Inquirer*: "'Food marvelous in Cuba—girls delightful stop could send you prose poems but don't feel right spending your money stop there's no war in Cuba signed Wheeler.' Any answer?" "Yes," says Kane. "'Dear Wheeler—you provide the prose poems—I'll provide the war.'" As is well known, the scene is closely based on an actual exchange between William Randolph Hearst and a correspondent he had sent to Cuba to cover the anticipated war. What is particular to our purpose is that the correspondent was Frederic Remington.[26]

The Spanish-American War had a direct influence upon the course of American domestic politics and, not coincidentally, upon the construction of "the West." The most famous figure to emerge from the conflict was Theodore Roosevelt.[27] Roosevelt had already acquired a reputation as a Westerner following his self-publicized exploits as a rancher, and Remington had illustrated his book *Ranch Life and the Hunting Trail* when it was serialized in *Century* in 1888. When war broke out with Spain, Roosevelt resigned his post as Assistant Secretary of the Navy to form a troop of cavalry. This troop, significantly dubbed the Rough Riders (a title previously used by Buffalo Bill for his performers), was composed largely of cowboys from the western states and a leavening of toffs from the smart clubs of New York. The Rough Riders were involved in the celebrated battle of San Juan Hill and Remington, present as a war correspondent, later painted a picture of Teddy leading the charge. It was not, unfortunately, "correct in every detail," since Teddy didn't actually take San Juan Hill, participating instead in a supporting action up nearby Kettle Hill, and cavalry were not employed since the terrain was unsuited to actions on horseback. But no matter; even if Remington's picture was more sober than some of the more imaginative portrayals produced by other artists, it was sufficiently in keeping with Teddy's view of the thing for it to decorate his account of the war published in 1903. Fittingly, at the ceremony to mark the disbanding of the Rough Riders, Teddy was presented with a cast of Remington's most famous bronze, "The Bronco Buster."

The fame engendered by his Cuban exploits undoubtedly helped Roosevelt secure the nomination as vice president in 1900, which led to his succession to the presidency when McKinley was assassinated the following year. The accession to the highest office in the land of the country's most visible Western and military hero can be said to have effected a seismological shift in the ideological construction of the West and its place in American cultural life. It fixed the West as the symbol of America's virility in contrast to the effete decadence of the old world. Specifically, Roosevelt brought before the public imagination a vision of a rough and ready army whose competence, based not upon the drill book but upon a whole way of life, was superior to the highly regimented and showy cohorts of the European powers (hence the scorn poured on Colonel Thursday's West Point training).

In this ideological shift, encapsulated in the political moment of Roosevelt, Remington undoubtedly played a part. Henceforth "the West" as an idea was both popular and culturally legitimate (a crucial combination, for without it would D. W. Griffith, ever the seeker after respectability, have made so many Westerns?). However, the view of the war which emerges from Remington's own writings is less than totally enthusiastic.[28] And his visual presentation of the cavalry, whether fighting Apache or Spaniards, generally lacks Roosevelt's swagger and bombast. In contrast to European battle scenes of the period his soldiers are weary and dusty, their uniforms battered. Instead of the might of a huge army they deploy only a thin line of blue. Ford's war films and Westerns alike are conceived in a similar spirit. *Rio Grande* ends, as it begins, with a cavalry column returning to the fort wounded and bedraggled, despite the victory that has been won. "Put out of your mind any romantic ideas that it's a way of glory," remarks Colonel York to his son. "It's a life of suffering and hardship." Ford's army, like Roosevelt's, is a place where the underdogs, the defeated Southerners, Irish immigrants, and the sons of ordinary NCOs can achieve dignity and self-respect alongside their supposed betters. Just as Teddy had united east and west, upper and lower classes, so Colonel Thursday's eastern snobbery is eventually overcome by the marriage of his daughter to the son of Sergeant Major O'Rourke. But what is different about both Remington and Ford, as exemplified in "The Last Stand" and *Fort Apache*, is that military glory belongs most truly to those who do not glory in it. This is why defeat is the apotheosis of triumph; only at the moment of his death against hopeless odds does Thursday achieve the heroic stature he had sought in victory.

"Charge of the Rough Riders at San Juan Hill" by Frederic Remington. Circa 1899. Courtesy of the Remington Art Museum, Ogdensburg, New York.

This paradox of a self-effacing inscription upon what *She Wore a Yellow Ribbon* calls "a cold page in the history books" can perhaps be related to a structure deep within American ideology. If the Spanish-American War marked the emergence of the United States onto the stage of world geopolitics (and the national myth of the West which Roosevelt helped construct served admirably to develop a growing national confidence), yet America was still able to present itself as an anti-imperialist power. This was possible because in the nineteenth century its imperialism had been internal, directed toward its own territory and the peoples who occupied it.[29] The variant of the Western myth which Remington and Ford represent, founded upon a popularly constituted soldiery and upon the glory attained by dignified defeat, may perhaps fit more easily with the anti-imperialist stance.

Critics who have attempted to relate the Western to movements in American society have generally preferred to connect the films to a particular set of conjunctural forces operating at the time of their production. Thus Will Wright sees plot structures as expressive of stages in the evolution of the capitalist

"The American Tommy Atkins in a Montana Blizzard" by Frederic Remington. Originally published in *Harper's Weekly,* 13 August 1892.
Courtesy of the Remington Art Museum, Ogdensburg, New York.

economy. Philip French reads films in terms of different political styles. John H. Lenihan finds that Westerns are really "about" such things as the Cold War.[30] All these approaches, whatever the ingenuity of their particular arguments, run the risk of short-circuiting a system of representation whose genesis actually predates the cinema and whose determinations and effectivity are therefore more extensive than such analyses propose. "The West," in the form in which we now have it, was essentially a nineteenth-century invention, and we cannot write the history of the cinema's treatment of the subject without taking this into account. This is not to say that the cinema merely reproduced what already existed; only that by the time Western films began to be made a corpus of work was in existence which already predefined what "the West" could be taken to mean. And to that work painting, especially the painting of Frederic Remington, made a decisive contribution.

NOTES

1. The second film in the cavalry trilogy, *She Wore a Yellow Ribbon,* opens with the words "Custer is dead."

2. See Robert Taft, *Artists and Illustrators of the Old West* (Princeton: Princeton University Press, 1982), 146.

3. Another notable example is Scotland, whose historical iconography was largely manufactured in the nineteenth century. See, for example, Colin McArthur, ed., *Scotch Reels* (London: British Film Institute, 1982).

4. For those with a taste for the byways of historical coincidence, Ford's *The Searchers* provides a labyrinthine example of the interconnections between the "real" West and the construction of its representations. The film was produced by Cornelius Vanderbilt Whitney, a distant descendant of the Eli Whitney who invented the system of mass-producing guns through the use of interchangeable parts and so provided cheap reliable weaponry for the conquest of the West. C. V. Whitney was also a cousin of the Gertrude Vanderbilt Whitney who founded the Whitney Gallery of Western Art in Cody, Wyoming, where some of Remington's pictures are preserved. McBride and Wilmington in their book on Ford (see below) speculate that the name of the hero of *The Searchers,* Ethan Edwards, is an amalgamation of Ethan Allen, the Revolutionary hero, and Jonathan Edwards, the preacher. They might have added that Eli Whitney was in fact married to Jonathan Edwards's granddaughter.

5. For discussions of popular literature and Wild West Shows see Henry Nash Smith, *Virgin Land* (New York: Vintage Books, 1950); John G. Cawelti, *The Six-Gun Mystique* (Bowling Green: Bowling Green University Popular Press, 1970); and essays by Kathryn Esselman and Richard W. Etulain in *Focus on The Western,* ed. Jack Nachbar (Englewood Cliffs: Prentice-Hall, 1974).

6. Peter Bogdanovich, *John Ford* (London: Studio Vista, 1967), 87.

7. Joseph McBride and Michael Wilmington, *John Ford* (London: Secker & Warburg, 1974), 164.

8. Though the parallels in the biographies of the two men are not without cultural resonances. Each abandoned university after a short period and lit out for the West;

each acquired a reputation for heavy drinking, gruff misanthropy, and awkwardness with women; both were fascinated by the military and became "war correspondents."

9. Quoted in Frank Getlein, *The Lure Of The Great West* (Waukesha, Wisconsin: Country Beautiful, 1973), 33.

10. Jean-Louis Comolli, "Machines of the Visible," in *The Cinematic Apparatus*, ed. Teresa de Lauretis and Stephen Heath (London: Macmillan, 1980), 122.

11. Remington was himself to make a trip to Morocco, where he painted Arab horses and French soldiers.

12. Quoted in William H. Goetzmann, *Exploration and Empire* (New York: Vintage Books, 1972), 225.

13. Quoted in G. Edward White, *The Eastern Establishment and the Western Experience* (New Haven: Yale University Press, 1968), 121.

14. In the *Brooklyn Eagle*, quoted in Gordon Hendricks, *Eadweard Muybridge: The Father of the Motion Picture* (London: Secker & Warburg, 1975), 202. I assume that Messonier is the same as the "Jean Louis Meissonier" referred to by Terry Ramsaye in *A Million and One Nights* (New York: Simon and Schuster, 1926), 38f. According to Ramsaye, it was Messonier who had the idea of projecting Muybridge's photographs in sequence, to create the illusion of movement, thus providing the essential link between Muybridge's still photographs and the cinema.

15. Not that it was ever that simple. Degas was greatly influenced by photography, while some kinds of photography actually became incorporated into an antinaturalistic style: "For artists working in the tradition of nineteenth-century naturalism the clarity of the Muybridge photographs was preferable to those of Marey. But for those seeking to obscure the literal identity of things, to give precedence to the more abstract realities of nature: the movements themselves rather than the objects in movement, the fundamental rhythms and patterns of the universe—so great a preoccupation in this century—Marey's images served admirably as a point of departure" (Aaron Sharf, *Art and Photography* [London: Allen Lane, 1968], 199).

16. Thus the Cowboy Artists of America, contemporary painters of Western subjects who would doubtless consider themselves the inheritors of the Remington tradition, pursue a style which has no points of contact at all with modern art.

17. André Bazin, *What Is Cinema?* vol. 2 (Berkeley: University of California Press, 1971), 141.

18. Jean Narboni and Tom Milne, *Godard On Godard* (London: Secker & Warburg, 1972), 117.

19. See Robert Anderson, "The Role of the Western Film in Industry Competition 1907–11," *Journal of the University Film Association* 31, no. 2 (Spring 1979).

20. Photography of the West was in any case itself greatly influenced by painting, the composition of the views taken owing much to artistic notions of what constituted a pleasing scene. The influence was then reciprocated; Bierstadt used photographs as the basis for some of his canvasses. See Weston J. Naef and James N. Wood, *Era of Exploration* (Boston: Albright-Knox Gallery and the Metropolitan Museum of Art, 1975).

21. Most of the information on photographic processes can be found in Robert Taft, *Photography and the American Scene* (New York: Dover Publications, 1964).

22. Photographs taken during the Spanish-American War are either of scenes comfortably behind the lines or, when farther forward, show only blurred figures in longshot. Artists' impressions were far more vivid.

23. See Peter Marzio, *The Democratic Art* (London: Scolar Press, 1980).

24. In earlier allegorical paintings, as for example those by Tiepolo in the middle of the eighteenth century, America was conventionally represented as a woman. Not until the arrival of Uncle Sam during the Civil War did the country change sex. See Hugh Honour, *The New Golden Land* (London: Allen Lane, 1975).

25. For a recent account see Sandra L. Myres, *Westering Women and the Frontier Experience, 1800–1915* (Albuquerque: University of New Mexico Press, 1982).

26. The actual exchange was "'Everything is quiet. There is no trouble here. There will be no war. I wish to return.'—Remington. 'Please remain. You furnish the pictures and I'll furnish the war.' —W. R. Hearst." Quoted in W. A. Swanberg, *Citizen Hearst* (New York: Charles Scribner's Sons, 1961), 127.

27. The general influence of Roosevelt upon the construction of "the West" has of course not gone unnoticed. See, for example, the study by G. Edward White, *Eastern Establishment*. White considers the role played by Roosevelt, Remington, and Owen Wister; yet inexplicably his comments on Remington are restricted to the painter's writings. Nothing is said directly about his pictures. Roosevelt is also cited as an important influence by Richard Etulain, "Cultural Origins of the Western," in *Focus on The Western*, 19–24, and an article by Raymond Durgnat and Scott Simon, "Six Creeds That Won The West," *Film Comment* 16, no. 5 (Sept./Oct. 1980), remarks in the course of a brisk romp through the historical roots of the Western's ideology that "Roosevelt's shadow falls long over John Ford." Kevin Brownlow in *The War, The West and The Wilderness* (London: Secker & Warburg, 1978) tells how Tom Mix invented a wholly fictitious role for himself in the Spanish-American War in order to boost his status as a hero. He also describes Edwin S. Porter's debunking film about Roosevelt, *Terrible Teddy, The Grizzly King*. Porter showed footage of Cuba during the war at the Eden Musee in New York.

28. See the account of Remington's experiences in the war in Peggy and Harold Samuels, *Frederic Remington: A Biography* (Garden City, New York: Doubleday, 1982).

29. This argument is developed further than I can take it here by Gareth Stedman Jones in "The History of U.S. Imperialism," in Robin Blackburn, ed., *Ideology in Social Science* (London: Fontana, 1972).

30. Will Wright, *Sixguns and Society* (Berkeley: University of California Press, 1975); Philip French, *Westerns* (London: Secker & Warburg, 1973); John H. Lenihan, *Showdown: Confronting Modern America in the Western Film* (Urbana: University of Illinois Press, 1980).

7

"THE SOUND OF MANY VOICES"
MUSIC IN JOHN FORD'S WESTERNS
Kathryn Kalinak

Huw Morgan in *How Green Was My Valley* describes his Welsh village as ring-ing "with the sound of many voices, for singing is in my people as sight is in the eye." It seems to me that something very similar might be said about the work of Huw's cinematic progenitor, John Ford, for singing is in John Ford's films "as sight is in the eye," endemic, inherent, defining. Given the genres that Ford gravitated toward—Westerns, war films, and literary adaptations—the predomi-nance of song and the emphasis on it are nothing short of remarkable. In fact, music, especially the use of song, has been labeled one of the most distinctive features of Ford's oeuvre by most of his critics from the initial wave of auteurist analysis in the fifties to recent reevaluation in the eighties and nineties. Ford's famous predilection for American hymnody and folk idioms is frequently cited in this context. I will argue that the musical scores for Ford's Westerns are cru-cial not only to these films' narrative trajectory and thematic exposition but to their ideological enterprise as well. In fact, one can chart the ideological terrain of a Ford Western through its use of music, and particularly through its songs.

Ford's Westerns are, among other things, concerned with defining an American nation. Given this agenda, it is not surprising that they are similarly preoccupied with matters of race, gender, and ethnicity and their relationship to an American identity. Music plays a vital role in these films, where it becomes a significant part of the process through which such ideologically loaded con-structs are created. In fact, music may be the most significant component in this process, since it taps into and reinforces emotionally loaded responses power-fully and, for most spectators, unconsciously.

What distinguishes Ford Westerns in this regard is the extent to which song carries the ideological payload. Perhaps this is why memories of Ford Westerns often hinge on their "production numbers": "The Girl I Left behind Me," throughout the cavalry trilogy and "She Wore a Yellow Ribbon" in the film of the same name (and elsewhere); "The Streets of Laredo" sung as a lullaby to an orphaned newborn in *3 Godfathers;* "Wagons West" sung by the Sons of the Pioneers in *Wagon Master;* the interrupted "Shall We Gather at the River?" at the Edwards family funeral in *The Searchers;* "Drill, Ye Tarriers, Drill," sung by the railroad workers in Ford's silent epic *The Iron Horse* and accompanied by intertitles complete with music and lyrics! One thinks, in this context, of the sequence cut from *Stagecoach,* where the assembled passengers sing "Ten Thousand Cattle," led by Doc Boone (Thomas Mitchell). More on this later.

Just as characteristic, if less immediately "audible," are those moments which quote from song: "Jeanie with the Light Brown Hair" as a leitmotif for Hatfield (John Carradine) in *Stagecoach;* "My Darling Clementine" played on a honky-tonk piano as the Earp brothers first enter Tombstone, and "Camptown Races" during the first meeting between Wyatt (Henry Fonda) and Doc Holliday (Victor Mature) in *My Darling Clementine* (and remember that Ford made not one but two Westerns bearing the names of songs); "I'll Take You Home Again, Kathleen," accompanying the appearances of Kathleen York (Maureen O'Hara) in *Rio Grande;* "Shall We Gather at the River?" in just about everything. And this list is only a beginning. No wonder Ford's recent biographer, Tag Gallagher, observes, "Ford's cinema can, without too much exaggeration, at times be likened to a trailer for a musical."[1]

How songs operate in Ford texts is a rich site for investigation, encompassing a number of questions from the broadest and most theoretical—how music operates in and through culture and what happens to music's function when it becomes channeled through a film score—to general questions relating to the genre—how the classical Hollywood film score works and how songs work in and in relation to the classical score—to textually specific questions—how songs work in individual films. Given the critical assumptions of this anthology, another question springs to mind: what part of these film scores is actually attributable to Ford himself?

Unfortunately, it is not a question that can be definitely answered at this point in time (if it ever was possible to answer it). Given the nature of artistic collaboration in Hollywood, in combination with both extremely spotty record keeping with regard to music and the notorious unreliability of personal recollection in a business known for self-promotion, the evidence is murky at best. Yet it is possible to reconstruct something of Ford's impact on the creation of these scores. Music credits, one source for documenting Ford's participation, make it appear unlikely that Ford exercised control over the choice of composer. As was typical in the Hollywood of the studio years, a composer under contract to the studio would routinely be assigned to score a film, and in Ford's case this meant that a wide variety of composers worked on his films. (Here the exception proves the rule: in the films produced by his own Argosy Productions, Richard Hageman is afforded a virtual monopoly—six out of seven Argosy films were scored by him—suggesting that when given the opportunity to choose a composer, Ford took advantage of it.) Thus, while it is tempting to try to articulate the typical Ford film score, it would be a gross oversimplification to categorize his films or even his Westerns within some kind of monolithic model.

Because of the Hollywood production system, Ford's films embrace a variety of musical styles, idioms, media, and practices, depending on the studio, the particularities of the production, and the composer. But this is not to say that Ford, arguably Hollywood's most prestigious director, was not able to influence the score.

To begin with, Ford was very knowledgeable about music. He owned and maintained an extensive collection of commercial recordings that included classics of nineteenth-century Romanticism (Brahms, Liszt, Wagner); Welsh, Mexican, and Irish ballads; Hawaiian and Tahitian music; American folk songs; opera; Artie Shaw; and soundtrack albums (all of which appear "well used").[2] According to Patrick Ford, the director's son, Ford would listen to his collection during scripting and production of a new film: "He'd lock himself in his 'den' with his old 'victrola' and play records to put himself in a scene-creating mood."[3] That so many of the scores for Ford's Westerns include hymns and folk songs that Ford owned can hardly be a coincidence.[4] Such anecdotal evidence also points to Ford's recognition of the power of music to stir emotion.

Ford's collection also contained the music track recordings of many of his films, and they form an interesting and revealing part of it. These reference disks were made at the recording sessions and include retakes, conductor's voice-overs, and the like; they are basically unlistenable-to as music. Ford's conservation of this material shows the extent of his interest not only in music but in the process of scoring as well. In addition, Ford used music during the production of his films as both entertainment and inspiration for cast and crew, both on and off the set. Anecdotes concerning Danny Borzage, the accordionist who became a fixture on Ford's sets, are legendary.

The most telling mark of Ford's influence, however, comes from the scores themselves. The recurrence of the same musical material across a number of films produced by different studios in different eras and scored by different composers suggests Ford's hand at work. I'm thinking here of the recurrence of such traditional tunes as "Shall We Gather at the River?" and "Cuckoo Waltz," or the use of Ann Rutledge's leitmotif from *Young Mr. Lincoln* in *The Man Who Shot Liberty Valance*, or "Ten Thousand Cattle," cut from *Stagecoach* only to reappear in *My Darling Clementine*.[5] I hasten to add, however, that Ford's influence was not absolute. One need only recall his vehement reaction to the score for *Cheyenne Autumn* to understand the limitations of directorial control or even influence with regard to the film score in the Hollywood production process. (Said Ford, "I thought it was a bad score and there was too much of it.")[6] Ford's antagonism toward lush scoring is legendary: "Generally I hate music in pictures—a little bit now and then, at the end or the start. . . . I don't like to see a man alone in the desert, dying of thirst, with the Philadelphia Orchestra behind him."[7] But there are times when this is, almost literally, what he got.

In fact, even a cursory examination of the scores for Ford films reveals an array of musical styles and production practices within the genre. On one hand there is Max Steiner's score for *The Searchers*. Heavily romantic in its orientation, the score depends upon a symphonic medium and a lush harmonic idiom, and saturates the film with music. On the other hand there is the multi-authored score for *Stagecoach*. Seeking an American idiom, it embodies sparse orchestration, a leaner harmony, and a less intrusive aesthetic. But what remains constant throughout Ford's scores and may well be the mark of Ford himself is the use of song.

In fact, Ford's films are so filled with songs that they invite comparisons to musicals. Yet it would be difficult to sustain that comparison much further. For despite the (omni)presence of song, Ford Westerns derive their musical design not from the conventions established for the presentation of production numbers in musicals (although they share some of the same strategies, as I will discuss later), but from the scoring conventions developed in Hollywood for the accompaniment of dramatic film. These included the use of music to sustain narrative structure and coherence, to illustrate narrative content, and to control narrative connotation; the privileging of dialogue over music; and the placement of music in such a way that it was rendered unobtrusive, indeed even "inaudible."[8]

The classical score depends for the successful achievement of these goals upon its ability to harness music's expressivity. It is largely able to do so by tapping into powerful associations culturally imbedded in both music and performance practice. Songs function as a kind of aural shorthand, quickly and reliably summoning up general cultural associations (the West, for instance, with cowboy songs) and even specific meanings, which are often encoded through but not necessarily dependent upon lyrics. (When we hear "Jeanie with the Light Brown Hair," for instance, we don't actually need to hear the lyrics for them to be summoned up in our minds.) In fact, songs are among the most reliable ways to access cultural associations, since they are often recognizable or at least familiar and, as such, tend to enter consciousness on a higher level than most background scoring.

An analysis of a film such as *My Darling Clementine* can serve as a window into the ideological project of a Ford Western, and the centrality of music and especially song to that enterprise.[9] The film chronicles the establishment of law and order in the frontier town of Tombstone through the agency of Wyatt Earp, who is driven to complete the task by the need to avenge the murder of his brother James at the hands of lawless Old Man Clanton (Walter Brennan) and his sons. Like so many other Ford Westerns, this one is ostensibly about civilization and its stabilizing effects on the American frontier. To be specific, it is about the power of the dominant community to, among other things, define a collective identity and in the process control definitions of citizenship and nationhood. But, as in so many other Ford Westerns, there exists a deep ambivalence about the power of, need for, and consequence of community on the American frontier.

The word "community" itself simply denotes a group of people with something in common. But it is important to remember that the mechanism by which that commonality is achieved is exclusion: a community exists in relation to what it is not, to what it has come together to eliminate. Ultimately defined by that thing which is "in common," community works selectively, by embracing some and rejecting others. I think that Annette Hamilton's concept of "the national imaginary" can be very useful in providing a theoretical framework for John Ford's communities. Working from Emile Durkheim's concept of "collective representations," Hamilton defines the national imaginary as "the means by which contemporary social orders are able to produce not merely images of themselves but images of themselves against others."[10] She argues that the last two centuries have produced a crisis in terms of distinguishing a national self, a crisis precipitated by a growing sense of internationalism that has undercut older forms of "national, ethnic, local, class or trade-specific identities."[11] It is the concept of the Other that has come to provide that cohesion in modern nations. The primacy of the mass media and particularly film in the construction of the national imaginary cannot be underestimated. As Hamilton states,

> What has come to distinguish a "national self" from "national others"—in a process which, in an older form, was described as stereotyping or even racism—emerges not from the realm of everyday concrete experience but in the circulation of collectively held images through multiple circuits of exchange typified by the print medium earlier and mass media today.[12]

In *My Darling Clementine* community is defined by a confluence of law, race, and ethnicity and is manifested through an Eastern value system dominated by a Protestant work ethic. Lindsay Anderson has pointed out that Ford's films depend upon distinctly Protestant values ("a philosophy that finds virtue in activity [and] see[s] struggle as a necessary element in life").[13] Interestingly, it seems to me, Anderson's collateral observation, that Ford's philosophy does not derive from Catholic values, holds true for both meanings of the word "Catholic." For Ford's communities are anything but universal and all-inclusive, and Tombstone is no exception. It includes lawman Wyatt Earp, schoolteacher Clementine Carter (Cathy Downs), and the law-abiding white inhabitants of Tombstone, and excludes the law-breaking, the non-working, the drunk, and the theatrical, the most visible manifestations of a failure to adopt the Eastern and Protestant value system Tombstone (and the film) privileges. This makes a character such as Doc Holliday triply disenfranchised: he operates outside the law (at least until the Earps arrive); drink has rendered him unfit for the work he was trained for; and he has a girlfriend who is decidedly Other.[14] Joining Doc outside the community are the cattle-rustling (and presumably shiftless) Clanton clan; the girlfriend of indeterminate racial and ethnic origin, Chihuahua (Linda Darnell); a drunken actor; and, of course, the entire Mexican and Native American populations.

In *Clementine*, community is established through the exclusion of the Other, defined through difference from the designated characteristics of the dominant community. In *Tombstone*, the Other encompasses the unlawful, like the Clanton clan, unable or unwilling to submit to authority, but also the racially or ethnically different. The extent to which Ford colludes in this textual operation has been a sticky point in Ford scholarship. Robert Lyons, for instance, notes that "Wyatt's sense of diversity . . . has significant racial limitations."[15] Especially revealing (or troublesome, as the case may be) is the extent to which the film confuses the Mexican population with Native American as if they are interchangeable: "Indian" Charlie speaks Spanish as he terrorizes the town on one of his tears; Chihuahua, whose very name bears the imprint of Mexican geography, is told to "get back on the reservation" by Earp. The Other is articulated in *Tombstone* through codes of language (English vs. Spanish) and music (typical "bad guy" music for the Clantons). It is also reflected in the clearly established borders that operate both inside and outside the town.

One border is geographic: the border that separates the Clanton homestead and the Native American encampment from what is defined as Tombstone. (In a revealing shot cut from the film's final release version, Wyatt Earp, in leaving Tombstone, walks past a Native American encampment located conspicuously outside the town limits.) Other borders are less geographic than ideological. Tombstone is divided between the world of the hotel and the world of the saloon. In fact, Wyatt's movement from one to the other as the film progresses becomes a mark of the emergent power of a dominant community. There is a further division within the latter world: a saloon for Tombstone's dominant community and one for the Mexican. (And it is interesting to note that the Clantons and Doc Holliday have the privilege of frequenting both.) That these borders, geographic and otherwise, are not fully in place when the Earps arrive testifies to the ongoing struggle of the community to establish itself and the need for a figure of authority, such as Wyatt, to complete the process.

A crucial part of that process is ritual, the cement that binds the community together and protects it against outsiders. In Ford Westerns these rituals are inherently musical: religious services, weddings and funerals, dances, marches, and singing. Much has already been written about the justifiably famous Sunday-morning church service and dance sequence in *My Darling Clementine* and about the function of music, and specifically dance, in creating and sustaining the emergent community of Tombstone. Peter Stowell, for instance, describes the dance as "Ford's ultimate expression of community cohesion . . . sealing civilization's compact."[16] And while dance is the most obvious signifier of the community's power to set Tombstone's moral agenda, song is equally, or perhaps even more, revelatory of the nature of that agenda and of who has the power to set it.

The dance sequence is preceded by a prologue in which Tombstone's citizenry gather at the site of the future church (a skeletal bell tower and woodplank floor) to enact a "regular church" service revolving around the singing of "Shall We Gather at the River?" It is represented as an instance of social integration, but who is "gathered" and who is not (most conspicuously Doc Holliday and Chihuahua) reflects the principles of exclusion by which the community works.

Camerawork here authorizes who and what are chosen through its selection of Wyatt and Clementine as the archetypal participants in this nascent community. Stunning use of mise en scène in the first glimpse of the "church" configures Tombstone, the community assembled in the "church," and the wilderness, from the foreground of the shot to the background, in a microcosm that defines the mythology of the West in this film. It is Clementine and Wyatt who enter the shot and move into the space of the community. Song furthers such distinctions by separating those who join the singers from those who do not.

The choice of the hymn could hardly be more appropriate or telling. "Shall We Gather at the River?" is a Methodist hymn built on a nexus of assumptions about salvation, predestination, and communal destiny. As Joseph Reed observes in *Three American Originals: John Ford, William Faulkner, and Charles Ives,* the river of the title is obviously the River Jordan, the crossing referred to is the crossing to the afterlife, and the gathering "is the assembly of Christian brothers and sisters to await the crossing."[17] Thus Ford's use of the hymn is most appropriate during funerals (as it is used in *The Searchers*). The lyrics tell of a chosen people, but it's clear that "chosen" refers as much to those gathering on this side of the river as it does to those who have already crossed to the afterlife. That process of selection and assemblage—some are chosen and presumably some are not—is crucial to an understanding of the hymn and underscores the antidemocratic and anti-egalitarian aspects of predestination. Thus the lyrics to "Shall We Gather" add resonance to *Clementine*'s scenario of inclusion and exclusion that form a community.

When the community members sing (and dance) together, they are bound not only by mutual purpose, but by camerawork that underscores their harmony. When those outside the community sing, however, it is a performance, shot in ways that inhibit social integration. When Chihuahua sings "Ten Thousand Cattle," codes typically used for the presentation of production numbers in musicals suspend narrative progression and position her as spectacle. The film is marked as a performance space and Chihuahua remains unconnected to the diegetic spectators through both the narrative construction (the diegetic audience is playing cards and paying little or no attention to her) and her position in the mise en scène (she is behind the cardplayers). Camerawork further isolates Chihuahua, separating her close-up from Earp's.

More than any other narrative element, the ending to *Clementine* points to the film's reservations about the function of community and the uneasy fit between the needs of social cohesion and the demands of individualism, both of which characterize the genre of the Western as a whole. This plays itself out in *Clementine* in Earp's leaving the very community he has given so much to establish (although he promises to return). In this way, *Clementine* mirrors other Ford Westerns, such as *Stagecoach* and *The Searchers,* which end with sympathy for the outsider and a certain amount of nostalgia for the outside. In general, Ford films tend more to complication than to resolution in their endings, and in the Westerns this tendency often displays itself in a tension between the ideals of the protagonists and the demands of the communities they have served and often leave.

Like many readers, I imagine, I came to the work of John Ford through the prism of auteurism. Ford's canonization in the sixties and seventies by auteurist critics not only established him as a "pantheon" director, in the words of Andrew Sarris, but created the impression—in fact, was generated from the supposition—that Ford's work exhibited a consistent style and thematics.[18] Certainly, I came to Ford's work in the nineties with just such a set of (largely unconscious) assumptions. There is an argument to be made, surely, for a visual style that can genuinely be defined as Fordian, at least as far as the Westerns are concerned. But I found Ford's thematic concerns to constitute a shifting, sometimes inconsistent, even contradictory body of evidence. (And I think this is one of the many reasons why an analysis of Ford's ideological concerns is so much more satisfying than an analysis of his thematics.)

Take *Stagecoach* and *My Darling Clementine,* for instance, the first and second sound Westerns Ford made, which are set in roughly the same time and geographic space. In *Clementine,* the protagonist is a man of the law, Wyatt Earp, whose heroic status is a direct result of the powerful legal authority he chooses to accept; in *Stagecoach,* the protagonist is an outlaw, the Ringo Kid, who must operate outside a largely ineffectual legal authority. In *Clementine,* Native Americans are little more than a public nuisance, easily disposed of by Earp, and, in a shot cut from the final release version, a passive, woebegone lot. In *Stagecoach,* Native Americans are a bloodthirsty threat, raping and massacring women and attacking a stagecoach bearing a mother and newborn child. In *Clementine,* civilization is a pacifying force of high moral purpose; in *Stagecoach,* it's what you escape from. *Clementine* ends with the solidification of borders, *Stagecoach* with their crossing.

The position of women in the films is particularly interesting. In both *Clementine* and *Stagecoach,* women are divided along stereotypical lines: those allied with civilization (the schoolmarm, Clementine, who arrives in Tombstone, and a soldier's wife, Mrs. Mallory [Louise Platt], traveling in the stagecoach, both from the East) and those outside it (the prostitutes, Chihuahua and Dallas). But each film treats its women in very different ways. *Clementine* exalts the loyal schoolmarm while *Stagecoach* reproaches the snooty Mrs. Mallory. In fact, *Clementine* and *Stagecoach* reverse one another's sexual dichotomies. In *Clementine*, the prostitute, Chihuahua, is dishonest, untrustworthy, and disloyal, a woman whose public humiliation in a horse trough is depicted by the film as humorous. She dies. In *Stagecoach*, the prostitute, Dallas (Claire Trevor), has a heart of gold: she's honest, trustworthy, forgiving, and loyal. Her public humiliation at the hands of the ladies of the Law and Order League is decried as unjust. She gets her man.

Yet *Stagecoach*'s ideological concerns mirror those of *Clementine:* the American nation and its relation to Otherness, and the place within this nation for racial and ethnic difference.[19] The first film follows the travails of a group of passengers journeying by stagecoach from Tonto to Lordsburg with Geronimo on the warpath somewhere in between. The assembled travelers represent a spectrum of the newly enfranchised American West: the sheriff, the banker, the salesman, the soldier's Eastern wife, the doctor, the driver, the Southern gambler, the prostitute, and the outlaw. And although the film's sympathies are clearly with the last two members of this list, its ideological project is to expel them (and others). *Stagecoach* is as much about fitting in as it is about freedom, about the necessity and cost of exclusion. Ultimately, its twin concerns with community—indeed, with the necessity of community on the frontier—and with the institutional authority of "civilization" clearly link it to *Clementine*.

Stagecoach is a film driven by tensions between inside and outside that permeate its narrative structure, visual design, and ideological enterprise. The film's first order of business is to consolidate the contentious group of white travelers assembled inside the coach. So many moments of community cohesion are celebrated through song in Ford Westerns that it comes as a bit of a surprise and a disappointment when the passengers in *Stagecoach* don't sing. But in an earlier version of the film, they did indeed. In a scene cut after previews, the assembled passengers sang "Ten Thousand Cattle."[20]

According to Dudley Nichols's final revised script of 11 November 1938, the passengers were to sing "Ten Thousand Cattle" (initiated by Doc Boone) after Ringo entered the coach, in an attempt to restore their fragile camaraderie.[21] But both the preliminary music cue sheet, undated, and the final cue sheet, dated 30 January 1939, position the song differently; in these documents "Ten Thousand Cattle" occurs as the passengers await the birth of Mrs. Mallory's baby, with a short, six-second snatch of the song sung by Doc Boone as the passengers leave Dry Fork. Since the final cue sheet postdates the final revised script by over two months and since *Stagecoach* was still filming in mid-December 1938, weeks after the "final" script was completed, it seems likely that the cue sheets provide the more reliable evidence.

Additionally, the placement of the song at Ringo's entrance is not only at odds with the music cue sheet but is puzzling in terms of the narrative. The song itself (the same one sung by Chihuahua in *Clementine*—Ford got to use it after all) is a slow ballad with melancholy lyrics. Its content seems much more appropriate for a tense, waiting scene than for Ringo's appearance. Additionally, a publicity still from the production shows the cast rehearsing a song (which would have to be "Ten Thousand Cattle") with an off-screen pianist. All the stagecoach passengers are in the photo (in costume) with the exception of Mrs. Mallory, another indication that it was meant to be sung in the waiting sequence, during which she would have been otherwise engaged.

I referred to *Stagecoach*'s score earlier in this article as "multi-authored," and here I would like to provide more detail about what that means. Hollywood's production model for musical scores encompassed a variety of practices, from the exceptional single author such as Bernard Herrmann, who composed and orchestrated his own film scores; to the more collaborative and characteristic composer-orchestrator team, such as Erich Wolfgang Korngold and Hugo Friedhofer; to several composers working simultaneously to create multi-authored texts, what Roy Prendergast has called "paste-pot-and-scissors" scores.[22] Prendergast argues that "paste-pot" scores constituted the typical model in the early years of sound film, and the practice continued well beyond the thirties, especially in low-budget films or ones that needed to be scored fast. What is unusual about *Stagecoach*, however, is the extent to which that collaboration is acknowledged, with five composers receiving screen credit (and the Oscar).[23]

In fact, it may have been just this collaborative effort that caused the demise of "Ten Thousand Cattle." Matthew Bernstein, in his critical biography of the film's producer, Walter Wanger, contends that Ford cut the scene himself after preview audiences reacted negatively.[24] Production records at Paramount Pictures (the score was farmed out to Paramount, not an untypical practice for an independently produced, low-budget film such as *Stagecoach*) indicate that there was concern about using "Ten Thousand Cattle" even before the previews.

On the preliminary music cue sheet, "Ten Thousand Cattle" was penciled in in the margin. Initially, it was assumed that "Ten Thousand Cattle" was in the public domain and that it necessitated no costly copyright fee. Given the number of people at work on this film and the murky copyright history of the song itself, it is not entirely surprising that the "Ten Thousand Cattle" sequence was filmed before it was discovered that the song was indeed under copyright.[25] (Its title was then hastily penciled in on the preliminary cue sheets.) Studio executives briefly considered reshooting the sequences with another song rather than pay what they felt to be an outrageous copyright fee.[26] But time was running short. The problem was discovered in mid-January; the recording of the score was scheduled for January 24, 1939, and previews for February 2nd. So

A publicity still for *Stagecoach* showing the cast rehearsing a musical number, presumably "Ten Thousand Cattle." The absence of Louise Platt, who plays Mrs. Mallory, is one indication that the song was meant to be sung during the birthing sequence. Copyright United Artists, 1939. Production still courtesy of the Wisconsin Center for Film and Theater Research.

"Ten Thousand Cattle" remained in the film for the previews and was still listed on the final music cue sheet of January 30th.[27] When audiences reacted badly, the song was cut, and it seems distinctly possible that copyright problems figured in the decision to eliminate it.

Inside the coach, the passengers establish their fragile community without the help of song. Soon, they are set in opposition to what is outside of the coach: Native Americans, Mexicans (and, like *Clementine*, the film confuses the two), and the threat of miscegenation. With Buck's Mexican wife, Juliette, who fills his life with culinary and other domestic woes as well as ever-multiplying relatives; with the comic stationmaster Chris with his heavy accent and oversize girth, and his Native American wife, Yakeema, who alerts Geronimo; with Luke Plummer's villainously coded and Spanish-speaking Mexican sidekick; and with the murderous Apache themselves, thundering down on the coach in the film's chase sequence, the film plugs into racist stereotypes. This discourse functions on the narrative level to reinforce the passengers' sense of alienation, but it also

10	TWO OUTCASTS AT TABLE (Part 2)	
:51	Leo Shuken	
	Irving Berlin, Inc.	inst. back
	no	no
11	TEN THOUSAND CATTLE	
:06	Owen Wister	partial
	Witmark	Vocal vis. & inst. back
	YES	YES
12	PARTING OF COACH AND TROOPS	
1:19½	John M. Leipold	
	Irving Berlin, Inc.	inst. back
	no	no
13	SNOW COUNTRY AND THIRSTY PASSENGERS	
4:30	John M. Leipold	
Reel 5	Irving Berlin, Inc.	inst. back
	no	no
14	APACHE WELLS ARRIVAL	
	John M. Leipold	
:31	Irving Berlin, Inc.	inst. back
	no	no
15	MRS. MALLORY FAINTS	
1:10	W. Franke Harling	
	Irving Berlin, Inc.	inst. back
	no	no
16	BIRTH OF A BABY	
:23	W. Franke Harling	
	Irving Berlin, Inc.	inst. back
	no	no
17	TEN THOUSAND CATTLE	
1:21	Owen Wister	partial
	Witmark	Vocal vis. & inst. back
	YES	YES
18	THE BABY IS BORN	
1:10	W. Franke Harling	
Reel 6	Irving Berlin, Inc.	inst. back
	no	no
19	THE KID PROPOSES	
3:29	Leo Shuken	
Reel 7	Irving Berlin, Inc.	inst. back
	no	no
20	OUTCASTS IN KITCHEN	
1:58½	Leo Shuken	
	Irving Berlin, Inc.	inst. back
	no	no
21	APACHE FIRES AND LEE'S FERRY	
5:52	Gerard Carbonara	
Reel 8	Irving Berlin, Inc.	inst. back
	no	no
22	GERONIMO THREATENS	
:55	Gerard Carbonara	
	Irving Berlin, Inc.	inst. back
	no	no

A page from the cue sheet for *Stagecoach* dated 30 January 1939, when "Ten Thousand Cattle" was still in the scene. It was cut sometime after the previews of February 2.

works to convince us in both subtle and obvious ways how Other the Mexican and Native American cultures are to Ford's definition of American-ness.

The score is part of this enterprise as well. Music accompanying Native Americans, for instance, exploits powerful musical codes (in particular certain rhythmic figures, intervals, and harmonic devices) to reinforce cultural stereotypes about Otherness and establish Native Americans as wild, powerful, primitive, and exotic. As Claudia Gorbman has demonstrated in her article on "Indian Music," Hollywood developed a specific vocabulary for representing Native Americans: a rhythmic figure of four equal beats with the accent falling on the first, often played by drums or low bass instruments; the use of perfect fifths and fourths in the harmonic design; and the use of modal melody.[28] As Gorbman notes, *Stagecoach* exemplifies this "Indian-on-the-warpath motif" with its tom-tom rhythmic figure in the bass and its exploitation of parallel fourths in the harmonic texture.[29]

Music, in *Stagecoach*, establishes Native Americans as Other; through its positioning, it also establishes them as intruders on the frontier landscape. In

The original cover for the sheet music of "Ten Thousand Cattle," composed in 1904 for the stage production of *The Virginian*.

Courtesy of the University of California Los Angeles Music Library, Special Collections Library.

one of the most oft-quoted sequences in Ford, the stagecoach, in extreme long shot, moves through the gigantic dimensions of Monument Valley; this shot is followed by a pan to a menacing group of Native Americans ready to ambush them. (In fact, the sequence is so stunning that Ford repeats it.) Stereotypes in the music establish Native Americans as menacing and threatening, but something much more insidious is going on here as well. Up until this point in the film, shots of Monument Valley have been accompanied by the stagecoach theme, building up an association, over the course of the film, between white civilization and the wilderness. In fact, in this very sequence, immediately prior to the appearance of Native Americans we hear the stagecoach's music. Thus it is the Indian music, ironically, that seems out of place in Monument Valley, and Native Americans who seem outside the natural order of things in *Stagecoach*. Thus music positions Native Americans not only as Other, but as intrusive, as not belonging.

Music continues its work in *Stagecoach* with Yakeema, the Apache wife of the jovial stationmaster, Chris. As in *Clementine*, when Other characters outside the privileged community of the coach sing, codes reminiscent of production numbers in the musical are used to impede the establishment of a sense of community. An interesting example from *Stagecoach* parallels Chihuahua's performance in *Clementine*. Yakeema entertains three *vaqueros* outside the station. Despite the fact that the four are "in cahoots" (she lets them know— in Spanish—when the coast is clear, presumably so they can alert Geronimo), the sequence borrows heavily from techniques used in production numbers, creating a performance space that severs the natural connections between Yakeema and her cohorts and repositions her as spectacle.

Importantly, I think, she sings in Spanish. While alienating (unless you know Spanish, you have no idea what's she's singing about), the Spanish language may also, as Edward Buscombe asserts, provide a context where "the voice of the Other forces its way through."[30] And I think there is something to this, but it is complicated. Spanish is presumably not Yakeema's native language, and the conflation of Native American and Mexican remains disturbing, as does Chris's remark that what he misses most about his wife's disappearance is the horse and the rifle she has taken (not to mention the veiled reference to her "uncivilized" sexuality—"she's a little bit savage, I think").

What makes *Stagecoach* an especially rich film, however, is not its rather simplistic us-vs.-them mentality, but its dissection of the community inside the coach. A veritable who's who of Western stereotypes, the passengers are initially defined by their occupational roles, but their fates are ultimately determined by their social roles, by the extent of their ability to participate in and serve the community. Hatfield, who cannot move beyond the value system of the antebellum South and embrace the more egalitarian ethos of the West, is killed. Gatewood, who refuses to set aside his selfish goals, is taken to jail. On the other hand, Mrs. Mallory, who accepts the help of Doc Boone and Dallas and learns to respect both, survives with her baby and will be reunited with her husband. Buck and Curley, whose primary missions are to serve and protect the passengers, survive, as does Mr. Peacock, meek though he may be, who is able to put his own physical needs behind those of the others, and who reminds all, "Let's have a little Christian charity one for the other." Drunken Doc Boone sobers up and does his duty. That leaves Dallas and Ringo.

Although Dallas is accepted by the passengers, she is excluded from reintegration into the larger community. Her fate bears the traces of and points to the power of patriarchal ideologies about female sexuality circulating in the culture. Despite her punishment and penance, the film cannot quite forgive her. The case with Ringo, I think, is more complicated. As Tag Gallagher has argued, Ringo "seems the most community-minded," and his appearance, with his Union cavalry garb (a subtle and continual reminder of Hatfield's outsider status), marks him as the hero of a new American order. Yet as Gallagher points out, "he gave vengeance priority over defense during the Indian chase."[31] It comes as a bit of a shock when Ringo announces to Curley, "I lied to you, Curley. Got three left." It's a telling detail, and not only because it points to Ringo's willingness to put his vengeance first. Three bullets for three men presumes either an extraordinary and reckless ego or superlative marksmanship. When the latter possibility is confirmed in the town's reaction to Ringo's arrival and especially in the shoot-out with the Plummer boys (it's three against one), it reminds us of just how dangerous Ringo is and points to a darker reading of his character than the innocent farm-boy persona he presents to the passengers. Gatewood goes to jail and Ringo gets to escape, but they both have to leave.

The opening credits for *Stagecoach* announce that the score is "Based on American folk songs."[32] *Stagecoach,* like *My Darling Clementine* and many other Ford Westerns, adopts a musical idiom that is somewhat atypical of Hollywood, although certainly not outside the possibilities available to Hollywood composers. Hollywood, of course, had largely adopted (and adapted) the Late Romanticism favored by the influential Viennese émigrés Max Steiner and Erich Wolfgang Korngold. The idiom affecting *Stagecoach,* however, was largely influenced by movements in contemporary American art music in the thirties and forties that rejected the abstraction of European Modernism and embraced a uniquely American sound characterized by simple harmonic structures and textures. A critical part of this enterprise was the search for an American form. Folk songs as well as traditional American music of all kinds became the inspiration for a generation of composers seeking a uniquely American idiom. Aaron Copland's *Rodeo* and *Appalachian Spring* could serve as master examples here. Thus *Stagecoach*'s use of indigenous American music drew power from a well-defined and vigorous discourse that attached American-ness to certain kinds of music, such as hymnody and folk song.

As in *My Darling Clementine* and other Ford Westerns, indigenous American music in *Stagecoach* supports the film's ideological project. Recognizable melodies, such as "Jeanie with the Light Brown Hair" and a parodic version of "Shall We Gather at the River?" tap into a set of ready-made and reliable cultural associations that can be activated to manipulate audience response. Using "Jeanie with the Light Brown Hair," for instance, as a leitmotif for the southerner Hatfield functions as a constant reminder of his own intrinsic Otherness in the new order of the American West. What is so powerful about this tune, however, is the nostalgia it carries for the antebellum South, softening Hatfield's harsh and inflexible persona when we are in danger of becoming totally alienated from him.[33] (The "If you see Judge Greenfield" line at his death functions in the same way.) "Shall We Gather at the River?" also functions by manipulating musical associations, this time in order to cast ridicule on the Ladies' Law and Order League. Heard initially on an organ, it is recast in weird instrumentation as accompaniment to the outraged womenfolk of Tonto. This parodic version functions by denying the listener the satisfaction of a familiar tune and transferring that discomfort to the on-screen characters associated with it.

The ways in which folk songs and popular music of the era are used in *Stagecoach,* however, are not always immediately apparent. Often heard in fragments, frequently cast into unfamiliar harmonic modes, integrated into a larger original composition, or—the most nebulous of all—"inspiring" original composition, folk tunes and popular music are often positioned in Ford Westerns to affect response without the auditor's conscious recognition of these sources.[34]

The way in which folk tunes became part of the musical tapestry of a Ford Western is aptly demonstrated by the stagecoach theme itself. Despite its aching familiarity, it is not an actual quotation of an American folk song. Edward Buscombe in his BFI monograph identifies its probable source as "The Trail to Mexico," a folk song that first appears in the 1910 John Lomax collection, *Cowboy Songs and Other Frontier Ballads.* Folk song as a musical form is characterized by a high degree of variation, ranging from simple embellishments of the melodic line to actual alternative melodies available for lyrics that themselves vary greatly depending on the era, geographic location, and performance setting. Thus Rudy Behlmer describes the stagecoach theme as the "somewhat altered 'Bury Me Not on the Lone Prairie'" while Buscombe calls it "a much jollier ballad, 'The Trail to Mexico.'"[35]

Archival records at Paramount Studio's Music Department, however, clearly point to "The Trail to Mexico" as the source for Paramount's composing team. Although the Press Book is not a definitive source (it lists some songs not used in the film and fails to list some that are), it does name "The Trail to Mexico" and not "Bury Me Not on the Lone Prairie." Additionally, the source for folk song in Paramount's Music Library in those days was Carl Sandburg's 1927

American Songbag. In that collection, the melody used for "Bury Me Not on the Lone Prairie" is unrelated to the stagecoach theme, while the melody of "The Trail to Mexico" bears a striking resemblance to it. Still, it would be inaccurate to describe the stagecoach theme as a literal quotation of "The Trail to Mexico." Folk tunes often work this way in Ford: exploited for their familiarity without being quoted so closely as to draw the audience's conscious attention. Thus the stagecoach theme is positioned to connote Western-ness without the audience's recognizing or needing to recognize the source.

The Lordsburg section of *Stagecoach* exemplifies this use of music to create a tapestry of Western-ness. What is especially interesting about the sequence is the way that diegetic music begins to function as non-diegetic background scoring does—to create specific moods, underscore particular actions, and provide commentary on the narrative activity—while the non-diegetic scoring begins to function as the diegetic folk tunes do, providing a recognizable melody to help anchor meaning.

The sequence begins as the first travelers arrive in Lordsburg: Mrs. Mallory and her baby, the wounded Mr. Peacock, and Dallas. The diegetic piano music functions exactly as non-diegetic background scoring would: the spirited and upbeat "Joe Bowers" as Mrs. Mallory is carried inside; the slower and highly sentimentalized Stephen Foster tune "Gentle Annie" as Dallas exits the wagon (what a coincidence—the pianist just happens to change numbers as she steps down with the baby); and, as the stagecoach itself enters the shot, the traditional song "Rosa Lee."

The saloon scene in which Luke Plummer learns of Ringo's return contains the piano player heard earlier, continuing "Rosa Lee." But something interesting is going on here as well, an almost antiphonal relationship played out through music between Nick Plummer and the piano player. As the sequence continues, the arrangement of "Rosa Lee" becomes increasingly jazzy, with the chromatic chordal progressions of ragtime. (This, of course, attaches to Plummer and helps to flesh out a very sketchily drawn character.) I say "antiphonal" because the music actually seems to respond to Nick's actions. When it is reported, for instance, that the "Ringo Kid's in town," the action stops while Luke glances around the room. The music stops here as well, the piano player hesitating while Luke digests the information. Later, the music dramatically stops when Luke cashes in his chips. There is a particularly nice example prior to Doc's entrance in which Luke casts a sidelong glance at the piano player, who looks him straight in the eye and responds with a jazzy, chromatic progression. This use of diegetic music to respond specifically to narrative is atypical of the classical Hollywood film score, in which non-diegetic music usually performs this function. That the score for *Stagecoach* reverses this convention is yet another of its distinctive features.

Non-diegetic music replaces diegetic for the first time when Dallas and Ringo meet in Lordsburg. Curley allows Ringo to settle his score with the Plummers and, before Ringo seeks them out, he accompanies Dallas "home." The sequence begins with the diegetic "Lilly Dale" heard in the background on the saloon piano. But the music quickly becomes non-diegetic, with strings prominently exploited both to reinforce the sentiment of the moment and to differentiate this non-diegetic music from the diegetic piano music heard prior to it. The non-diegetic music associated with Dallas and Ringo (their leitmotif) is actually based on the song "I Love You" from the 1923 Broadway production of *Little Jesse James*. In fact, the musical material quoted in *Stagecoach* is from the chorus, whose refrain, unvoiced here, contains the lyrics "I love you." Thus non-diegetic music here works as diegetic music often does: associations attached to the song and especially to the lyrics are harnessed to the images, anchoring their meaning in a particular way. As Ringo walks Dallas "home," their leitmotif yields to the diegetic music emanating from the open doors of the bordellos they pass, first the popular "Up in a Balloon, Boys," and then "She Is More to Be Pitied Than Censured"[36] (an obvious commentary on Dallas for those who recognize the tune). But the non-diegetic love theme reappears for their touching farewell.

Non-diegetic music accompanies the shoot-out as well, and here the score exploits several conventional scoring practices of the era: a rising musical line, tremolo strings, and even mickey mousing. After a reiteration of Dallas and Ringo's leitmotif at the conclusion of the gunfight, the score ends the diegetic portion of the film with a variation on the stagecoach theme as Dallas and Ringo leave the "blessings of civilization." If we are to believe the theme's inspiration or source to be "The Trail to Mexico" (and I think we should), then on one level at least, the theme turns out to be literally true: Dallas and Ringo are indeed on the trail to Mexico, where Ringo's ranch is located.[37]

One needs to consider at least one other level of meaning in investigating how music and especially song work in a Ford Western. I am particularly interested here in music's ideological function and its relationship to nationhood and national identity. My thinking on this issue has been inspired by Caryl Flinn's work on gender and nostalgia and their connection to the Hollywood film score. Of all the elements in a filmic text, music has remained the most resistant to critical analysis. Part of this resistance may be due to the fact that a specific knowledge of musical analysis is presumed necessary to understand a film score. But part emanates from a particular set of culturally determined values attached to music: that it is timeless and autonomous, the embodiment of individual expression untouched by social and historical forces. The work of the Frankfurt School, and in particular the text *Composing for the Films,* by Hans Eisler and Theodor Adorno, has deconstructed this network of cultural assumptions and exposed the ideological function of music. Yet music's image as apart from worldly influences and constraints has had a remarkable resilience. (And any-

The chorus from "I Love You," the hit song from the 1923 production of *Little Jessie James.*
Courtesy of the University of California Los Angeles Music Library, Special Collections Library.

one doubting this resilience should peruse the pages of a traditional musicology journal.) Caryl Flinn argues that one of the most potent and persistent of the discourses attached to music has been that music "has the peculiar ability to ameliorate the social existence it allegedly overrides, and offers, in one form or another, the sense of something better. Music extends an impression of perfection and integrity in an otherwise imperfect, unintegrated world." Flinn labels this music's "utopian function": music purportedly offers listeners a "fullness of experience," "an ability to return . . . to better, allegedly more 'perfect' times and memories."[38] It is this discourse that films absorb through their scores, transporting listeners from the technological, fragmented experience of a postindustrial and mechanically reproduced art form such as film to an idealized past of imagined plentitude and unity. Thus music always carries with it a kind of nostalgia, which Hollywood films have been particularly adept at exploiting for their own purposes.

The concept of music's utopian function can be extremely helpful in coming to terms with Ford film scores, in which music is ideally positioned to tap into the powerful notions of nostalgia that are already circulating in these films about an idealized American past. This is especially true of songs that, for a number of reasons described earlier, have a heightened ability both to reach listeners and, in doing so, to particularize the utopian promise contained in film music. In the case of Ford Westerns, music's rather general utopian promise is transformed, largely through song, into Ford's specific notion of the nineteenth-century American West, an idealized, mythic past that never actually existed. Songs both make that past real and create a nostalgia for it. In this way, song becomes the critical component of the particular way that Ford defines the West.

Thus the folk and traditional tunes used in *Stagecoach* provide more than a tapestry of Western-ness. They harness the nostalgic power of film music to authenticate Ford's particular version of the settling of the American frontier and his particular definition of what it means to be an American. From the stagecoach theme, to the period songs emanating from the bordellos in Lordsburg, to the non-diegetic background scoring of the final sequence (and other scenes), music not only convinces us that Ford's vision of the American past is authentic, it makes us long for it and what is attached to it: a particular way of thinking about what makes us a nation, about who is included and who is not in our definition of American-ness. This process takes place in all of Ford's Westerns. Indeed, one need only look over the list of Ford's "production numbers" with which I began this article to appreciate this point and to recognize the centrality of song to the process of mapping Ford's ideological terrain.[39]

Ford's name has become inextricably linked to his Westerns, although they represent only a portion of his prodigious output. There are, in fact, a significant number of films in Ford's oeuvre devoted to frontiers of a different sort, to the reaches, near and far, of the British Empire: Ireland, Scotland, Wales, India. Here one sees a reflection of the processes within the Westerns, particularly with regard to music, where sentiment is exploited through the use of song and harnessed to ideological purpose. Within and across Ford's work, musical definitions and demarcations of ethnicity, race, and nation interact, negotiated by a complex process that both connects to and plays off larger cultural notions about national identity. Song's particular potency is its ability to function within this network while seeming to transcend it, and in this way it becomes one of the surest markers of culture's work.

NOTES

I would like to extend my thanks to Sandy Flitterman-Lewis and Krin Gabbard for inviting me to give a version of this article at the Columbia University/Museum of

Modern Art Colloquium Series, where I received generous and valuable feedback. Special thanks to Elizabeth Weis, whose extremely insightful comments as respondent helped me to reshape the article in important ways.

1. Tag Gallagher, *John Ford: The Man and His Films* (Berkeley: University of California Press, 1986), 55.

2. James D'Arc, "What's in a Name: The John Ford Music Collection at Brigham Young University," *The Cue Sheet* 5 (1988), 115.

3. Patrick Ford, quoted in D'Arc, "What's in a Name," 116.

4. And, in at least one case, Ford's participation in the choice of period music was exploited in studio publicity. For *The Searchers,* Warner Brothers proudly announced that "The Yellow Rose of Texas" was Ford's own selection. Warner Brothers Archive, University of Southern California.

5. William Darby analyzes the repeated use of Ann Rutledge's theme, as does Tag Gallagher. See William Darby, "Musical Links in *Young Mr. Lincoln, My Darling Clementine,* and *The Man Who Shot Liberty Valance,*" *Cinema Journal* 31, no. 1 (Fall 1991): 22–36; and Gallagher, *John Ford,* 170 n, 387, 398, 413.

6. Ford, quoted in Peter Bogdanovich, *John Ford* (Berkeley: University of California Press, 1978 [revised edition]), 104.

7. Ford, quoted in Bogdanovich, *John Ford,* 99.

8. For a more detailed description of the conventions and practices of the classical Hollywood film score, see my *Settling the Score* (Madison: University of Wisconsin Press, 1992), 66–110.

9. The score for *My Darling Clementine* was composed by Cyril J. Mockbridge.

10. Annette Hamilton, "Fear and Desire: Aborigines, Asians and the National Imaginary," *Australian Cultural History* 9 (1990): 16.

11. Hamilton, "Fear and Desire," 16.

12. Hamilton, "Fear and Desire," 16.

13. Lindsay Anderson, *About John Ford* (New York: McGraw-Hill, 1981), 114.

14. I like Corey Creekmur's reading of *My Darling Clementine,* which goes outside the framework of the binary oppositions that have informed much of the criticism of this film. Creekmur draws attention to the "erotic tensions" arising from the triangular structure of desire among Wyatt, Doc, and Clementine and reads Doc as a figure who troubles normative definitions of masculinity. Thus Creekmur offers yet another way in which Doc is constituted as an outsider and Other, especially when he is compared to the more conventionally masculine Wyatt. See Creekmur, "Acting like a Man: Masculine Performance in *My Darling Clementine,*" in *Out in Culture: Gay, Lesbian, and Queer Essays on Popular Culture,* ed. Corey Creekmur and Alexander Doty (Durham and London: Duke University Press, 1995), 167–182.

15. Robert Lyons, "Introduction: *My Darling Clementine* as History and Romance," in *My Darling Clementine,* ed. Robert Lyons (New Brunswick: Rutgers University Press, Rutgers Films in Print, 1984), 12.

16. Peter Stowell, *John Ford* (Boston: Twayne, 1986), 106.

17. Joseph Reed, *Three American Originals: John Ford, William Faulkner, and Charles Ives* (Middletown, Conn.: Wesleyan University Press, 1984), 21.

18. See Andrew Sarris, *The American Cinema: Directors and Directions, 1929–1968* (New York: Dutton, 1968), 43–49. It may be worth pointing out that it was the British and American auteurist critics who first championed Ford, not the French.

19. There are obviously other ways to read *Stagecoach* ideologically, as an allegory, for instance, of the Depression or the coming war.

20. It is interesting to note that the moment of communal singing in *Stagecoach* is pure Ford (via Dudley Nichols). The original short story by Ernest Haycox, "Stage to Lordsburg," upon which the screenplay is based, contains no reference to song.

21. Dudley Nichols, final revised screenplay for *Stagecoach*, 11 November 1938, in the Walter Wanger Collection, Wisconsin Center for Film and Theater Research, Madison, Wisconsin. Perhaps this is the evidence that led Rudy Behlmer to report that "Ten Thousand Cattle" is sung after Ringo makes his entrance into the stagecoach. See Behlmer, *Behind the Scenes: The Making of America's Favorite Movies* (New York: Ungar, 1982), 117–118.

22. Roy Prendergast, *Film Music: A Neglected Art* (New York: Norton, 1977), 29.

23. Musical direction is credited to Borris Morros; five composers share screen credit for arrangement: Richard Hageman, Franke Harling, John Leipold, Leo Shuken, and Louis Gruenberg. Gerard Carbonara also contributed to the score but did not receive screen credit. The Academy Award went to all except Gruenberg and Carbonara.

24. Matthew Bernstein, *Walter Wanger, Hollywood Independent* (Berkeley: University of California Press, 1994), 149.

25. Although the song certainly does sound as if it was written in the nineteenth century, it was in fact composed by Owen Wister and used in stage adaptations of his novel *The Virginian*. (The song, with words and music by Wister, was first published in 1904.) Several sources have argued that Wister based the song upon folk ballads circulating in the northern Plains states in the years following the notorious winter of 1886–1887, which killed thousands of cattle. To complicate matters, Wister's version was published in numerous anthologies without attribution, even though the song was copyrighted. It appears, for instance, in Margaret Larkin's *Singing Cowboy* in 1931, where it was attributed to a Colorado source, and in Lomax's revised and updated *Cowboy Songs and Other Frontier Ballads*, 1938, where it was also not attributed to Wister. Little wonder, then, that Paramount found itself, at a very late date in the production, using a song that turned out to be copyrighted after all. For the thorny history of Wister's song, see Jim Bob Tinsley, *He Was Singin' This Song* (Orlando: University Presses of Florida, 1981), 88–91; Glenn Ohrlin, *The Hell-Bound Train: A Cowboy Songbook* (Urbana: University of Illinois Press, 1973), 15–17; and John I. White, *Git Along, Little Dogies: Songs and Songmakers of the American West* (Urbana: University of Illinois Press, 1975), 27–37.

26. That fee was initially $2500.

27. Even the Press Book lists "Ten Thousand Cattle" as part of the catalogue of traditional American music used in the film.

28. For work in this area, see Claudia Gorbman, "Indian Music in the Liberal Western," paper presented at the Society for Cinema Studies Conference, New York, 1995.

29. Gorbman, "Indian Music," 2.

30. Edward Buscombe, *Stagecoach* (London: British Film Institute, 1992), 54.

31. Gallagher, *John Ford*, 150.

32. Although based on American folk songs (and other traditional sources), the score for *Stagecoach* is not historically accurate. *Stagecoach* takes place sometime during the years 1881 to 1886, when Geronimo was on the warpath in the American South-

west. Certain of the folk songs do belong to this period, such as "Joe Bowers," a Gold Rush song; "The Trail to Mexico," a frontier ballad; and "Gentle Annie," a Stephen Foster tune. But other songs postdate the time period of the film. Most notably, some of the bordello songs heard in the Lordsburg section were composed around the turn of the century, such as "She Is More to Be Pitied Than Censured" and "Up in a Balloon, Boys." "I Love You," the song that becomes Dallas and Ringo's leitmotif, turns up in the 1923 Broadway musical *Little Jesse James.* I suspect that this song is itself derived from traditional sources.

33. Stephen Foster, composer of source music for both *My Darling Clementine* ("Camptown Races") and *Stagecoach* ("Jeanie with the Light Brown Hair" and "Gentle Annie"), has as complicated a relationship to the South as he does to the West. Not only did Foster never travel west of Kentucky, he only traveled south of it once in his lifetime, on a riverboat trip to New Orleans, and that was only after he had composed the bulk of his work. Foster was a Northerner and an Easterner, born and bred. There is much evidence to suggest that he was, in fact, growing uncomfortable with the minstrel songs (such as "Camptown Races") that earned him his livelihood and connected him in the public mind to the South. In later years, he turned to sentimental ballads, such as "Jeanie," but these never enjoyed the success of the minstrel songs. I think there has been a great deal of slippage in Foster's oeuvre between his minstrel songs and his sentimental ballads in terms of Southern-ness. Although the ballads were never written in dialect, they nonetheless carry the connotations of Southern-ness attached to the minstrel songs. The relationship among blackface minstrel songs, the South, and the West is an extremely complicated one and a subject for an article, if not a book, of its own.

34. Music department correspondence at Paramount reveals that nineteen songs were initially considered for possible use in the film, depending on their copyright status. (The studio obviously didn't want to pay copyright fees when so much traditional music was in the public domain.) The only song title to appear on the cue sheet, however, is "Ten Thousand Cattle." This is somewhat misleading. Cue sheets were in-house documents used to determine screen (and sometimes Academy Award) credits and copyright obligations. If a song was in public domain, there was no legal obligation to pay any fees. Thus songs in the public domain were often listed on the cue sheet under the title of the cue. "Shall We Gather at the River?" for instance, appears on the cue sheet as "The Two Outcasts." This helps to explain why "Ten Thousand Cattle" was penciled in the margins of the preliminary cue sheet. The music department was working under the assumption that the song was in the public domain, and when that turned out not to be the case, its title was hastily added to the cue sheet.

35. Behlmer, *Behind the Scenes,* 117; Buscombe, *Stagecoach,* 48.

36. Written on the cue sheet as "She's More to Be Pitied Than Censored."

37. On the basis of the title of the song and Ringo's description of his ranch as across the border, one might be tempted to argue that at the end of the film Ringo, in fleeing the American West for Mexico, is embracing the very culture of the Other that Ford disenfranchises. On this point I agree with Richard Slotkin when he argues that "Mexico" in Westerns in general, and in *Stagecoach* in particular, is a nebulous, "disembodied" place unrelated to the historical Mexico. He describes it as a "mythic space par excellence: outside the frame of 'history'." See Richard Slotkin, *Gunfighter Nation: The Myth of the Frontier in Twentieth-Century America* (New York: Atheneum, 1992), 310–311.

38. Caryl Flinn, *Strains of Utopia: Gender, Nostalgia, and Hollywood Film Music* (Princeton: Princeton University Press, 1992), 9.

39. Song and its ideological function can be traced across a number of other Ford Westerns, even those which may seem antithetical, musically, to *My Darling Clementine* and *Stagecoach*. Even Max Steiner's highly conventionalized and romantically inflected score for *The Searchers* uses music to evoke community or, in this case, lost community. (Think of how many communal moments accompanied by music are interrupted in the film.)

8

JOHN FORD AND JAMES FENIMORE COOPER
TWO RODE TOGETHER
Barry Keith Grant

Writing about the deficiencies of most film genre criticism, both Alan Williams and Steve Neale have called for more attention to be paid to what Williams refers to as a film genre's "pre-history" and "its roots in other media."[1] But with few exceptions, critics have not pursued this line of investigation, continuing instead to treat film genres apart from other aspects of popular culture.[2] In regard to the Western specifically, little more has been done than Henry Nash Smith's *Virgin Land* (1950), John Cawelti's *The Six-Gun Mystique* (1970), and, more recently, the epic three-volume exploration of the American frontier as cultural myth by Richard Slotkin.[3]

It is now more than twenty years since Peter Wollen, in the chapter on auteurism in his influential *Signs and Meaning in the Cinema*, advised film critics that "We need comparisons with authors in the other arts: Ford with Fenimore Cooper, for example, or Hawks with Faulkner."[4] While some scholars have in fact gone on to investigate the stylistic and thematic connections between the work of Hawks and Faulkner,[5] there have been no extended examinations of Cooper and Ford, despite the fact that they are the two most significant figures in the Western genre, artists who tower over the rest of the posse like John Waynes striding among a multitude of nondescript cowboys.

Their work was instrumental in defining the genre itself, and while both artists also created more overtly "socially conscious" fictions, both are primarily remembered for their forays into the apparently more escapist Western. Cooper's novels of social criticism as well as his polemical tracts such as *The American Democrat* (1838) have been generally forgotten, while his Western series, the Leatherstocking Tales, is canonized within American literature. Cooper himself accurately predicted that "If anything from the pen of the writer of these romances is at all to outlive himself, it is, unquestionably, the series of 'The Leather-Stocking Tales.'"[6] Similarly, Ford's place in film history has come to rest more on his Westerns than on either the movies of Americana (the Will Rogers films, *The Last Hurrah* [1958]); the "art films" (*The Informer* [1935], *The Long Voyage Home* [1940]); or even the prestige pictures of social conscience (*The Grapes of Wrath* [1940]).

But while Cawelti has observed that the work of both men shares a sense of "elegiac nostalgia" and Robert B. Ray has compared Ford's *The Man Who Shot Liberty Valance* (1962) to Cooper's *The Pioneers* (1823),[7] no one has considered the remarkable parallels between their Western oeuvres. This lack constitutes a surprising critical gap, given the comparable significance of each in the history of the genre. Their similar skill at exploiting the constituent elements of the Western, as well as their similarly evolving attitudes toward those elements, makes a comparison of their work especially important to understanding the history of the genre as a whole. Indeed, any comparative examination of the Westerns of Cooper and Ford is necessarily an examination of the Western itself as well.

In the following analysis of the Westerns of Cooper and Ford I shall focus on three areas that have been of particular concern to critics writing on the Western genre: their function as cultural myth and their aesthetic relation to issues of realism; their representation of the Western hero and his relation to action and landscape; and the relation between myth and history. As we shall see, the connections between the works of Cooper and Ford, the striking parallels in the way the two conceived of and worked through the genre's central thematic oppositions despite the different media and historical contexts in which they worked, are profound indeed and ultimately challenge conventional wisdom about genre "evolution."

MYTH AND REALISM

It is true that some elements of the Western were already present in the earlier captivity narratives of the Puritans.[8] But it is in his five Leatherstocking Tales featuring Natty Bumppo—*The Pioneers* (1823), *The Last of the Mohicans* (1826), *The Prairie* (1827), *The Pathfinder* (1840), and *The Deerslayer* (1841)— that Cooper combined the appeal of such stories with the historical romance in the manner of Sir Walter Scott and the actual figure of Daniel Boone as popularized in John Filson's *Discovery, Settlement, and Present State of Kentucke* (1784) to forge a new genre. By appropriating and combining these sources, Cooper was able to charge what has become the Western with the iconographic and mythic power that is at the heart of the genre as we understand and appreciate it today.

With the very first novel in the series, *The Pioneers,* Cooper's prose sought to reach beyond realism for the grand abstraction of myth. For example, at the end of the novel, Leatherstocking leaves the townsfolk and moves on. Cooper adopts the viewpoint of the genteel heroine, who

> . . . saw the old hunter standing, looking back for a moment, on the verge of the wood. As he caught their glances, he drew his hand hastily across his eyes

again, waved it on high for an adieu, and uttering a forced cry to his dogs, who were crouching at his feet, he entered the forest. . . . This was the last that they ever saw of the Leatherstocking. . . He had gone far towards the setting sun—the foremost in that band of pioneers who are opening the way for the march of the nation across the continent.[9]

In these two concluding paragraphs Cooper manages to capture one of the essential conventions of the genre, the tragic quality of the stoic Western hero who, in helping others meet the dangers of the frontier, inevitably displaces and sacrifices himself. It is hardly possible to read this passage without thinking of young Brandon de Wilde imploring Alan Ladd's Shane to stay as he rides out of town at the end of that most self-consciously classic of Westerns.[10] Because so many of the genre's conventions can be traced in like manner to the Leatherstocking Tales, Leslie Fiedler claims that in these five books Cooper virtually "invented" the Western, and Cawelti that he "originated the Western as we know it."[11]

Just as Cooper provided the narrative conventions of the Western as well as its iconography, so Ford defined much of its look, the way the material of the Western was translated from page to screen. For example, Ford contributed significantly to the development of John Wayne as the ideal iconographic embodiment of the Western hero, making him in the national imagination a mythic figure equal to Cooper's Natty Bumppo. As well, his use of landscape has been so influential that no subsequent film may show Monument Valley without invoking his work in the viewer's mind. Ford shot nine movies there, beginning with *Stagecoach* (1939), working the images of its distinctive contours to the extent that, as Joseph McBride and Michael Wilmington have enthused, the place transcends its geographical location to become a "state of mind . . . point[ing] toward Eternity."[12]

The Western has been commonly perceived as a system of binary oppositions, largely as the result of the influential structural analysis of Jim Kitses and the more historically based work of Cawelti. For Kitses, the genre crystallizes the conflicting attitudes about the West that have pervaded American cultural thought in a series of "antinomies" between the wilderness and civilization. These oppositions are possessed of clusters of opposing values (individual/community, nature/culture) derived from a multitude of cultural discourses, which in turn generate its function as cultural myth. In any given Western, the respective representations of the wilderness and of civilization determine its ideology, its attitude toward the genre's dialectical thematic. The central question of the Western, says Kitses, is this: "Is the West a Garden of natural dignity and innocence offering refuge from the decadence of civilization? Or is it a treacherous Desert stubbornly resisting the gradual sweep of agrarian progress and community values?"[13]

Immediately in the opening scene of *The Pioneers,* Cooper initiates the action of a scene that is now a familiar one in the genre. It is the beginning of the deer-hunting season, and two men, Bumppo and Judge Temple, having shot at the same buck at approximately the same time, claim ownership of the animal. Natty's claim is based on empirical pragmatism as he explains why the Judge could not possibly have hit the buck from his position, but Judge Temple, the founder of the town in the wilderness and the embodiment of Law, rhetorically confounds the issue for the plain-dealing Natty by resorting to obfuscating legal language ("'what we call an act of supererogation'"[14]) in order to take it. In Cooper's handling of this scene, many of the binary oppositions enumerated by Kitses are mobilized and amplified in the ensuing narrative conflict.

It is Ford's comparable ability to animate the genre's binary elements that has made, for example, the dance scene in *My Darling Clementine* (1946) so justly famous.[15] Ford views the character of Wyatt Earp (the appropriately cast Henry Fonda) as a proud individualist who accepts the inevitable coming of civilization. After accepting the marshal's badge and the values it represents, Earp goes to the barber, who shears the visible sign of Earp's uncivilized existence. The artificial scent of the honeysuckle perfume that the barber uses on him is commented upon more than once in the dialogue.

Shortly after his visit to the barbershop, Earp meets Clementine (Cathy Downs). They exit the hotel to the street, the avenue of social discourse, link arms, and walk toward the church. When the male hero, the individual, joins with the woman (a schoolmarm), the Western icon of social responsibility, the frame is neatly balanced by the desert behind Earp on one side and the hotel behind Clementine on the other. The genre's alternatives, typically represented by town and desert, are, at least temporarily, reconciled in the linked arms of the two characters.

The church at the other end of the street—the immediate destination of the characters as well as the ethical and spiritual goal of the new civilization they represent—has only its foundation built, but an American flag on a pole rising from this foundation billows in the wind. Earp and Clementine join in the dance on the church floor, a Fordian ritual of community and a celebratory image of civilization's incipient victory over the wilderness of unregenerate individualism (represented in *My Darling Clementine* by the brutish self-interest of the Clantons). Here, as in so many other places in Ford's Westerns, action, dialogue, iconography, and mise en scène all work within the generic context to provide meaning. The communal harmony that the scene so gloriously depicts is, for Ford, the base of true civilization and its establishment on the frontier. But the brevity of this pastoral lyricism perhaps only underscores the ultimate irreconcilability of wilderness and civilization that Cooper also explores. The celebratory gathering of the townsfolk is, finally, an experience that the individual Earp cannot be a permanent part of, and he, like Hawkeye, lights out for the territory at the end.

Wyatt Earp (Henry Fonda) and Clementine (Cathy Downs) walking to the church dance in *My Darling Clementine* (1946).
Courtesy of Barry Grant.

In the Leatherstocking Tales, truly Romances in Northrop Frye's sense, Cooper takes every opportunity to demonstrate the ability of Natty Bumppo and "his red associates" to practice "the art of the forest." Cooper sacrifices verisimilitude at the snap of a proverbial dry twig for the sake of mythic scope. In *The Last of the Mohicans,* for example, Hawkeye, Chingachgook, and Uncas are able to read footprints in the bank of a stream after diverting its path and to sneak through enemy lines around the tightly besieged Fort Henry by following the furrows of cannonballs through a thick fog. As befits the hero of Romance, Hawkeye is "superior in *degree* to other men and to his environment";[16] he is larger than life, like the Westerners of Ford silhouetted against the setting sun.

In *The Prairie,* Bumppo ("the trapper") and his accompanying band of assorted character types are engaged in a debate about the scientific basis of the biblical version of creation when they observe a buffalo stampede on the horizon. But even the imminent danger posed by the advancing herd cannot halt the hero's philosophical musing:

> Clouds of dust shot up in little columns from the centre of the mass, as some animal, more furious than the rest, ploughed the plain with his horns, and, from time to time, a deep hollow bellowing was borne along on the wind, as if a thousand throats vented their plaints in a discordant murmuring.
>
> A long and musing silence reigned in the party, as they gazed on this spectacle of wild and peculiar grandeur. It was at length broken by the trapper,

who, having been long accustomed to similar sights, felt less of its influence, or rather, felt it in a less thrilling and absorbing manner, than those to whom the scene was more novel.

"There go ten thousand oxen in one drove, without keeper or master, except Him who made them, and gave them these open plains for their pasture! Ay, it is here that man may see the proofs of his wantonness and folly! Can the proudest governor in all the States go into his fields, and slaughter a nobler bullock than is here offered to the meanest hand; and when he has gotten his sirloin or his steak, can he eat it with as good a relish as he who has sweetened his food with wholesome toil, and earned it according to the law of natur' by honestly mastering that which the Lord hath put before him?

"But the herd is heading a little this-a-way, and it behoves us to make ready for their visit."[17]

At the last moment, when the herd is bearing down upon them, Natty smartly leads his intrepid band to shelter under an outcropping of rock, which, conveniently located on the flat expanse of the plains, helps divide the thundering herd into flanking streams.

Mark Twain interpreted such prose as failings on Cooper's part in his (in)famous essay "Fenimore Cooper's Literary Offenses." By Twain's reckoning, Cooper was guilty of violating eighteen rules of literary art, out of a possible nineteen. Twain had great fun at Cooper's expense, observing, for example, that

> A favorite one [of Cooper's "tricks"] was his broken twig. He prized his broken twig above all the rest of his effects, and worked it the hardest. It is a restful chapter in any book of his when somebody doesn't step on a dry twig and alarm all the reds and whites for two hundred yards around. Every time a Cooper person is in peril, and absolute silence is worth four dollars a minute, he is sure to step on a dry twig. There may be a hundred handier things to step on, but that wouldn't satisfy Cooper. Cooper requires him to turn out and find a dry twig; and if he can't do it, go and borrow one.[18]

Perhaps the first instance of deconstructionist criticism, Twain's essay unravels in impressive detail the absurdities of the passage in *The Deerslayer* in which a group of six Indians, apparently neither very bright nor well coordinated, attempt to ambush the floating Hutter home by dropping onto it from overhanging branches—with amazingly improbable results. Twain concludes that this episode "does not thrill, because the inaccuracy of the details throws a sort of air of fictitiousness and general improbability over it."[19]

Today, however, we might regard Cooper's improbabilities more charitably as conventions, no more or less believable finally than any other, like breaking into song and dance in a musical or having a showdown on Main Street (an event which did not happen very often in the real West but does consistently in the Western, including several of Ford's). Twain's attack is a somewhat unfair (though very funny) roast by a realist writer operating within a different aesthetic tradition. His criticism of Cooper's skill at characterization, for example, that one cannot distinguish the living persons from the corpses, assumes that Cooper failed to create psychologically rounded characters; yet Cooper himself explicitly acknowledged a preference for depicting classes or types rather than rounded individuals in his work.[20] His characters, not unlike most in Ford's Westerns, are generic types. Leslie Fiedler's comment that "Cooper had, alas, all the qualifications for a great American writer except the simple ability to write" is more appreciative of the mythic quality of Cooper's prose.[21]

Choosing not to present ethnographically accurate representations of Western peoples and places, which for Twain constituted an artistic failure of basic "observation,"[22] Cooper established a powerful national myth, the Western, discovering in the process the first truly American story. American writers before him (Charles Brockden Brown, Washington Irving) had imitated their European and British models too closely, and it was Cooper who first recast the British novel into American terms, infusing the form with native materials (forests, Indians, issues of wilderness ethics). Cooper was the first writer whose work examined the nature of what historian Frederick Jackson Turner would later call the "crucible" of the wilderness and its significance in shaping both American history and a distinctive American national character.

For Turner, the existence of the frontier tested American settlers with unique challenges and experiences that encouraged the development of certain character traits required for their survival. Such qualities as self-reliance and rugged individualism, combined with a "unifying tendency" needed to maintain the frontier's "nucleus of settlement," in turn "promoted the formation of a composite nationality for the American people."[23] The Western, beginning with the Leatherstocking Tales, articulated a cultural myth because the books are largely about the definition and evaluation of these qualities, particularly the difficulty of striking a balance between the "unifying tendency" (civilization) and rugged individualism (wilderness), and the relation between this "new product that is American" and the unique shaping of American democracy.[24] The Westerns of both Cooper and Ford have been fundamental in establishing this conflict, which has become "the dialectical structure of the Western."[25]

Ford, too, takes frequent liberties with realism, similarly striving to create a mythic space rather than an actual one. Occasionally Ford violates the norms of the classical Hollywood style (narrative cinema's equivalent of realism), such as the conventional continuity of screen direction. Such violations are sometimes motivated to achieve a particular effect, as Ray argues about the shootout in *Liberty Valance*,[26] but at other times are diegetically unmotivated. In *The Iron Horse* (1924), for example, the Indian scouts, waiting to ambush the train, are shown looking off screen left, the same direction in which the train is shown to be traveling. In the same film, more than once Ford violates Hollywood's nor-

mally sacrosanct 180-degree rule, reversing the direction in which Indians ride
their horses within the same scene. Perhaps the most famous example of this
liberty with screen direction occurs during the climactic chase in *Stagecoach*.
As the stage is being pursued by the Apache across the dry lake bed, Ford films
the action from both sides, with the effect that the coach and the pursuing Indians seem suddenly to reverse direction. Ford's preference for mythic over real
space is revealed in his explanation of the construction of this scene: the sun was
setting, so that if he had maintained the camera's position "the horses would
have been back-lit, and I couldn't show their speed in back light."[27] Because of
such constructions, John Baxter goes so far as to claim that Ford frequently
displays a "total disregard for visual consistency," as in his alternation between
real exteriors and artificial interiors. He even claims this stylistic trait as the
distinctive feature of Ford as auteur, for in such moments the director's personal
vision transcends conventional codes of expression.[28]

Indeed, if Twain were to critique, say, *Stagecoach,* he probably would question why the Apache did not simply shoot the stage's lead horse during the
climactic chase across the salt flats, or how Ringo is able to shoot two Apache
off their horses with one bullet from the roof of the speeding coach. One might
also consider the timely arrival of the cavalry in the climax, coming to the rescue as if in answer to Mrs. Mallory's prayers, *deus ex machina* (a scene borrowed from Griffith's 1914 Western, *The Battle of Elderbush Gulch*), to be an
even more amazing coincidence than the timely appearance of Ringo in the
stagecoach's path carrying his rifle and saddle. Similarly, the perfectly timed
arrival of the Kansas cattle in the Wyoming Rockies in *The Iron Horse* just as
the railroad workers are about to rebel because of hunger requires a willing
suspension of disbelief as great as when Natty divides that buffalo stampede
like Moses parting the Red Sea. If Ford, like Cooper, sometimes stretches cre-
dulity in what Twain would call narrative "situations," it is because the mythic
dimension of the Western requires the hero to be associated with the wilderness
and to have the opportunity to demonstrate in some spectacular fashion "the
art of the forest."

Ford does provide his Westerns with a greater sense of verisimilitude than
Cooper (although the degree of the writer's anthropological accuracy concerning Native Americans has been a subject of some debate), and he was known
for employing Native Americans when making his Westerns. But his greater
attention to historical detail is in large part attributable to the differences between literature and film as media, for where language tends toward the abstract, the camera has the inevitable power of documenting the visible surface
of things. Ford told Peter Bogdanovich that because he had known Wyatt Earp
personally he was able to do the climactic gunfight at the OK Corral "exactly
the way it had been," and that the Grand March in *Fort Apache* (1948) was
"typical of the period. . . . I try to make it true to life."[29] An insert title in *The*

Iron Horse tells us that for the reenactment of the completion of the transcontinental railroad in 1869, the original two locomotives were used. The mise en scène of the climactic ceremonial driving of the golden spike closely resembles that in photographs of the actual event. But these details may be less the result of the auteur's vision than standard studio practice for providing historical films with a sense of accuracy, a practice made famous by Griffith in *Birth of a Nation* (1915).

In any event, the historical specificity of Ford's images is always informed with larger mythic resonance. Ford is frequently viewed as one of the few American film "poets"—the term is used by, among others, Bogdanovich, Lindsay Anderson, Andrew Sarris, Robin Wood, and even Orson Welles, who claimed to have watched *Stagecoach* forty times in preparation for making *Citizen Kane* (1941)[30]—and his films are called "poetic" largely because they possess a "double vision," the concrete immediacy of narrative events reverberating with the abstraction of history. In Sarris's famous words, Ford alternates "between close-ups of emotional intensity and long shots of epic involvement, thus capturing both the twitches of life and the silhouette of legend."[31]

This quality is common to all of Ford's Westerns, but it appears perhaps most emphatically in *The Man Who Shot Liberty Valance,* with its main nar-

Silhouetting de-emphasizes the particulars of character
for the larger historical view.
Directorial credit for *Rio Grande* (1950).

rative framed as a flashback from the present, a time when the glory days of the old West have passed. Ford's fondness for silhouetting his characters against expanses of sky and land graphically de-emphasizes the particulars of character in favor of the larger historical view. Such shots appear, pointedly, as the first image in *The Horse Soldiers* (1959) and behind the directorial credit in *Rio Grande* (1950). *Stagecoach* is the best example of Sarris's contention, as structurally it expresses what he terms Ford's "double vision" in its alternation of tight shots of characters in the coach with panoramic shots of Monument Valley. The long shots of the coach moving through the valley reveal the dangers facing this particular group of travelers even as they visually attest to civilization's tenuous toe-hold in the wilderness.

LANDSCAPE, ACTION, AND HEROES

In their approach to the Western myth, both Cooper and Ford treated the landscape and defined their heroes' relation to it through action. As their imagination was focused less on naturalistic depictions of Western life than on exploring the mythic potential of their stories, both artists sought to embellish their work for pictorial effect. The visual richness of Cooper's prose and of Ford's distinctive imagery have been the subject of much scholarly work,[32] but not the degree to which both artists use the Western landscape to similar purpose, as an index of their characters' moral worth.

Consistently in their Westerns, action is played out in terms of its appropriateness to the American landscape's unique qualities. Marius Bewley has observed that action in Cooper's Western novels is "the intensified motion of life in which the spiritual and moral faculties of men are no less engaged than their physical selves."[33] In other words, what men *do* in these books is a direct expression of their beliefs and values. This idea, I think, applies equally to the action in Ford's Westerns, and is another sense in which the works of both men express that mythic "double vision." The ability to perceive the American landscape on its own terms, seeing both its unique beauties and the particular challenges it engenders, and the relation between this ability and moral worth, are themes that unite many of Ford's Westerns as strongly as they do all five of the Leatherstocking narratives.

Cooper was well aware of the distinctive landscapes that characterized the work of the Hudson River School painters (1825–c. 1880), a few of whom he knew personally. Some of them illustrated scenes in early editions of Cooper's books. According to Howard Mumford Jones, the principal theme informing the work of the Hudson River School was the naturally immanent grandeur of God working within the universe, represented by the glorious sublimity of the American landscape.[34] Following these artists, Cooper invested his landscapes with metaphorical import and used the landscape as concrete instances of the frontier's crucible. In *The Pathfinder,* for example, the most frequent topic of conversation concerns how to sail through the fresh water of Lake Ontario despite its deadly undertow, a phenomenon repeatedly said to be unique to the Great Lakes. The issue is metaphorically related to the main plot, which features the gradual realization that a spy is present in disguise, hiding "below," among the crew of this microcosmic ship of state.

In *The Pioneers,* wherein "The actors are as unique as the scenery,"[35] the thematic conflict between Judge Marmaduke Temple, founder of the town of Templeton, and the elderly trapper Natty is embodied in their respective apperception and appreciation of the glorious Catskill landscape. The Judge, representing the letter of the law, first envisions founding the town when looking down from atop the significantly named Mt. Vision. In order to facilitate the town's progress, he inevitably has the trees cleared from a portion of the site. The Judge cannot see the trees for the forest, and so later is almost killed when one falls directly in front of him. In other words, he is blind to the dangers of his own "Vision" and so, during the climactic fire, unaware of his daughter's possible immolation, the Judge is unable to act, frozen in "contemplation" of the flaming mountain.[36] By contrast, Natty also gazes from a spot in the mountains, but his vantage point is so much higher than the "Vision" that Natty can see not only all the "manufactories, bridges, canals, [and] mines" of Templeton, but nothing less than "Creation, all creation."[37]

Because Natty is consistently attuned to the unique properties of the land, he is able to offer different but successful strategies for dealing with the crucibles of the wilderness and fulfilling the Western hero's code, which he phrases as "Life is an obligation which friends often owe to each other in the wilderness."[38] In *The Last of the Mohicans,* his understanding of the land is consistently opposed to the less attentive view of Duncan Heyward, a British officer charged with conducting Alice and Cora Munro to safety. Just as Heyward dislikes the taste of the wild water of an American stream, a taste that, as Natty says, must be acquired,[39] so Heyward is initially opposed to Natty's military philosophy but by the end comes to accept it.

At one point, when he is supposed to be on watch, Heyward falls asleep and dreams, significantly, "that he was a knight of ancient chivalry, holding his midnight vigils before the tent of a recaptured princess." When the party is besieged by the Hurons at the Falls, Heyward's impulse is to rush forward to meet them, a knight protecting his lady fair, but he must be restrained by Hawkeye, Chingachgook and Uncas. But he is, in Cooper's words, "an adventurer in empiricism" who must learn the inappropriateness of such chivalric defense in the context of the American forest, which requires a more pragmatic approach ("dodge and cover," Hawkeye calls it). Facing imminent capture by Magua, Cooper's trio of American heroes are willing to exploit the cover provided by the Falls and abandon the rest of the party, since, as Cora notes, to stay will serve only "to increase the horror of our capture, and to diminish the chances of our release." Heyward, however, steadfastly remains behind because he considers it his duty to do so, and is saved, along with the rest of the party, only because Hawkeye was able to escape in the first place.[40]

Ford, too, had a particularly strong feeling for the wilderness landscape, which he often depicted in an admirably epic mise en scène, and he similarly linked it to character through action. Like Cooper, Ford was clearly influenced by Western painters, especially the work of Frederic Remington, whom the director specifically identified as an influence on the look of *She Wore a Yellow Ribbon* (1949).[41] Remington's influence on Ford has been explored in detail by Edward Buscombe, whose research suggests that scenes such as the climactic chase in *Stagecoach* were likely modeled in part on paintings such as Remington's 1907 "Downing the Nigh Leader."[42]

Ford did much of his Western shooting on location rather than in the studio or on the backlot, and the landscape figures prominently in his Westerns. Sometimes it is absolutely central to the action in his films, even in such non-Westerns as *The Lost Patrol* (1934) and *The Hurricane* (1937). This emphasis on landscape is evident in his striking outdoor compositions, particularly in the numerous long shots in which land and sky dominate. His landscape shots often encapsulate theme, as in the "epic" long shots of *Stagecoach* and the famous opening shot of *The Searchers* (1956), which frames the expanse of Monument Valley within the ranch house doorway.

Ford's Westerns often express a sublime regard for nature and landscape that marks him as a direct descendant of such Hudson River painters as Albert Bierstadt. This is perhaps most explicit in *3 Godfathers* (1948), wherein the Western desert becomes the backdrop to and cause of a Christian transformation among three bank robbers who must purge themselves of their selfish desire for filthy lucre in order to deliver the baby they have rescued to the nurturing "bosom" (as Mr. Peacock in *Stagecoach* would call it) of civilization. But even without the obvious Christian overtones of *3 Godfathers*, Ford, like Cooper, often used the landscape as a Turneresque crucible to test through action the moral and political values his characters represent. As Baxter has observed, Ford had a penchant for using nature in a "precise and symbolic" manner[43]—as in the ending of *Young Mr. Lincoln* (1939), in which the future president walks alone over a hill toward a gathering storm. Storms also appear symbolically in Ford's Westerns, like the one in *Drums along the Mohawk* (1939) that represents Lana's psychological low point as she attempts to come to grips with the realities of frontier life.

J. A. Place has noted that *Drums along the Mohawk* "makes full use of weather symbolism," consistently reflecting the narrative issue of Lana's development from an Easterner to a hardy pioneer and the development of the Western community in qualities of the land and weather.[44] *Stagecoach, Fort*

Apache, Wagon Master (1950), and *The Searchers* also emphasize their characters' appreciation for and perception of the distinctive Western landscape in relation to the moral and political values appropriate to the frontier. Actually this is
true even in lesser Ford Westerns, such as *Rio Grande*, for example, where there
is no doubt that trooper Tyree (Ben Johnson) is not only innocent of manslaughter
but a man of moral integrity because, as Ford shows, he can handle horses ably
and puts himself in danger to rescue another trooper during an Indian attack.

The journeys through the wilderness in *Stagecoach* and *Wagon Master* serve
the same function as the journey in *The Last of the Mohicans*—to define and
test a democratic, pragmatic social ethic in the context of the wilderness. In
Stagecoach, the characters who represent such values (Ringo, Doc Boone, Dallas)
or adopt them (Peacock, Mrs. Mallory) survive the journey and reach Lordsburg,
while outworn and corrupt values, embodied respectively by the fallen Southern aristocrat Hatfield (John Carradine) and the embezzling banker Gatewood
(Berton Churchill), are eliminated from the fledgling democratic society aboard
the stage. Similarly, in *Wagon Master* civilization, as represented by the west-
ward-bound Mormon wagon train, must negotiate between the materialism
represented by the primal horde of the Cleggs on the one hand, the physical desire
represented by the show troupe on the other, and also their own internal intolerance, as caricatured in Russell Simpson's portrayal of the staunch Elder Adam.
Successfully doing so, in the end the wagon train reaches the promised land of
the fertile San Juan Valley to establish its settlement.

But that goal could not have been reached without the help of the cowboy
Travis (Ben Johnson), for it is his decisive action that is needed to expel the Cleggs
from the nascent society. Indeed, no wagon train can complete its journey, no
group of British gentry can arrive safely back at the fort, without the help of the
Western hero, the embodiment of the genre's ideal ethical "code."[45] In Ford's
Westerns, as in Cooper's, this code defines the hero as the ideal American so
enthusiastically described by Hector St. John de Crevecoeur: "*He* is an American, who, leaving behind him all his ancient prejudices and manners, receives
new ones from the new mode of life he has embraced. . . . The American is a
new man, who acts upon new principles."[46] Both artists examine these principles in the context of the heroic action required of the landscape's crucible.

In *Stagecoach,* this code is embodied by Ringo (John Wayne, in his first
starring role), whose relationship to the land is emphasized by his startling first
appearance, and then by the open window behind where he sits in the coach—
between the other characters, as befits his role as mediating hero. In Wayne's
famous introductory shot in the film, in which he suddenly emerges out of the
desert, the camera dollies in for an emphatic close-up, one of the few instances
in Ford's work of the camera moving in relation to a stationary subject (another,
equally emphatic, example occurs when Lucy [Pippa Scott] realizes the Indian
attack is coming in *The Searchers*). "One of the most stunning entrances in all

of cinema,"[47] Ringo's first appearance is a worthy equivalent to Natty's grand entrances in the Leatherstocking Tales, such as the one which opens *The Prairie:* "The sun had fallen below the crest of the nearest wave of the prairie, leaving the usual rich and glowing train on its track. In the centre of this flood of fiery light a human form appeared, drawn against the gilded background as distinctly, and seemingly as palpable, as though it would come within the grasp of any extended hand. The figure was colossal."[48]

Like Hawkeye, Ringo is the most perceptive about the landscape, so he is the first to observe the Indians in the distance at the Apache Wells way station (the "war signals" he points out to Curley [George Bancroft] are in fact difficult to discern in Curley's subsequent point-of-view shot of the surrounding landscape). And, again like Hawkeye, Ringo believes in communal responsibility for survival, so at the last moment he abandons his escape even as he is making it, in order to defend the other passengers. Ringo's code is set in explicit opposition to the "civilized" code of chivalry represented by the aristocratic Hatfield, much as Heywood is contrasted to Hawkeye in *Mohicans.* Hatfield offers water (a central metaphor in Ford's Westerns, as his frequent use of the song "Shall We Gather at the River?" suggests) to Mrs. Mallory (Louise Platt) from a silver cup, while refusing the same offer to the "fallen woman," Dallas (Claire Trevor); Ringo, however, democratically shares the communal canteen with her. Hatfield saves one bullet for Mrs. Mallory, and is about to kill her so that the "angel in the jungle" will not meet "a fate worse than death" at the hands of Indians; Ringo

The introductory shot of Ringo (John Wayne) in *Stagecoach* (1939). Courtesy of Barry Grant.

saves three bullets, one for each of the Plummer Brothers. Tellingly, Hatfield is killed before he can pull the trigger, before he can act upon his code,[49] while Ringo is able to defeat the three Plummers, one of whom is even armed with a shotgun, in the film's final showdown.

Wayne in Ford's Westerns (with the notable exception of *The Searchers*) tends to be a hero in the mythic mold of Natty, who is described in another Cooper novel, *Home as Found* (1838), as "a man who had the simplicity of a woodsman, the heroism of a savage, the faith of a Christian, and the feelings of a poet."[50] Such idealization applies as well to Ford's Wayne (unlike Hawks's Wayne), who also, as Fiedler says of Natty, has "detached" himself from his texts and "entered the free domain of our dreams."[51] Both are figures of mythic proportion, like the imaginary ideal of Captain Buffalo in *Sergeant Rutledge* (1960). And like Hawkeye in *Mohicans*, Ford's Wayne tends to display a difficult but necessary pragmatism, as when his Ethan Edwards in *The Searchers*, in opposition to the Heyward-like impetuous idealism of Martin Pawley (Jeffrey Hunter), insists on watering the horses before returning to the ranch where he knows his brother's family has been attacked in order ultimately to get there more quickly.

As part of Cooper's and Ford's mythic approach to the Western, then, landscape is presented as the iconographic embodiment of the frontier "crucible," and heroic action, the concrete expression of a character's relation to the landscape, is symbolic of the democratic values forged in that crucible. For both artists, the ideal Western hero is able to perceive and have a special appreciation for the particulars of the landscape.

MYTH AND HISTORY

Both Leatherstocking and the Fordian Wayne attained their mythical status in part through the accumulation of multiple appearances. Cooper's Leatherstocking is in fact a composite of five different Natty Bumppos who evolve, in Frye's terms, from low mimetic comic relief in the first of the Leatherstocking Tales, *The Pioneers*, to mythic hero eighteen years later in the last book of the series, *The Deerslayer*, where he appears in his prime and the wilderness is Edenic.[52] Ford's vision of the Western hero is represented in different films by such actors as Harry Carey Jr., Ben Johnson, and Henry Fonda, as well as Wayne, although it is of course the latter who achieved iconographic weight comparable to Hawkeye's, having appeared in a total of seventeen of Ford's films over a span of four decades. Wayne's screen persona has come to stand as the embodiment of Ford's ideal of the American rugged individualist.

Naturally the depiction of these heroes and their heroic codes changed over time. Both men made their later Westerns feeling somewhat out of step with the American democracy that their work in the genre had earlier explored so enthusiastically. Natty, who had proudly proclaimed that he never saw the sky but through the branches of the forest trees, dies on the flat expanse of *The Prairie*, while Wayne's Tom Doniphon meets a similarly inglorious fate in *Liberty Valance*, buried by the county in a plain pine box without his boots or spurs. Thus the two artists moved from an initial optimism about America and democracy toward increasing doubt and disillusionment.

Both Cooper and Ford toward the end of their careers fell out of favor with the American public and experienced a profound sense of disenchantment. Cooper was embraced by the nation as a popular writer in the 1820s but only two decades later found himself the object of public ridicule and scorn, the victim, as he saw it, of the vagaries of public opinion. The administration of Andrew Jackson (1829–1837) marked the demise of the conservative politics of Federalism and the consequent rise of both capitalist materialism (in the new Whig party) and populism as dominant political forces in American life. So profound and rapid were these changes that Van Wyck Brooks dubbed the period "the nation's awkward age."[53] In 1826 Cooper left America for a seven-year tour of Europe (*The Last of the Mohicans* was published upon his arrival in England, and a good deal of *The Prairie* was written in Paris), which only served to heighten his sense of culture shock later. While abroad, he found himself defending the unpopular side of what was known as the Finance controversy, and upon his return to the United States he became embroiled in a legal dispute over a small tract of land known as Three Mile Point, an area that his family legally owned but that the people of Cooperstown claimed for their public use. These issues entangled Cooper in a series of libel cases that lasted for the rest of his life.[54]

Cooper came to regard himself as a voice of principle against the democratic recklessness that assumed the majority ("public opinion") was always right. It is no coincidence that in *The American Democrat* (subtitled *A Treatise on Jacksonian Democracy*) the chapter devoted to the "disadvantages of Democracy" is twice as long as those concerned with the drawbacks of either an aristocracy or a monarchy. The author's many legal battles were depicted in the popular press as a conflict between an aristocrat and the people. Even Walt Whitman, the good poet of democracy, publicly criticized Cooper as an "enormous ape" for his perseverance in libel prosecutions.[55] Raised as a conservative who believed that a virtuous gentry (a class that included himself) was best qualified for political leadership ("It takes a first-class aristocrat to make a first-class Democrat," he once wrote[56]), Cooper was left behind by these sweeping changes of Jacksonian democracy. By the late 1840s, Cooper's opinion of the "people" had degenerated to the point that he "would as soon confide in convicts."[57]

Critics have often noted that the diegetic chronology of the Leatherstocking Tales is almost the exact reverse of the books' order of composition. This evolution is usually explained as a progressive retreat into a mythic past while real experience increasingly disillusioned Cooper about American society and politics. As Cooper found himself increasingly at odds with the Jacksonian masses, his hero Natty moved further away, both spatially and temporally. *The Deerslayer,* the last of the series, even as it depicts the beauties of the natural environment, tells us in the very first paragraph that the process of "rescuing the region from the savage state" had begun two centuries ago.[58] *The Deerslayer* ends with a brutal incursion of the forces of civilization into its pastoral beauty, like Eisenstein's Cossacks on the Odessa Steps, as hyperbolic in its description as Lee Marvin's characterization of the eponymous villain in *Liberty Valance,* whose very name suggests the danger he embodies of shattering democratic freedoms:

> The sound was regular and heavy, as if the earth were struck with beetles. Objects became visible among the trees of the background, and a body of troops was seen advancing with measured tread. They came upon the charge, the scarlet of the king's livery shining among the bright green foliage of the forest. . . . A general yell burst from the enclosed Hurons; it was succeeded by the hearty cheers of England. . . . that steady, measured tramp continued, and the bayonet was seen gleaming in advance of a line that counted nearly sixty men.

Cooper, like his Natty, is forced in *The Deerslayer* to the conclusion that "The Law—'tis bad to have it, but I sometimes think it is worse to be entirely without it."[59]

Cooper's last published novel, *The Crater, or Vulcan's Peak* (1847), is an ironic utopia about an attempt to establish an ideal democratic society on a remote island. Built literally upon a shaky foundation of bird guano, it is clearly doomed from the start. In the narrative this hopeful society is gradually subverted until finally the author, seemingly impatient with its inevitable corruption—a clear parable of his own unfortunate experiences with the Jacksonian masses—sinks it to the bottom of the sea, all evidence of it vanishing without a trace. All that remains is what was there before the hand of man, the peak of the Crater, which Cooper describes as a "sublime rock" in the manner of Thomas Cole's landscapes. Recalling Shelley's "Ozymandias," this fate, Cooper warns in the concluding paragraph, is poetic justice for such political hubris: "Let those who would substitute the voice of the created for that of the Creator, who shout 'the people, the people,' instead of hymning the praises of their God, who vainly imagine that the masses are sufficient for all things, remember their insignificance and tremble."[60]

The similar evolution in Ford's vision is often cited as one of Ford's prime auteurist virtues, as in Wollen's celebrated preference of Ford over Hawks.[61] Critics have often noted the ambiguity of Doc Boone's (Thomas Mitchell) penultimate remark in *Stagecoach*—"Well, they're saved from the blessings of civilization"—as he and the sheriff send the wagon with Ringo and Dallas out into the Western landscape, away from the town to Ringo's wilderness ranch. Certainly Ford's early Westerns, like Cooper's, possess such moments of doubt about civilization—indeed, it is this very ambiguity that animates these Westerns in the first place—but still Ford's work through the 1930s remained essentially optimistic. *Drums along the Mohawk,* for example, concludes with a sentimental montage of rapturous faces gazing up at the first raising of the new American flag that is an unambiguous endorsement of civilization's blessings as white folk, blacks, and Indians all reverently salute together.

Like Cooper's in Jacksonian America, by the late 1940s Ford's particular blend of nostalgic pastoralism and sentimentality became out of step with the prevailing cultural mood. While *Wagon Master* in 1950 may be seen, as Bogdanovich says, to represent Ford's "height of optimism,"[62] already in the 1948 *Fort Apache* the optimistic acceptance of civilization—embodied so of-

The optimism, nostalgic pastoralism, and sentimentality of *Wagon Master* (1950):
out of step with the prevailing cultural mood.
Courtesy of the Museum of Modern Art Film Stills Library.

ten by Ford in the icon of the cavalry—is seriously questioned. In the famous coda of the film, new commander Kirby York (John Wayne) deliberately perpetuates the legend of "Thursday's Charge" rather than reveal the truth of the military debacle, in order to provide the necessary inspiration for the cavalry now and in the future. Whether Wayne's Captain York in the end has suddenly become a spokesman for Washington or, as Leland Poague argues, merely maintains his unwavering loyalty to the troop in opposition to Eastern bureaucracy is a moot point: in either case, for the viewer the "official story" is deconstructed as myth rather than truth.[63]

In *Two Rode Together* (1961), the initially mercenary marshal Guthrie McCabe (James Stewart) chooses to head west and leave the town that, in its racism and hypocrisy, is more immoral than even he had been. With men like Mr. Wringle, who offers to pay for any captive white boy in order to satisfy his wife's fervent desire to be reunited with her son, it is indeed the case that in society, as among the ladies of the Law and Order League in *Stagecoach,* in Dallas's words "there are worse things than Apaches." Ford's final Western, *Cheyenne Autumn* (1964), reverses the director's, as well as the genre's, own earlier colonialist and racist treatment of Native Americans. Anticipating the cycle of disillusioned Vietnam Westerns such as Arthur Penn's *Little Big Man* (1970) by several years, the film depicts the Indians as helpless victims, the cavalry as callous victimizers. Ford explained to Bogdanovich that he wanted to atone for the fact that he had "killed more Indians than Custer, Beecher, and Chivington put together."[64] Civilization's blessings here are, at best, mixed.

Yet this revisionism did not capture the popular imagination the way, say, *Little Big Man* would do a few years later. Moreover, at the same time as many Americans (the sixties "counterculture") now assumed the validity of questioning authority, Ford's stated view was that orders must be followed. In this context, Ford endorsed York's action in *Fort Apache*, telling Bogdanovich in 1968 that "it's good for the country to have heroes to look up to."[65] Ford also defended the historical Pat Garrett as a hero, while only a few years later he would be exposed as a man who compromised his integrity, "selling out" to the Eastern establishment, in Sam Peckinpah's *Pat Garrett and Billy the Kid* (1973).

Joseph McBride has described the second half of Ford's pro–Vietnam War documentary, *Vietnam! Vietnam!* (shot in 1968 but not released until 1972), as "a presentation of the debate between American hawks and doves which is loaded to make the doves seem naive, glib, and even treasonable," and observes that such a "jingoistic and hawkish" vision "is charming in the archaic context of the Western genre, but debilitating and ridiculous in a documentary of modern war."[66] Ford's vision, infused with the love of community that is articulated in his fondness for scenes of social dancing and celebration, was clearly out of step with contemporary America, violently polarized by Vietnam, racism, and other issues. As Sarris puts it, by the sixties Ford came "to mean Old Guard politi-

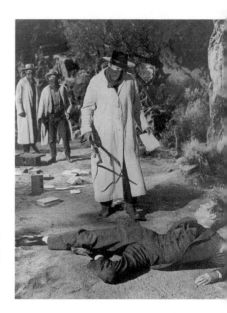

Liberty Valance (Lee Marvin) gives Ranse Stoddard (James Stewart) a taste of "Western law" in *The Man Who Shot Liberty Valance* (1962).
Courtesy of The Lilly Library, Indiana University, Bloomington, Indiana.

cally and old hat artistically."[67] In a way, Ford, like Cooper, must have felt like a defender of tradition in the face of youthful rabble. And if, in his imagination, Cooper fled further into the uncivilized wilderness, Ford fled the country altogether, as only one of his last four features is set in America.

By the time of *The Man Who Shot Liberty Valance* Ford would seem to agree with Cooper's conclusion that Law was necessary. The moment Ranse Stoddard (James Stewart) enters the West, he is robbed and whipped by Valance (Lee Marvin), who tears up Stoddard's law books and gives him a taste of "Western law." The violent defeat of the villainous Valance is necessary for the territory to achieve statehood through the democratic process, even though it means that Wayne's Westerner Tom Doniphon must be sacrificed ("Hallie's your girl now," he acknowledges to Stoddard). In the optimistic conclusion of *The Iron Horse*, the transcontinental railroad is completed while simultaneously the nuclear family is established through the unification of the couple, Davy and Miriam (George O'Brien and Madge Bellamy), and the erasure of ethnic differences (the Italian worker Tony, earlier referred to by the Irish as a "furriner," informs everyone that he has married an Irish girl). But the locomotive, which Leo Marx calls the primary icon of American progress,[68] becomes more of an intrusive machine in the garden in the opening of *Liberty Valance*, as it is shown belching thick black smoke into the pure air of the frontier, hardly the welcoming beacon of capitalism's advance it is in, say, Hawks's *Red River* (1948).

Donovan's Reef (1963), made the year before *Cheyenne Autumn*, is in a sense Ford's version of *The Crater*. Its fantasy Polynesian island setting is Ford's West in disguise, its maker's regressive vision of paradise: a mascu-line adolescent fantasy, with a saloon as town center and where barroom brawling, that comic business of which Ford is so fond, is institutionalized as an annual ritual. On Haleokaloa, the Fordian hero, Michael Patrick Donovan (Wayne), maintains a benevolent and untroubled patriarchal imperialism over all others (women, dark-skinned natives, Chinese workers, and perhaps even the French, who legally govern the island).

In the film's conclusion Donovan and Amelia Dedham (Elizabeth Allen), the heiress from Boston (the traditional locus of Old World culture and values), are betrothed, and Donovan seems finally to receive all the blessings of civilization as he marries a very rich and beautiful woman. But the stultifying nature of Boston (shown early on in the company boardroom scene with a row of stern, similarly dressed executives on either side of the frame) is clearly antipathetic to the robust individualism of the brawling Donovan. And if Amelia is converted to Donovan's values, he is nonetheless returning stateside with her, so the film's "happy ending" seems little more than an obligatory concession to conventional closure. Only on the surface, then, is this apparent comedy less acerbic than Cooper's novel. As Robin Wood discerns, "The tiresome and protracted buffoonery of *Donovan's Reef* . . . merely conceals an old man's disillusionment at the failure of his ideals to find fulfilment."[69]

The evolution in the Leatherstocking series from realism to myth—in D. H. Lawrence's lovely phrase, from "a decrescendo of reality to a crescendo of beauty"[70]—works backward to depict Natty in his prime. But even when reading of young Deerslayer's prowess in the wilderness, we know that he will eventually become a toothless old man marginalized in the developing society of Templeton and that he will die far from home, on the Great Plains. Similarly, in *Rio Grande* the Wayne character is also named Kirby Yorke, here older than in the earlier *Fort Apache;* in the same film the trooper played by Ben Johnson is named Tyree, and is depicted as younger than the Tyree that Johnson played in the earlier *She Wore a Yellow Ribbon.* The nostalgic appeal operates whether we understand these characters as the same as in the earlier films, or if, as in the work of Ingmar Bergman, we regard the repetition of the names as creating a network of intertextual meanings. Also, the extended flashbacks that make up most of *Liberty Valance* function, as Ray notes, like the reverse chronology of the Leatherstocking Tales, to give us "a double time-consciousness that determined that our perception of earlier events would be shaped by our knowledge of their ultimate outcome."[71]

Both Cooper and Ford imbued "present" events in their Westerns with a sense of retrospection, tingeing them with the poignancy of inevitable decline and passing that they themselves were feeling. In response to their sense of a widening gap between history and myth, both artists followed the advice of the newspaper editor in *Liberty Valance:* "When the legend becomes fact, print the legend." Ford's imagery—already relying heavily on caricature, or what Tag Gallagher calls "vignetting"—tended to become, as Sarris notes, increasingly archetypal.[72] Janey Place observes of the desert in *The Searchers*, for example, that "Almost nothing is seen of the men working the land; even their cattle are barely in evidence. The land exists and functions only in a mythical way."[73] Sarris goes so far as to attempt to defend the flat, undetailed depiction of the town of Shinbone in *Liberty Valance* as thematically resonant, like a zealous Hitchcockian attempting to read significance into the obviously two-dimensional backdrops in Hitchcock's *Marnie* (1964).[74] However, whether Ford's landscape in his later work was gloriously transcendent or merely lazy, its characteristic "abstraction" is clearly analogous to the forests of Cooper, where characters "flee or pursue through woods which contain not oaks or beeches or maples, only unnamed archetypal trees."[75]

CONCLUSION

Given their similar approach to the Western as cultural myth, Cooper and Ford in their Westerns both perfectly capture what John Cawelti calls the "epic moment" of American history that is so crucial to the genre.[76] Yet this is not to suggest that the artistic visions of the two are identical. Indeed, the sensibility each brings to the Western is distinctly different, as a brief consideration of *Drums along the Mohawk* in relation to the Leatherstocking Tales makes clear.

As an "Eastern Western" set in New York State during the American Revolution, *Drums along the Mohawk* is on the surface the Ford Western most closely resembling Cooper's fiction. But their similarities are less significant, finally, than their differences. Gil Martin (this is Ford's Fonda, not Wayne) is the Westerner as common man rather than as mythic hero. He loves the frontier, fights for it heroically, and like Natty in *The Pioneers* has a grander vision. But whereas Natty sees an Emersonian transcendent truth in the landscape, Gil, more like Judge Temple, sees the promise of a future house and thriving farm. Here and typically in his work Ford embraces family, industry, and progress, quite unlike Cooper, for whom domesticity and family are almost entirely absent. Home and hearth constitute a central value in *Drums along the Mohawk*, emphasized everywhere in the film: from the loss of the Martins' farm to the feisty Mrs. McKlennan (Edna May Oliver), who demands to be carried out of her bedroom by the Iroquois in her marriage bed before they burn the house. By contrast, the only home in the Leatherstocking Tales is the Hutter family fortress in *The Deerslayer*, which is, tellingly, an unfixed floating boat.

D. H. Lawrence has suggested that Cooper imagined the relationship between Hawkeye and Chingachgook as an ideal male substitute for his marriage, a liberating imaginative alternative to living in the country manor with his wife.[77] Certainly there is no sense of yearning in the Leatherstocking Tales for the domestic comfort that taming the wilderness inevitably brings. Hawkeye has only a mild, chaste flirtation with Hetty Hutter in *The Deerslayer*, whereas, for

The embracing of domesticity and family in counterpoint to Cooper:
Gil and Lana Martin (Henry Fonda and Claudette Colbert) in
Drums along the Mohawk (1939).
Courtesy of Barry Grant.

example, Ringo leaves town on a buckboard with Dallas for his ranch at the end of *Stagecoach* and Gil is married in the opening scene of *Drums along the Mohawk*. There is nothing in Cooper to match the poignant but unstated sense of yearning with which Ethan Edwards regards his sister-in-law Martha (Dorothy Jordan) in the farmhouse scenes at the beginning of *The Searchers*.

Rather, the continuities in the Westerns of Cooper and Ford illuminate our understanding both of the Western and of genre history in general. Steve Neale has identified three models of genre history, the first two of which, he notes, are generally assumed by genre critics: that of "growth, flowering and decay" and that of "progress towards self-conscious formalism."[78] But Neale rejects both models on several grounds—philosophical, aesthetic, historical. Still, these models have prevailed as the common view of the genre system generally and of the Western in particular, which is commonly said to have developed from naive optimism and affirmation ("white hats vs. black hats") to a more complex moral vision and ambivalence (the postwar cycle of "adult" Westerns). However, the parallel careers of Cooper and Ford, both of which trace this broad trajectory although they are separated by almost a century, indicate that this is hardly true of the genre itself. Rather, this comparative analysis of Ford's Westerns and Cooper's would seem to support Tag Gallagher's view, to which Neale also subscribes, that "A superficial glance at film history suggests cyclicism rather than evolution."[79]

Once upon a time the Western was considered the glory of American popular cinema, a genre that seemed able with equal ease to accommodate both studio hacks and the pantheon (male) film auteurs. The Western was the primary focus of early genre criticism, and has received, with the possible exception of the horror film, more attention than any other genre since. In recent years, however, the genre has been neglected, perhaps because of its traditional patriarchal and colonialist ideology. Yet despite the sometimes fierce winds of critical change, Ford, like Cooper, has staunchly remained a figure of consistent interest; like one of the sturdy palm trees in *The Hurricane,* his work has proved important to ongoing theoretical debates about such central issues as authorship, ideology, classic narrative construction, literary adaptation, and, of course, genre theory. For all their importance to the history of the Western, Cooper and Ford do not "transcend" the genre, as Kitses would argue, so much as embody it.[80]

NOTES

1. Alan Williams, "Is a Radical Film Criticism Possible?" *Quarterly Review of Film Studies* 9, no. 2 (Spring 1984), 124; and Steve Neale, "Questions of Genre," *Screen* 31, no. 1 (Spring 1990), 66.

2. These few exceptions include John G. Cawelti, *Adventure, Mystery, and Romance: Formula Stories as Art and Popular Culture* (Chicago and London: University of Chicago Press, 1976); Mark Jancovich, *Horror* (London: Batsford, 1992); and Henry Jenkins III, *What Made Pistachio Nuts? Early Sound Comedy and the Vaudeville Aesthetic* (New York: Columbia University Press, 1993).

3. Richard Slotkin, *Regeneration through Violence: The Mythology of the American Frontier, 1600–1860* (Middletown, Conn.: Wesleyan University Press, 1973); *The Fatal Environment: The Myth of the Frontier in the Age of Industrialization, 1800–1900* (Middletown, Conn.: Wesleyan University Press, 1986); and *Gunfighter Nation: The Myth of the Frontier in Twentieth-Century America* (New York: Harper Collins, 1993). Also notable here is Edward Buscombe's analysis of the influence of Frederic Remington's Western art on Ford's Western films, "Painting the Legend: Frederic Remington and the Western," *Cinema Journal* 23, no. 4 (Summer 1984): 12–27 (reprinted in this volume).

4. Peter Wollen, *Signs and Meaning in the Cinema,* rev. ed. (Bloomington and London: Indiana University Press, 1972), 115.

5. Bruce Kawin, *Faulkner and Film* (New York: Ungar, 1977); and Peter Hogue, "Hawks and Faulkner: *Today We Live,*" *Literature/Film Quarterly* 9, no. 1 (1981): 51–58.

6. James Fenimore Cooper, "Preface to *The Leatherstocking Tales*" (1850), reprinted in *The Last of the Mohicans* (Cambridge, Mass.: Riverside, 1958), 11.

7. John Cawelti, *The Six-Gun Mystique* (Bowling Green, Ohio: Popular Press, 1970), 36; Robert B. Ray, *A Certain Tendency of the Hollywood Cinema, 1930–1980* (Princeton: Princeton University Press, 1985), 243.

8. For a discussion of captivity narratives, see, for example, Roy Harvey Pearce, "The Significance of the Captivity Narrative," *American Literature* 19, no. 1 (March

1947): 1–20; and Alden T. Vaughan and Edward W. Clarke, eds., *Puritans among the Indians: Accounts of Captivity and Redemption, 1676–1724* (Cambridge and London: Harvard University Press, 1981).

9. James Fenimore Cooper, *The Pioneers* (New York: New American Library, 1964), 435–436.

10. Some of Ford's Westerns (*My Darling Clementine, The Searchers*) clearly follow this model, although others do not (*Stagecoach, Wagon Master, 3 Godfathers*). The cavalry films, focusing on soldiers rather than the individual Western hero, are different in this respect.

11. Leslie Fiedler, *Love and Death in the American Novel*, rev. ed. (New York: Delta, 1966), 191; Cawelti, *The Six-Gun Mystique*, 91. Fiedler discusses Cooper's adaptation of the historical romance to the Western in great detail in chapter 7.

12. Joseph McBride and Michael Wilmington, *John Ford* (New York: Da Capo Press, 1975), 36–37.

13. Jim Kitses, *Horizons West* (Bloomington and London: Indiana University Press, 1970), 10.

14. Cooper, *The Pioneers*, 21.

15. This sequence is discussed in some detail in Stefan Fleischer's essay "A Study through Stills of *My Darling Clementine*," *Journal of Modern Literature* 3, no. 2 (April 1973): 241–252.

16. Northrop Frye, *Anatomy of Criticism: Four Essays* (New York: Atheneum, 1970), 33.

17. James Fenimore Cooper, *The Prairie* (San Francisco: Rinehart Press, 1950), 228–229.

18. Mark Twain, "Fenimore Cooper's Literary Offenses," in *The Writings of Mark Twain*, vol. 22, *How to Tell a Story and Other Essays* (New York and London: Harper & Brothers, 1899), 82.

19. Twain, "Fenimore Cooper's Literary Offenses," 85–86, 88.

20. Kay Seymour House, *Cooper's Americans* (Athens: Ohio State University Press, 1965), 10.

21. Fiedler, *Love and Death in the American Novel*, 191.

22. Twain, "Fenimore Cooper's Literary Offenses," 88.

23. Frederick Jackson Turner, "The Significance of the Frontier in American History," in *Frontier and Section: Selected Essays of Frederick Jackson Turner*, ed. Ray Allen Billington (Englewood Cliffs, N.J.: Prentice-Hall, 1961), 46–47, 51.

24. Turner, "Significance of the Frontier," 39.

25. Cawelti, *Six-Gun Mystique*, 73.

26. Ray, *A Certain Tendency*, 215–243.

27. Quoted in Peter Bogdanovich, *John Ford* (Berkeley: University of California Press, 1968), 70.

28. John Baxter, *The Cinema of John Ford* (New York: A. S. Barnes; London: Zwemmer, 1971), 27.

29. Bogdanovich, *John Ford*, 85, 86.

30. Bogdanovich, *John Ford*, 30–31.

31. Andrew Sarris, *The John Ford Movie Mystery* (London: Secker & Warburg/ British Film Institute, 1976), 85.

32. For example, on Cooper's pictorialism, see Blake Nevius, *Cooper's Landscapes: An Essay on the Picturesque Vision* (Berkeley: University of California Press, 1976);

and on Ford's, see Michael Budd, "A Home in the Wilderness: Visual Imagery in John Ford's Westerns," *Cinema Journal* 16, no. 1 (Fall 1976): 62–75.

33. Marius Bewley, *The Eccentric Design: Form in the Classic American Novel* (New York and London: Columbia University Press, 1963), 73.

34. Howard Mumford Jones, "James Fenimore Cooper and the Hudson River School," *The Magazine of Art* 45, no. 6 (October 1952), 250. For more on this period in American painting, see John K. Howat, *The Hudson River and Its Painters* (New York: Viking Press, 1972). See also Donald A. Ringe, "Chiaroscuro as an Artistic Device in Cooper's Fiction," *PMLA* 77, no. 4, pt. 1 (September 1963): 349–357; and Howard Mumford Jones, "Prose and Pictures: James Fenimore Cooper," *Tulane Studies in English* 3 (1952): 133–154.

35. Cooper, *The Pioneers*, 204.

36. Cooper, *The Pioneers*, 392.

37. Cooper, *The Pioneers*, 279.

38. James Fenimore Cooper, *The Last of the Mohicans* (Boston: Houghton Mifflin, 1958), 43.

39. Cooper, *The Last of the Mohicans*, 73.

40. Cooper, *The Last of the Mohicans*, 48, 41, 149, 196, 88.

41. Bogdanovich, *John Ford*, 87.

42. Buscombe, "Painting the Legend," 17–20 (158–161 in this volume).

43. Baxter, *The Cinema of John Ford*, 11.

44. J. A. Place, *The Western Films of John Ford* (Secaucus: Citadel Press, 1974), 49.

45. On the Western hero's code, see Cawelti, *The Six-Gun Mystique;* Robert Warshow, "Movie Chronicle: The Westerner," in *Focus on the Western*, ed. Jack Nachbar (Englewood Cliffs, N.J.: Prentice-Hall, 1974), 45–56; and Peter Homans, "Puritanism Revisited: An Analysis of the Contemporary Screen-Image Western," in Nachbar, ed., *Focus on the Western*, 84–92.

46. Hector St. John de Crevecoeur, *Letters from an American Farmer* (New York: Dutton, 1957), 39–40.

47. Edward Buscombe, *Stagecoach* (London: British Film Institute, 1992), 9.

48. Cooper, *The Prairie*, 8.

49. J. P. Telotte, "A Fate Worse Than Death: Racism, Transgression, and Westerns," *Journal of Popular Film and Television* 26, no. 3 (Fall 1998): 120–127, offers an informative analysis of this scene's ideological implications.

50. James Fenimore Cooper, *Home as Found* (New York: Capricorn Books, 1961), 196.

51. Fiedler, *Love and Death in the American Novel*, 192.

52. Frye, *Anatomy of Criticism*, 33–35.

53. Van Wyck Brooks, *The World of Washington Irving* (New York: Dutton, 1944), 401.

54. Cooper's politics and his actual party affiliation have been matters of considerable discussion. That this is an open question is a further illustration of how alienated from mainstream America Cooper became. For details of Cooper's politics and legal battles, see, for example, Dorothy Waples, *The Whig Myth of James Fenimore Cooper* (New Haven: Yale University Press, 1938); Granville Hicks, "Landlord Cooper and the Anti-renters," *Antioch Review* 5, no. 1 (Spring 1945): 95–109; Donald A. Ringe, *James Fenimore Cooper* (New York: Twayne, 1962); and Robert E. Spiller, *Fenimore Cooper: Critic of His Times* (New York: 1931).

55. Walt Whitman, editorial of 19 April 1842, reprinted in *Walt Whitman of the New York Aurora*, ed. Joseph Jay Rubin and Charles H. Brown (State College, Pa.: Bald Eagle Press, 1950).

56. Quoted in Waples, *Whig Myth*, 50.

57. James Fenimore Cooper, *Correspondence of James Fenimore Cooper*, vol. 2, ed. by his grandson James Fenimore Cooper (New Haven: Yale University Press, 1922), 732.

58. James Fenimore Cooper, *The Deerslayer* (New York: New American Library, 1963), 9 (my emphasis).

59. Cooper, *The Deerslayer*, 507, 225.

60. James Fenimore Cooper, *The Crater, or Vulcan's Peak*, ed. Thomas Philbrick (Cambridge, Mass.: Harvard University Press, 1962), 456, 459.

61. Wollen, *Signs and Meaning*, 102.

62. Bogdanovich, *John Ford*, 34.

63. Leland Poague, "'All I Can See is the Flags': *Fort Apache* and the Visibility of History," *Cinema Journal* 27, no. 2 (Winter 1988): 8–26.

64. Bogdanovich, *John Ford*, 104.

65. Bogdanovich, *John Ford*, 86.

66. Joseph McBride, "Drums along the Mekong," *Sight and Sound* 41, no. 4 (Autumn 1972): 214–215.

67. Sarris, *John Ford Movie Mystery*, 14.

68. Leo Marx, *The Machine in the Garden: Technology and the Pastoral Ideal in America* (New York: Oxford University Press, 1964), 24–33.

69. Robin Wood, "'Shall We Gather at the River?': The Late Films of John Ford," in John Caughie, ed., *Theories of Authorship* (London and Boston: Routledge & Kegan Paul, 1981), 99–100 (reprinted in this volume).

70. D. H. Lawrence, *Studies in Classic American Literature* (New York: Penguin, 1977), 55.

71. Ray, *A Certain Tendency*, 240.

72. Tag Gallagher, *John Ford: The Man and His Films* (Berkeley: University of California Press, 1986); Sarris, *John Ford Movie Mystery*, 161.

73. Place, *The Western Films*, 171.

74. Sarris, *John Ford Movie Mystery*, 176.

75. Fiedler, *Love and Death in the American Novel*, 183.

76. Cawelti, *Six-Gun Mystique*, 39.

77. Lawrence, *Studies in Classic American Literature*, 54.

78. Neale, "Questions of Genre," 58–59.

79. Tag Gallagher, "Shootout at the Genre Corral: Problems in the 'Evolution' of the Western," in *Film Genre Reader II*, ed. Barry Keith Grant (Austin: University of Texas Press, 1996), 252; Neale, "Questions," 59–60.

80. Kitses, *Horizons West*, 7.

9

FROM AESTHETE TO PAPPY
THE EVOLUTION OF JOHN FORD'S PUBLIC REPUTATION
Charles J. Maland

Avid moviegoers today associate John Ford primarily with the Western, Monument Valley, and John Wayne. As a number of contributors to this volume have pointed out, Ford himself encouraged that view with his statement at a Directors Guild meeting of 15 October 1950. Standing to challenge Cecil B. DeMille's anti-Communist charges against guild president Joseph L. Mankiewicz, Ford prefaced his comments by saying, "My name's John Ford. I make Westerns."[1] As Edward Buscombe has noted in *The BFI Companion to the Western,* Ford's connection to the Western has become widely accepted in film culture: "No other major director identified himself so closely with the genre, and in the public mind the association between Ford and the Western is so close that one seems to merge into the other."[2] Indeed, one especially familiar image is of Ford standing by a director's chair wearing an eye patch and a rumpled-brimmed hat, with the vast Western skies, punctuated by Monument Valley buttes, in the back-ground. The image conjures up *Stagecoach* (1939), *My Darling Clementine* (1946), *Fort Apache* (1948), *The Searchers* (1956), and others. How fully that image seems to encapsulate the public reputation of John Ford.

Yet that image, however familiar and comforting it may be today, is incomplete, even misleading. At times in his career Ford himself downplayed his Westerns, not least because many held the genre in such low esteem. Once, responding to a critic who claimed the director was a poet of the Western saga, Ford replied, "I am not a poet, and I don't know what a Western saga is. I would say that is horseshit."[3] Although Ford's association with Westerns became the dominant view among most *cinéastes* from the early 1960s on, filmgoers in 1935, if they knew about Ford at all, would more likely have thought of him as an artistic director interested in exploring Irish culture using expressionist film style. Such an apparent contradiction raises the broad question of just how a film director's public reputation emerges and evolves in the American film industry and the context of American culture.[4] This essay will explore the question by tracing the evolution of director John Ford's public reputation in the United States, focusing particularly on his reputation from the 1920s to the middle 1970s and on the way his status as the preeminent Hollywood director of Westerns became so deeply entrenched.

Pappy Ford on location in Monument Valley, 1964: a familiar and
comfortable image of the director.

How have the public reputations of directors emerged in American movies
and American culture? Although frequently the topic of discussion today, directors didn't deeply engage the attention of critics and reviewers until the 1950s
in France and the 1960s in the United States, when shifts in the "art world" of
film and the broader sociopolitical climate of American culture began to change
the way people talked about and evaluated directors and their movies.[5] Before
that time a number of factors discouraged filmgoers from paying attention to
the director. Stars, story, spectacle, and genre were all used to sell movies as early
as the 1910s, but not until the 1960s did it become a widespread practice to use
the director's name to help sell the film.[6] Except for director-performers like
Chaplin, Welles, and Woody Allen, or a director like Alfred Hitchcock, who
always made a cameo appearance in his films, directors don't appear in films.
Moviegoers don't experience their images and voices the way that they see stars
and hear their voices. Finally, with the exception of a few major names—like,
for example, D. W. Griffith, Erich von Stroheim (also an actor-director), and
Cecil B. DeMille—directors of movies generally are not highlighted in critical
reviews and feature articles the way stars are, and certainly were not through
most of the 1940s. Thus, any director before 1935 who was well known to the
public was the exception rather than the rule.

   Yet the situation began to change in the 1950s and 1960s. The widespread
attention given to European art-film directors like Bergman, Antonioni, Fellini,
Kurosawa, and Godard in the late 1950s and early 1960s tended to attribute

the central creative role in filmmaking to the director. Accompanying the art-film movement was a critical perspective called the auteur approach; emerging in France in the 1950s and popularized in the United States by Andrew Sarris, it also celebrated directors, even Hollywood studio directors who specialized in genre films. Finally, the continued breakdown of the studio system and the rise of the package-unit production system in the American film industry made it more possible for some directors to assume significant creative control of their productions.[7] The situation had so changed that by 1970 an anthology appeared titled *The Film Director as Superstar*.[8] Some American films began to be marketed by highlighting the directors, and criticism and commentary as well as publicity about directors were becoming common enough that committed moviegoers chose to attend a film—such as Kubrick's *2001: A Space Odyssey* (1968)—because of its director's reputation. For these reasons, more discourse about directors was circulating by the 1960s than before.

What about John Ford specifically? How did his public reputation develop, and what qualities were associated with that reputation over time? To begin to answer these questions, it's instructive to compare the attention given to Ford as a director with that given to other Hollywood directors of his generation. One way to do this is to estimate how often Ford was a featured subject of articles in magazines and periodicals. Table 9.1 tabulates the number of magazine and periodical articles that featured Chaplin, Capra, Hitchcock, Ford, and Hawks from the decade of the 1910s to the 1960s and from 1970 to 1972.[9]

The chart invites several observations. As suggested above, a director who also acts in his films generates more attention than one who only directs. Granted, Chaplin is an exceptional case as one of the chief icons in the history of cinema, but even in the 1930s, when he directed only two films—*City Lights* (1931) and *Modern Times* (1936)—he was featured in fifty-six articles. In contrast, Frank Capra—who directed fifteen films in the decade, at one point was president of both the Directors Guild and the Academy, appeared on the cover of *Time* in 1938, and was certainly one of the most famous American directors by the late 1930s—had fourteen essays written about him. Ford, who directed twenty-six features, garnered the attention of only four articles in that same time period.

Table 9.1

Director	1910s	1920s	1930s	1940s	1950s	1960s	1970–1972
Chaplin	27	55	56	38	45	50	16
Capra	0	0	14	15	2	7	8
Hitchcock	0	0	9	2	39	48	19
Ford	0	0	4	7	15	25	16
Hawks	0	0	2	2	3	7	9

With the exception of Chaplin, who received relatively constant attention from the 1920s on, and Capra, whose career declined precipitously after *State of the Union* (1948), directors received more attention from the middle 1950s on as their careers advanced and the auteur approach became more common. Astonishingly, more articles were written on Howard Hawks between 1970 and 1972 than in the entire period before 1960, when he had already been directing for over thirty years. It's also clear that attention to Ford as a filmmaker expanded rapidly in the 1950s and even more so in the early 1960s, an increase related not only to the growing popularity of the auteur approach but also to Ford's increased willingness to talk with interviewers from the 1950s on. Before that time Ford had rarely made himself available to interviewers or sought publicity for himself.

The table suggests that a director was much more likely to gain the attention of filmgoers and the press before 1960 if his films were associated with a particular genre. Chaplin's tramp-centered comedies, Frank Capra's blend of screwball comedy and social-problem film, and Hitchcock's signature thrillers all elicited a great deal of attention compared to the directors (like Hawks and Ford) who worked in a wide variety of genres. It was simply easier for a journalist to pigeonhole a director who worked primarily in one genre. Only after World War II, when Ford began to direct a higher proportion of Westerns, did he begin to garner more critical attention. Although Ford directed in a wide variety of genres in the 1930s (he made no Westerns until *Stagecoach* in 1939), six of his eight films between 1946 and 1950 were Westerns. He also directed five consecutive Westerns between 1959 and 1962, starting with *The Horse Soldiers* and ending with *How the West Was Won*. It seems that in the studio era it was particularly difficult for any director who worked in many genres, even an especially gifted one, to gain the attention of the press.[10]

A chronological overview of the criticism of and commentary on Ford and his films paints a mural of how Ford's public reputation developed. Looked at globally, it suggests that Ford's public reputation was composed of a shifting variety of qualities, some persisting, some dropping away, and some emerging. Not until the 1950s and 1960s did Ford's status as a maker of Westerns really achieve its present dominance. Very early in his career, he was not well known but definitely associated with Westerns. Later he was written about and even presented himself as an aesthete and intellectual—a "high art" director in a popular medium—although this image diminished somewhat as the 1930s wore on. (Granted, it's tough maintaining a high-brow reputation when you direct films with titles like *Wee Willie Winkie*, as Ford did in 1937; it was a Shirley Temple vehicle.) He was sometimes considered an important realist or a gifted film stylist; at other times he was seen as an Irish genius particularly engaged in making films about Irish history, culture, or politics. *The Informer* (1935) was crucial in fashioning both aspects of Ford's image. In the late 1930s and early

1940s he occasionally received praise for making realist, even socially conscious, films. From the war years on, he was sometimes the patriotic defender of traditional American values. But especially from the late 1940s on, he was the maker of Westerns—the "poet of the Western saga"—or "Pappy" Ford, the paternalistic Hollywood veteran who ruled his set during production with an iron hand but still managed to create a sense of community among the cast and crew.

The 1920s offer a good starting point for a consideration of the changes in Ford's public reputation. Although Ford had directed about sixty films by 1927, nearly three-quarters of which were Westerns, he wasn't widely known outside the film industry. On rare occasions he was mentioned—usually positively— for his work on Westerns. One early reference can be found in a *Motion Picture News* review of *Straight Shooting* (1917), which notes that Ford directs with "terrifically fast action, particularly when he is dealing with horses and riders."[11] Probably Ford's greatest success in the silent era was *The Iron Horse* (1924), a Western about the transcontinental railroad. For that film Fox publicity highlighted Ford's interest in the West. It pointed out that the director had earlier worked with Tom Mix: "With Mix he spent countless hours talking of the glorious figures of the early west. . . . Together they lived again in imagination those fascinating days. Then Ford came to know Theodore Roosevelt, Frederic Remington, and Russell, the cowboy artist, and the golden splendors of the old west lived again."[12] Some reviews of *The Iron Horse* praised Ford. *Variety,* for example, observed that "John Ford, who directed, put his story over on the screen with a lot of punch," adding that Ford handled the actors well; he "touched them with just a bit of pathos in the end that made them stand out as real humans."[13] The *New York Times* reviewer agreed when he wrote, "John Ford, the director of this film, has done his share of the work with thoroughness and with pleasing imagination."[14] Clearly *The Iron Horse* was an important project for Ford. *Variety* wrote that another Ford-directed Western, *3 Bad Men* (1926), "falls just short of being a terrific knockout" and that the director "has turned out a special in the fullest sense of the word. This is a superwestern and every bit as big as *The Iron Horse* was."[15]

Yet even with the financial success of *The Iron Horse,* Ford garnered little publicity outside the film industry in the silent era. Andrew Sarris opens his admiring sketch of Ford in *The American Cinema* by saying, "If John Ford had died or retired at the end of 1929, he would have deserved at most a footnote in film history."[16] This overstates the case a bit—Ford was known for not only *The Iron Horse* but also a World War I film, *Four Sons* (1928), and he had been elected president of the Motion Pictures Directors Association in 1927. His public reputation began to grow around this time because of changes in his aspirations and his involvement with the industry. Tag Gallagher sees the late 1920s as a key turning point for Ford: "suddenly in 1927 he began to make pictures on an altogether more ambitious level of artistry, the true characteris-

(Above) Ford's greatest success in the silent era was a Western—*The Iron Horse* (1924). John Ford (on right) and actor Will Walling on location.

Courtesy of the Museum of Modern Art Film Stills Archive.

(Left) In the 1920s, Ford was not widely known outside the film industry. Directors William Beaudine (on far left) and John Ford (on far right) flank Hollywood superstars Douglas Fairbanks and Mary Pickford, circa 1925.

Courtesy of The Lilly Library, Indiana University, Bloomington, Indiana.

tics of his mature work began to emerge, and, with smashing commercial successes, his position at Fox became preeminent."[17]

Ford's artistic ambitions were fueled by the example of F. W. Murnau, the distinguished German Expressionist director who was hired at Fox to help raise the studio's prestige. Ford, after seeing a rough cut of Murnau's *Sunrise* in March 1927, told the press that it was "the greatest picture that has been produced" and that he doubted "whether a greater picture will be made in the next ten years."[18] Later that year, Ford traveled to Germany, and while in Berlin he visited Murnau and learned more about the director's production methods.

Perhaps under the spell of the Murnau mystique, Ford wrote an article for the *New York Times,* "Veteran Producer Muses," in June 1928.[19] This was an uncharacteristic act for the director, who very rarely wrote for publication.[20] Ford opens the essay by listing the Seven Wonders of the World, the "seven stamping grounds of civilization," and noting that "no other monument of man's migratory spirit has arisen to contest their supremacy until the last decade." Since the World War, Ford writes, a "remarkable hegira" has been occurring; the "creative artistic brainpower of modern civilization has been making a pilgrimage to a town on the California coast . . . until today the eighth great stamping ground of the world's relentless horde is Hollywood."[21]

The essay goes on to make the case that film is a creative and artistic medium that speaks the universal language of mankind, a familiar claim in the 1920s—at least until the talkies arrived. Ford looks back at "the great trail blazer of films," D. W. Griffith, who devised methods and secured effects "that were to make pictures a real artistic medium." A great film, Ford believes, "must have its theme of universal appeal but its people vivid." The settings—like the Germany of *Four Sons* or the Ireland of *Mother Machree,* Ford's two most recent films at the writing—should also be true and vivid. Noting that the introduction of sound will make substantial changes in the film industry, Ford argues that filmgoers will still remember most "the heart-interest stories of plain people interpreting vital emotions." Ford concludes by saying that Hollywood and the other Seven Wonders of the World have not been "high monuments of man's accomplishment but turbulent plazas of man's unceasing search for something he can never find."

Poised at the beginning of the sound era, director Ford presents himself as a creative artist, even something of an intellectual, as he "muses" about the film industry. The somewhat elevated diction of the essay, as well as Ford's belief in the creative promise of the movies, presents an image that certainly contrasts with the gruff, informal pragmatist that we more often associate with the later Ford. Yet a similar image of Ford as artist and intellectual is conveyed in a picture accompanying one of the first feature articles on Ford in a film magazine, "Meant for Martyrdom," which appeared in *Motion Picture Classic* in 1930. The picture shows a somber, bookish-looking man wearing round horn-rim glasses, a dark double-breasted suit, and a dark tie with tiny white dots. One hand rests in a coat pocket; the other holds a pipe in front of him, slightly above waist level. The man looks more like a young, erudite college professor than a director of dusty Westerns. As a picture of a director who later in his career was annoyed at those who took his work seriously, protesting that he was just doing a "job of work," this image of Ford the artist and intellectual comes as something of a surprise.[22]

Between the beginning of the 1930s and the American entry into World War II, John Ford became increasingly well known, particularly because of several films that were very well received by the critics and the Motion Picture Academy. Between 1935 and 1941 the New York Film Critics voted him best director four times, for *The Informer* (1935), *Stagecoach* (1939), *The Grapes of Wrath* and *The Long Voyage Home* (1940), and *How Green Was My Valley* (1941). The Motion Picture Academy awarded him the Best Directing Oscar for *The Informer, The Grapes of Wrath,* and *How Green Was My Valley.* This was the period of his career when his films generated the greatest positive response from the Academy, and except for *Stagecoach*—Ford's return to the Western after nearly a decade's hiatus—these films were *not* Westerns. Three, in fact, were set in Ireland or Wales. Ford's public reputation in the 1930s and into the 1940s was distinctly shaped by this fact.

Several feature articles in fan magazines of the 1930s, as well as Lewis Jacobs's portrait of Ford in *Rise of the American Film* (1939) and a 1941 sketch in *Current Biography* drawn partly from those sources, give us an idea of the qualities publicly attributed to the director on the eve of World War II. It's clear

A 1930 portrait of Ford shows the director as a serious, even elite, artist. Courtesy of Tag Gallagher.

that Ford was not yet a "film director as superstar," nor had his public reputation become closely associated with the Western.[23] Nevertheless, he had attained some stature in the culture: Lewis Jacobs, for example, discusses Ford along with Vidor, Lang, von Sternberg, Mamoulian, Capra, Leroy, and Milestone in a chapter of his pioneering film history titled "Contemporary Directors."[24] Together, these discussions from the 1930s and early 1940s associate four qualities with Ford: 1) his Irish heritage and personal interest in Irish concerns; 2) his casual informality; 3) his status as a careful film stylist; and 4) the social-realist, even progressive, nature of his films. The first two relate more to Ford the person, the last two to his movies.

Cruikshank, in "Meant for Martyrdom," opens by saying that if it had not been for Ford's father's immigration to America, "John Ford doubtless would have dangled from the end of a rope, or faced British bullets in an Irish village square." Emphasizing the strong-willed Galway ancestry of Ford's family, Cruikshank, like Lewis Jacobs, suggests that Ford's best films are still in the future and writes that "it is safe to say that the best of these pictures will be painted with the green hills of Ireland as a background."[25] This tendency to emphasize Ford's Irish heritage grew following the success of *The Informer*. In his 1936 *Photoplay* essay, Howard Sharp calls this film "the greatest motion picture ever filmed" and writes that Ford "represents all that is best of Hollywood and its industry."[26] Ford's work on *The Plough and the Stars* (1936) and *The Long Voyage Home* only strengthened the image of him as a director particularly drawn to Irish or Irish American subjects.

These profiles of Ford describe him in ways that counter the intellectual, even pompous, image found in his 1928 essay and his 1930 portrait. The 1936 *Motion Picture* essay exemplifies this tendency: "Always garbed in old flannel trousers, tennis shoes with holes in the toes, shirt open at the throat, no necktie, and collar turned up in the hottest weather, Ford would never be selected from a crowd as one of the greatest directors ever to handle a picture in cinemaland."[27] *Current Biography* perpetuates the image of a Ford who is "all the time dressed in shabby clothes, his feet in sneakers with holes in the toes."[28] This emerging image of Ford as casual, even sloppy, counters the formality associated with publicity from 1928 through 1930, bringing us closer to the more commonly held modern image of Ford, especially as he appeared on Western locations.

After *The Informer* Ford the director also began to be known as a film stylist deeply involved in the whole filmmaking process. The *Photoplay* essay, in fact, was the first of a series of articles that explored the important role of the director, and the essay reported on Ford's involvement with all phases of production: wardrobe, sets, scripting, acting, camera, sound, and editing. In 1939 Jacobs emphasized Ford's attention to style. In a passage later quoted in the *Current Biography* sketch, he alludes to Ford's "distinct flair in the use of the camera, care in composition, a feeling for mood, a deft cutting style, an appreciation of movement as the prime element of the movies, an eye for colorful characterization and a great ease in the manipulation of all these elements."[29] He admires, among other moments, a scene from *The Informer* in which Ford dissolves from a subjective shot of Gypo Nolan staring at a poster on the wall to a shot of his friend's face to suggest that Gypo is getting the idea of betraying him. Or, to take another example, he praises Ford's use of internal diegetic sound from Gypo's perspective, like the accusatory sound of Frankie's voice that Gypo hears as he stares at a model of the steamship and thinks of escaping to the United States.[30]

Finally, besides being portrayed as a gifted film stylist, Ford was often praised for the realism in his films. "Realism" denoted at least two different things to these critics. On the narrowest level, it meant that Ford included incidents borrowed from real-life experience in his movies or sought to represent human behavior in a plausible, accurately observed manner. Sharp, for example, commends Ford's assertion that "a good many of the most outstanding incidents I have filmed have been things that members of the company have actually seen or actually done during their lives."[31]

More importantly, however, the critics commenting on Ford's realism were referring to an approach to film that became highly valued among many film critics from the Depression to the early post–World War II years. In his history of the origins of American film criticism, Myron Lounsbury discusses what he calls the "modern liberal" approach to film criticism that emerged in the Depression.[32] This approach valued serious films with artistic aspirations over slick entertainment, terming the first "realist" and the second "commercial." To the modern liberal critic, serious films like *The Informer* or *The Grapes of Wrath* were prized. "Escapist" genre films like screwball comedies or horror films or even Westerns generally were not.[33] In this context, Ford came to be valued as a realist. The journalist who wrote "Men Behind the Stars," for example, notes approvingly that "Mr. Ford believes that there is a definite trend in motion picture production towards realism and stories that deviate from the conventional theme." The *Current Biography* sketch similarly affirms that most of his films "are distinguished by a certain vital realism that Ford has made his own."[34]

This broader sense of realism could even extend to a filmmaker's political perspective and a movie's overt social or political messages. Modern liberal critics during the Depression tended to praise filmmakers whose films developed reformist or populist themes, and Ford was also on occasion considered a realist on these criteria. Jacobs, for example, argues that Ford "has not only King Vidor's earnestness, versatility and craftsmanship but as sincere a purpose and social awareness of the times."[35] By comparing Ford with the director of social critiques of American culture like *The Crowd* (1928) and *Our Daily Bread* (1934), Jacobs presents Ford as a socially conscious, realist filmmaker with populist or liberal social views. Although that perception never became dominant, it did create complications for later critics who considered Ford a social and political conservative.

A good way to encapsulate the public reputation John Ford had achieved by 1941 is to look at the picture of him that emerges in the observations of Otis Ferguson, who regularly reviewed for the *New Republic* from 1934 to 1942. That Ferguson thought highly of Ford at his best is evident in a review in which he groups Ford with other directors, such as Capra, Clair, Milestone, Lubitsch, Lang, and Pudovkin, whose work shows "flash of genius." However, Ferguson sometimes was hard on Ford's films and even on the director himself. For example, in a review of *Tobacco Road* (1941) Ferguson writes, "The difference between John Ford's bad pictures and his good pictures is so wide that you have to assume he neither knows actors nor how to hold them down, and that he is never sure whether he is working on a good story or not." Calling *Four Men and a Prayer* (1938) "a flop" and "a turkey," Ferguson says that "without a story having the kind of message to his liking . . . John Ford hasn't the patient skill in his own trade to place among the first ten or a dozen" directors in Hollywood. Yet he adds that Ford's *Arrowsmith* (1931) was "among the masterpieces" of the "dark early thirties."[36]

Ferguson considered Ford's chief contribution to be mainly stylistic, not thematic. In *The Prisoner of Shark Island* (1936) Ford's "genius shows in the management not only of the action, but of the actors in it." Ferguson praises Ford's "slow drawling tempo" in *Young Mr. Lincoln* (1939), manifested in the camera's presentation of the ambling Lincoln or in the fair-day scene. In his rave review of *The Grapes of Wrath* Ferguson attributed to Ford the film's "feeling of space and large movement," generated by so many long shots, as well as its use of music and of silence. To Ferguson, John Ford's chief contributions to his movies were in stylistic elements like framing, lighting, acting, and the soundtrack to develop a sense of emotion and narrative tempo. And like other observers in the 1930s and early 1940s, Ferguson admired the realistic detail of Ford's best films. He writes of the "sense of reality" that made *Young Mr. Lincoln* "so vivid and seeming-true," as well as the "half-lighting and dark masses—together with the realism of detail—Ford likes so much" in *The Long Voyage Home*.[37]

Ferguson's Ford is thus much like the Ford that emerges in the feature articles on the eve of World War II. He's a gifted and efficient director whose films are sometimes successful, sometimes not. He's concerned about a sense of realistic detail. He attends to the camera, lighting, and narrative pace, the effect of music and sound. Add to these qualities the two personal characteristics particularly connected to Ford—his Irish ancestry and his informally casual dress and manner on the set—and we have a pretty accurate portrait of Ford's public reputation as of 1941.

One curiosity is how little Ford was associated with the Western by 1941, particularly given the success of *Stagecoach*, which André Bazin would praise in the 1950s as the prototypical classical Hollywood Western.[38] Ferguson did not even bother to review the film in the *New Republic*, and among national mass magazines, only *Time* and *Newsweek* did. In neither of these reviews was *Stagecoach* the only Western discussed. The *Time* review concentrates on producer Walter Wanger, "in the forefront of Hollywood's crusade for social consciousness," discussing him in more detail than the film, and Ford is mentioned, in only one sentence, as having contributed, with writer Dudley Nichols, to the film's "admirable pace." The *Newsweek* review, titled "High-Toned Hoss Operas," discusses the film with *The Oklahoma Kid* (1939). It praises Ford and the film, but associates Ford as much with an earlier, non-Western, film: "The film's success is more fully explained by the names of its adapter and director—Dudley Nichols and John Ford. This team has brought to a Western some of the rare quality that made *The Informer* a screen masterpiece."[39] Probably Ford was given the greatest praise by the *New York Times* reviewer, Frank Nugent, who later would write screenplays for the director. Commenting on those involved in the film, Nugent wrote, "They've all done nobly by a noble horse opera, but none so nobly as its director. This is one stagecoach that's powered by a Ford."[40] Despite this praise, Ford turned next to non-Westerns like *The Grapes of Wrath* and *How Green Was My Valley*, and his public reputation as of 1941 still was not closely associated with the Western.

Ford's public reputation began to shift in the 1940s for a variety of reasons. After directing *How Green Was My Valley* in 1941, Ford, a U.S. Navy reservist, was asked to head a Field Photographic unit for William Donovan's Office of Strategic Services (OSS). He spent the rest of the war involved in making and supervising the making of documentary films, the most successful of which were *The Battle of Midway* (1942) and *December 7* (1943), which both won Academy Awards for best documentary in their year of release.

The country's shift to a more patriotic and conservative political climate in the early years of the Cold War coincided with Ford's own growing conservatism and patriotism during and after the war. Some of the political conservatism evident in Ford's cavalry trilogy—*Fort Apache* (1948), *She Wore a Yellow Ribbon* (1949), and *Rio Grande* (1950)—may be related to the fact that they were all based on short stories by James Warner Bellah. According to Bellah's son, his father's politics "were just a little right of Attila. He was a fascist, a racist, and a world-class bigot." Celebrations of the cavalry in the Old West, particularly the sense of community it generated, and critiques of the Indians who challenged it, Bellah's short stories provided the fodder for Ford's trilogy, which, according to Ford biographer Ronald Davis, "reflects Ford's war experiences, his love for the military, and the sense of community he felt exists among fighting men and military families."[41]

Perhaps most important, after the war Ford concentrated on making Westerns again. In the second half of the decade he directed eight films, from *My Darling Clementine* in 1946 to *Rio Grande* in 1950; six of the eight were Westerns. This also contributed to the shift in his public reputation and intensified the process by which he came to be associated with Westerns. Besides the two already mentioned, the Westerns were *3 Godfathers* (1948), *Fort Apache* and *She Wore a Yellow Ribbon*—the first two films of the cavalry trilogy—and *Wagon Master* (1950). All of these but *My Darling Clementine*, a 20th Century–Fox release, were made for Ford's independent production company, Argosy Pictures. Ford's move toward independence could have garnered him more publicity and more widespread recognition. Yet unlike Frank Capra, a director who sought out and often received publicity and recognition, Ford generally showed an aversion to publicity in the 1930s and 1940s, an aversion that continued well into the 1950s.

These Westerns were reviewed a little more widely than *Stagecoach* had been. Among the mass magazines indexed in the *Reader's Guide*, *Stagecoach* was reviewed in only two, while *3 Godfathers* and *Wagon Master* were reviewed in four, *Fort Apache* in five, *My Darling Clementine* and *She Wore a Yellow Ribbon* in six, and *Rio Grande* in eight. However, this attention was significantly less than "prestige" pictures of the era received; Olivier's *Hamlet* (1948), for example, was reviewed in eighteen periodicals, and even some of Ford's mid-1950s films received considerably more attention, notably *The Searchers* (1956, eleven reviews) and *The Long Gray Line* (1955, fifteen reviews). This suggests that attention to and respect for Ford's films, including his Westerns, increased as the emergence of "adult Westerns" like *High Noon* (1952) in the 1950s helped raise the cultural status of the genre.

A look at the reviews of *My Darling Clementine* and the cavalry trilogy gives us a sense of how the evolution of Ford's reputation proceeded. At times these reviews portray Ford as a director with artistic pretensions, much like some commentary from the 1930s. Reviewing *Clementine*, *Variety* wrote that the "trademark of John Ford's direction is clearly stamped on the film with its shadowy lights, softly contrasted moods, and measured pace, but a tendency is discernible towards stylization for stylization's sake without relationship to the screen material. At several points, the pic comes to a dead stop to let Ford go gunning for some arty effect. As usual in a Ford pic, the photography is brilliantly conceived."[42] This picture of Ford is very like the image inherited from the late 1920s and early 1930s. It was also commonplace for the reviews to praise the photography of Ford films. In a brief review of *Rio Grande* in *Christian Century*, the reviewer observed that, "directed by John Ford, a master at this sort of thing, [the] film is no masterpiece, but it has *sweep* and *motion*, is beautifully photographed."[43] Sometimes reviewers even compared a Ford Western negatively to his earlier work. Robert Hatch, in his mixed-to-negative review of *Rio Grande*, wrote that "Ford should not use McLaglen in his popcorn operas; too many people still remember *The Informer*."[44] Similarly, even though *Time* praised Ford's "thoroughgoing craftsmanship" in *Rio Grande*, it concluded that the film "no longer quite makes up for his shoddy taste in material, nor can it satisfy moviegoers who remember him as the director of *The Informer* or *The Grapes of Wrath.*"[45]

Like Otis Ferguson's occasional critiques from the 1930s, some reviews of the late 1940s dismissed the Westerns in a single paragraph. John McCarten in the *New Yorker* was often condescending, as when he wrote that "it's a pleasure, therefore, to report that the American aborigines in John Ford's *Fort Apache* are all as well bred as Groton graduates and that they are led by chaps who want nothing more than to stand around with some smoke and a blanket and chat with a neighboring chieftain about old times."[46] McCarten reviewed *Yellow Ribbon* with four other films—he titled the review "No Aces"—and called it "completely unremarkable" in comparison with *Stagecoach,* adding that the film was all right as long as the characters kept moving, which was "about half the time."[47] In a similar vein, *Time* called *Fort Apache* an "unabashed potboiler," and concluded in another review, "Mostly *Yellow Ribbon* is a waste of talent and Technicolor."[48]

And even when Ford received critical praise for his Westerns, this praise was couched in acknowledgment that he was working in a disparaged genre. Bosley Crowther, who regularly gave Ford's Westerns positive reviews in the *New York Times* during this period, usually deprecated the genre even as he praised Ford. His reviews suggested to his readers that he didn't take Westerns all that seriously. *Fort Apache* was a "rootin', tootin' Wild West show, full of Indians and United States cavalry, dust and desert scenery and a nice masculine trace of romance." *She Wore a Yellow Ribbon* was "a dilly of a Cavalry picture. Yeehoo."[49] While even those critics who liked Ford's Westerns in the late 1940s at times looked down on them, others paid no attention. James Agee, well-known reviewer for *The Nation* from 1943 to mid-1948, didn't even bother to review *My Darling Clementine.*[50]

Occasional reviews of *Clementine* and the cavalry trilogy, however, hinted at a shift in Ford's reputation: reviewers began to speak positively of John Ford as a director especially known for his Westerns. Philip T. Hartung often praised Ford in his *Commonweal* reviews and associated him with Westerns. In his review of *My Darling Clementine,* Hartung wrote that "The 'western' is a manifestation of modern art in which movies excel. And when John Ford makes a 'western,' it's good." *Yellow Ribbon,* Hartung wrote, "is the kind of outdoor melodrama that Producer-director John Ford makes to perfection." He added that "Ford has mixed his ingredients well and he uses the camera expertly to tell an interesting story." Still later he wrote, "Even when Director John Ford does what he has done before, he does it so well it bears re-seeing. *Rio Grande* has many of the old Ford elements: fast riding, tough fighting, vivid characterization, warm sentiment."[51] In a similar vein, *Variety* called *Yellow Ribbon* "a western meller done in the best John Ford manner," and *Newsweek* wrote of the same film that "the fine, forceful hand of the John Ford who made *Stagecoach* is apparent."[52] The association of Ford and Westerns was starting to merge.

In the postwar era reviewers began to speak positively of John Ford as a director known for his Westerns. Ford and cast on the set of *My Darling Clementine* (1946).

Courtesy of The Lilly Library, Indiana University, Bloomington, Indiana.

Around this time a feature article appeared that was a key part of publicizing Ford as one of the premiere directors of American Westerns. That essay, "Hollywood's Favorite Rebel," appeared in the large-circulation *Saturday Evening Post* in 1949 and was written by Frank Nugent, the former *New York Times* film reviewer who had praised *Stagecoach* so highly in 1939 and had become Ford's screenwriter.[53] The admiring essay was crucial, I believe, in elevating Ford's public reputation, not only through its praise of his directorial skills but also via its vivid portrait of Ford as a masculine, individualist, rebellious spirit.

The essay's opening page featured a picture of the grizzled, cigar-chomping Ford at the poker table with seven other men, including Ward Bond, John Wayne, and "Ford's favorite leading man," Henry Fonda. Ford is hatless, wearing a Western neckerchief with his shirt, and reaching for the cards at the middle of the table, an empty glass at his side. Calling Ford a "big, shambling man with a corrugated face . . . and a gift for making pictures which uncomfortably remind Hollywood that the movies are not just an industry but an art," Nugent adds that "among the cinema's *cognoscenti* he is considered one of the greatest directors who ever lived." Listing Ford's impressive array of awards, Nugent also points out that although Ford was proud of his awards, he never showed up at the dinners to claim them because "he hates publicity."[54]

Nugent's Ford blends the image of the 1930s with an emerging new one. Contrary to the image of the 1930s, Ford's "specialties are period Westerns and sea pictures, the two most masculine brands of movie fiction."[55] Countering the image of Ford as an intellectual, artistic director, Nugent tells us "he still is unmistakably the product of a rough-and-tumble movie school" who, even after thirty-four years in the business, probably hasn't "been interviewed a half-dozen times." He chews his pipe stems "to jagged stumps" and often works with a "handkerchief dangling from one corner of his mouth."[56] All these factors, along with the picture at the start of the essay, emphasize Ford's masculine toughness, an image quite removed from the sensitive stylist who made 1930s movies like *The Informer* or *Mary of Scotland*.

Anticipating the auteur approach, Nugent writes that although not all of Ford's films have been successful, "none of them has been without some touch of distinction—or call it genius—which stamps it indelibly as his." Although he is a great stylist, the style is simple, never calling attention to itself. Nugent quotes Ford: "I don't want [the audience] to be conscious of a camera or a screen. I want them to feel that what they're seeing is real."[57]

Emphasizing biographical details, Nugent sketches Ford's childhood in Maine, his early years in Hollywood, and his career's high points. He emphasizes Ford's distaste for producers and his independent spirit, quoting a producer's assistant: "You don't handle Ford. You turn the reins loose and you try to hang on." Ford himself is quoted: "A producer's function has always seemed to me

to be a casual one. Pictures should be the result of a writer and a director getting together with the producer merely standing by in a fatherly, benevolent way
to chide them if they spend too much money."[58] Prouder of the U.S. government Field Photography citations he received during World War II than of all
his Oscars, Ford is, in Nugent's portrait, "Pappy" Ford: a tough, independent-
minded director of Westerns and sea stories, indifferent to the whims of authority,
one of the greatest directors of all time. With such praise appearing in a large-
circulation magazine like the *Saturday Evening Post,* Ford's public reputation
was surely becoming more firmly anchored in American culture.

Following close on the heels of Nugent's article was the commentary of the
British critic and future director Lindsay Anderson. His writing on Ford provided for *cinéastes* what Nugent gave the broad readership of mass magazines.
Anderson co-edited *Sequence,* which was an influential British film journal from
1947 until its demise in 1952. In it he called for a decisive reorientation in British cinema by defending Hollywood rebels like John Ford. Even though Anderson did not locate Ford's greatness squarely in his Westerns, Anderson's commentary on Ford deserves attention as some of the earliest of what would by
the 1960s become an avalanche of articles in film magazines and journals discussing and praising Ford and his films.

Noting the "baffling diversity" of Ford's films, Anderson aims "to set his
career in perspective and evaluate his achievements" in his 1950 *Sequence* essay on Ford.[59] Following a brief survey of the contours of Ford's career, Anderson argues that Ford's greatness lies not with his serious adaptations, such as
The Informer, The Long Voyage Home, and *The Fugitive* (1947), but rather
with his American films, particularly those set in the American past, such as
Young Mr. Lincoln, The Prisoner of Shark Island, and *Drums along the Mohawk*
(1939). Ford's films exhibit a number of qualities, Anderson argues: they "re-
vive the manners and appearances of past times" through their care with mise
en scène; their dances and other community rituals suggest a yearning for simpler but more lively times; they have strong narratives, vivified by Ford's "own
humane inspiration"; their characterizations are rich and memorable; and Ford's
"control of the medium," while unobtrusive, includes a "pictorial flair," effective use of lighting and composition, smoothly rhythmic editing, and inspired
use of traditional music. Anderson sums up Ford's style in a sentence: "Rich in
phrasing, simple in structure, it is a style which expresses a sure, affirmative
response to life—the equivalent to that Biblical prose which, today, it takes
greatness of spirit to sustain."[60]

Taking a cue from some of the 1930s commentary on Ford, Anderson
opposes Ford's art to the debasing qualities of Hollywood's commercialism, but
he also contrasts it to what he terms the "elegant despair" of *The Third Man*
(1949) or the "compassionate defeatism" of *The Bicycle Thief* (1947). Unlike
the "increasingly sophisticated and eclectic" art of Western societies, Anderson
argues, Ford's films seem to be from another era:

His art is not intellectual; his impulse is intuitive, not analytical. Unsophisticated and direct, his work can be enjoyed by anyone, regardless of cultural level, who has retained his sensitivity and subscribes to values primarily humane. . . . Ford's art is inspired by an optimistic faith in man's nature, a reverence for the human creature which is evident always in choice of subject and manner of treatment; but this is combined with a firm emphasis on discipline, an implicit stress on moral and social duties which may properly be described as classical.

At their most intense, Anderson claims, Ford's films attain "poetry." These American films, which have the "creative vigor" of his recent *Wagon Master* and *She Wore a Yellow Ribbon,* "stand among the few truly noble works of art of our time."[61] This praise by a prominent intellectual seriously interested in film helped set the stage for the auteurist embrace of Ford, which would occur in the United States a decade later. It appeared to take an intellectual from another country to tell Americans that Ford's films of the American past were more moving and valuable than the more consciously "artistic" films for which he was often praised in the 1930s.[62] Both Nugent and Anderson set the stage for the acceptance of Ford as the great director of Westerns.

Although French artists and intellectuals have sometimes taught Americans to value their popular artists, as they did with Edgar Allen Poe in the nineteenth century, this was not the case with Ford. Around the time that *Sequence* was helping to solidify a serious film culture in England, a group of young critics attached to André Bazin's *Cahiers du cinéma* were attacking the "tradition of quality" in French cinema, partly by celebrating American genre directors via their *politique des auteurs.* These critics, including François Truffaut, Jean-Luc Godard, Claude Chabrol, and Eric Rohmer, opposed a prevailing tendency in the French film industry to prize films based on literary adaptations and the screenwriters responsible for the scripts. Instead, they argued via their *politique* that a director, particularly one deeply involved in the screenwriting process, was or should be the central creative force in making a film. This led the *Cahiers* critics to value not only distinctive French directors like Renoir, Bresson, and Tati but also a variety of Hollywood directors who achieved artistic expression despite the constraints of the studio system. However, the *Cahiers* critics did not seem to embrace Ford in the early, heady days of 1950s auteurism. Although an occasional reference to Ford's gift with composition might pop up, Ford was not the poet of the cinema to these critics, as he was to Lindsay Anderson. Between 1955 and 1959, *Cahiers* issued lists of the top films of each year; no Ford film appeared on any of them, even though other American directors were acknowledged regularly, among them Nicholas Ray (five films), Alfred Hitchcock (five), Fritz Lang (three), and Frank Tashlin (three). When *Cahiers* issued a list of top films and directors in its December 1958 issue, Ford's name was not among the twenty-two directors listed.[63] François Truffaut in particular failed to appreciate Ford. Even in a review of Westerns, he did not single Ford out for praise. Discussing Anthony Mann's *The Last Frontier*, Truffaut—who seems to be thinking of Ford as the 1930s director of quality adaptations—calls Mann "more clever than Ford," able to make his Westerns "less literary and less theatrical and more subtle. The characters seem more real and the relationships between them more true." Amazingly, Truffaut even dismissed *The Searchers* and used it on one occasion to say that among directors of Westerns, he preferred Lang, Mann, Aldrich, Walsh, and even Allan Dwan to Ford. Ford represents an earlier Hollywood, Truffaut writes, "the one when good health prevailed over intelligence, craftiness over sincerity." Where Nicholas Ray and Elia Kazan provide "poetry," Ford offers only "entertainment." He is "senile and repetitive, [and] bores us."[64]

It's jolting to see Ford dismissed so harshly for a film that has subsequently achieved such canonical status. The road of Ford's rising reputation in the 1950s would run through England and the United States rather than through France.

It is worth noting, however, that *The Searchers* did not get very strong reviews in the United States when it first appeared. *Variety* called it "overlong and repetitious at 119 minutes" and complained that "there are subtleties in the basically simple story that are not adequately explained." Although he liked Ford's photography, the usually supportive Philip T. Hartung similarly found the film "quite thin on plot." Robert Hatch's moralistic review in *Nation* criticized the sadism of Ethan Edwards, calling the film "long on brutality and short on logic or responsible behavior." *Time* felt that the "John Ford Stock Company" may be getting "too practiced and familiar" in *The Searchers*: "Even John Wayne seems to have done it once too often."[65] Ford's reputation didn't get any boost from these magazine and journal reviews of *The Searchers*.

Yet, following the groundwork laid by Lindsay Anderson, a number of American auteurist critics began to solidify Ford's public reputation in the early 1960s. Significantly, the articles and defenses began to appear after Ford had begun a late run of four Westerns: *The Horse Soldiers* (1959), *Sergeant Rutledge* (1960), *Two Rode Together* (1961), and *The Man Who Shot Liberty Valance* (1962). I'd like to focus on a number of representative documents that seem particularly important: Michael Barkun's "Notes on the Art of John Ford" in *Film Culture* (1962); Bogdanovich's "The Autumn of John Ford" in *Esquire* (1964) and his 1967 critical book and interview, *John Ford*; and several writings by Andrew Sarris, including his sketch of Ford in *The American Cinema* (1968).[66]

Film Culture, a serious New York–based film journal, devoted considerable attention to Ford in 1962, including a review of *The Man Who Shot Liberty Valance* by auteurist Andrew Sarris. Also reproduced were eight photographs of Ford at work (shooting *Stagecoach*, he's wearing a beret and holding a walking stick; shooting *Liberty Valance*, his accoutrements include a Dodger's cap, eye patch, and cigar). The most significant of these articles is Michael Barkun's "Notes on the Art of John Ford." Barkun's essay echoes Lindsay Anderson in assuming that Ford is an important artist fulfilling auteurist values. Ford's work, he writes, "constitutes one of the very few large groups of films stamped with a single creative vision." Barkun's aim is to "abstract his notion of the world" from the films. Also like Anderson, Barkun argues that Ford's "is not a 20th century view"; rather, it's a universe "bathed in light, rosy light at that," which would seem more suited to the eighteenth or nineteenth centuries: idealistic, optimistic about human nature, "more emotional than intellectual," focused on ordinary people and ordinary life.[67] Even at this relatively late date in Ford's career, the critic offers no sense of Ford's growing pessimism, a view that would later become commonplace.

Unlike Anderson, however, Barkun posits that Ford's artistry is not incompatible with his Westerns but inseparable from them. Although Anderson located Ford's greatness in his films of the American past generally—*The Prisoner of Shark Island, Drums along the Mohawk, Young Mr. Lincoln*, and some of the Westerns—Barkun locates Ford's greatest achievements squarely in his Westerns. In the most forceful and direct assertion of this position to this point,

For critics like Andrew Sarris, Ford was an auteur with a personal vision perhaps best expressed through his Westerns. Ford directing James Stewart and John Wayne in a scene from *The Man Who Shot Liberty Valance* (1962). Courtesy of The Lilly Library, Indiana University, Bloomington, Indiana.

Barkun writes that even though many critics have found it "faintly demeaning" for a director to devote himself to the genre, "John Ford's Westerns are their own justification. They stand as one of the few genuinely American examples of film art."[68]

Barkun elaborates by stating first that Ford's vision is incapable of dealing with contemporary society; rather, his work revolves around two subjects— Ireland and the American West. The Irish films, however, constitute "a succession of minor triumphs. . . . For all of Ford's obvious sympathy with the Irish, this has not turned out to be his *métier.* The further expression of his talents lay closer at hand, in the American West." As Barkun sees it, although American audiences prefer to think of Ford as the director of *The Informer,* Europeans are more interested in the Western, for they, and Ford, see the Western in a "strangely European way." This "classic European view of America" considers the United States a place where fresh starts could be made, free from the social barriers and customs of the Old World. The New World, particularly the Western frontier, "attracted and developed a peculiarly direct, unsubtle person, with just that combination of virtues that Ford considers important."[69] Although uncited, Frederick Jackson Turner's frontier thesis hovers over this analysis. After associating Ford centrally with his Westerns, Barkun points out a number of their narrative, thematic, and stylistic aspects. Most of these had already become familiar in the discourse about Ford: a distinctive heroism, the presence of the Irish, rich characterizations, memorable performances, effective lighting and composition, use of folk music, and so on. Yet the chief contribution of the essay lies in the way it attaches Ford's greatness and his public reputation to his Westerns. It's a crucial moment in the evolution of Ford's public reputation.

Nearly two years later auteur critic and soon-to-be director Peter Bogdanovich also associated Ford's greatness directly with the Western. His "The Autumn of John Ford" in *Esquire* (a large-circulation magazine with a primarily male readership) was precipitated by his visit to Monument Valley during the shooting of *Cheyenne Autumn* (1964), Ford's last Western.[70] More a portrait of Ford the man and his directing methods than an analysis of his "vision," the essay opens with the picture of Ford described in the opening paragraph of this essay. It equates Ford and the West through descriptions of what Bogdanovich saw on and off the set, anecdotes that crew members told about Ford, descriptions of Ford's relationship with the Navajo, and details of Ford's past.

The article's portrait of Ford is vivid, stressing a number of familiar motifs. His dress is informal and even sloppy. He speaks to the Navajo in their own language and leads applause for their dances and chants. We learn that the Navajo even have a special name for him, "Natani Nez"—Tall Leader. His set is filled with old friends and compatriots. On the set he has Danny Borzage constantly playing folk songs on the accordion. He's gruff. He tells Bogdanovich, "I love making pictures, but I don't like talking about them," and, in a moment of rare self-revelation, he adds, "It's been my whole life." When Bogdanovich asks the director's son, Pat Ford, if the rumor that *Cheyenne Autumn* would be his last Western contained any truth, Pat replies, "Hell, no! Why, he'll be makin' Westerns a couple a years after he's dead."[71] The essay is an affectionate tribute to a humane and creative director who is most at home in—even inseparable from—his Westerns.

In 1967 Bogdanovich expanded on this sympathetic view of Ford by publishing *John Ford*. This monograph included a revised version of the *Esquire* article, along with a chapter on Ford's vision and "genius" called "Poet and Comedian"; a transcript of an extended interview with Ford from 1966; and a detailed filmography. Throughout the book are dozens of production stills and photographs from the sets of a range of Ford's films, although the opening chapter is illustrated almost exclusively with stills from Ford Westerns. As the first book in English devoted exclusively to Ford and his films, it is a milestone. In addition, it shaped Ford's public reputation further when it was reissued in a second edition following Ford's death; this edition included a brief chapter, "Taps," that discussed Ford's final years and Bogdanovich's last visit with him. It also summed up well Bogdanovich's attitude toward the director: "His best movies—and there are many of them—are for *all* our days. They are the size of legends and possess the soul of myth."[72]

Extended interview books like these and directors' autobiographies were important in building the public reputations of a number of American directors in the 1960s and early 1970s. Among these books were François Truffaut's *Hitchcock* (1967), John Halliday's *Sirk on Sirk* (1971), and Frank Capra's *Name Above the Title* (1971). Each of these books helped gain its subject additional critical attention and raise his status in the art world of film. Bogdanovich's book crucially performed a similar function for Ford.

Just as influential in raising Ford's reputation through praise for his Westerns and devaluation of his more serious art or social-problem films was Andrew Sarris.[73] Following a trip to France in 1961, Sarris became a polemical defender of the auteur approach. "Notes on the Auteur Theory in 1962" was one of his first widely discussed essays, while his *The American Cinema: Directors and Directions, 1929–1968* (1968) provided an influential ranking of nearly two hundred directors who worked in American cinema during the sound era.[74]

Just how highly Sarris valued Ford's movies is clear from "Notes." In it, Sarris lists his top twenty auteurs "at this moment." Overall, Ford was sixth; of directors who worked primarily in Hollywood, he was third, after only Hitchcock and Chaplin but before Welles, Griffith, Sternberg, Stroheim, Hawks, and Lang.[75] His ranking remained high in *The American Cinema*, where Ford is one of fourteen directors in Sarris's "Pantheon." Despite this high ranking, Sarris refused to value most highly the films for which Ford had been most praised in the 1930s and 1940s. In doing so Sarris embodied an important shift in critical approaches to movies that was evolving in the 1950s and early 1960s. Whereas the modern liberal critics of the Depression and war years tended to value "realism" over "entertainment," weighty thematic explorations over genre films, subject matter over style, Sarris reversed these priorities.[76] Like many early auteur critics reacting against the modern liberal approach typified by Bosley Crowther, he tended to emphasize style over subject matter, genre films over social realism.

For example, in his 1961 essay devoted partly to Ford Sarris wrote, "It can be argued that *Wagon Master* is John Ford's greatest film. If I choose not to argue the point at this time, it is because there are too many other candidates, and these do not include *The Informer* and *The Grapes of Wrath.*"[77] Characteristically, Sarris devalued two serious literary adaptations praised highly by modern liberal critics, one a consciously arty film and the other a social-problem film, in favor of a Western—a good Hollywood genre film. Although his sketch of Ford in the book does not say flatly that his Westerns are his greatest films, it's clear that Sarris's sympathies are more with the Westerns than with his other films. Predictably, the only Western that Sarris calls a failure in the Ford entry in *The American Cinema* is *Cheyenne Autumn,* "simply because Ford cannot get inside the Indians he is trying to ennoble." That's no surprise, given Sarris's distaste for socially conscious films at this point in his career.[78]

As these writings and Sarris's 1962 review of *The Man Who Shot Liberty Valance* suggest, Ford's vision is perhaps best expressed through his Westerns. Sarris's Ford, like Anderson's and Barkun's, is not a modernist artist, but a conservative hoping to maintain "the memories of old values even if they have to be magnified into legends. The legends with which Ford is most deeply involved ... are the legends of honorable failure, of otherwise forgotten men and women who rode away from glory toward self-sacrifice."[79] In such a formulation the Ford Westerns *Fort Apache* and *The Man Who Shot Liberty Valance* immediately spring to mind as quintessential Ford.

Anderson, Barkun, Bogdanovich, and Sarris were thus crucial in helping to revise John Ford's public reputation in the 1950s and 1960s; he was no longer "the man who directed *The Informer.*" He was no longer the socially conscious director of *The Grapes of Wrath.* He was, as he presented himself in the 1950 Directors Guild meeting, John Ford, who made Westerns.

By the early 1970s, that reputation had spread widely and solidified. Between 1965 and 1972 five film magazines devoted special issues to Ford and his films.[80] Two documentaries about him appeared in 1971: the American Film Institute–sponsored *Directed by John Ford,* written and directed by Peter Bogdanovich, and *The American West of John Ford,* which Ford's grandson Dan Ford helped to produce. John Baxter's *The Cinema of John Ford* appeared the same year, as did two elegant essays praising the director, one by the prominent British auteurist Robin Wood and the other by William Pechter.[81] In 1973 Ford received the first Life Achievement Award granted by the American Film

Institute. At the event President Richard Nixon presented Ford with the Medal of Freedom, the nation's highest civilian honor, and promoted the director from rear admiral to admiral. A substantial number of new books devoted to Ford and his films appeared before the end of the decade, including J. A. Place's *The Western Films of John Ford* (1974) and *The Non-Western Films of John Ford* (1979), Joseph McBride and Michael Wilmington's *John Ford* (1975), Andrew Sarris's *The John Ford Movie Mystery* (1975), and two biographies in 1979: Andrew Sinclair's *John Ford: A Biography*, and *Pappy*, by Ford's grandson Dan Ford. In 1981 Lindsay Anderson's *About John Ford*, some of which was originally written in the 1950s for an abortive British Film Institute project, was published with new material and a number of interviews with those who worked with Ford.

Yet attention to Ford peaked in the 1970s, then began to diminish in the 1980s, for several reasons. In the latter part of his career, Ford began to grant more interviews than he ever had before. One study lists twenty-seven interviews through 1972: one each in the 1930s and 1940s, five in the 1950s, thirteen in the 1960s, and seven between 1970 and 1972.[82] Auteurist readings thrive on the personalizing of art that interviews encourage, but with Ford's passing in 1973, potential biographers and critics could no longer ask him about his career. After Ford's public reputation grew in the 1960s, the fruits of that attention ripened into the critical studies and biographies of the 1970s. In the wake of that flurry of books, it seemed less pressing or necessary to write another. Also, Ford's perceived political conservatism and his close association with John Wayne distanced him from many in a generation that reached political maturity during the years of Vietnam and Watergate.

Finally, as film studies began to gain a firmer foothold in the academy in the 1970s, auteur analysis itself came under closer scrutiny. Some urged revision, others urged scrapping auteurism altogether. Peter Wollen, in *Signs and Meanings in the Cinema* (1969), offered a structuralist discussion of Ford that drew on the work of Claude Levi-Strauss, particularly his notion of cultural myths. Rejecting the kind of polemical ratings game of some 1950s French auteurism, Wollen sought instead to look for recurring patterns and dichotomies in a director's films. "The richness of the shifting relations between antinomies in Ford's work," wrote Wollen, "makes him a great artist, beyond being simply an undoubted *auteur*."[83] In 1972 a translation of the *Cahiers du cinéma* essay on *Young Mr. Lincoln* appeared in the British film journal *Screen*. Politicized by the events of May 1968 in France, the *Cahiers* critics sought to place the film within the context of Hollywood and the Fox studio in the late 1930s, as well as within the broader sociopolitical climate in the United States, and then to consider in greatest detail the narrative and its ideological implications.[84] An even more substantial challenge to auteurism came from the ripples created by Roland Barthes's essay "The Death of the Author," which challenged the notion that an easily discernable author was embedded in any text and urged critics to turn attention to texts and to the *reception* rather than the *creation* of art works—to works and audiences, not artists.[85] To those who heeded Barthes's call, auteurism as a critical approach was as dead as the author. Finally, as film studies evolved in the 1980s and 1990s, many scholars turned toward close examination of how the Hollywood film industry functioned, developing more complicated understandings of how Hollywood films were made than early auteurism had had. These later shifts helped temper the enthusiasm for Ford that had reached such heights in the late 1960s and the 1970s.

Despite these challenges, though, John Ford remains a figure of much interest to film studies. Robin Wood's essay on Ford in Richard Roud's *Cinema: A Critical Dictionary* (1980) gives a good portrait of John Ford after some of these challenges to auteurism.[86] "Few would now wish to question that Ford is among the greatest artists the cinema has so far produced," Wood writes, "yet the nature of his greatness has proved difficult to define." Wood particularly points out the seeming contradiction between Ford's comments that his film-making was "just a job of work" and his assertion to Bogdanovich that it was his "whole life." Any full account of Ford's work, Wood adds, would "involve writing not only the history of Ford but the history of Hollywood, and placing both in the wider context of the history of America—the America of Ford's contemporary background as well as the America of his subject matter." Rather than simply attributing Ford's films to his "genius" or his "vision," Wood argues that the situation is more complicated. In Wood's view, "the Hollywood system itself—a complex interaction of studios, stars, genres, topical themes and attitudes—clearly played a role in his development that must not be underestimated."[87] But even as he urges this more complex understanding of Ford and his career, Wood still devotes in his essay far more attention to Ford's Westerns than to any of his other films.

If we dolly back into an extreme long shot to survey the overall evolution of John Ford's public reputation, several insights come into sharper focus. The establishment of John Ford's public reputation was hindered both by the tendency not to publicize directors in the studio era and by Ford's personal aversion to interviews and publicity, which lasted through much of his career. His greater willingness to be interviewed, particularly from the early 1960s on, coincided with the growth of his reputation. Compared to the reputations of self-promoters like Capra or Hitchcock, Ford's reputation developed more because of his films and criticism of and commentary on them, and much less through promotion or publicity, at least until Ford began to be more receptive to critics who wanted him to talk about his work.

Two changes in the "art world" of film beginning in the 1950s contributed to the growth of Ford's public reputation. The first was the increased emphasis on the importance of the director in the creation of effective films. Observers like Lindsay Anderson in *Sequence,* the *Cahiers* critics (even if they didn't value Ford too highly), the British *Movie* critics in the early 1960s, Peter Bogdanovich, and Andrew Sarris all contributed to the notion that our critical attention should be focused on the films of a demonstrably effective director, which in turn spotlighted a director with such longevity as Ford's. Ford's increased willingness to talk with interviewers during this period, and the eagerness of his male collaborators to discuss Pappy, helped win Ford auteur status. In addition, the 1950s and 1960s were a period—termed by Andreas Huyssen "the great divide"—in which rigid distinctions between high culture and popular culture began to break down in American society. One manifestation of that change was that critics became willing to give previously disparaged genres serious aesthetic consideration and higher artistic value. This, as Robert Kapsis demonstrated so well, is when Alfred Hitchcock's thrillers began to be elevated from entertainment to art status. And it also helped make it possible for a director like Ford, long associated with the sometimes critically despised Western, to be called a great artist.[88]

Shifts in the broader culture that influenced Ford also contributed to the longevity of Ford's career, the shifts in his public reputation over time, and the complexity of determining the core of his work. For example, the leftist edge that some critics discerned in Ford's work in the late 1930s emanated from and spoke to American culture in the late Depression years. This related to the fact that Ford was then working with liberal screenwriters like Dudley Nichols and Nunnally Johnson and adapting works by leftist writers like John Steinbeck. His war documentaries surely spoke to American moviegoers during World War II. After the war, as Richard Slotkin has argued, Ford's celebrations of the cavalry, military authority, and American patriotism touched a chord in the early Cold War years.[89] The perspective of those films was also rooted in the conservative politics of James Warner Bellah, who wrote the short stories upon which the films were based. Finally, the greater sympathy shown to African Americans in *Sergeant Rutledge* and to Native Americans in *Cheyenne Autumn* coincided with the growth of the civil rights movement in the United States. Ford's ability to continue directing films and to work with different creative personnel, particularly screenwriters, who were sensitive to shifts in the broader sociopolitical climate helped to extend his career and to enhance his public reputation, particularly from the early 1950s on, when he began to elicit greater critical attention and to respond by being less averse to publicity than he had been through most of his career.

So John Ford *was,* according to his public reputation at different points in his career, the aesthete, the Irish genius, the chronicler of the West, and Pappy. He was also, according to observers at various times, a realist, a master film stylist, a liberal, a conservative, a patriot, and more. But he wasn't the chronicler of the West to almost anyone in 1935. That came years later, as auteurism and an increased appreciation for genre films filtered into the art world of cin-ema discourse. However much Ford may have resisted being labeled the "poet of the Western saga," he is today inextricably linked to that genre. And even as critics in coming years heed Robin Wood's call to define the particular great-ness of John Ford within the contexts of the Hollywood system and American society, where he faithfully did his job of work for a half-century, I suspect that the Western and John Ford will continue to ride down the trail together.

NOTES

1. Robert Parrish provides a full account of that meeting, and the events that led up to it, in *Growing Up in Hollywood* (New York: Harcourt, 1976), 201–210. Ford followed his now-famous opening comments with a critique of DeMille's actions and a motion for the resignation of DeMille and the board of directors and a vote of con-fidence in Mankiewicz.

2. Edward Buscombe, ed., *The BFI Companion to the Western* (New York: Atheneum, 1988), 344. The opening chapter of Peter Bogdanovich's *John Ford* (Ber-keley: University of California Press, 1968), 6, uses the epigraph as its title.

3. Quoted in Ronald L. Davis, *John Ford: Hollywood's Old Master* (Norman: University of Oklahoma Press, 1995), 12.

4. The recent scholarly interest in the history and operations of the American film industry has included several studies of how filmmakers have been perceived throughout their careers. Perhaps the best book on the making of a director's public reputation is Robert E. Kapsis's *Hitchcock: The Making of a Reputation* (Chicago: University of Chicago Press, 1992). Matthew Bernstein's *Walter Wanger: Hollywood Independent* (Berkeley: University of California Press, 1994) examines the evolution of that long-time producer's career. My own *Chaplin and American Culture: The Evolution of a Star Image* (Princeton: Princeton University Press, 1989) explores a similar topic, focusing on a director who was also a performer.

5. On the notion of "art world" and its application to American film, see Rob-ert Kapsis, *Hitchcock,* particularly chapters 1 and 7. Kapsis draws specifically on Howard Becker's *Art Worlds* (Berkeley: University of California Press, 1982), in which Becker suggests that artists produce an art work, "at least in part, by anticipating how other people will respond, emotionally and cognitively, to what they do. That gives them the means with which to shape it further, by catering to already existing dispositions in the audience, or by trying to train the audience into something new" (200). Becker argues that no matter what the art form, "reputations develop through a process of consensus building in the relevant art world" (359–360): the reputations of both genres and art-ists rise and fall over time because of those involved in the particular art world. Although Becker seems primarily interested in arts like painting and sculpture, Kapsis usefully applies the concept to the movies.

6. See David Bordwell, Janet Staiger, and Kristin Thompson, *The Classical Hollywood Cinema* (New York: Columbia University Press, 1985), 97–102.

7. See Bordwell, Staiger, and Thompson, *The Classical Hollywood Cinema,* chapter 26, on the package-unit system.

8. Joseph Gelmis, ed., *The Film Director as Superstar* (New York: Doubleday, 1970).

9. The chart is drawn from Mel Schuster's *Motion Picture Directors: A Bibliography of Magazine and Periodical Articles, 1900–1972* (Metuchen, N.J.: Scarecrow Press, 1973), which surveys English-language, primarily American periodicals, both mass magazines like the *Saturday Evening Post* and *Harper's* and more specialized film journals and magazines like *Film Quarterly* and *Film Culture*.

10. This is not to argue that a director of genre films was necessarily held in higher esteem than directors who worked in a variety of genres in the 1930s and 1940s. Some would argue, in fact, that directors of genre films—horror films, or Westerns, or thrillers—would not have been considered artists during that period but rather skilled entertainers. We will return later to the question of the changing attitude of commentators toward Hollywood film genres from the 1960s onward.

11. Peter Milne, review of *Straight Shooting, Motion Picture News* 16 (8 September 1917), 1668; reprinted in *Selected Film Criticism: 1912–1920,* ed. Anthony Slide (Metuchen, N.J.: Scarecrow, 1982), 249–250.

12. "William Fox Presents *The Iron Horse,*" John Ford clippings file, Academy of Motion Pictures Arts and Sciences Library. The Russell referred to is Charles Marion Russell (1864–1926), with Remington one of the two best-known painters of Western subjects. After 1919 he spent winters in California with his wife and met movie actors like William S. Hart, Harry Carey, Douglas Fairbanks, and Will Rogers, who bought paintings from him.

13. *Variety,* 3 September 1924, 23.

14. *New York Times,* 29 August 1924, 6.

15. *Variety,* 18 August 1926, 18.

16. Andrew Sarris, *The American Cinema* (New York: Dutton, 1968), 44.

17. Gallagher, *John Ford: The Man and His Films* (Berkeley: University of California Press, 1986), 47; see also Gallagher's chart of Ford's pre-1928 films, 36.

18. *Moving Picture World,* 3 March 1927, 35.

19. The essay is conveniently reprinted in Richard Koszarski, *Hollywood Directors, 1914–1940* (New York: Oxford, 1976), 199–204.

20. Gallagher cites only three articles written by Ford in his bibliography: this one; the introduction to Frank Capra's 1971 *Name Above the Title,* which Gallagher says is ghost-written; and a 1951 article in an Italian magazine praising John Wayne. Gallagher could find no English-language source for the last one (it is reprinted in translation in this volume). Ford is also credited with "How We Made *The Long Voyage Home,*" *Friday,* 9 August 1940: 21–26.

21. The essay appeared in the *Times,* 10 June 1928, sec. VIII, 4. All other quotations from this article are from this page. The essay is also reprinted in Koszarski, *Hollywood Directors,* 199–204.

22. Herbert Cruikshank, "Meant for Martyrdom," *Motion Picture Classic* 30 (January 1930), 45, 86. The same photo, although mirror-reversed, serves as the frontispiece of Gallagher's *John Ford.*

23. "Men Behind the Stars: John Ford, Director of *Mary of Scotland,*" *Motion Picture* (October 1936), 62; Howard Sharp, "The Star Creators of Hollywood," *Photoplay* (October 1936), 166–167, 333–335; Lewis Jacobs, *Rise of the American Film* (New York: Teacher's College Press, 1939), 479–486; "John Ford," *Current Biog-*

raphy (1941), 296–298. Sharp's piece is reprinted in Richard Griffith, ed., *The Talkies: Articles and Illustrations from a Great Fan Magazine, 1928–1940* (Dover, 1971).

24. In a good summary of Ford's reputation in 1939 among those seriously interested in the American film industry, Jacobs writes, "John Ford is best known today as the director of the celebrated film *The Informer.* Until 1935, when that film was made, Ford was hardly known outside the trade; yet for twenty-one years he had been directing, turning out good, bad, and indifferent films, changing his style in each to meet the demands of his employers" (*Rise of the American Film,* 479). Jacobs adds that although Ford was "not yet a great director," he was "always proficient" and was once, with *The Informer,* "exceptional." Emphasizing Ford's craftsmanship and promise, Jacobs concludes that Ford "may yet produce a great picture" (486).

25. Cruikshank, "Meant for Martyrdom," 45, 86.

26. Sharp, "The Star Creators," 167.

27. "Men Behind the Stars," 62.

28. "John Ford," 297.

29. Jacobs, *Rise of the American Film,* 485–486.

30. Jacobs, *Rise of the American Film,* 482.

31. Sharp, "The Star Creators," 334.

32. On the "modern liberal" approach to film criticism, as well as a related "social radical" perspective, see Myron Lounsbury, *The Origins of American Film Criticism* (New York: Arno, 1973), chapters 4–5 passim. For Lounsbury, Jacobs's *The Rise of The American Film* is a kind of culmination of this approach to movies, and one later carried on by influential *New York Times* film critic Bosley Crowther.

33. One exception may prove the rule. A key reason for Frank Capra's preeminence in the later 1930s was his ability to blend the social-problem film with the screwball comedy in movies like *You Can't Take It With You, Mr. Smith Goes to Washington,* and *Meet John Doe.* In a sense he could satisfy both audiences seeking entertainment and critics valuing realism. I'd argue that without the social-problem probing, Capra would never have reached the preeminence he achieved in the late 1930s: he never would have satisfied the modern liberal critics who did so much to help elevate his reputation.

34. "Men Behind the Stars," 62; "John Ford," 297.

35. Jacobs, *Rise of the American Film,* 485.

36. See Robert Wilson, ed., *The Film Criticism of Otis Ferguson* (Philadelphia: Temple University Press, 1971), 195, 345, 226–227.

37. Wilson, *Film Criticism,* 121, 258, 283–284, 288, 314.

38. André Bazin, "The Evolution of the Western," in *What Is Cinema?,* vol. 2, trans. and ed. Hugh Gray (Berkeley: University of California Press, 1971): 149–157. The article was originally published in French in the 1950s. Bazin wrote that in *Stagecoach* John Ford "struck the ideal balance between social myth, historical reconstruction, psychological truth, and the traditional theme of the western mise-en-scene" to create a Western of "classical perfection" (149).

39. *Time* 33 (13 March 1939), 31; *Newsweek* 13 (6 March 1939), 27. These are the only two reviews cited in the *Reader's Guide to Periodical Literature;* in contrast, *Wuthering Heights* was reviewed in eight sources the year before.

40. *New York Times,* 2 March 1939, 19.

41. Both quotations are from Davis, *John Ford,* 204.

42. *Variety,* 9 October 1946, 14.

43. *Christian Century* 67 (6 December 1950), 1471.

44. *New Republic* 123 (11 December 1950), 28.

45. *Time* 56 (11 December 1950), 98.

46. *New Yorker* 24 (3 July 1948), 58.

47. *New Yorker* 25 (3 December 1948), 74.

48. James Agee probably wrote the anonymous *Time* review of *Fort Apache;* it criticized the Irish comedy in much the same vein that Agee did in his *Nation* review. See *Time* 51 (10 May 1948), 102, 104; and 54 (24 October 1949), 103.

49. *New York Times,* 25 June 1948, 26; 18 November 1949, 35.

50. Agee concisely disposed of *The Fugitive* (1947) by calling it "a bad work of art, tacky, unreal, and pretentious," even though he admired its "sobriety of ambition." See James Agee, *Agee on Film,* vol. 1 (New York: Putnam, 1958), 89.

51. *Commonweal* 45 (6 December 1945), 205; 51 (16 December 1949), 294; and 53 (24 November 1950), 173.

52. *Variety,* 27 July 1949, 12; *Newsweek* 34 (12 December 1949), 88.

53. Frank Nugent, "Hollywood's Favorite Rebel," *Saturday Evening Post* 222, no. 1 (23 July 1949): 26, 96–98 (reprinted in this volume). When he wrote the article, Nugent had just finished serving as Ford's screenwriter on *Fort Apache, 3 Godfathers,* and *She Wore a Yellow Ribbon.* He would later work with Ford on *Wagon Master, The Quiet Man, The Last Hurrah, Two Rode Together,* and *Donovan's Reef.* A similar article in another mass magazine, albeit one with a smaller circulation, is David A. Smart's "John Ford, Maker of Hollywood Stars," *Coronet* 35 (December 1953): 133–140. The article covers much the same ground as Nugent's article and some of the earlier essays, including his early days, his indifference to what people think of him, his shabby dress (he "dresses like an elegant bum" [139]), his patriotic service during World War II, and his many awards.

54. Nugent, "Hollywood's Favorite Rebel," 26.

55. Nugent, "Hollywood's Favorite Rebel," 98.

56. Nugent, "Hollywood's Favorite Rebel," 97.

57. Nugent, "Hollywood's Favorite Rebel," 98.

58. Nugent underlines Ford's clashes with producers via an anecdote about a production manager who chided Ford for being ten days behind schedule during the shooting of *How Green Was My Valley.* In response, according to Nugent, Ford grabbed a script, ripped out twenty pages, and told the manager, "Now we're on schedule. Feel happier?" (96). The film, thirteen days over schedule, grossed $5.75 million on a cost of $1.25 million. Nunnally Johnson disputes this story in his interview for the UCLA oral history project.

59. Lindsay Anderson, *"They Were Expendable* and John Ford," *Sequence* 11 (Summer 1950): 18–31. I will be quoting from Anderson, "John Ford," *Films in Review* 2, no. 2 (February 1951): 5–16, a slightly briefer version of the same article, which was probably read by a wider audience and which surely was read by more serious filmgoers in the United States than the *Sequence* article.

60. Anderson, "John Ford," 10–14 passim.

61. Anderson, "John Ford," 14–16, 16.

62. Anderson must have been somewhat disappointed when he was granted an interview with Ford during the shooting of *The Quiet Man* (he writes that "Ford is pretty well interview-proof"—a perspective shared by many interviewers and frustrated would-be interviewers of Ford over the years). His report of that interview (Lindsay Anderson, "The Quiet Man," *Sequence* 14 [New Year's Issue 1952]: 23–27) is at times highly

amusing, a telling portrait of Ford's disdain for having his work taken seriously and his glee at thwarting those who did. Anderson, who had celebrated *They Were Expendable* as a "heroic poem" in the 1950 *Sequence* article, heard Ford respond, "You really think that's a good picture? I just can't believe that film's any good." When Anderson said he was horrified to learn that Ford hadn't even seen the film, Ford replied, "I'll use the same word. I was horrified to have to make it" (24). Often countering and contradicting Anderson throughout the interview, he tweaks him again at the end of their conversation. He tells Anderson he'll run *They Were Expendable* when he gets back to California: "The kids will like the boats, anyway." But Anderson, as compiler of the interview, gets the last word. The final line of the interview is, "God made him a poet, and he must make the best of that" (27). The image of the crusty, unpretentious Ford is certainly alive and well in this interview.

63. Many directors who worked often in Hollywood were on this list of top directors, including Griffith, Welles, von Stroheim, Hitchcock, Chaplin, Lang, Hawks, Keaton, and Ray. The *Cahiers* lists are included in Jim Hillier, ed., *Cahiers du cinéma: The 1950s* (Cambridge: Harvard University Press, 1985), 284–288.

64. Both reviews are included, translated into English, in Wheeler Winston Dixon's *The Early Film Criticism of François Truffaut* (Bloomington: Indiana University Press, 1993), 43–45. Truffaut's opinion of Ford had changed by the early 1970s. As he points out in the introduction to *The Films in My Life* (New York: Simon and Schuster, 1978), a collection of film criticism, "About Ford I have had a complete turnabout. When I was a critic, I hardly liked anything of his and I wrote two or three vicious articles about him. I had to become a director and watch *The Quiet Man* on television to realize one day how blind I had been" (17–18). Later in the same collection, Truffaut includes his obituary of Ford, "God Bless John Ford" (reprinted in this volume), which praises Ford's attention to characterization, his invisible film style, and the "royal ease" that enabled him to "make the audience laugh and . . . cry" (63). But by that time, Ford was firmly canonized as a pantheon director.

Despite Ford's low esteem in *Cahiers*, one French film critic and historian did write admiringly of Ford in the 1950s: Jean Mitry, whose brief monograph, *John Ford*, was published in Paris in 1954. Mitry was also able to interview Ford, although not much more successfully than Anderson. Originally appearing in *Cahiers* as "Rencontre avec John Ford" in March 1955, the interview was also translated into English and published as "John Ford," in *Films in Review* 6, no. 7 (August–September 1955): 305–309.

65. *Variety*, 14 March 1956, 6; *Commonweal* 64 (15 June 1956), 274; *Nation* 182 (23 June 1956), 536; *Time* 67 (25 June 1956), 58, 60.

66. I might note in passing that in the mass magazines and journals of opinion, *The Man Who Shot Liberty Valance* was not widely reviewed, nor were the few reviews very positive. In the *New York Times* (24 May 1962), A. H. Weiler, the second-string critic, not Crowther, reviewed the film: "The Old West, ravaged by repetition and television, has begun to show signs of age, to judge from *The Man Who Shot Liberty Valance*" (29). *Commonweal* 76 (18 May 1962) wrote that it took "Mr. Ford much too long to tell us [that the John Wayne character was a 'somebody']; and it wears us out in the telling" (211). Brendan Gill briefly dismissed the film in the *New Yorker* 38 (16 June 1962), calling the film an unintentional parody of Ford's best work. When the critic writes that "nothing is working as it should except the sets" (102), you know you're in trouble. Ultimately, auteur critics like Sarris and Wood played a larger role in raising Ford's critical reputation.

67. Michael Barkun, "Notes on the Art of John Ford," *Film Culture* 25 (Summer 1962), 9.

68. Barkun, "Notes," 11.

69. Barkun, "Notes," 9–10 passim.

70. Peter Bogdanovich, "The Autumn of John Ford," *Esquire* 61 (April 1964): 102–107, 144–145.

71. Bogdanovich, "Autumn," 106, 144.

72. Peter Bogdanovich, *John Ford,* revised edition (Berkeley: University of California Press, 1978), 109.

73. Sarris, who began writing for *Film Culture* in its second issue in 1955, later became the influential film reviewer for the *Village Voice.* He discusses his early years at *Film Culture* in his foreword to *Confessions of a Cultist: On the Cinema, 1955–1969* (New York: Simon and Schuster, 1970).

74. "Notes on the Auteur Theory in 1962" first appeared in *Film Culture* 27 (Winter 1962–1963) and is reprinted in Andrew Sarris, *The Primal Screen* (New York: Simon and Schuster, 1973), 38–53; Andrew Sarris, *The American Cinema* (New York: Dutton, 1968).

75. Sarris, "Notes on the Auteur Theory in 1962," 52.

76. See Lounsbury, *The Origins of American Film Criticism,* 4, 5, and 484–486.

77. Sarris, "Rossellini, Renoir, and Ford," *New York Film Bulletin* (27 March 1961), in *Confessions of a Cultist,* 41–42.

78. Sarris, *The American Cinema,* 48.

79. Review of *The Man Who Shot Liberty Valance, Film Culture* 27 (Summer 1962), reprinted in Sarris, *The Primal Screen,* 149.

80. The magazines were *Presénce du Cinéma* (March 1965), *Cahiers du cinéma* (October 1966), *Focus on Film* (Spring 1971), *Velvet Light Trap* (August 1971), and *Filmkritik* (January 1972).

81. John Baxter, *The Cinema of John Ford* (New York: A. S. Barnes, 1971); Robin Wood, "'*Shall* We Gather at the River?': The Late Films of John Ford," *Film Comment* 7, no. 3 (Fall 1971): 83–101 (reprinted in this volume); William Pechter, "Persistence of Vision," in *Twenty-Four Times a Second: Films and Film-Makers* (New York: Harper, 1971), 226–241.

82. Joseph McBride and Michael Wilmington, *John Ford* (New York: Da Capo Press, 1975), 228–229.

83. Peter Wollen, *Signs and Meanings in the Cinema* (Bloomington: Indiana University Press, 1969), 102.

84. "John Ford's *Young Mr. Lincoln,*" *Screen* (Autumn 1972); reprinted in Philip Rosen, ed., *Narrative, Apparatus, Ideology* (New York: Columbia University Press, 1986): 444–482. The essay originally appeared in the August–September 1970 issue of *Cahiers.*

85. Many of the challenges to and revisions of auteurism precipitated by Barthes's work, as well as selections from Barthes himself, are contained in a useful anthology: John Caughie, ed., *Theories of Authorship* (London: Routledge and Kegan Paul, 1981). The selection from Barthes, "The Death of the Author," is found on pages 208–213. First published in Paris in 1968, the piece was published in English translation in *Image-Music-Text* in 1977.

86. Robin Wood, "John Ford," in *Cinema: A Critical Dictionary,* vol. 1, ed. Richard Roud (New York: Viking, 1980): 371–387.

87. Wood, "John Ford," 371, 372, 372. Some of the work done on Ford and his films since 1980, like Tag Gallagher's ambitious and insightful critical biography *John Ford,* has begun the work Wood calls for, of looking at Ford in the context of that complex Hollywood system.

88. Andreas Huyssen, *After the Great Divide: Modernism, Mass Culture, Postmodernism* (Bloomington: Indiana University Press, 1986); Kapsis, *Hitchcock,* chapters 3 and 4.

89. In *Gunfighter Nation: The Myth of the Frontier in Twentieth-Century America* (New York: Atheneum, 1992), Richard Slotkin argues that in *Fort Apache* Ford goes so far as to call "for the willed retention of patriotic belief in the teeth of our knowledge that such belief has been the refuge of scoundrels and the mask of terrible death-dealing follies" (342). Such a use of the frontier myth, writes Slotkin, was "designed to build national solidarity in the face of the threatening advance of Soviet Communism" (343).

PART TWO
DOSSIER

10

JOHN FORD

FIGHTING IRISH

Emanuel Eisenberg

Mr. Ford wasn't in to anybody, the information clerk assured me; the secretary had just told him so. But I had been granted an appointment the day before. The clerk shrugged and called the secretary again. All right, I could go into the office, and he pressed a releasing button with an expression that said: for all the good it'll do you.

The secretary was extremely considerate and greatly concerned for my sanity. See Mr. Ford *today?* Did I know that he was making tests of Hepburn? That the filming of *Mary of Scotland* was to begin the day after tomorrow? She could conceive of no urgency impressive enough for disturbing him. I really must have made a mistake. Or Mr. Ford had not been aware of his own involvements in suggesting the appointment. It was quite hopeless. No one could see him today.

I wandered out of the building and there was the publicity department. Maybe they could help me: I knew the head. An interview with Ford? Ford never granted them to anyone: couldn't be bothered: there wasn't the dimmest chance. And TODAY: test day. I must be mad. Interruption was practically a criminal offence. He himself, the head publicity man, wouldn't dare to break in. Oh, no. Just forget the whole idea.

By now I was pretty depressed. John Ford had promised me no more than five minutes, but I wanted those five minutes and I was particularly piqued by the wonderful studio set-up of inaccessibility. It was impossible to believe that Ford himself had dictated this situation. Yet I had no way of finding out.

I walked on the mock streets of the enclosed studio city. Deserted. What would I do with the morning? I had made no more than two turns when suddenly, incredibly, there stood the unobtainable Mr. Ford, chatting leisurely with a couple of men. It was too good, too much like the mechanical ending of a joke with an overheavy buildup. I managed to catch his eye; he winked in recognition; we strolled over to the office; Dudley Nichols soon joined us; and we sat for almost two hours in an easy, informal, wandering talk.

"John Ford: Fighting Irish" by Emanuel Eisenberg originally appeared in *New Theater,* April 1936. Reprinted by permission.

I offer the preliminary details of the meeting simply because they are so representative of the man Ford, his style and his methods. In the middle of an abnormally busy day he had found time to hang around on the sidewalk for some gossip. Officially he could be located or approached by no one in the studio, yet a stranger wandering illegitimately around the lot might bump into him and attract him away from schedule for a period. The nongiver of interviews found NEW THEATRE and its point of view so challenging that he stretched five minutes to 120 and extended a further invitation to come down to the set next week and watch him direct (something Dudley Nichols described as a distinct rarity).

For Ford is Irish and a fighter. He has fought for this way of living within the film industry and he has had to fight for the stories that interested him and the methods he believed in.

Pictures like *The Informer* do not come into existence lightly. To the frantic but still hopeful devotee its appearance—or the appearance of any other film on such a high level—is revelation, oasis, and consummation, a sudden reward in the stoical pilgrimage of picturegoing; but to one whose eyes have been exposed ever so briefly to the mechanics and finances of Hollywood production, the sheer physical emergence of *The Informer* is a small miracle. It began over the dead bodies of all the money lads; it was permitted to carry through in the periodic embarrassed concession to Art, an essence relied upon to secure the equally obscure quality of Prestige; and when it broke across the tape not only with high critical acclaim but with $100,000 of profit, almost the sum it had been expected to lose, confusion was intense. Such reckless and audacious efforts are not supposed to make good.

John Ford is among the startling handful of men in films who believe that a picture, to make any sense, must be conceived from the first day of action by a fixed group of workers dedicated to seeing it through from beginning to end. This is so violently in contrast to the anarchist principles of putting anybody to work who happens to be around and never quite knowing the next week's program of operation (creatively speaking) that Ford is considered something of a forbidding fanatic and accordingly permitted—but not too often—to function severely in his own way. He wisely takes advantage of this reputation to insist upon a courageous individualism of attack which is denied even the most impressive directors in circulation.

He has been in pictures since 1914, thinks entirely in terms of cinema, and works as a craftsman. The conception of a frame, a composition, and a camera angle is rarely something he simply hands over to the highly skilled technicians around him; it has validity and completeness only after he has scrambled up the ladder to the platform and studied the actual register inside the box. His consistent participation in all of the aspects of production sometimes makes it difficult to distinguish him from among the property men, electricians, and

Ford is a "clear-eyed craftsman" whose "consistent participation in all of
the aspects of production sometimes makes it difficult to distinguish him from
among the property men, electricians, and camera workers." Director Ford (in beret)
on location for *Stagecoach* (1939).
Courtesy of the Museum of Modern Art Film Stills Archive.

camera workers. Ford's high talent for simultaneous leadership and collaboration is conceded by everyone who has ever worked with him to be almost without parallel in the movies.

"After all, there's nothing surprising about the difficulty of doing things you
yourself believe in in the movies," he said, "when you consider that you're
spending someone else's money. And a lot of money. And he wants a lot of profit
on it. That's something you're supposed to worry about, too."

"Trouble is, most of them can't imagine what'll make them money outside
of what's already been made and what's already made them money before."

"Exactly! That's why it's a constant battle to do something fresh. First they
want you to repeat your last picture. You talk 'em down. Then they want you
to continue whatever vein you succeeded in with the last picture. You're a comedy director or a spectacle director or a melodrama director. You show 'em
you've been each of these in turn, and effectively, too. So they grant you range.

Another time they want you to knock out something *another* studio's gone and cleaned up with. Like a market. Got to fight it every time. Never any point where you can really say you have full freedom for your own ideas to go ahead with."

"How do you explain such a crazy setup?" I asked. "By block booking? The star system? The fact that it's first an industry and second an art?"

"I used to blame it largely on the star system," the large genial Irishman told me. "They've got the public so that they want to see one favorite performer in anything at all. But even that's being broken down. You don't think *The Informer* went over because of McLaglen, do you? Personally, I doubt it. It was because it was about something. I'm no McLaglen fan, you know. And do you know how close *The Informer* came to being a complete flop? It was considered one, you know—until you fellows took it up. You fellows *made* that picture. And that's what the producers are going to learn, are already learning, in fact: there's a new kind of public that wants more honest pictures. They've got to give 'em to 'em."

"How do you think they'll go about it?" I wanted to know. "That is, if they go about it at all."

"Oh, they will," he assured me. "They've got to turn over picture making into the hands that know it. Combination of author and director running the works: that's the ideal. Like Dudley Nichols and me. Or Riskin and Capra."

The point startled me. "I thought directors were running the works completely now."

Ford snorted, amused. "Oh, yeah? Do you know anything about the way they're trying to break directorial power now? To reduce the director to a man who just tells actors where to stand?" He proceeded to describe a typical procedure at four of the major studios today. The director arrives at nine in the morning. He has not only never been consulted about the script to see whether he likes it or feels fitted to handle it but may not even know what the full story is about. They hand him two pages of straight dialogue or finally calculated action. Within an hour or less he is expected to go to work and complete the assignment the same day, all the participants and equipment being prepared for him without any say or choice on his part. When he leaves at night, he has literally no idea what the next day's work will be.

"And is that how movies are going to be made now?" I asked, incredulous. "Like a Ford car?"

He smiled wryly. "Not if the Screen Directors Guild can help it, boy. Hang around and watch some fireworks."

This Guild, of which Ford is one of the most embattled members, if and when it aligns itself with the Screen Actors' Guild and the Screen Writers' Guild, a not-too-distant possibility, will offer the autocratic money interests of the movies the most serious challenge of organization they have known to date.

Talk shifted to *The Informer.* Ford spoke of the great difficulty of persuading the studio that it ought to be tackled at all. He and Nichols arranged to take a fraction of their normal salaries for the sheer excitement of the venture; also, of course, to cut down production cost. Now, of course, the studio takes all the credit for the acclaim and the extraordinary number of second runs and for the Motion Picture Academy award—although Dudley Nichols's formal rejection of the award created considerable ructions. Nichols, it need scarcely be added, is one of the leading spirits of the Screen Writers Guild.

But what about the ending of the picture? I asked. Wasn't that a concession? So many of the criticisms had objected to it. Yes, said Ford, it was a compromise: the plan had been to show Gypo dying alone on the docks, and this had been just a little too much for the producers. Still, the religious ending was so much in keeping with the mystical Irish temperament, Ford maintained, that it was pretty extreme to characterize it as superimposed sentimentality.

How about more such pictures? What were the chances?

"If you're thinking of a general run of social pictures, or even just plain honest ones, it's almost hopeless. The whole financial setup is against it. What you'll get is an isolated courageous effort here and there. The thing to do is to encourage each man who's trying, the way you fellows have done. Look at Nichols and me. We did *The Informer.* Does that make it any easier to go ahead with O'Casey's *The Plough and the Stars,* which we want to do after *Mary of Scotland?* Not for a second. They *may* let us do it as a reward for being good boys. Meanwhile we're fighting to have the Abbey Players imported intact and we're fighting the censors and fighting the so-called financial wizards at every point."

"Actually tackling social themes would be marvelous, of course," I put in at this point. "But what seems to us almost as important right now is to give the straight version of any aspect of life the movies do choose to handle. To avoid distortion and misrepresentation in favor of one interest or another. Don't you think that can be managed *within* this setup?"

"It can and should!" he exclaimed. "And it's something I always try to do. I remember a few years ago, with a Judge Priest picture, putting in an antilynching plea that was one of the most scorching things you ever heard. They happened to cut it, purely for reasons of space, but I enjoyed doing that enormously. And there can be more things like that."

"Then you do believe, as a director, in including your point of view in a picture about things that bother you?"

He looked at me as if to question the necessity of an answer. Then: "What the hell else does a man live for?"

Ford, who is on record as having directed about a hundred pictures, selects *Men Without Women* as his favorite. His desire is to do a film about the men and women workers in the wings of film production; they are the only people in "the industry" who interest him at all. That this is not remotely near being the affectation it may sound like to some is attested by Dudley Nichols, who admires John Ford as one of the most fearless, honest, and gifted men in Hollywood. Ford's house, says Nichols, is the same one he has lived in for fifteen years now: it has never occurred to him to "gold it up" or change it. No movie star or executive may ever be found visiting it. Electricians, property men, and camera men are the people invariably hanging around—and in this choice of unprominent and unsung companions may very well be found the key to the fighting Irishman's life as a clear-eyed craftsman.

11

HOLLYWOOD'S FAVORITE REBEL
Frank S. Nugent

John Ford is a big, shambling man with a corrugated face, red hair that has faded with the years, a temper that hasn't, and a gift for making pictures which uncomfortably remind Hollywood that the movies are not just an industry but an art. Among the cinema's *cognoscenti* he is considered one of the greatest directors who ever lived; some call him the greatest. He has won three personally inscribed Academy Oscars—only Frank Capra among the directors has as many—and is an unequaled four-time winner of the New York Film Critics' annual awards for direction. Ford is proud of his trophies, even though he never showed up at the Academy dinners or the critics' broadcasts to accept them. He hates publicity.

Ford started copping prizes in 1935, when he made *The Informer*, but it didn't become a habit until 1939. Then, his *Stagecoach* got the critics' award as the best-directed picture of the year. In 1940 his *The Grapes of Wrath* took both the critics' scroll and the Academy Oscar. In 1941 he won his third Oscar for *How Green Was My Valley,* and he put the enraptured critics in a pretty dilemma: they couldn't decide between that picture and *The Long Voyage Home.* As Ford had directed them both, it really didn't matter.

In Navy uniform commanding the Field Photographic Branch of the OSS, he was out of the competition for a while. But he still managed to knock off two Oscars at long range for the Navy. His film of the Battle of Midway won a special award as the best short documentary of the year. Ford shot it himself, standing on an exposed water tower and, according to onlookers, yelling at the attacking Zeros to swing left or right—and cursing them out when they disobeyed directions. The film jumps in one spot: the moment a fragmentation bomb exploded close by and drove its steel splinters into his arm. He kept on shooting. He got a second Oscar for the Navy with a film called *December 7,* which recorded the damage done to Pearl Harbor.

Uncle Sam had to credit him with another—although less direct—assist in connection with the big war-crimes trials. One of the jobs of the OSS had been

"Hollywood's Favorite Rebel" by Frank S. Nugent originally appeared in the *Saturday Evening Post,* July 23, 1949. Reprinted by permission of the Saturday Evening Post © 1949.

to round up film, which might document the guilt of the Nazi war conspirators. Two young Navy officers got wind of a treasure trove; the negatives of all German newsreels were stored in the Reich Film Archives at Babelsberg, in the Soviet zone of occupation. The Russian officer in charge, a Major Arinarius, looked suspiciously at the two Navy men, one of whom happened to be Hollywood writer Budd Schulberg, author of *What Makes Sammy Run.*

"What is a naval officer doing looking for films in Germany?" Arinarius asked.

"Well, it's a little hard to explain," Schulberg said, "but I belong to a naval unit headed by Captain John Ford which has been put in charge of photographic evidence for the Nuremberg trial."

"John Ford, the director?" asked the major.

"You've heard of him?" blurted Schulberg.

"In my book on the history of motion pictures," said Arinarius, "I gave Ford two chapters. *The Iron Horse* is still one of my favorite motion pictures." And the former professor of film history at the Cinematic Institute in Moscow went on from there to name and analyze *The Informer, Arrowsmith, The Lost Patrol* and a dozen other famous Fords. When he had finished, he clapped Schulberg on the back and told him to come around next day with a jeep.

When the Navy men left Babelsberg two days later, they required not a jeep but a truck to cart away the film. It was to prove a fatal link in the chain of evidence against Goering and his crew.

From all the foregoing it might be inferred that Ford, at fifty-four, is the darling of Hollywood's producers, the one director every glamour girl would like to have on her set. Fortunately or otherwise, Ford is neither of these. He has no truck with glamour girls on or off the set, because he refuses to believe in the boy-meets-girl theme. He sheepishly admits that he once met a Mary Smith at a St. Patrick's Day shindig in the Hollywood Hotel and, after a brisk, three-months courtship, married her. But that was twenty-nine years ago, and if Mrs. Ford were ever to refer to their romance as boy-meets-girl, the chances are he would leave home for at least a fortnight.

Producers squirm uncomfortably when his name is mentioned. "He's a difficult man to handle," one of them said. His assistant waited for the boss to leave the room, then snickered. "You don't handle Ford," he said. "You turn the reins loose and you try to hang on."

Ford made many of his best pictures by the simple expedient of ramming them down Hollywood's reluctant throat. It took him five years to persuade a studio to let him make *The Informer.* Neither Twentieth Century–Fox nor David O. Selznick would back *Stagecoach* or *The Long Voyage Home;* he carried the fight to Walter Wanger and finally won him over. RKO had so little confidence in his womanless *Lost Patrol* that it restricted him to virtually a Class C budget; Ford shot the picture in the quickie time of three weeks. Producers always reserve the right to edit and recut a director's work; Ford clips their wings by shooting his pictures so they can be cut only one way—his way. "A producer's function has always seemed to me to be a casual one," he says. "Pictures should be the result of a writer and a director getting together with the producer merely standing by in a fatherly, benevolent way to chide them if they spend too much money."

Chiding does not always work, and Ford once actually mutinied against his producer. It happened when he was making *The Iron Horse*. He had gone off into the Nevada Sierras with a company of 300 and a four-weeks shooting schedule. The troupe had barely made camp between Pyramid Lake and Reno when a blizzard struck. Ford decided it was easier to change the script than the weather, and began shooting. The first blizzard was followed by a second and a third. Temperatures of twenty below were common. At the end of the allotted month the producer ordered his return. Ford tore up the wire and sent his railroad builders out into the drifts to lay another mile of track.

They laid three miles, built three shack towns and hauled their vintage iron horse over the spine of the Sierras before Ford was through. This was five weeks after receipt of the first recall order; it had been repeated, on a rising note of outrage, at weekly and then daily intervals thereafter. The producer was all but biting chunks out of his desk when Ford reported back to Hollywood. He relented when he saw the film they had shot. One day's footage had been overexposed. "That must have been the day the sun came out," Ford apologized. *The Iron Horse* cost $280,000 and grossed more than $3,000,000.

During the making of *How Green Was My Valley*, the production manager approached him on the set and nervously reminded him that he was ten days behind schedule. Ford reached for a copy of the script and calmly tore twenty random pages from it. "Now we're right on schedule," he said. "Feel happier?" The production man admitted that he didn't. "Make up your mind," Ford told him then. "Do you want it fast or do you want it good?" The man from the front office decided they wanted it good. Ford was thirteen days over schedule when he finished. The picture cost $1,250,000; to date it has grossed $5,750,000.

Two years ago Ford decided he had had enough front-office interference and set up his own production organization, Argosy Pictures, in partnership with Merian Cooper, the man who made *Grass, Chang* and *King Kong*. Caution dictated the choice of a good, safe commercial film as their first venture; instead Ford went off to Mexico and made *The Fugitive*, an artistic, religious parable filmed without a single concession to the box office. Having thus thumbed his nose at convention, Ford then buckled down to *Fort Apache, 3 Godfathers* and *She Wore a Yellow Ribbon*—all of them outdoor Westerns.

Ford's flair for rebellion was inherited, says his family, from an uncle, Mike Connolly, who made the crossing from Ireland early in the spring of '62. As he descended the gangplank he was approached by two smiling strangers. "How would you like to be a streetcar conductor?" one of them asked. Mike said that would suit him very well. So they gave him a uniform, and the next thing he knew he was in the Battle of Shiloh. The duplicity of all this so annoyed him that he deserted forthwith to the rebel side and served with great distinction against a force which he sometimes identified as the Union, but more often as the traction interests.

Ford has always been proud of his Uncle Mike, and remains a Confederate sympathizer in spite of having been born in Cape Elizabeth, Maine, of a Galway-bred father and a mother from the Aran Isles. Ford says his birth date was February 1, 1895, and claims to be the youngest of thirteen children. His birth date may be accurate, but the Feeneys had only eleven children according to John's two brothers and one sister in Hollywood. Feeney is the official family name. Originally it had been O'Fienne. The name of Ford was adopted by brother Francis when he ran off to become an actor, and John accepted it, to avoid confusion, when he followed Francis to Hollywood. But there was no escaping confusion when brother Eddie came out later, calling himself O'Fearna, which Frank and John insist is neither fish, flesh nor Gaelic.

O'Fearna, a stocky assistant director at Fox, never has completely emerged from the doghouse Ford once consigned him to for bawling "Quiet!" in the middle of a take. It is, of course, an assistant's job to enforce silence on the set but reprimanding a gurgling water cooler seemed to Ford to be carrying authority too far. O'Fearna had trod on John's toes before. Their mother had come to Hollywood on a visit, and naturally, wanted to see her sons at work. She arrived on the set as they were lining up the next shot. Ford, having given the order, was quietly sitting back while Eddie was everywhere, shouting at the top of his lungs. Mrs. Feeney was impressed. Months later, she was a guest at the picture's New York première. Ford made an exception to his rule and attended. The producer called her attention to the large photograph of John in the lobby.

"Your boy, Mrs. Feeney," he said. "Aren't you proud?"

"Yes," she admitted, and then, after a troubled examination of the other photographs in the lobby display asked, "But where's my Eddie?" It since has become a pet phrase with the Fords, but O'Fearna doesn't see the humor of it.

John grew up in and around Portland, Maine, sailed its bays and resisted his mother's prayers that he turn to the priesthood. Mrs. Feeney had prayed thus for each of her boys. One by one, they ran away from home. John was the youngest and her last hope; he was the subject of incessant memos to the Almighty. There may have been a slip-up in the celestial bureaucracy: John's cousin, Daniel Feeney, became Bishop of Maine. John, three weeks after his enrollment in the University of Maine, cut loose and fled to Hollywood.

Francis Ford had preceded him there by several years and, when John arrived in 1914, was a well-established serial star and director. Frank never had notified the family of his new name or occupation. In fact, Mrs. Feeney once had read a description of a highwayman operating in Yellowstone Park and had decided it could be none other than her missing son. She began following the highwayman's exploits with a certain maternal pride. John punctured this bubble one day when, in the course of a summer's service as usher in a Portland movie house, he recognized his brother on the screen. That night the Feeneys went to the theater in a body. Mrs. Feeney made only one comment. "He'd have been smarter to have stayed a highwayman," she said.

Frank put Jack to work as a twelve-dollar-a-week prop boy. He soon became a stunt man, not because he wanted to, but because Frank would shame his reluctant actors by saying, "What d'ye mean, it's dangerous? Here, I'll have my kid brother do it!" Once he seated young Jack at a dynamite-wired desk in a tent, fired a cannon ball through the tent and blew the desk—and the kid brother— five yards in the air. Another time he deputized him to make a seventy-five-foot dive off the roof of a freight car rolling over a trestle. Jack made the leap all right, but carefully blessed himself before jumping—and spoiled the shot.

Frank had magnificent faith in his brother's durability. He staged an automobile chase through Cahuenga Pass and from the camera car bellowed instructions at Jack in the careening flivver ahead: "Now you're shot! The car gets out of control! It swings to the right! . . . More to the right! . . . Get ready for the blowout!" Jack woke up in the hospital. The "blowout" had been guaranteed by mining the road with dynamite hooked to a series of trip wires.

When Jack's broken arm had knit, he reported back to work, and found himself in Confederate uniform dodging shot and shell on a hell's half acre of battleground. Frank was pitching the powder bombs. He saved the last for a bang-up close shot. It bounced off Jack's head and exploded just beneath his chin. "That was a close thing," Frank told him later, when the nurses began admitting visitors. "Another second and audiences would have realized I was using a double."

Jack never was one to hold a grudge, but the bomb incident rankled. Nineteen years later, when he was directing *Judge Priest*, he gave Frank the part of a village loafer, a bewhiskered old character in a Civil War cap whose chawing-and-whittling perch was a wheelbarrow in front of the general store. When Frank was not looking, Ford had an assistant tie a rope from the wheelbarrow to the axle of a carriage. The first half of the scene was played as written, but when the heroine drove off in her carriage, Frank went for the ride of his life. Worst of it was that the first jolt made him swallow his chaw of tobacco.

When he came limping back, Jack shook his finger under his nose. "That was for the grenade!" he scolded, just as if he had been conked only the day before.

Ford's first year in Hollywood ended in a blaze of glory. The company was shooting a circus sequence to be climaxed by the inevitable fire in the big top. As the tent had been rented for the occasion, Producer Carl Laemmle begged everyone to treat it with respect. A spare flap of canvas would be ignited at a safe distance from the tent walls; a stand-by crew with buckets of water would douse the flames the second the action had been shot. As prop boy, it was John's job to provide the water buckets. The more he thought about it, the more depressed he became. He went around mumbling about a two-bit fire. He was up at dawn on the morning of the big scene: When the company arrived, he was standing guard over a platoon of red painted fire buckets. Soon the torch was put to the kerosene-soaked canvas flap. It flamed beautifully.

"Fine!" yelled the director. "You can douse it now!"

The fire brigade swung the buckets. There was a roaring explosion as the gasoline they contained hit the burning flap and turned the circus tent into an inferno. Horses stampeded and roustabouts ran for their lives.

Ford had stationed himself next to the camera. "Don't stop! Keep cranking!" he yelled an instant after the blast.

The cameraman numbly did what he was told. John went into hiding. He didn't have to be told that he was fired. Two days later, Laemmle hired him back as an assistant director.

"A spectacle like that is worth a circus tent," he told him. "But don't do it again."

Ford promised to behave, but when he was promoted to full director, the glory went to his head. It couldn't have been the salary, because Laemmle cut him from fifty dollars a week to thirty—the honor of being a director at twenty-one was supposed to compensate. He was sent out to make a two-reeler with Harry Carey. Ford ignored the script Laemmle had given him and wrote one of his own. He called it *The Sky Pilot* and proudly led his company on location to the sand dunes of Playa del Rey, then subbing for Arizona. There he proceeded to shoot a five-reeler, instead of a two, and refused to let anyone cut an inch of it. Word of his revolt reached Laemmle's ears.

"Did he go over the budget?" was his first, producer-like question. The studio manager admitted Ford hadn't.

"Humh," grunted Laemmle, his eyes lighting. "And what, offhand, is wrong with making a five-reeler for the price of a two? I'll see it."

He liked what he saw, and released *The Sky Pilot* as a feature. It was a hit. Carey's salary skyrocketed almost overnight from $150 a week to $1800. Ford's skyrocket lacked oomph; his pay hopped only to seventy-five dollars a week. But his days as a prop boy, extra and stunt man were over.

Ford's salary has increased meteorically since then, but he still is unmistakably the product of a rough-and-tough movie school. He has none of the Hollywood mannerisms. He goes to no previews, not even of his own pictures. In his thirty-four years in the movies, it is doubtful if he has been interviewed a half-dozen times. He wouldn't be found dead or alive at Ciro's or the Mocambo and still lives in the comfortable but unpretentious hillside home he bought for his bride almost thirty years ago.

Unlike some of Hollywood's showman directors, he seems to find it unnecessary to wear riding boots, a monocle or plaid sport jacket to work. True, he has a habit of chewing his pipestems to jagged stumps and frequently works with a handkerchief dangling from one corner of his mouth, which gives him something of the look of a bulldog playing retriever. But this is a matter of nerves rather than self-dramatization. On the set he is a veritable Captain Bligh, demanding the impossible of his crews, and grunting the merest acknowledgment when they achieve it. They love him for it.

He's just as tough on actors. Once he grew weary of a leading lady's constant demurrers and suggestions. "Honey," he said, for the assembled company to hear, "they pay me to direct. What do they pay you for?" During the making of *My Darling Clementine,* he kept a troupe standing in a driving rainstorm for three hours, waiting for enough light to break through the clouds to give him a shot he wanted. In *3 Godfathers,* he took his company out in the middle of a Death Valley sandstorm and shot scenes that not even his cameraman believed could be photographed. John Wayne and the other actors exposed to the sandblast got a bitter laugh later out of one critic's blithe reference to "one of the biggest sandstorms ever whipped up by Hollywood's wind machines."

Ford has directed more than eighty features during his Hollywood lifetime, which is possibly a record for directors still active in the business. Not all of them were good, many were box-office flops, but none of them has been without some touch of distinction—or call it genius—which stamps it indelibly as his. He has been called the greatest stylist in pictures, yet the essence of his style is its simplicity. He rarely moves his camera, never indulges in those long crane shots starting from the rafters and ending in a close-up of a woman's eyebrow. He hates process shots and scenes taken from weird, eccentric angles. He despises— his word—directors' touches.

"I try to make people forget they're in a theater," he says. "I don't want them to be conscious of a camera or a screen. I want them to feel that what they're seeing is real."

For that reason, if an actor stumbles over a word in an emotion-packed scene he generally lets the stammer stand; it's more natural that way. He rehearses his players as often as necessary, but rarely shoots more than three takes and usually is content with one. Shooting a scene twenty or thirty times, as some directors do, robs it of all spontaneity, he feels.

He still uses "mood music" on his sets to get his players in the right frame of mind. Any time there is a sad scene in a Ford picture you can bet that Danny Borzage was softly playing "Red River Valley" on his accordion during the rehearsals. Ford uses "Red River Valley" the way most of the oldtimers used "Hearts and Flowers." When he feels good, he whistles it in jig tempo. Borzage's accordion supplied almost all the music you heard in *The Grapes of Wrath.* Ford recorded it along with the dialogue as he shot the picture—and then fought for days with the music department, which wanted to substitute the usual swelling

"I want them to feel that what they're seeing is real": cast and crew on location in Monument Valley setting up a shot for *Stagecoach* (1939). Courtesy of Wisconsin Center for Film and Theater Research.

symphonic background. "All I want is that wheezy old 'Red River Valley,'" Ford insisted. Reluctantly the studio surrendered, and that wheezy old tune, played on Borzage's wheezy old accordion, tugged at a million hearts.

Ford never has formally surrendered to the talkies. His writers are under standing orders to keep dialogue to an "irreducible minimum." Ford usually manages to trim the "irreducible" still more. He always works with his writers on a script, but never lets them forget who holds the whip hand. In one script a writer referred to a Sharps repeater.

"I like the sound of 'Winchester repeater' better," Ford said.

"But they didn't have Winchester repeaters at this period," the writer protested.

"Very well," said Ford, eying the ceiling. "Leave 'Sharps' in the script . . . but it's going to sound mighty like 'Winchester' on the sound track!"

Another time Ford was describing how he visualized his first shot of the Apache chief, Cochise. "I see him standing straight against the sky line, one hand clutching his pipe and pressed against his chest—"

"Wait a minute," protested the hapless writer, who had spent seven weeks at Ford's orders on period research. "The Apaches never used pipes. They smoked cigarettes rolled with corn husks at first, then with Mexican corn paper."

Ford listened patiently, then resumed in the same tones, "I see Cochise standing straight against the sky line, one hand pressed to his chest . . . and in that hand he may have a flute, he may have an ax, I don't give a damn what he has . . . But he isn't smoking any cigarette!"

Perhaps Ford's best attribute as a director is his ability to get superlative performances out of run-of-the-mill actors. "Ford could win an Oscar for a wooden Indian," one of his cameramen once said. This reputation is tough on actors like Henry Fonda—Ford's favorite leading man—who doesn't have to be Svengalied into giving a performance. "Hank's a real pro," says Ford. It's a tribute he reserves for only a half dozen of the players he has directed. Ford's Stock Company is a famous Hollywood institution. It is made up of twenty or thirty supporting actors, bit players and extras who manage to get into most of his pictures—and are wonderful—but who can't seem to do much for anyone else.

The classic example of Ford's casting genius was Victor McLaglen's unforgettable portrayal of Gypo Nolan in *The Informer.* Ford literally double-crossed him into his Academy-award performance. He browbeat him until Gypo's truculent expression couldn't come off. At the close of a long day's shooting, he suggested a quick run through of a scene scheduled for the next morning.

"But I'm not up in my lines," McLaglen protested.

"It's only a rehearsal," Ford assured him, and then signaled the cameraman and soundman to get busy.

McLaglen groped his way through the scene, trying to catch his cues from his fellow players. It played as Ford had known it would: no one in the theater could miss the fact that Gypo was bluffing, making up his story as he went along.

When he shot Gypo's carouse through the Dublin pubs, Ford primed Vic for the sequence by seeing that his whisky glasses contained whisky. Jack Pennick, the ex-marine who has been Ford's man Friday for years, was McLaglen's greatest sympathizer during the trying days of the picture. He took him to dinner, seemed to have an inexhaustible supply of liquor, kept him from sleep night after night. "We'll show the Old Man," he'd say. "We'll show him he can't boss us around."

On the set, after a few days of this, Gypo's guilt-ridden, remorseful face was the mirror of a Gargantuan McLaglen hang-over. Not until long after did he discover that the car they drove and the liquor they drank were Ford's, that Pennick had been working under the Old Man's orders.

Ford's specialties are period westerns and sea pictures, the two most masculine brands of movie fiction. His fondness for the westerns can be attributed to their relative indifference to romance, their opportunity for action and pictorial splendor. His love for sea stories goes deeper; it springs from his love of the sea itself. Ford spends most of his free time aboard his 110-foot ketch, the Araner, which he refuses to call a yacht. Before the war, the Fords—son Pat is a writer and Barbara an assistant film editor—would sail her to Honolulu every August and spend the winter there. Between pictures he took shorter cruises along the Mexican coast, usually with such cronies as Fonda, Ward Bond, Pennick and Dudley Nichols.

Both the Araner and Ford joined the Navy when war began, but not together. Ford's war record is not widely known; it would not be known at all if you depended on him to talk about it. As early as 1939, he was certain the United States would be drawn into the struggle, and began talking up the importance of a motion-picture unit which could be used for reconnaissance, combat photography and documentaries showing the public the kind of war their men were fighting.

Ford took his plan to some Navy friends. The best they could do was assure him of their personal interest; officially it was turned down. Undiscouraged, Ford set about recruiting his volunteers from among Hollywood cameramen, soundmen, cutters and editors. They had no status—only the possibility that the Navy might take them in as reservists. They had no equipment, so Ford went out and borrowed it from the studios. They needed drillmasters—so ex-Marine Pennick and old-time Chief Boatswain's Mate Ben Grotzky, a veteran of thirty years in the Navy, were brought in to whip the volunteers into some semblance of military order.

By midsummer of '41, the Navy decided to take a chance, accepted the group as a reserve unit, and ordered it to Washington. There it was broken up into combat camera teams. Ensign Ray Kellogg took a small group to Iceland. The detail was one of the first Navy units to see action when their convoy was attacked by German submarines in the North Atlantic. When Pearl Harbor was hit, members of the unit were serving in every quarter of the globe. Cameramen from Field Photo filmed the Jap sneak attack. Others, serving with famous Navy Patrol Wing 10, brought back some of the first pictures of the defense of the Philippines. Ford's unit had proved its worth before the war was a week old.

There were 180 men in Ford's unit and he knew every one of them personally. "One thing I'll promise you," he told them during their training days. "I'll never send any of you on a job I wouldn't tackle myself." He proved it when he gave himself the Battle of Midway assignment. He was on the U.S.S. Salt Lake City filming the Navy's part in the Jimmy Doolittle raid on Tokyo. He went along on the raids on Marcus Island and Wotje and, among many other assignments, filmed the Normandy landing at Omaha Beach on D Day.

Thirteen men from Field Photo were killed in action. More than half the men of the unit won decorations. Ford is prouder of his unit's citations than he is of all his Oscars. When the Navy gave him leave, late in '44, to make *They Were Expendable,* a story of PT boats, he accepted the assignment with the stipulation that his entire salary of $225,000 be used to set up a recreation farm for the men of Field Photo. The comfortable six-bedroom farmhouse stands today on an eight acre tract in Encino, in the San Fernando Valley. It has a swimming pool, tennis court, baseball field, paddock, horses, chickens, memorial chapel and endowment fund to guarantee its permanence. No man of Ford's unit will ever lack shelter, and there's no cover charge.

Ford's recent spate of outdoor westerns has put his Argosy Company well into the black, and he and Cooper now are nursing plans for a few roving ventures—possibly *The Quiet Man,* to be filmed in Ireland, or a South Seas yarn to be made in the French Marquesas. But whether these or another will be the next to reach the screen, don't bother to look for Ford at the première. He'll probably be off somewhere on the Araner or locked up in his room with a stack of mystery stories beside his chair and his back to the Oscars on his shelf.

12

JOHN WAYNE–MY PAL
John Ford
Translated by Gloria Monti

Now that Duke Wayne sits on top of the world, the time has come to declare that he is, has always been, and always will be my pal. I have liked Duke's style since the first time I saw him in 1928, when I went to USC to recruit a bunch of athletes to play in a football game in *Salute,* a film I was shooting at the Annapolis Naval Academy.

Duke was not as strong or as developed as the other young men I saw. He was just a lanky kid who had grown too fast and was wearing clothes that were too small for him. However, I was struck by his self-assured manner. I also liked his smile—easy and natural. So, that same evening, in the university hall, I asked him to choose the young men that would join the film set in Annapolis. I have never regretted my decision because that moment marked the beginning of a friendship that has brought joy into my life.

The following summer, Duke came to visit me in Newhall, where I was shooting a Western, and asked me for a job. He started as a truck driver and before the end of the summer, he became a props assistant. He liked that job so much that he never went back to school and his choice probably saved the campus furniture from wear and tear.

Duke possesses a tremendous energy. He is convinced that an athletic looking person can challenge him/herself to do anything better, harder, and longer than anybody else can. He never feared hard work. On the other hand, I remember the day I scared him to death when I asked him to replace an actor who hadn't shown up on the set for a bit part.

"Yes, you, big boy," I yelled back. "Come here and put this jacket on."

Duke was far from memorable in his early acting career, especially when it came to love scenes. It is not easy being romantic when your heart is pounding. However, he displayed that masculine ease which is the secret of success on the silver screen.

Duke has made more than one hundred fifty films; he is a well-respected actor and one of the most bankable Hollywood names. Over the last two years,

From *Hollywood,* no. 287 (17 March 1951).

"Duke" Wayne is "on top of the world" and Ford is on the camera elevator with cinematographer William H. Clothier for *The Man Who Shot Liberty Valance* (1962). Courtesy of The Lilly Library, Indiana University, Bloomington, Indiana.

he went from relative obscurity to the top of everybody's list. Every studio executive is convinced that casting Duke in a film guarantees financial success. I have always believed it. In fact, I have often wondered what took the public and the Hollywood executives so long to realize that.

You see it is not enough for an actor to look the part or to know the lines well. Something else needs to reach the audience, something intangible that no director can impart or create: the ability to be a real man.

Even today, I wouldn't call Duke an actor. He is rather a "reactor." When acting in a dramatic role, he behaves in the same way as he would in real life. It is this kind of acting that makes a film both beautiful and believable.

For this reason, I wanted John Wayne in the lead role for *Stagecoach*. Although he was not an experienced actor, I felt that he was the only one who could express great strength and willpower without much talking.

This trait might seem easy, but it is not. It is a talent that one either has or hasn't. One cannot acquire it.

Duke's human gifts contributed enormously to the dignity of the adventure films he made with me: *Stagecoach, The Long Voyage Home, Fort Apache, She Wore a Yellow Ribbon, Rio Grande,* and others.

Even when Duke was a big kid just out of school, I enjoyed his company. I tried a million times to get him angry, but I only succeeded about a hundred times . . . which is a very low score for an Irishman.

I spent most of my free time fishing in Mexico with John Wayne. You can tell a lot about people when you watch their behavior as they fish. I am not talking about the way they bait the hook or reel in the fish, and not even about how many fish they catch; instead I mean their ability to enjoy themselves and relax, to put manners aside and be completely carefree.

Duke has always been able to savor life, to swallow and digest it in big bites, without chewing them. Depending on the situation, he can be either reckless or a perfect gentleman. He plays very risky and costly games of poker. As far as fighting goes, he has had enough fist fights to give conclusive proof that he is the kind of man you don't want to come to blows with. However, he has also learned, effortlessly, to behave with dignity and manly kindness.

I am happy to say that my affection for this man is well placed. My time in Hollywood would be quite trying if he did not come by my office every day, or if he didn't call me on the phone to discuss a problem, an idea, or an interesting piece of news.

Therefore, my claim that Duke's lively mind and enthusiasm for new projects makes him a dear friend should come as no surprise.

I might sound overly sentimental when I remark that for years Duke has been trying to make his hats look as worn out as mine are. He has sat down on them, dipped them in water, furiously stepped on them, and he has even managed to switch his with mine when I wasn't looking. Yet, those hats look ill at ease on his head.

I told him a thousand times that until a hat grows with the man who wears it, it will not belong to his head.

Duke has been able to learn a decent amount of things about filmmaking by keeping his eyes and ears open. During a career that spanned twenty years, he was a props assistant, an electrician, a stuntman, an extra, a bit part actor, an assistant director, a producer, and a star. I would not be surprised if one day he directed a film that will induce jaw dropping among the Hollywood establishment.

Over the past two years, Duke has devoted an inordinate amount of energy to his work; he acted in a half dozen films while also working on production. Any other man in his place would have collapsed. Last year he installed some workout equipment in his garage because he did not have time to go to the gym, and then realized that he did not have time to work out either. I could not help but laugh. Moreover, if physical fitness were the only criterion to measure life, Duke would probably be the last man to leave this earth.

However, he has started to pay close attention to his health lately. From time to time, he convinces himself that he is at the end of his rope and walks around looking like he cannot even breathe. Then he jumps in his car and drives to a spa in La Jolla, where he stays for a couple of days at the most. When he comes back to Hollywood, he tells everybody he has never felt better. That place must be extraordinary. . . .

Actually, Duke is always so busy that he cannot even afford the leisure activities he enjoys most. With the exception of last year's brief vacation in Santa Catalina, he has heroically given up his favorite pastimes: hunting and fishing.

A few years ago, however, he resolved that he needed a hobby that would allow him to work with his hands. He kept thinking and thinking about it until he met a screenwriter who made pottery in his garage in his spare time. Duke decided that pottery was the ideal hobby. As his birthday was coming up, his wife Chata bought him all the necessary equipment: an oven, shelves, clay, and pyrometric cones.

The other day, at lunchtime, the screenwriter happened to be sitting at the same table as Duke and asked him about his progress in the art of pottery. Duke replied that he had not yet had time to try it but that the oven was an ideal storage space for his shoes!

While shooting a film it is customary to have one day when everything seems to go wrong; a horse whinnies right as the hero is whispering very important sweet nothings into the heroine's delicate ear; the stuntmen miss their cue; or the sun hides behind the clouds as the camera starts filming the most difficult long shot of the day.

When things go wrong, Duke's presence becomes very important. He is the one who runs to the opposite side of the plain to tell the second crew that we are going to do another take of the same scene. He rarely asks somebody else to do something that he is capable of doing himself and for this reason, the technicians adore him.

We went to the most desolate places to film our Westerns. We shot *Rio Grande* near Moab, in Utah, and Duke was able to spend time outdoors in close contact with nature. I am sure that he would have been quite unhappy had he been confined to work in the studio sets; it would be the equivalent of putting a mountain lion in a cage. On the other hand, Duke needs to challenge and be challenged by nature.

When Duke works in interiors or in a studio set, it becomes very difficult to make him sit still. I have read somewhere that homemakers walk an average of three miles per day while they perform domestic duties. Duke walks an equal distance, and smokes half a dozen cigarettes, while he is waiting to shoot a scene.

I could not think of a more cruel torture than tying Duke to a chair and forcing him to watch people walking on a screen. He would go insane, I think.

Duke is now at a point in his career where all the honors that Hollywood and the fans can bestow upon an actor are coming his way.

Last summer I went to Reno with him to attend John Wayne Day, during which he received the yearly award that the city gives him for his role in a Western. That year he was honored for *She Wore a Yellow Ribbon*. Duke was far more interested in the people he met than in the trophy he received. "Nice, eh?" he said as he showed me the award. "But it is not as important as the ideas behind it."

Quite frankly, I am convinced that Duke can wear any prize with dignity as the gentleman he really is, despite his stern appearance.

A few years ago, just before *Stagecoach,* I told Duke that a great future lay ahead of him. If it were not so obvious, I would say the same thing today.

He is my pal.

13

THE OLD WRANGLER RIDES AGAIN
Bill Libby

Not unlike a person from another place and another time, a displaced character out of his beloved Old West, director John Ford swept from the sun-baked
streets of Sunset Boulevard into his small, plush Hollywood offices. He was a
picture of khakied inelegance, preceded by two wildly barking dachshunds. One
of the office girls rushed to corral the dogs; the others pressed their backbones
to the wall to clear a path for the briskly striding figure.

He is an old Navy man, frequently referred to as "The Skipper" by his associates. His office is walled with pictures and mementos of the West and the
sea, his two passions, and of the actors, mostly cowboy actors, with whom he
has been associated. He has won six Oscars, more than any other director, but
not one of these trophies is among those on display.

Ford settled into a chair behind his desk, cupped his hands, and a secretary
rushed to shove a huge, steaming mug of coffee into them. He swallowed from
his cup, lit a cigar, flipped the match on the rug, and turned to me: "I've been
damned as a 'Western director,'" he said. "Every time I start to make a Western, they say: 'There goes senile old John Ford out West again,' but I just don't
give a damn. I've done a lot of pictures in my lifetime that weren't Westerns,
but I've also done a lot that were, and I'm going to do a lot more. I don't think
they need any defense at all, but if you do, and you want me to give one, I sure
as hell won't hesitate to do so."

SEX, CRIME AND SUBTITLES

Ford is not an easy man to see. He says he can count on the fingers of one
hand the full interviews he's granted in the last ten years. He succumbed to me
simply because I held out as lure this defense of his favorite topic. "You're supposed to be an illiterate if you like Westerns," he growled. "What nonsense! Is
it more intelligent to prefer pictures about sex and crime, sex maniacs, prosti-

"The Old Wrangler Rides Again" by Bill Libby originally appeared in *Cosmopolitan*, March
1964. Reprinted by permission.

Not giving a damn when they say, "There goes senile old John Ford out West again,"
director Ford relaxes with his cast while on location for *Two Rode Together* (1961).
From left to right in the foreground: Henry Brandon, John Ford, James Stewart,
Linda Cristal, Richard Widmark, and David Kent.

Courtesy of The Lilly Library, Indiana University, Bloomington, Indiana.

tutes and narcotics addicts? Is it more in-telligent to prefer a picture simply because it's a foreign film and has subtitles? It may be more fashionable, but it
isn't more intelligent. I'm not a vain man. I don't like talking about my own
work. But it's time those of us who make Westerns, or go to them, or enjoy them
in any way, stopped ducking into dark alleys when the subject is brought up.
It's time we spoke up."

Speak up he did, drinking one hot mug of coffee after another, chain-smoking
cigars and tossing the butts roughly and often inaccurately in the direction of
an ash tray a little smaller than the Grand Canyon. He is a thin, tough old man,
a strong, almost forbidding personality. He owns a master's degree, has served
both in the ranks and eventually as an admiral through two wars. He is world-
traveled. But he enjoys disguising himself in postures of illiteracy. He has a
reputation as a rugged, two-fisted man's man, but he is an Irishman who usu-

ally drinks sparingly, curses without profane intention and speaks of women with respect. He takes pride in his toughness, and takes pride in recalling the time he beat a Navajo Indian in a footrace.

His worn face, which reminded me of Somerset Maugham's, and which Ford calls "ugly," betrays a continuous amusement with the world around him. He wears glasses and one black patch over his blind left eye. He has such poor sight in the other eye he must hold what he is reading very close to see. He is so hard of hearing that others must shout at him to be heard, and he shouts at them in return. When he barks orders at his associates, they are respectfully obedient, but they smile uneasily all the while, for they are never quite sure if he is putting them on, and they do not want to seem foolish.

MAKING MOVIES FOREVER

It is easy to be fooled by such a man. His outer senses are dulled and he is no longer young. He has been making movies forever. When you ask him a question, you must wait against a long silence for a reply, until you begin to wonder if he has forgotten or even heard you in the first place. But when he has considered your question carefully, he will give you your answer, and if it has been a foolish question, his answer will mock you and make you seem a fool, and if it has been a good question, his answer will be good and make you feel good.

"When a motion picture is at its best," he said, "it is long on action and short on dialogue. When it tells its story and reveals its characters in a series of simple, beautiful, active pictures, and does it with as little talk as possible, then the motion picture medium is being used to its fullest advantage. I don't know any subject on earth better suited to such a presentation than a Western.

"The people who coined that awful term 'horse opera' are snobs. The critics are snobs. Now, I'm not one who hates all critics. There are many good ones and I pay attention to them and I've even acted on some of their suggestions. But most criticism has been destructive, full of inaccuracies and generalizations. Hell, I don't think the leading newspaper reviewers even go to see most of the Westerns. They send their second string assistants. And they're supposed to be very nasty and very funny in their reviews. Well, it's a shame, because it makes it a crime to like a Western. Sure, there have been bad and dishonest Westerns. But, there have been bad and dishonest romantic stories, too, and war stories, and people don't attack all romantic movies or war movies because of these. Each picture should be judged on its own merit. In general, Westerns have maintained as high a level as that of any other theme.

"The critics always say we make Westerns because it's an easy way to make money. This is hogwash. They're not cheap or easy to make. They have to be done on location, which is damned hard work, the most expensive and most difficult form of movie-making. It's true Westerns generally make money. What the hell's wrong with that? They make money because people like them. And what the hell's wrong with that? If there was more concern with what the public wants and less with what the critics want, Hollywood wouldn't be in the awful fix it's in right now. This is a business. If we can give the public what it wants, then it's a good business and makes money. The audience is happy and we're happy. What the hell's wrong with that?"

PRESIDENTS PREFER COWBOYS

"Some of our greatest Americans have been Western fans. I guess in many cases it provided them with an escape, a relief, but I see nothing wrong with that. Woodrow Wilson, Franklin Roosevelt, Jack Kennedy were all Western fans.

"Yes, that's right, they *were* all Democrats, and I'm a Democrat, too. I don't try to hide that, either. But some Republicans have been great Western fans— Douglas MacArthur. I flew from Korea into Tokyo once, years ago, and MacArthur sent for me. He said they were showing movies that night, and that the picture was one of mine, *She Wore a Yellow Ribbon*. He said he was showing it in my honor, that he watched it least once a month and never got tired of seeing it. Now that *is* an honor."

I asked Ford who attends Westerns. "Everyone," he said brusquely. Then he smiled. "Actually, we've taken surveys and we've found that most of our audience is made up of children and fathers taking their children. The fathers enjoy Westerns and the children give them an excuse to go. It's a shame most persons feel they have to sneak in to see a Western by the side door. There's nothing wrong with anything being 'family entertainment,' you know. But now Hollywood has found it can pull a lot of people to the box office and make a lot of money with a lot of different types of pictures. Lately, they've been doing it with 'dirty pictures.' I don't like to use that term, but I don't know what else you can call them."

WESTERNS NOT FOR ADULTS ONLY

"Now, I'm a Roman Catholic. But, I'm Irish, too. I think I'm fairly masculine and I don't think I'm a prude, but I do think there are certain things that don't belong on the screen. I wouldn't take anyone to see some of the pictures that are being put out today. I wouldn't even take them to see the billboards outside of the movie houses. These and other ads, lurid come-ons with half-naked women, are dishonest and cater to our worst instincts. They aren't making Hollywood any friends.

"When I come back from making a Western on location, I feel a better man for it. I don't think some of the modern trash makes anyone feel better for having read or seen it.

"I don't recall a Western which ever had to carry a 'For Adults Only' sign. When you go to a movie today, you feel guilty, as though you were going to a striptease. It all runs in cycles. Tomorrow, someone will make a picture about a boy and a dog and it'll make money and then everyone will start making boy-and-dog pictures again.

"Actually, I'm certainly not against sex on the screen if it's done in the right way. Many Westerns have a gusty sort of sex. And I think I made the sexiest picture ever, *The Quiet Man.* Now this was all about a man trying to get a woman into bed, but that was all right, they were married, and it was essentially a moral situation, done with honesty, good taste and humor. These things are all fundamental to a good Western, too. In a Western, you can make a strong picture which is reasonably adult, yet a man can still take his children to see it, which is the way it should be. After all, we're not in the burlesque business.

"I know the term 'morality play' has been applied to Westerns, but I won't go that far, nor be so high-toned about it, but I do feel they have a basically moral quality, and I applaud this and think it's the way it should be.

"We use immoral characters. In *Stagecoach,* we had Claire Trevor playing a woman of easy virtue and Thomas Mitchell playing a drunken doctor. We don't deny that there are such persons; we just aren't out to glorify them or build every story around them. Incidentally, these have become stock characters in Westerns and maybe they've become what you call 'clichés,' but they weren't always clichés, and I keep trying to do things fresh or different, just as many others in this business do.

"There are no more clichés in Westerns than in anything else, and this applies to our moral approach, too. I don't think I, nor anyone else, have always garbed my heroes in white and my villains in black and so forth. Good doesn't always triumph over evil. It doesn't in life and it doesn't in all Westerns. Usually it does, but I think this is the way it should be. I have depicted some sad and tragic and unjust things in my Westerns, as have others.

"I remember once I was seated in a screening room with someone viewing the rushes of a picture I was shooting. In an early scene, there was a background shot of a man on a horse. It was background, mind you; he wasn't important and the scene wasn't. This person turned to me and said he knew that was the villain. He was wearing black or riding a black horse or some such fool thing. I threw him the hell out. I had to cut the scene out. It's not fair. It's one of those unfair generalizations made about Westerns."

BRINGING BACK WILL ROGERS

What, I wondered, were the men of the West really like?

"They were like Will Rogers," Ford said, waving at the wall. He stood staring at a blank spot on the wall. He buzzed his secretary and she came rushing in, thrusting another steaming mug of coffee into his hands and turning to run. He pinned her to the door with a shout: "Where the hell is my Will Rogers picture? When am I going to get it back? When I loaned it out, they promised to return it. Would you be kind and generous enough to get those kind and generous people on the phone and ask them when can I kindly have my Will Rogers picture back?"

"Yes, sir, Mr. Ford," she shouted back. "Right away, sir."

When she had made her escape, he looked down to find coffee in his hands, and raised the cup to his lips. He flipped a cigar butt away, missing the Grand Canyon, lit another, puffed it, and stared at the wall. "I had a picture of Will Rogers and, by God, I'll get it back," he said. He turned to me. "The men of the West were like Will Rogers. They were rugged and imperfect men, but many were basically gentle, and most were basically moral and religious, like most people who live with the land.

"They had their own language, but it was not profane. They had a warm, rugged, natural good humor. Strong people have always been able to laugh at their own hardships and discomforts. Soldiers do in wartime. The old cowboy did in the Old West. And today, in the hinterlands, in places like Montana and Wyoming, there are working cowboys, and they even carry guns, usually .30-30 Winchesters, though for protection against animals, such as coyotes, not to shoot each other."

WALTER MITTY'S WESTERN HERO

"We've studied the history of these cowboys, past and present, and we've had some true Western characters, such as Pardner Jones, serving as technical experts on our films. I think some of the personality things I've mentioned have been very well portrayed in our Western film heroes. These men are natural. They are themselves. They are rugged individualists. They live an outdoor life, and they don't have to *conform*.

"I think one of the great attractions of the Western is that people like to identify themselves with these cowboys. We all have an escape complex. We all want to leave the troubles of our civilized world behind us. We envy those who can live the most natural way of life, with nature, bravely and simply. What was that character's name? Mitty, that's it. We're all Walter Mittys. We all picture ourselves doing heroic things. And there are worse heroes than the Westerners for us to have.

"The Western heroes may be 'larger than life,' but so are many of our historical heroes, and we hate to dispel the public's illusions. If we cast handsome men and attractive women in semibiographical roles, portraying persons who were really homely, we are doing no worse than has always been done in movies. I myself am a pretty ugly fellow. The public wouldn't pay to see me on film.

"It is probable that the Westerns have been most inaccurate in overglamorizing and overdramatizing the heroes and villains of the period, and in playing up the gunfights. We could do without such stock characters as the hero who leaps from two stories onto his horse, fires twenty shots at a time from his six-shooter and has a comical, bearded rascal for his sidekick. But again, these are generalizations which don't apply to all Westerns.

"We have been charged with using too much violence, with too often achieving a good end through the unfortunate use of violent means, and this charge has merit, but, after all, those *were* violent times. I've tried not to overdo this and so have a lot of men who have turned out good Westerns. The very term 'gunslinger' makes us cringe, and we try to hold shoot-downs to a minimum. But men did carry guns and did shoot at each other. There wasn't much law for a long while, after all.

"It is wrong to make heroic the villainous characters, such as Billy the Kid, who were more ruthless and vicious than anyone can imagine today. However, it is true that much of the conversion to law and order was accomplished by reformed criminals, who got sheriffs' jobs because of their strong reputations. Men like Wyatt Earp had real nerve. They didn't have to use their guns. They overpowered the opposition with their reputations and personalities. They faced them down. They were lucky. A .45 is the most inaccurate gun ever made. If you've handled one, you know. Pardner Jones told me if you put Wild Bill Hickok in a barn with a six-shooter, he couldn't have hit the wall.

"It is equally wrong for the heroes to have been made out to be pure Sir Galahads in so many cases, which is nonsense. However, those were different times than we know today. Mere survival took something a little out of the ordinary, and the men who dominated the time *were* out of the ordinary, really big men."

SHOWMEN AND SADDLE TRAMPS

"Some of the early Western stars, such as William S. Hart and Buck Jones, were real Western types, either from the West or naturals for the part. They were great and courageous athletes and horsemen, skills which deserve some credit. Tom Mix was a great athlete and, I think, next to C. B. De Mille, our greatest showman. I worked often and happily with George O'Brien, a fine Western actor. And also Harry Carey, through whom we brought the real saddle tramp to the screen for the first time. He was natural and rugged, but he had an innate modesty. He was a great, great actor, maybe the best Westerner ever. Will Rogers was a real Westerner, a truly outstanding character actor, humorist and person, who did much to popularize the real cowboy. I used to have a fine picture of him up there on the wall and I intend to get it back.

"Because the roles such actors played were natural roles and because they played them naturally and simply, they have never been given enough credit for their acting skills. Even those that date back to the silents seem less exaggerated, more natural to us than the romantic heroes of that period, as we see these early films once again. But the critics seem to think you have to be conscious of acting for it to be acting. Actually, the less conscious you are that it is acting, the better it usually is."

COOP WAS A REAL WESTERNER

"There have been many fine Western actors in recent years damned with this casual acceptance. Henry Fonda has been one. Gary Cooper was another. Coop even came not to believe in himself. But if Coop said he wasn't a great actor, he was wrong. And he was a real Westerner. He was just as fine in *High Noon* as he was in *Sergeant York,* and I'm glad the critics saw fit to reward him equally for both.

"Many of our fine Western actors, such as Jimmy Stewart, who is terrific, have had to go outside Westerns to get their rewards. Two who have never received anywhere near the credit they deserve are two of my closest friends and men with whom I've made many films, John Wayne and Ward Bond.

"Wayne is one of our most popular actors and a great box office draw, something which should not be disregarded. And he is superb. As long ago as *The Long Voyage Home,* he proved he was a fine actor. When I made *She Wore a Yellow Ribbon,* we had Wayne playing an old man. The critics announced in advance Wayne wasn't capable of playing an old man. Then they didn't bother to judge for themselves. But he did it, and beautifully. It was a very moving performance.

"I miss old Ward Bond very much. He played *Wagon Master* for me in the early days, and it's possible his very successful TV *Wagon Train* role was modeled after this. He was a great human being and a wonderful actor who was taken for granted because he played Westerns.

"It has been said that we haven't always portrayed women fairly in Westerns, and I think there's some truth in that, though not a great deal. It is a sort of a sore spot. The men were dominant in settling the West. The women played a somewhat lesser role, though certainly an important one. There were the saloon women. There always will be wherever there are rugged and lonely men. And some of these were not such terrible characters. And there were the home women who helped break the land, bear and raise children and make a home for their families. These were hard times for women and they acquitted themselves nobly. And I think they've generally been portrayed very well by actresses. Claire Trevor is one example. Jane Darwell, a grand person and a grand actress, is another."

I was reminded that Deborah Kerr played a wonderful Western sort of character in *The Sundowners* a couple of years ago, but missed getting an Oscar as she had several times previously. No actress, featured or supporting, has ever won an Oscar for a Western role. The only Western to win the "best picture" award was *Cimarron,* back in 1931, and the only featured Western actors to win were Warner Baxter for *In Old Arizona,* vintage 1929, and Gary Cooper for *High Noon,* in 1952. A few supporting actors—Thomas Mitchell, Walter Brennan and Burl Ives—have won Oscars for roles in Westerns and one director, George Stevens, for *Giant,* in 1956 (and that was not a classic type Western).

IN PURSUIT OF OSCAR

Ford has won six Oscars, two for wartime documentaries, and four for feature films. He was honored for *The Informer* in 1935; *The Grapes of Wrath* in 1940; *How Green Was My Valley* in 1941; and *The Quiet Man* in 1952. But he has never been honored as director for any of his great Westerns.

"It is hard for me to judge," he says, "but I would say *Stagecoach, She Wore a Yellow Ribbon* and *The Searchers* were my best Westerns. I also remember *The Iron Horse* and *Wagon Master* fondly. And I think some of my more recent ones, such as *The Man Who Shot Liberty Valance,* stand up very well, too. I like to think *Stagecoach* set a trend, sort of blazed a trail, for the adult Western, and it *is* appreciated, but it did not win me an Oscar. I don't like to say 'I'm proud' of the pictures that did win, but I do remember them fondly. Still, I'll be darned if I worked any less seriously on some of my Westerns, and I think they're just as good."

He pointed out that of the pictures that had brought him Oscars for the best direction, only *How Green Was My Valley* was also selected as the best picture. And he threw in the names of some of his other pictures that didn't win him Oscars but which he felt were just as good as those that did: *The Long Voyage Home; Young Mr. Lincoln;* Irvin Cobb's *The Sun Shines Bright;* and *When Willie Comes Marching Home* with Dan Dailey, which he considers "the funniest film ever made." He also noted that some great Westerns made by other men also lost out in the quest for Hollywood's major awards. These include *The Ox-Bow Incident, Shane* and *Red River.*

"Oscars aren't the end-all of our business," he growled nastily. "The award those of us in this profession treasure most highly is the New York Film Critics Award. And those of us in the directing end treasure the Directors Guild of America Award. These are eminently fair."

Yet it is a fact that even these have been snobbish about Westerns. *High Noon,* and its director, Fred Zinnemann, did win the New York Film Critics Award. Ford won it four times, for *The Informer, Stagecoach, The Grapes of Wrath* and *The Long Voyage Home* (the same year) and *How Green Was My*

Valley. Miss Kerr did win this prize for her woman of the soil in *The Sundowners.* George Stevens won the Directors Guild Award for *Giant* (also *A Place in the Sun*), while Ford won it for *The Quiet Man,* but never for a Western.

"Well, the applause of the critics isn't the end-all of our business, either," Ford said, his voice cracking with contempt. "But when awards and such things influence public opinion, it's damned unfortunate. Do you think I let Oscars influence me? What is the Academy Award anyway? Who is a member? Who votes? I'm not a member. Do you know that only a couple of hundred people vote each year? Is that supposed to represent all of us? None of us really give a good damn about the Academy. I've never even been to one of their shindigs, not even to receive one of my awards."

He stared reflectively into his mug of coffee. His voice mellowed for a moment. "Oh, I'm pleased when I'm honored," he said. "I'm just not fooled by it. I don't think it's the measure of my success. I don't think John Wayne thinks his lack of awards is the measure of his success. I hope not. I love that damn Republican," he grinned.

FUNDAMENTAL FIGHT

He pointed to some pictures of Indians on the wall, and had me look at them. "The Indian is very close to my heart," he said. He had a deer hide inscribed to him with affection from the Navajo, and he asked me to pick it up and feel it and read the gracious inscription.

"There's some merit to the charge that the Indian hasn't been portrayed accurately or fairly in the Western, but again, this charge has been a broad generalization and often unfair. The Indian didn't welcome the white man, you know, and he wasn't diplomatic. We were enemies and we fought. The fight against the Indian was fundamental to the story of the West. If he has been treated unfairly by the whites in films, that, unfortunately, was often the case in real life. There was much racial prejudice in the West. Some of it was directed against the Negro, too, by the way, something I touched on in *Sergeant Rutledge.*

"The Indians are wonderful people. I have come to know best the Navajo of Monument Valley. The Navajo can ride like a son of a gun and they're the greatest damn fighters in the world. They were tough to beat in the Old West and they've been tough to beat in modern war, in which many of them fought with us and performed heroically. But even today, although the Indian has a better civilized understanding of us, we do not have a much better understanding of him. There is still a lot of prejudice.

"When we first went into the Indian reservations, they were poor and starving. The pay from the shooting of *Stagecoach* helped put them on their feet. Since then, many movies on location have helped and rewarded the Indian. I don't mean we should take too much credit for this, or that it makes up for our treatment of them on film, but it is a fact and it's been important to them. Many of the Indians are wealthy now, through the discovery of oil on their property but except for a few luxuries, they actually still live as they always have, simply and close to the land. They're not greatly different than they were, particularly not at heart."

WORKING THE INDIAN ANGLE

"I am doing now a particular story I've wanted to do which stresses the Indian angle. It's called *Cheyenne Autumn*. It won't be the first film to deal sympathetically with them. Since the early years, a lot of movie-makers have tried to see at least some of the Indians' side of the problem. Television hasn't dealt too much with the Indian, but has concentrated more on the whites in the Old West. Under the handicaps it faces TV has done a wonderful job with Westerns in general.

"However, when you get down to the matter of treating various phases of the Old West inaccurately, TV has been a worse offender than the movies. More than the movies, TV has glamorized and dramatized their heroes inaccurately. And many of the TV Westerns are just plain bad, just like many of the movie Westerns. I don't sympathize with anyone who sits glued to his set for hours on end watching any of this that comes along. In this respect, I guess it's just as well my eyesight prevents me watching more.

"But in general, I don't think there is any aspect of our history that has been as well or completely portrayed on the screen, particularly in movies, as the Old West.

"Ambitious projects along this line are constantly coming along. One of the latest is *How the West Was Won,* which was done in separate segments. I was one of the directors on one section, a very short piece of material in which a boy returns to the farm from the Civil War, then leaves to head West. I have seen it on the screen and was pleased to find it touching and strong. And it is more or less a very true situation.

"There have to be some compromises with historical fact and accuracy in all movies. The public will simply not accept certain things which seem strange to them, true as they may be. You cannot, for example, show a general heading into battle, riding a mule, wearing corduroys and a pith helmet, and shielding himself from the sun with an umbrella, yet General Crook actually did that.

"Most Westerners really dressed in simple, rugged clothing, and were often very dirty. You got dirty on the range, you know, and laundries and bathrooms were sometimes hard to come by. Some time ago we reached the point where they would let our characters get out of the elaborate dress that once passed in movies for cowboy clothes, and let us put John Wayne, for example, into a part without a coat and with suspenders showing, as in *The Horse Soldiers.*

"Actually, the thing most accurately portrayed in the Western is the land. I think you can say that the real star of my Westerns has always been the land. I have always taken pride in the photography of my films, and the photography of Westerns in general has often been outstanding, yet rarely draws credit. It is as if the visual effect itself was not important, which would make no sense at all.

"When I did *She Wore a Yellow Ribbon,* I tried to have the cameras photograph it as Remington would have sketched and painted it. It came out beautifully and was very successful in this respect, I think. When I did *The Searchers,* I used a Charles Russell motif. These were two of our greatest Western artists, of course."

ODE TO THE OUTDOORS

"Is there anything more beautiful than a long shot of a man riding a horse well, or a horse racing free across a plain? Is there anything wrong with people loving such beauty, whether they go to experience it personally, or absorb it through the medium of a movie? Fewer and fewer persons today are exposed to farm, open land, animals, nature. We bring the land to them. They escape to it through us. My favorite location is Monument Valley, which lies where Utah and Arizona merge. It has rivers, mountains, plains, desert, everything the land can offer. I feel at peace there. I have been all over the world, but I consider this the most complete, beautiful and peaceful place on earth. I'm shooting some of *Cheyenne Autumn* there.

"There should never be any shame in liking Westerns," he said. "Westerns are understood and appreciated the world over, as much or more in other countries as here. When I go to Japan, I am more readily recognized and treated more as a celebrity than I am in my own country. When I go to England, I am often paid the respect of being asked to lecture, as I have at Oxford and Cambridge, and am often asked to discuss in particular a film such as *Wagon Master,* which is totally forgotten here. This is all to the good. As a movie-maker, my audience is the world, not just the US.

"And if one small segment of the population, the critics, paid and unpaid, professional and amateur, prefer to be snobs and to sneer, I'm certainly not going to worry about it. As long as I can remember these pictures affectionately and with a little pride, as long as people like them and come to see them, as long as they make money, as long as they are good and honest and attractive and decent films, I'm not going to worry, I'm going to figure they're wrong and we're right."

14

ABOUT JOHN FORD

John Ford died August 31, 1973, after a life full of honors. A President had come to California to present him with the Medal of Freedom. The Academy of Motion Picture Arts and Sciences had named him four times as best director of the year. The Directors Guild of America, which he helped found, three times named his direction the year's best. In addition, he was given the D. W. Griffith Award—many chroniclers have declared Ford to have been the Griffith of the sound era.

He was not a man who took well to praise, but John Ford respected the opinions of his fellow directors. A number of them have sent to *ACTION* their feelings about Ford and his work.

WILLIAM WYLER

One of John Ford's earliest pictures was a silent film with Harry Carey called *3 Godfathers*. One of my first feature films was a remake of this film with talk and sound and retitled *Hell's Heroes*. Many years later Ford made it again, this time with John Wayne. The last time I saw Jack he said to me, "It's your turn to make *3 Godfathers* again."

Among all the film directors—old and new—there are very few John Fords—if any. I am proud that he called me his friend.

FRANK CAPRA

John Ford was the Compleat Director *(Arrowsmith, The Informer, Stagecoach, The Grapes of Wrath, The Long Voyage Home, How Green Was My Valley, The Quiet Man)*, undoubtedly the mightiest and most versatile in films. A megaphone was to John Ford what the chisel was to Michelangelo: his life, his passion, his cross.

Ford cannot be pinned down and analyzed. He was pure Ford—which means pure great. John was half-tyrant, half revolutionary; half-saint, half-satan; half-possible, half impossible; half-genius, half-Irish—but *all* director, and for all time.

"About John Ford" originally appeared in *Action* 8, no. 8 (Nov.–Dec. 1973). Reprinted by permission.

After the director's death, the "visual gratification" of films like
Wagon Master (1950) continues to provide eloquent testimony of a man
"who lived for the cinema."
Courtesy of The Lilly Library, Indiana University, Bloomington, Indiana.

FEDERICO FELLINI

What I like most in John Ford is the artist in a state of purity, unaware and raw, deprived of sterile and farfetched cultural intermediations, immune from intellectualistic contaminations. I like his strength and his disarming simplicity. When I think of Ford I sense the smell of barracks, of horses, of gunpowder, I visualize silent and alarming flatlands, the unending trips of his heroes. But, above all, I feel a man who liked motion picture, who lived for the cinema, who has made out of motion picture a fairy tale to be told to everyone, but—in first place—a fairy tale to be lived by himself, a dwelling in which to live with the joyous spontaneity of entertainment and passion.

For all this I esteem him, I admire him and I love him.

WILLIAM FRIEDKIN

Like almost every other director of my generation, I am inescapably under John Ford's influence. Anyone who's ever seen a movie or tried to direct one owes something to Ford. In my own case I owe him much more than something, though we had never met. Most of all, Ford represented both challenge and inspiration to filmmakers.

Inspiration, in that having seen one of his many great films you were moved to try to go out to do the same thing. The challenge will always be there, reminding those who were inspired that they had little chance of equalling the output of this master filmmaker.

When we have colonized the moon, people will still be watching and loving John Ford's films.

MERVYN LEROY

In regards to John Ford's passing, I can only say he was a diamond in the rough, one of the greats of our business, and will be missed by everyone who knew him or appreciated his wonderful work on the movie screens of the world.

ALFRED HITCHCOCK

A John Ford picture was a visual gratification—his method of shooting, eloquent in its clarity and apparent simplicity. No shots from behind the flames in the fireplace towards the room—no cameras swinging through chandeliers, no endless zooming in and out without any discernible purpose. His scripts had a beginning, a middle and an end. They are understood all the world over and [stand] as a monument to part of the land he loved: Monument Valley.

STANLEY KRAMER

Before a film is screened at the Kremlin Palace in Moscow, the director is asked to comment about his film. Any comment is, of course, gratuitous. The film speaks for itself.

That's what we face in discussing John Ford. There is nothing to be said—his films roar through our times.

JEAN RENOIR

Talent is rare. Technical skill is not common. Leadership on a set is not found on every street corner. A quality even more scarce is nobility. John Ford was a king: he knighted all those who had the immense luck to work with him. His loss is irreparable.

LEWIS MILESTONE

What else can anyone say that hasn't already been said about Jack Ford? Perhaps I can tell a couple of stories that illustrate his unique qualities.

One day Jack dropped in at the Rolls Royce dealer on Sunset Boulevard. He was dressed in his usual attire, looking like a bum. The salesman paid no attention to him, so he went over to one of the cars and started opening and shutting doors, and examining the upholstery. Finally a salesman came over, very annoyed, and asked, "What do you want, Mac?"

"Can you deliver this particular car to me today?" Jack asked.

The salesman was amused and he replied, "Yes, sir. Can you deliver a certified check for $35,000?"

"Yes," Jack replied, handing him a card. "Deliver it at this address to Mrs. John Ford. Be sure you do it today. It's her birthday."

The other story happened when Jack was doing a remake of *What Price Glory?* Everybody from Darryl Zanuck down thought it would be a good idea to make it as a musical, and that was the plan. But when Jack finished the picture, it had no musical numbers. "If you want music, you put it in," he told Zanuck and walked out.

The story was told by Zanuck himself, with much amusement.

ELIA KAZAN

Bless Jack Ford. In 1945 I came to Hollywood out of the N.Y. Theatre. After I'd done half a dozen films, I looked at them in a very unfriendly way. They seemed to me to be photographed stage plays. They were pretty well directed but in the same ways I'd done shows on Broadway. Hitchcock says film is not photographs of people talking. Mine were. Mostly in medium shots. The films were well received, better received than some of the films I've made since. But I was dissatisfied with them. I decided to turn around. I began to run Jack's films one after the other. You've all done that, haven't you? Why Jack? Because of all our filmmakers I admired him most. He taught me to tell it in pictures. Only. A truism? Of course. I knew it theoretically the first day I stepped on a sound stage. But knowing something is one thing, breaking old habits another. Jack taught me to trust long shots. I watched a scene in *Young Mr. Lincoln,* a killing in the woods. Jack played it in LS. Far back in a clearing I could see small figures. Then I heard a distant report, a pistol? This shot was held, not cut into. A thin plume of smoke rose slowly till it passed out of sight. Jack held it that long. I would not have. I would have cut in. The face of this one, the face of the other, the impact, the fall. Today I don't remember the details of the scene and I'm probably describing it incorrectly. What I remember is how Jack conceived the scene. I made up my mind to change my way, do something drastic. I decided to make a film that was in effect a silent. I would not rely on dialogue to tell the story, not at all. I would tell it as if I was still in the time of titles. But I'd leave out the titles too. Especially the last reels. Pictures, not words. That way I might kick my habit, move away from my stage technique, begin to make films. I talked to Jack about this experience, trying to thank him. It was at a party and we were both a little drunk. He sort of nodded, gave me the single fish-eye, made a grumpy sound. I think he might have been flattered, but damn if he'd say so.

I had a feeling he didn't think much of my awakening. Why had I spent so much time discovering the obvious? It was second nature to him, should have been to me. It wasn't, I told him. He'd changed my working life, I told him. I was never the same after. (Except once. Tennessee Williams' *Streetcar* is a perfect stage play; I didn't touch it.) There was one other thing I didn't ever say to Jack Ford. What he brought to the screen that made me admire him more than any other film-maker was a kind of poetry, specific to the screen and specific to men. Granted his women were not his best creations, but his men, those in *The Long Voyage Home,* for instance, were presented with such poetry and feeling and not one bit of sentimentality. Much deep sentiment, no self-favoring. That's why so many of us think of Jack as a kind of father. Once I tried to engage as many of his old bunch as possible, not the actors, I had my own actors, but his crew. *Viva Zapata* was made with Jack's staff heads. I learned more about his ways from them. Get out early, before anyone else—they remembered he did. Use the day as it comes up. The accident of each day's weather is a dramatic effect, don't duck it, use it. Keep your eye, hour by hour, on the movement of the sun. Go with it! Plan your shots to fit in. Get out on the set before anyone else, walk around it. Look this way, look that. The set is your main source. I asked him once, at another party, where he got his ideas about how to stage scenes. He said from the set. Not from the script, not from the actors, not from the theme. *From the set.* The settings he chose were already poetry. He lifted his action to fit them. I adored the old man, though, of course, I never dared tell him that in words, either. He would have hated it. But it's the truth, I did. Among us all, he's still my main man.

SATYAJIT RAY

In my youth I admired John Ford for almost exactly the same reasons that I admired Beethoven: for his strength and simplicity; for his warmth, his lyricism and his breadth of vision; for his heroic stance, and his unbounded faith and optimism. Even in their outbursts of boisterousness and their occasional emotional excesses, the two had much in common.

Ford was among the half-a-dozen or so directors, mostly American, who instilled in me a love of the cinema and taught me its rudiments. It was he more than anyone else who made me realize that a film could live and breathe and behave like a sane and healthy human being, and that the art that infused this life was often—like the air that surrounds and sustains us—invisible, and the better for being so.

One does not regret the passing of an artist who worked so fruitfully over such a length of time, but one does regret, deeply, the passing of an era that made John Ford possible, and the coming of one when the very air that we breathe has become polluted.

JOHN SCHLESINGER

As a school boy I marvelled at *Stagecoach* and *The Grapes of Wrath*. I had no idea then that I was to become a director. At University the name of John Ford meant a great deal more. He was to us then the most influential American Director. Perhaps he will always remain so.

What I have never ceased to wonder at is the personal vision he remained true to throughout such a prodigious number of films. His humanism shone through all of them.

I met him finally at the Venice Film Festival in 1971 when he was awarded a special prize. His daughter told me he would like to meet me. On the last day of the Festival I plucked up courage to go up to his suite, somewhat nervous of the meeting. Words of admiration always seem inadequate at such a moment. He was sitting up in bed smoking a cigar and drinking coffee and brandy. I shook his hand. He stared at me with his one good eye. "Shake it properly," he said.

FRANÇOIS TRUFFAUT

John Ford was one of the most celebrated directors in the world, while everything about him—his deportment, and his observations—gave the impression that he never sought this fame nor even that he accepted it. This man, who has always been described as surly and secretly tender, was surely closer to the characters that he had Victor McLaglen play than to the leading parts that John Wayne interpreted.

John Ford was one of those artists who never used the word "art" and was one of those poets who never used the word "poetry."

What I like in the work of John Ford is that he always gave priority to the characters. For a long time, I criticized his view of women—which I found too 19th century. Then I realized that, thanks to John Ford, a splendid actress like Maureen O'Hara has been able to play some of the best women's roles of the American cinema between 1941 and 1957.

John Ford could receive—*ex aequo* with Howard Hawks—the prize for "invisible direction." I want to mention that the camera work of these great storytellers is not discernible to the spectator's eye: very few camera movements—only in order to follow a character—a majority of stationary camera shots, always filmed at an exact distance, this created a supple and fluid literary style that one can compare to that of Guy de Maupassant or Turgenev.

With a royal ease, John Ford knew how to make the audience laugh and knew how to make it cry. The only thing that he did not know how to do was to bore it!

And, since John Ford believed in God, "God Bless John Ford."

FILMOGRAPHY

The following listing of major credits is for convenience of reference. For ex-
haustive credits (including uncredited work), consult the filmography in Tag
Gallagher's *John Ford: The Man and His Films* (Berkeley: University of California Press, 1986).

Stagecoach (Walter Wanger/United Artists, 1939).
Producer: John Ford. Executive Producer: Walter Wanger. Screenplay: Dudley
Nichols, from the story "Stage to Lordsburg" by Ernest Haycox. Cinematog-
raphy: Bert Glennon. Editors: Otho Lovering, Dorothy Spencer, and Walter
Reynolds. Art Direction: Alexander Toluboff. Costumes: Walter Plunkett.
Music: Richard Hageman, W. Franke Harling, John Leipold, Leo Shuken, and
Luis Gruenberg (seventeen American folktunes of the 1880s). 95 min.

Cast: Claire Trevor (Dallas). John Wayne (Ringo Kid). Thomas Mitchell (Dr.
Josiah Boone). John Carradine (Hatfield). Andy Devine (Buck). Donald Meek
(Samuel Peacock). Louise Platt (Lucy Mallory). Tim Holt (Lieutenant
Blanchard). George Bancroft (Sheriff Curley Wilcox). Berton Churchill (Henry
Gatewood). Chris Martin (Chris). Elvira Rios (Yakeema, his wife). Francis
Ford (Billy Pickett). Marga Daighton (Mrs. Pickett). Jack Pennick (barman).
Brenda Fowler (Mrs. Gatewood). Tom Tyler (Luke Plummer). Joseph Rickson
(Ike Plummer). Vester Pegg (Hank Plummer). Chief White Horse (Indian chief).

Drums along the Mohawk (20th Century–Fox, 1939).
Producer: Raymond Griffith. Executive Producer: Darryl F. Zanuck. Screen-
play: Lamar Trotti and Sonya Levien, from the novel by Walter D. Edmonds.
Cinematography: Bert Glennon and Ray Rennahan (Technicolor). Editor:
Robert Simpson. Sound Effects Editor: Robert Parrish. Art Direction: Richard
Day and Mark Lee Kirk. Costumes: Gwen Wakeling. Music: Alfred Newman.
103 min.

Cast: Claudette Colbert (Lana Borst Martin). Henry Fonda (Gilbert Martin).
Edna May Oliver (Mrs. McKlennan). Eddie Collins (Christian Reall). John
Carradine (Caldwell). Dorris Bowdon (Mary Reall). Arthur Shields (Rever-
end Rosenkranz). Robert Lowery (John Weaver). Jessie Ralph (Mrs. Weaver).
Roger Imhof (General Nicholas Herkimer). Francis Ford (Joe Boleo). Ward

Bond (Adam Hartmann). Russell Simpson (Dr. Petry). Chief Big Tree (Blue Back). Jack Pennick (Amos). Robert Grieg (Mr. Borst).

My Darling Clementine (20th Century–Fox, 1946).
Producer: Samuel G. Engel. Screenplay: Samuel G. Engel and Winston Miller, from a story by Sam Hellman, based on Stuart N. Lake's book *Wyatt Earp, Frontier Marshal.* Cinematography: Joseph P. McDonald. Editor: Dorothy Spencer. Art Direction: James Basevi and Lyle R. Wheeler. Costumes: René Hubert. Music: Cyril J. Mockridge. Special Effects: Fred Sersen. 97 min.

Cast: Henry Fonda (Wyatt Earp). Linda Darnell (Chihuahua). Victor Mature (Doc John Holliday). Walter Brennan (Old Man Clanton). Tim Holt (Virgil Earp). Ward Bond (Morgan Earp). Cathy Downs (Clementine Carter). Alan Mowbray (Granville Thorndyke). John Ireland (Billy Clanton). Grant Withers (Ike Clanton). Fred Libby (Phin Clanton). Russell Simpson (John Simpson). Francis Ford (Dad). Danny Borzage (accordionist).

Fort Apache (Argosy Pictures/RKO, 1948).
Producers: John Ford and Merian C. Cooper. Screenplay: Frank S. Nugent, from the story "Massacre" by James Warner Bellah. Cinematography: Archie Stout (William Clothier, second unit). Editor: Jack Murray. Art Direction: James Basevi. Costumes: Michael Meyers and Ann Peck. Music: Richard Hageman. Special Effects: Dave Koehler. 127 min.

Cast: John Wayne (Captain Kirby York). Henry Fonda (Lieutenant Colonel Owen Thursday). Shirley Temple (Philadelphia Thursday). John Agar (Lieutenant Michael O'Rourke). Ward Bond (Sergeant Major O'Rourke). George O'Brien (Captain Sam Collingwood). Victor McLaglen (Sergeant Mulcahy). Pedro Armendáriz (Sergeant Beaufort). Anna Lee (Mrs. Collingwood). Irene Rich (Mrs. O'Rourke). Guy Kibbee (Dr. Wilkins). Grant Withers (Silas Meacham). Miguel Inclán (Cochise). Jack Pennick (Sergeant Dan Schatuck). Mae Marsh (Mrs. Gates). Dick Foran (Sergeant Tim Quincannon). Frank Ferguson (newspaperman). Francis Ford (Fink). Ray Hyke (Gates). Movita Castaneda (Guadalupe). Hank Worden (Southern recruit).

3 Godfathers (Argosy Pictures/M-G-M, 1948)
Producers: John Ford and Merian C. Cooper. Screenplay: Laurence Stallings and Frank S. Nugent, from a novel by Peter B. Kyne. Cinematography: Winton C. Hoch (Technicolor). Editor: Jack Murray. Art Direction: James Basevi. Wardrobe: Michael Meyers and Ann Peck. Music: Richard Hageman. 106 min.

Cast: John Wayne (Robert Marmaduke Sangster Hightower). Pedro Armendáriz (Pedro Roca Fuerte). Harry Carey Jr. (William Kearney, "The Abilene

Kid"). Ward Bond (Perley "Buck" Sweet). Mildred Natwick (mother). Charles Halton (Mr. Latham). Jane Darwell (Miss Florie). Mae Marsh (Mrs. Perley Sweet). Guy Kibbee (judge). Ben Johnson, Michael Dugan, and Don Summers (men in posse). Fred Libbey and Hank Worden (deputy sheriffs). Jack Pennick (Luke). Francis Ford (drunk).

She Wore a Yellow Ribbon (Argosy Pictures/RKO, 1949).
Producers: John Ford and Merian C. Cooper. Screenplay: Frank S. Nugent and Laurence Stallings, from the stories "War Party" and "The Big Hunt" by James Warner Bellah. Cinematography: Winton C. Hoch (Technicolor). Editor: Jack Murray. Art Direction: James Basevi. Costumes: Michael Meyers and Ann Peck. Music: Richard Hageman. Special Effects: Jack Caffee. 103 min.

Cast: John Wayne (Captain Nathan Brittles). Joanne Dru (Olivia). John Agar (Lieutenant Flint Cohill). Ben Johnson (Sergeant Tyree). Harry Carey Jr. (Lieutenant Pennell). Victor McLaglen (Sergeant Quincannon). Mildred Natwick (Mrs. Abby Allshard). George O'Brien (Major "Mac" Allshard). Arthur Shields (Dr. O'Laughlin). Francis Ford (Irish barman). Chief Big Tree (Pony That Walks). Noble Johnson (Red Shirt). Jack Pennick (sergeant major). Michael Dugan (Hochbauer).

Wagon Master (Argosy Pictures/RKO, 1950).
Producers: John Ford and Merian C. Cooper. Screenplay: Frank S. Nugent and Patrick Ford. Cinematography: Bert Glennon. Editor: Jack Murray. Art Direction: James Basevi. Costumes: Wes Jeffries and Adele Parmenter. Music: Richard Hageman. Songs sung by the Sons of the Pioneers; words and music by Stan Jones. Special Effects: Jack Caffee. 86 min.

Cast: Ben Johnson (Travis Blue). Harry Carey Jr. (Sandy Owens). Joanne Dru (Denver). Ward Bond (Elder Wiggs). Charles Kemper (Uncle Shiloh Clegg). Alan Mowbray (Dr. A. Locksley Hall). Jane Darwell (Sister Ledeyard). Russell Simpson (Adam Perkins). James Arness (Floyd Clegg). Fred Libby (Reese Clegg). Hank Worden (Luke Clegg). Mickey Simpson (Jesse Clegg). Francis Ford (Mr. Peachtree).

Rio Grande (Argosy Pictures/Republic, 1950)
Producers: John Ford and Merian C. Cooper. Screenplay: James Kevin McGuinness, from the story "Mission with No Record" by James Warner Bellah. Cinematography: Bert Glennon. Editor: Jack Murray. Art Direction: Frank Hotaling. Costumes: Adele Palmer. Music: Victor Young. Songs sung by the Sons of the Pioneers. Special Effects: Howard and Theodore Lydecker. 105 min.

Cast: John Wayne (Lieutenant Colonel Kirby Yorke). Maureen O'Hara (Mrs. Yorke). Ben Johnson (Trooper Travis Tyree). Claude Jarman Jr. (Trooper Jeff Yorke). Harry Carey Jr. (Trooper Daniel "Sandy" Boone). Chill Wills (Dr. Wilkins). J. Carrol Naish (General Philip Sheridan). Victor McLaglen (Sergeant Major Tim Quincannon). Grant Withers (deputy marshall). Alberto Morin (Lieutenant).

The Searchers (C. V. Whitney Pictures/Warner Bros., 1956).
Producers: Merian C. Cooper and C. V. Whitney. Screenplay: Frank S. Nugent, from the novel by Alan LeMay. Cinematography: Winton C. Hoch (Technicolor). Editor: Jack Murray. Art Direction: Frank Hotaling and James Basevi. Costumes: Frank Beetson and Ann Peck. Music: Max Steiner (title song by Stan Jones). Special Effects: George Brown. 119 min.

Cast: John Wayne (Ethan Edwards). Jeffrey Hunter (Martin Pawley). Vera Miles (Laurie Jorgensen). Ward Bond (Captain Reverend Samuel Clayton). Natalie Wood (Debbie Edwards). John Qualen (Lars Jorgensen). Olive Carey (Mrs. Jorgensen). Henry Brandon (Chief Scar). Ken Curtis (Charlie McCorry). Harry Carey Jr. (Brad Jorgensen). Antonio Moreno (Emilio Figueroa). Hank Worden (Mose Harper). Dorothy Jordan (Martha Edwards). Pat Wayne (Lieutenant Greenhill). Dan Borzage (accordionist).

The Horse Soldiers (Mirisch Company/United Artists, 1959)
Producers-Screenwriters: John Lee Mahin and Martin Rackin, from the novel by Harold Sinclair. Cinematography: William Clothier (Deluxe Color). Editor: Jack Murray. Art Direction: Frank Hotaling. Costumes: Frank Beetson and Ann Peck. Music: David Buttolph (song by Stan Jones). Special Effects: Augie Lohman. 119 min.

Cast: John Wayne (Colonel John Marlowe). William Holden (Major Hank Kendall). Constance Towers (Hannah Hunter). Althea Gibson (Lukey). Hoot Gibson (Brown). Anna Lee (Mrs. Buford). Russell Simpson (Sheriff Captain Henry Goodboy). Stan Jones (General U. S. Grant). Carleton Young (Colonel Jonathan Miles). Ken Curtis (Wilkie). Denver Pyle (Jagger Jo). Strother Martin (Virgil). Hank Worden (Deacon). Jack Pennick (Sergeant Major Mitchell).

Sergeant Rutledge (Ford Productions/Warner Bros., 1960)
Producers: Patrick Ford and Willis Goldbeck. Screenplay: Willis Goldbeck and James Warner Bellah. Cinematography: Bert Glennon (Technicolor). Editor: Jack Murray. Art Direction: Eddie Imazu. Costumes: Marjorie Best. Music: Howard Jackson (song by Mark David and Jerry Livingston). 111 min.

Cast: Jeffrey Hunter (Lieutenant Tom Cantrell). Constance Towers (Mary

Beecher). Woody Strode (Sergeant Braxton Rutledge). Billie Burke (Mrs. Cordelia Fosgate). Juano Hernandez (Sergeant Matthew Luke Skidmore). Willis Bouchey (Colonel Otis Fosgate). Carleton Young (Captain Shattuck). Mae Marsh (Nellie). Fred Libby (Chandler Hubble). Jack Pennick (sergeant). Hank Worden (Laredo).

Two Rode Together (Ford-Sheptner Productions/Columbia, 1961) Producer: John Ford. Associate Producer: Stan Sheptner. Screenplay: Frank Nugent, from the novel *Comanche Captives* by Will Cook. Cinematography: Charles Lawton Jr. (Pathecolor). Editor: Jack Murray. Art Direction: Robert Peterson. Costumes: Frank Beetson. Music: George Duning. 109 min.

Cast: James Stewart (Guthrie McCabe). Richard Widmark (Lieutenant Jim Gary). Shirley Jones (Marty Purcell). Linda Cristal (Elena de la Madriaga). Andy Devine (Sergeant Darius P. Posey). John McIntire (Major Frazer). Paul Birch (Edward Purcell). Willis Bouchey (Harry J. Wringle). Henry Brandon (Quanah Parker). Harry Carey Jr. (Ortho Clegg). Ken Curtis (Greely Clegg). Olive Carey (Abby Frazer). Anna Lee (Mrs. Malaprop). Jeanette Nolan (Mrs. McCandless). John Qualen (Ole Knudsen). Woody Strode (Stone Calf). Mae Marsh (Hannah Clegg). Jack Pennick (sergeant).

The Man Who Shot Liberty Valance (Ford Productions/Paramount, 1962) Producers: John Ford and Willis Goldbeck. Screenplay: Willis Goldbeck and James Warner Bellah, from the story by Dorothy M. Johnson. Cinematography: William H. Clothier. Editor: Otho Lovering. Art Direction: Hal Pereira and Eddie Imazu. Costumes: Edith Head. Music: Cyril J. Mockridge (theme from *Young Mr. Lincoln* by Alfred Newman). 122 min.

Cast: James Stewart (Ransom Stoddard). John Wayne (Tom Doniphon). Vera Miles (Hallie Stoddard). Lee Marvin (Liberty Valance). Edmond O'Brien (Dutton Peabody). Andy Devine (Link Appleyard). Ken Murray (Doc Willoughby). John Carradine (Starbuckle). Jeanette Nolan (Nora Ericson). John Qualen (Peter Ericson). Willis Bouchey (Jason Tully). Carleton Young (Maxwell Scott). Woody Strode (Pompey). Denver Pyle (Amos Carruthers). Strother Martin (Floyd). Lee Van Cleef (Reese). Jack Pennick (barman).

How the West Was Won (Cinerama/M-G-M, 1962) "The Civil War." Producer: Bernard Smith. Screenplay: James R. Webb, suggested by a series in *Life* magazine. Cinematography: Joseph LaShelle (Technicolor, Ultra Panavision/Cinerama). Editor: Harold F. Kress. Art Direction: George W. Davis, William Ferrari, and Addison Hehr. Costumes: Walter Plunkett. Music: Alfred Newman and Ken Darby. 25 min.

Cast: Spencer Tracy (Narrator). George Peppard (Zeb Rawlings). Carroll Baker (Eve Prescott Rawlings). Russ Tamblyn (Confederate deserter). Claude Johnson (Jeremiah Rawlings). Andy Devine (Corporal Peterson). Willis Bouchey (surgeon). Henry Morgan (General U. S. Grant). John Wayne (General Sherman). Raymond Massey (Abraham Lincoln).

Cheyenne Autumn (Ford-Smith Productions/Warner Bros., 1964)
Producers: John Ford and Bernard Smith. Screenplay: James R. Webb, from the book by Mari Sandoz and Howard Fast's novel *The Last Frontier*. Cinematography: William Clothier (Technicolor, Super Panavision 70). Editors: David Hawkins and Otho Lovering. Art Direction: Richard Day. Music: Alex North. 159 min.

Cast: Richard Widmark (Captain Thomas Archer). Carroll Baker (Deborah Wright). James Stewart (Wyatt Earp). Edward G. Robinson (Secretary of the Interior Carl Schurz). Karl Malden (Captain Wessels). Sal Mineo (Red Shirt). Dolores Del Río (Spanish Woman). Ricardo Montalban (Little Wolf). Gilbert Roland (Dull Knife). Arthur Kennedy (Doc Holliday). Pat Wayne (Second Lieutenant Scott). Elizabeth Allen (Guinevere Plantagenet). John Carradine (Major Jeff Blair). Victor Jory (Tall Tree). Mike Mazurki (Top Sergeant Stanislaw Wichowski). George O'Brien (Major Braden). Ken Curtis (Joe). Harry Carey Jr. (Trooper Smith). Ben Johnson (Trooper Plumtree). Carleton Young (Schurz's aide). Denver Pyle (Senator Henry). John Qualen (Svenson).

SELECTED BIBLIOGRAPHY

Aleiss, Angela. "A Race Divided: The Indian Westerns of John Ford." *American Indian Culture and Research Journal* 18, no. 3 (1994): 167–186.

Anderson, Lindsay. *About John Ford.* New York: McGraw-Hill, 1981.

Barkun, Michael. "Notes on the Art of John Ford." *Film Culture* 25 (Summer 1962): 9–15.

Bataille, Gretchen M., and Charles L. P. Silet, eds. *The Pretend Indians: Images of Native Americans in the Movies.* Ames: Iowa State University Press, 1980.

Baxter, John. *The Cinema of John Ford.* New York: A. S. Barnes, 1971.

Bazin, André. "The Evolution of the Western." In *What Is Cinema?* vol. 2, ed. and trans. Hugh Grey. Berkeley: University of California Press, 1971, 149–157.

Bogdanovich, Peter. "The Cowboy Hero and the American West . . . as Directed by John Ford." *Esquire* 100, no. 6 (1983): 417–425. Rpt. as "The America of John Ford" in Bogdanovich, *Pieces of Time: Peter Bogdanovich on Movies.* New York: Arbor House, 1985, 291–305.

———. *John Ford.* Berkeley: University of California Press, 1968.

Browne, Nick. "The Spectator-in-the-Text: The Rhetoric of *Stagecoach.*" *Film Quarterly* 29, no. 2 (Winter 1975–1976): 26–38.

Budd, Michael. "Genre, Director and Stars in John Ford's Westerns: Fonda, Wayne, Stewart and Widmark." *Wide Angle* 2, no. 4 (1978): 52–61.

———. "A Home in the Wilderness: Visual Imagery in John Ford's Westerns." *Cinema Journal* 16, no. 1 (Fall 1976): 62–75.

Buscombe, Edward. *Stagecoach.* London: British Film Institute, 1992.

———, ed. *The BFI Companion to the Western.* London: British Film Institute, 1988.

Buscombe, Edward, and Roberta E. Pearson, eds. *Back in the Saddle Again: New Essays on the Western.* London: British Film Institute, 1998.

Cameron, Ian, and Douglas Pye, eds. *The Book of Westerns.* New York: Continuum, 1996.

Campbell, Russell, ed. "John Ford." Special issue of *The Velvet Light Trap,* no. 2 (1971).

Card, James. "'The Searchers': By Alan LeMay and by John Ford," *Literature/Film Quarterly* 16, no. 1 (1988): 2–9.

Carey, Harry, Jr. *Company of Heroes: My Life as an Actor in the John Ford Stock Company.* Metuchen, N.J.: Scarecrow Press, 1994.

Cawelti, John. *The Six-Gun Mystique.* Bowling Green, Ohio: Popular Press, 1970.

Combs, Richard. "At Play in the Fields of John Ford." *Sight and Sound* 51, no. 2 (1982): 124–129.

Coyne, Michael. *The Crowded Prairie: American National Identity in the Hollywood Western.* New York: I. B. Taurus, 1996.

Darby, William. *John Ford's Westerns: A Thematic Analysis, with a Filmography.* Jefferson, N.C.: McFarland, 1996.

———. "Musical Links in *Young Mr. Lincoln, My Darling Clementine,* and *The Man Who Shot Liberty Valance.*" *Cinema Journal* 31, no. 1 (Fall 1991): 22–36.

Davis, Ronald L. *John Ford: Hollywood's Old Master.* Norman: University of Oklahoma Press, 1995.

Dempsey, Michael. "John Ford: A Reassessment." *Film Quarterly* 28, no. 4 (Summer 1975): 2–15.

Directors Guild of America. "Special Issue on John Ford." *Action* 5 (September–October 1971).

Eckstein, Arthur M. "Darkening Ethan: John Ford's *The Searchers* from Novel to Screenplay to Screen." *Cinema Journal* 38, no. 1 (Fall 1998): 3–24.

Ellis, Kirk. "On the Warpath: John Ford and the Indians." *Journal of Popular Film and Television* 8, no. 2 (1980): 34–41.

Eyman, Scott. *Print the Legend: The Life and Times of John Ford.* New York: Simon and Schuster, 1999.

Fenin, George N., and William K. Everson. *The Western: From the Silents to the Seventies.* New York: Grossman, 1973.

Ford, Dan. *Pappy: The Life of John Ford.* Englewood Cliffs, N.J.: Prentice-Hall, 1979.

Gallafent, Edward. "Four Tombstones, 1946–1994." In *The Book of Westerns,* ed. Ian Cameron and Douglas Pye. Westport: Greenwood Press, 1996, 302–311.

Gallagher, Tag. *John Ford: The Man and His Films.* Berkeley: University of California Press, 1986.

———. "John Ford's Indians." *Film Comment* 29, no. 5. (1993): 68–72.

———. "Shoot-Out at the Genre Corral: Problems in the 'Evolution' of the Western." In *Film Genre Reader II,* ed. Barry Keith Grant. Austin: University of Texas Press, 1995, 246–260.

Gomery, Douglas. "Mise-en-scene in John Ford's *My Darling Clementine.*" *Wide Angle* 2, no. 4 (1978): 14–19.

Hardy, Phil. *The Western.* New York: William Morrow, 1991.

Henderson, Brian. "*The Searchers:* An American Dilemma." *Film Quarterly* 34, no. 2 (Winter 1980–1981): 9–23. Rpt. in *Movies and Method: An Anthology,* vol. 2, ed. Bill Nichols. Berkeley: University of California Press, 1985, 429–449.

Lehman, Peter. "An Absence Which Becomes a Legendary Presence: John Ford's Structured Use of Off-Screen Space." *Wide Angle* 2, no. 4 (1978): 36–42.

———. "Texas 1868/America 1956: *The Searchers.*" In *Close Viewings: An Anthology of New Film Criticism,* ed. Peter Lehman. Tallahassee: Florida State University Press, 1990: 387–415.

Leutrat, Jean-Paul, and Suzanne Liandrat-Guigues. "John Ford and Monument Valley." In *Back in the Saddle Again: New Essays on the Western,* ed. Edward Buscombe and Roberta E. Pearson. London: British Film Institute, 1998, 160–169.

Levy, Bill. *John Ford: A Bio-bibliography.* Westport: Greenwood Press, 1998.

Lourdeaux, Lee. *Italian and Irish Filmmakers in America: Ford, Capra, Coppola and Scorsese.* Philadelphia: Temple University Press, 1990.

Luhr, William, and Peter Lehman. *Authorship and Narrative in the Cinema.* New York, Capricorn Books, 1977.

Lyons, Robert, ed. *My Darling Clementine.* New Brunswick: Rutgers University Press, 1984.

Maltby, Richard. "A Better Sense of History: John Ford and the Indians." In *The Book of Westerns,* ed. Ian Cameron and Douglas Pye. Westport: Greenwood Press, 1996, 34–49.

McBride, Joseph and Michael Wilmington. *John Ford.* New York: Da Capo Press, 1975.

McCarthy, Todd. "John Ford and Monument Valley." *American Film* 3, no. 7 (1978): 10–16.

Mitchell, Lee Clark. *Westerns: Making the Man in Fiction and Film.* Chicago: University of Chicago Press, 1996.

Nachbar, Jack, ed. *Focus on The Western.* Englewood Cliffs, N.J.: Prentice-Hall, 1974.

Nolley, Ken. "Printing the Legend in the Age of MX: Reconsidering Ford's Military Trilogy." *Literature/Film Quarterly* 14, no. 2 (1986): 82–88.

———. "The Representation of Conquest: John Ford and the Hollywood Indian (1939–1964)." In *Hollywood's Indian: The Portrayal of the Native American in Film*, ed. Peter C. Rollins and John E. O'Connor. Lexington: University Press of Kentucky, 1998, 73–90.

Palmer, R. Barton. "A Masculinist Reading of Western Films: *High Noon* and *Rio Grande*." *Journal of Popular Film & TV* 12, no. 4 (1984/1985): 156–162.

Pilkington, William T. "Fort Apache (1948)" In *Western Movies*, ed. William T. Pilkington and Don Graham. Albuquerque, N.M.: University of New Mexico Press, 1979, 40–49.

Place, J. A. *The Western Films of John Ford*. Secaucus: Citadel Press, 1974.

Poague, Leland. "'All I Can See Is the Flags': *Fort Apache* and the Visibility of History." *Cinema Journal* 27, no. 2 (Winter 1988): 8–26.

Pye, Douglas. "Double Vision: Miscegenation and Point of View in *The Searchers*." In *The Book of Westerns*, ed. Ian Cameron and Douglas Pye. New York: Continuum, 1996, 229–235.

———. "Genre and History: *Fort Apache* and *The Man Who Shot Liberty Valance*." *Movie* 25, no. 1 (Spring 1976). Rpt. in *The Book of Westerns*, ed. Ian Cameron and Douglas Pye. New York: Continuum, 1996, 111–122.

Roth, Lane. "Ritual Brawls in John Ford's Films," *Film Criticism* 7, no. 3 (1983): 38–46.

Roth, Marty. "'Yes, My Darling Daughter': Gender, Miscegenation and Generation in John Ford's *The Searchers*." *New Orleans Review* 18, no. 4 (Winter 1991): 65–73.

Sarris, Andrew. *The John Ford Movie Mystery*. Bloomington: Indiana University Press, 1975.

Schatz, Thomas. *Hollywood Genres: Formulas, Filmmaking, and the Studio System*. New York: Random House, 1981.

Schickel, Richard. "Ford Galaxy." *Film Comment* 20, no. 2 (1984): 24–27.

Sinclair, Andrew. *John Ford: A Biography*. New York: Lorrimer, 1979.

Skerry, P. J. "Space and Place in John Ford's *Stagecoach* and *My Darling Clementine*." *New Orleans Review* 14, no. 2 (1987): 87–91.

———. "What Makes a Man to Wander? Ethan Edwards of John Ford's *The Searchers*." *New Orleans Review* 18, no. 4 (1991): 65–73.

Slotkin, Richard. *Gunfighter Nation: The Myth of the Frontier in Twentieth-Century America*. New York: Atheneum, 1992.

Stowell, Peter. *John Ford*. Boston: Twayne, 1986.

Tavernier, Bertrand. "Notes of a Press Attache: John Ford in Paris, 1966." *Film Comment* 30, no. 4 (1994): 66–75.

Telotte, J. P. "A Fate Worse Than Death: Racism, Transgression and Westerns." *Journal of Popular Film and Television* 26, no. 3 (Fall 1998): 120–127.

Tuska, Jon. *The American West in Film: Critical Approaches to the Western*. Westport, Conn.: Greenwood Press, 1985.

Westbrook, Max. "The Night John Wayne Danced with Shirley Temple," *Western American Literature* 25, no. 2 (1990): 157–169.

White, Armond. "Stepping Forward, Looking Back." *Film Comment* 36, no. 2 (March–April 2000): 32–39.

Wills, Garry. *John Wayne's America*. New York: Simon and Schuster, 1997.

Wood, Robin. "Drums along the Mohawk." *Cineaction* 8 (Spring 1987): 58–64. Rpt. in *The Book of Westerns*, ed. Ian Cameron and Douglas Pye. New York: Continuum, 1996, 174–180.

———. "John Ford." In *Cinema: A Critical Dictionary*, vol. 1, ed. Richard Roud. New York: Viking, 1980, 371–387.

CONTRIBUTORS

CHARLES RAMÍREZ BERG is Associate Professor and University Distinguished Teaching Professor of Film Studies in the Department of Radio-Television-Film at The University of Texas at Austin. He is author of two books on Mexican cinema and numerous articles on Latino imagery in Hollywood film.

MATTHEW BERNSTEIN is author of *Walter Wanger, Hollywood Independent,* editor of *Controlling Hollywood: Censorship and Regulation in the Studio Era,* and, with Gaylyn Studlar, co-editor of *Visions of the East: Orientalism in Film.* He teaches Film Studies at Emory University.

EDWARD BUSCOMBE is Visiting Professor in Media Arts at Southampton Institute. He has written on *Stagecoach* in the BFI Film Classics series and, together with Roberta Pearson, edited *Back in the Saddle Again: New Essays on the Western.* He is currently writing a volume on *The Searchers* for BFI Film Classics.

JOAN DAGLE is Professor of English and Film Studies and Chair of the English Department at Rhode Island College. She has published essays on narrative theory, narration in film and literature, and the representation of race in film.

BARRY KEITH GRANT is Professor of Communication, Popular Culture and Film at Brock University in Ontario, Canada. He is author of *Voyages of Discovery: The Cinema of Frederick Wiseman, Near Death,* and *The Film Studies Dictionary* (with Steve Blandford and Jim Hillier, forthcoming), and editor of such volumes as *Film Genre Reader, The Dread of Difference: Gender and the Horror Film,* and *Documenting the Documentary: Close Readings of Documentary Film and Video* (with Jeanette Sloniowski). His writing has appeared in numerous anthologies and journals. He is editor of the Genres in American Cinema Series for Cambridge University Press and of the Contemporary Film and Television Series for Wayne State University Press.

KATHRYN KALINAK is Professor of English and Film Studies at Rhode Island College. She has published numerous articles on film music and is author of *Settling the Score: Music and the Classical Hollywood Film.* She is currently at work on a book entitled *How the West Was Sung,* about music and the Western.

PETER LEHMAN is Professor in the Interdisciplinary Humanities Program and the Hispanic Research Center at Arizona State University and editor of *Defining Cinema.*

CHARLES J. MALAND is Chair of the Cinema Studies Program at the University of Tennessee and Lindsay Young Professor of American Studies, Cinema Studies, and American Literature in the English Department. He is author of three books: *American Visions: The Films of Chaplin, Ford, Capra, and Welles, 1936–1941; Frank Capra;* and *Chaplin and American Culture: The Evolution of a Star Image.* The latter won the Theater Library Association Award for best book that year in film studies.

GLORIA MONTI recently completed her dissertation in the American Studies Program at Yale University, and currently teaches in the Audio/Video/Film Department at Hofstra University.

GAYLYN STUDLAR is Rudolf Arnheim Collegiate Professor of Film Studies and Director of the Program in Film and Video Studies at the University of Michigan, Ann Arbor. She is author of *This Mad Masquerade: Stardom and Masculinity in the Jazz Age* and *In the Realm of Pleasure: Von Sternberg, Dietrich, and the Masochistic Aesthetic,* as well as co-editor of three volumes, most recently *Titanic: Anatomy of a Blockbuster.* She is currently working on a social history of American women and Hollywood film culture.

ROBIN WOOD is author of *Hollywood from Vietnam to Reagan, Hitchcock's Films Revisited,* and *Sexual Politics and Narrative Film.* He is also co-editor of and a frequent contributor to *Cine-Action.*

INDEX